The Corinthian Correspondence

The Corinthian Correspondence

Redaction, Rhetoric, and History

Frank W. Hughes
Robert Jewett

LEXINGTON BOOKS/FORTRESS ACADEMIC
Lanham • Boulder • New York • London

Published by Lexington Books/Fortress Academic
Lexington Books is an imprint of The Rowman & Littlefield Publishing Group, Inc.
4501 Forbes Boulevard, Suite 200, Lanham, Maryland 20706
www.rowman.com

6 Tinworth Street, London SE11 5AL, United Kingdom

Copyright © 2021 by The Rowman & Littlefield Publishing Group, Inc.

All rights reserved. No part of this book may be reproduced in any form or by any electronic or mechanical means, including information storage and retrieval systems, without written permission from the publisher, except by a reviewer who may quote passages in a review.

British Library Cataloguing in Publication Information Available

Library of Congress Cataloging-in-Publication Data

Names: Hughes, Frank Witt, 1954– author. | Jewett, Robert, author.
Title: The Corinthian correspondence : redaction, rhetoric, and history / Frank W. Hughes, Robert Jewett.
Description: Lanham : Lexington Books/Fortress Academic, [2021] | Includes bibliographical references and index. | Summary: "In The Corinthian Correspondence, Frank W. Hughes and Robert Jewett argue that the Apostle Paul wrote eight letters to the church in Corinth, and that those letters were edited and reshaped into 1 and 2 Corinthians. This analysis, using redaction and rhetorical criticism, provides many insights into Paul's difficult relationship with the Corinthians"—Provided by publisher.
Identifiers: LCCN 2021027651 (print) | LCCN 2021027652 (ebook) | ISBN 9781978705197 (cloth) | ISBN 9781978705203 (epub) | ISBN 9781978705210 (paper)
Subjects: LCSH: Bible. Corinthians—Criticism, interpretation, etc. | Bible. Corinthians—Criticism, Redaction. | Bible. Corinthians—Language, style.
Classification: LCC BS2675.52 .H79 2021 (print) | LCC BS2675.52 (ebook) | DDC 227/.206—dc23
LC record available at https://lccn.loc.gov/2021027651
LC ebook record available at https://lccn.loc.gov/2021027652

Contents

Figures   vii

Preface   ix

PART ONE: THE REDACTION OF THE CORINTHIAN LETTERS   **1**

1   Introduction   3

2   The Partition and Redaction of 2 Corinthians   11

3   The Need to Partition 1 Corinthians   43

4   The Redaction of 1 Corinthians   85

PART TWO: THE PROVENANCE AND RHETORIC OF THE ORIGINAL LETTERS   **105**

5   Letter A: Troubles in Worship (1 Cor 11:2, 17-34a + 11:3-16 + 16:1-4 + 11:34b)   107

6   Letter B: The Body Matters (2 Cor 6:14–7:1 + 1 Cor 6:12-20 + 1 Cor 9:24–10:22 + 1 Cor 15:1-58 + 1 Cor 16:13-24)   121

7   Letter C: Arguing for Unity (1 Cor 1:1–6:11 + 7:1–8:13 + 9:19-23 + 10:23–11:1 + 12:1-31a + 14:1c-33a + 12:31b–13:13 + 16:5-12)   151

8   Letter D: Reorganizing the Offering (2 Cor. 8:1-24)   167

9   Letter E: Apology for Paul's Apostleship (2 Cor 2:14–6:13 + 7:2-4)   175

10	Letter F: Anguish of Heart and Many Tears (2 Cor 10:1–11:9 + 1 Cor 9:1-18 + 2 Cor 11:10-13:13)	193
11	Letter G: Consolation for the Afflicted (2 Cor 1:1–2:13 + 2 Cor 7:5-16 + 13:11-13)	211
12	Letter H: An Appeal to the Achaians (2 Cor 9:1-15)	231

PART THREE: REFLECTIONS ON THE REDACTION OF THE ORIGINAL LETTERS — 241

13 Redirecting Paul's Ministry — 243

PART FOUR: HISTORICAL IMPLICATIONS — 253

14 The Publication of 1 and 2 Corinthians: From Scroll to Codex — 255

APPENDICES — 263

Appendix I: Summary of the Jewett-Hughes Partition Theory in Relation to the Canonical 1 and 2 Corinthians — 265

Appendix II: Schematic Representations of the Redactional Process — 267

Appendix III: Previous Partition and Redaction Theories — 271

Appendix IV: Translations of the Eight Original Letters — 275

Bibliography — 309

Subject Index — 353

Author Index — 355

Index of Biblical Citations — 361

About the Authors — 373

Figures

2.1	The Bornkamm Hypothesis	24
2.2	Our Hypothesis about the Redactional Composition of 2 Corinthians	33
2.3	The Result: Canonical 2 Corinthians	34
2.4	The Result: Canonical 2 Corinthians, Showing the Order of Composition of Materials	35
5.1	The Double Chiasm Argument in 1 Cor 11:11-12	112
A-II.1	The Formation of 1 Corinthians	267
A-II.2	The Formation of 2 Corinthians	268
A-II.3	The Result: Canonical 2 Corinthians	269

Preface

After many years of work on the Corinthian correspondence, and after several visits to each other's residence and places of research, this jointly authored book now makes its appearance. In this book, we argue in favor of a partition theory of the Corinthian letters that includes the material in both 1 and 2 Corinthians. We argue, primarily through the use of redaction criticism and rhetorical criticism, the probability of the existence of eight original letters, which Paul wrote to the Corinthian church he had founded. These letters and letter-fragments, which we identify as Letters A to H, are embedded in the form of 1 and 2 Corinthians in the canonical New Testament. Thus, 1 and 2 Corinthians reflect very substantial editing by people, most likely in the late first century or early second century, who wished to modify the theological and ecclesial legacies of Paul.

This book had its origins in Jewett's article "The Redaction of I Corinthians and the Trajectory of the Pauline School," published in 1978, in which Jewett applied redaction criticism to 1 Corinthians. In 1980, Jewett and Hughes met, and in 1982, Hughes entered the joint doctoral program at Garrett-Evangelical Theological Seminary and Northwestern University, graduating in 1984. Hughes was ordained in 1981 in Chicago, and much of his career has been devoted to pastoral ministry in Episcopal churches, while it also included his tenure as a senior lecturer at Codrington College in Barbados, in affiliation with the University of the West Indies, where he taught graduate, undergraduate, and diploma students. He also taught in diocesan programs in the United States for the training of lay ministers, deacons, and priests. Jewett came to Garrett-Evangelical in 1980 and served there until 2000, when he went to the University of Heidelberg where he was a guest professor and where he completed his quarter-century of work on his large Romans commentary.¹ Thus, the conversation between Hughes and Jewett about the Corinthian correspondence has been going on since 1982.

In studying the letters and letter-fragments of the Corinthian correspondence, as Jewett reconstructed them, Hughes analyzed most of them according to traditions of Greek and Roman rhetoric, as he was later to do with 1 and 2 Thessalonians.² We were both intrigued to discover that Corinthian Letter C works out as a rhetorical document extremely well, with a three-part *probatio* and a very finely crafted *peroratio* which recapitulated all the matters in Corinthian Letter C but, very importantly, not all the topics in the canonical 1 Corinthians. Out of this work with Jewett, Hughes also wrote two articles on Corinthian Letters G and E, which were published in 1991 and 1997.³ Jewett and Hughes also had the privilege of including several graduate students as well as seminarians in that conversation at different times.

In the present work, we aim to present all the arguments in favor of our position about the origins, collection, and redaction of the Corinthian correspondence. Since this is an involved proposal, we supply a summary of the book at the beginning of chapter 1.

We have many people to thank. First of all are the many librarians who have helped us for many years. These include librarians at the Styberg Library at Garrett-Evangelical Theological Seminary and the libraries of the University of Heidelberg. As this project was nearing its end, Mary-Carol Riehs of Garrett-Evangelical, Linda Frasier of the Webster Parish Library in Minden, Louisiana, and Summer Crow of the Nacogdoches Public Library in Texas deserve special thanks. Another former student of Robert Jewett, John E. Phelan, Jr., assisted Frank Hughes with the translations of the eight original Corinthian letters as reconstructed. The errors that may remain are those due to Hughes alone. The students we have taught at Garrett-Evangelical Theological Seminary, Codrington College, the School of the Diaconate of the Diocese of Pennsylvania, the School of Christian Studies of the Diocese of Central Pennsylvania, the Diocesan School of Theology of the Diocese of Western Louisiana, the Church of the Holy Cross, Shreveport, Louisiana, Grace Church, Monroe, Louisiana, St. John's Church, Minden, Louisiana, Trinity Church, Longview, Texas, and Christ Church, Nacogdoches, Texas, have patiently listened to our ideas about multiple Corinthian letters and what Paul thought he was doing as he wrote them. We have also discussed our partition theory with several other Pauline scholars. Members of our families and many friends have also provided much encouragement and help over many years.

In the past five years, our progress has been slowed by Jewett's Parkinson's disease, as well as Hughes's work as an interim rector in several parishes before his recent retirement. Robert Jewett passed away on December 4, 2020, at the age of eighty-six years, which were well and generously lived.

We are grateful for the patience of Neil Elliott of Fortress Academic and Rowman and Littlefield and for his support of this project. We are grateful for the feedback we have received at all the stages of the writing and editing of this book.

F. W. H.
January 2021

NOTES

1. Robert Jewett, *Romans: A Commentary,* edited by Eldon J. Epp (Hermeneia; Minneapolis: Fortress Press, 2008).
2. Frank W. Hughes, *Early Christian Rhetoric and 2 Thessalonians* (JSNTSup 30; Sheffield: JSOT Press, 1989).
3. See Frank W. Hughes, "The Rhetoric of Reconciliation: 2 Corinthians 1.1-2:13 and 7.5-8.24," in Duane F. Watson, editor, *Persuasive Artistry: Studies in New Testament Rhetoric in Honor of George A. Kennedy* (JSNTSup 50; Sheffield: Academic Press, 1991), 246–61; idem, "Rhetorical Criticism and the Corinthian Correspondence," in Thomas H. Olbricht and Stanley E. Porter, editors, *The Rhetorical Analysis of Scripture: Essays from the 1995 London Conference* (JSNTSup 146; Sheffield: Sheffield Academic Press, 1997), 336–50.

Part One

THE REDACTION OF THE CORINTHIAN LETTERS

Chapter 1

Introduction

In this introduction, we give a brief summary of what we argue in this book, followed by our statement of the fundamental problem that caused us to develop a partition theory of 1 and 2 Corinthians. At the end of this introduction, we describe our use of rhetorical criticism and redaction criticism.

THE ARGUMENT OF THIS BOOK

In chapter 2, we deal with the understanding that 2 Corinthians contains more than one letter embedded within the form that we have it in the canonical New Testament. Much has been written about such partition theories regarding 2 Corinthians, and we bring to the attention of our readers both older and contemporary scholarship on this letter. In chapters 3 and 4, we will argue that the originality of the canonical 1 Corinthians is equally as problematic as the originality of the canonical 2 Corinthians. In chapter 3, we will bring forward older arguments against understanding the canonical 1 Corinthians as an integral letter; these arguments include those of several scholars, most notably Johannes Weiss from the early twentieth century. We will argue that it is highly unlikely for Paul to "unknow" in 1 Cor 11:18-19 what he clearly knew in 1 Cor 1:1–4:21 about the pervasive disunity of the Corinthian congregation, and which he strongly corrects in these four chapters. We will show the probability that several passages are best understood as having been used to make ostensibly smooth transitions. What we argue here has a major bearing on why the original Corinthian letters of Paul were edited. In chapter 5, we will present our proposal concerning the redaction of what became known as 1 Corinthians, which is that the redactors took Letter C and used it as the "frame" letter; their motive in doing so was to take the original Letter

C out of the hands of proto-gnostics, so that Paul's statements about some church members having wisdom, among other statements, could not be used by proto-gnostics to disrupt the church in either the late first century or early second century CE.

In chapters 5 through 12 of this book, we turn to the rhetorical analysis of the eight letters and letter-fragments we call Letters A through H. The alphabetical order of our titles for these letters and letter-fragments indicates our understanding of their relative chronology. We found that several of the letters and letter-fragments exhibited patterns of persuasion that are very amenable to analysis according to precepts of arrangement, invention, and style, according to ancient Greek rhetoric and its appropriation in Latin rhetoric. Letter A is incomplete, but it includes what appears to be a *probatio* with two parts. Letter B also lacks an epistolary prescript, and yet we found that the most difficult section of all, 2 Cor 6:14–7:1, comes into focus when we interpret it as part of the *exordium* of Letter B, which includes the material against immorality as well as Paul's detailed refutation of those who deny the resurrection of the dead. Letter C, the "frame letter" standing behind the canonical form of 1 Corinthians, is a complete letter, with a three-part *probatio*, and a striking *peroratio* in 1 Cor 13:1-13. Letter D, 2 Cor 8:1-24, is a fragment of a letter Paul wrote to encourage the Corinthians to collect money for the offering for the relief of fellow believers in Jerusalem. We believe that this letter is earlier in the Corinthian correspondence rather than later. It appears to us to follow Letter C closely in time. Letter C was a plea for unity, and it appears that Paul asked the congregation to raise the money thereafter in Letter D, thinking that the plea for unity in Letter C would have been successful.

By the time Paul wrote Letter E, he now understood that he must defend himself and prosecute his opponents. This he does in a measured way in 2 Cor 2:14–6:13 + 7:2-4, still proclaiming in the *peroratio* of this letter his love for the Corinthian congregation. After he wrote Letter E, Paul made his second visit to Corinth, and this was the painful visit, to be sure. Paul and his apostleship—which was his legitimate and historical connection with the Corinthian congregation—were rejected in Paul's presence. Paul then wrote Letter F. After Letter F was read to the Corinthians, the congregation, or perhaps the major portion of it, realized that a serious turnaround was necessary. They did indeed repent, and they proceeded to punish the evildoer, apparently a ringleader of the opposition to Paul. Then Paul wrote Letter G, 2 Cor 1:1–2:13 + 7:5-16, + 13:11-13, the letter that uses the well-known topics of consolation as a way to help effect a reconciliation between the Corinthian congregation and Paul. Paul in 2 Cor 2:6-11 tells the Corinthian congregation that the evildoer has now been punished enough, and that they should welcome this person back into the fellowship of the church. In Corinthian Letter H, 2 Cor 9:1-15, we have a fragment of yet another fundraising letter; the circumstance and probably the addressees of this letter appear to be different from those of Letter D.

Chapter 13 of this book is a summary of what our hypothesis about the redaction of the several original Corinthian letters into the canonical form of 1 and 2 Corinthians suggests about how the image of Paul needed to be altered. In chapter 14 of this book, we relate the editing of these eight letters and letter-fragments to the problem of how and under what circumstances believers in Jesus turned away from the use of the scroll to the use of the codex to transmit and preserve their writings.

THE BASIC PROBLEM OF THE CORINTHIAN LETTERS

There has been a working consensus, a view held by many if not most critical New Testament scholars, that 2 Corinthians contains a letter and fragments of one or more other letters. The most important reason for partitioning 2 Corinthians between chapters 9 and 10 is the fact that 2 Cor 1:1–2:13 and 7:5-16 are heavily taken up with consolation, Paul's pastoral follow-up to a severe letter Paul wrote to correct the Corinthians, in order to foster reconciliation. Paul says that he wrote this severe letter "with much affliction and anguish of heart and with many tears" (2:4). This severe letter, which we identify as 2 Cor 10:1-11:9 + 1 Cor 9:1-18 + 2 Cor 11:10-13:13 (our Letter F), was written, as Paul believed, because it was necessary to correct the Corinthians, to get them "back on track" in their relationship with their founding apostle and—as Paul saw it—with God. It is fundamentally difficult to imagine that anyone with sense of how persuasion worked would have written a letter about reconciliation at the beginning of the letter, using the topics of consolation, which were well known in the ancient world, and then in the very same letter, launch a bombastic attack on the very congregation for whose recent correction and reconciliation with himself he has just given thanks. We do not believe that it could ever have been to Paul's rhetorical advantage to write such a strange and unclear letter such as what we read in the canonical form of 2 Corinthians. Is it likely that the Paul, who wrote such finely crafted rhetorical letters as 1 Thessalonians, Galatians, and Romans, would have written 1 and 2 Corinthians in the form in which we have them in the New Testament? We do not believe so. There are other good reasons for partitioning 2 Corinthians at other places, and we present our argument in favor of this partitioning in chapter 2 of this book.

THE RHETORIC OF PAUL'S LETTERS

In the study of the New Testament, we are now in an era in which multiple methods of interpretation are quite explicitly being employed. As we show in this book, the use of rhetorical criticism to identify the arguments of particular Corinthian letters actually confirms many of the results of literary criticism as practiced over a century ago by Johannes Weiss as well as other scholars both before and after him.

This brings us to the whole matter of how we may best understand Paul's method or methods of doing persuasion by letter. Much has been written about rhetorical criticism of letters, and the two authors of this book have done rhetorical criticism on Romans and on 1 and 2 Thessalonians. Other colleagues have done some similar things with other letters in the New Testament. There has been an ongoing conversation since about 1974, when Hans Dieter Betz delivered his lecture on the rhetoric of Galatians.[1] We need not reproduce this conversation in full here,[2] yet in this introductory chapter, we wish to give a brief glimpse of our use of rhetorical criticism.

Paul founded churches mostly made up of Gentiles. Paul seems to have favored urban areas, probably because he wanted to evangelize as many people as possible before the second coming of Christ. After his call as an apostle, he started out as an associate of Barnabas in Antioch, and then later Paul did mission with other coworkers. Paul's missionary strategy included his founding of churches primarily in cities relatively near the Mediterranean Sea. After Paul would leave one city to go found or minister in a church in another city, certain churches in which he was previously ministering would experience problems of one kind or another. Sometimes Paul sent Timothy or Titus, who were his chief deputies, and sometimes Paul attempted to straighten out the problems by one or more letters to the church involved, which one of his deputies would actually read (and interpret) to the gathered congregation. These letters, which Paul dictated and sent when he could not be physically present, needed to be as persuasive as possible; otherwise, they would not be effective to correct the problems or answer the concerns in the churches to which Paul had written. It was natural for Paul to use rhetoric in his letters, for his letters were the substitute for his physical presence and personal ministry in the churches to which he wrote.[3] If Paul would use the precepts of rhetoric when he addressed congregations in person, when Paul could not be in Corinth or Galatia or Thessalonica in person, it is not surprising that various features of rhetoric can be found in letters to churches in those cities. Why would Paul not use every means available to make his letters persuasive to those congregations, which had problems that needed his attention, even at long distance? Thus, in rhetorical criticism of Paul's letters based on Greek rhetoric along with its appropriation in Latin rhetoric, models drawn from handbooks of rhetoric and visible in speeches of Demosthenes, Cicero, and many others, along with the letters of Demosthenes, can be used as parallels to illuminate what Paul was doing as he wrote some of his letters. Several scholars have done rhetorical criticism on quite a few of the letters of the New Testament.[4] We do so on Corinthian Letters A through H in chapters 5 through 12 of this study. Rhetorical criticism of segments of the Corinthian correspondence is being used here along with more traditional historical criticism and other methods of historical reconstruction of texts of early Jesus-believing communities.[5]

REDACTION CRITICISM

In chapter 4 of this study, we are making explicit use of redaction criticism of 1 and 2 Corinthians, as we show the editorial interests that redactors of the multiple Corinthian letters had. Although we do not know of the explicit uses of redaction criticism per se outside the gospels and the traditions standing behind the gospels in the New Testament,[6] there is no reason why redaction criticism cannot be used on the letters of the Pauline corpus, given, for example, that the author or editor of Ephesians most likely made use of Colossians.[7] In using Colossians as a source and then changing it and adding other material, the writer of Ephesians transformed Colossians into Ephesians. The same can be said, for example, of how the writer/editor of Matthew used Markan material. In using it, the writer of Matthew both preserved it and transformed it. Our study argues that the redactor of the Corinthian correspondence inserted various passages into Corinthian Letter C, to take it out of the hands of proto-gnostic followers of Paul. By means of several insertions of other authentic Pauline material into the original Letter C, the canonical form of 1 Corinthians was created.

It is not news in our guild that the use of multiple methods of analysis is both desirable and necessary for the most plausible exegesis and interpretation of early texts written by Jesus-believers. Yet none of the methods we might use, new or old, can ever replace the method of common sense. Common sense, upon which detection of forgeries must be based, tells us that it is highly unlikely for Paul to "unknow" something in 1 Cor 11:18-19 (or to deal with it in a way that suggests that it is not a major problem) for which he has raked the Corinthians over the coals in the first four chapters of 1 Corinthians.[8] Precisely on rhetorical grounds, it seems extremely unlikely to make rhetorical sense for Paul to dismiss the importance of unity and to declare that disunity is not so bad after all (1 Cor 11:18-19), in the very same letter where he has previously pleaded at length for unity and in which he will describe disunity as childish behavior in 1 Cor 13. Thus, as we are arguing for the plausibility, including the rhetorical coherence, of what we have of the original Corinthian letters of Paul, we are also using redaction criticism to account for the transformation of the eight original letters and letter-fragments into the two Corinthian letters as we know them in the New Testament.

THE PAULINE CORPUS AND THE RESHAPING OF PAUL

We see in the Corinthian letters, along with the other writings in the Pauline corpus in the New Testament, a rich and complex collection of writings. This complexity naturally causes us, as historical critics, to ask what the reasons were for the complexity of the Pauline corpus. The Pauline corpus includes the fourteen texts from Romans to Hebrews in the New Testament, and the thirteen texts from Romans to Philemon imply a variety of situations within Pauline churches, both during Paul's lifetime and afterwards. As we read and study these letters, one of our goals must surely be to investigate the situational character of each letter. In our view, it is equally important to analyze the situation of the reconstructed letters to the Corinthians as it is to analyze them in their canonical form.

Paul dictated many original letters. We know very well that we do not possess all of Paul's letters; sadly, we do not know whether we even possess most of them or not. As for the letters we do possess, we have always known that it was the early church that collected and preserved these precious texts. Paul's letters, like other ancient texts, were preserved by making copies of them, and thus creating new manuscripts, which contained Paul's original words, along with some copyists' mistakes. Along with these manuscripts of Paul's own letters were also texts, which reflect intentional reshapings of Paul's legacy in particular ways. The impetus to reshape of the Pauline legacy did not only cause certain letters of the Pauline corpus to be created; they also caused, in our view, some of the letters written by Paul to be edited and thus transformed. If 2 Thessalonians 2:2 is part of a letter written by Paul himself, then even during the Apostle's lifetime he was being careful about how his *ethos* was being affected and shaped by the textual creations of others, who were writing and propagating "a letter as from us."

In sum, we are proposing that it is historically likely that, after Paul's martyrdom, subsequent leaders of Pauline churches used methods of reshaping and focusing Paul's legacy in ways of their own choosing, because of new challenges in the late first-century or early second-century Pauline churches—difficulties that Paul himself had not faced. When we read certain letters in the Pauline corpus, classic and current scholarship tells us that we are likely reading portions of the persuasive literature of the late first-century or early second-century church, not letters from Paul himself. If we accept that part of the Pauline corpus is pseudonymous, despite the fact that we do not agree on the extent to which pseudonymity was used, it remains logical for us to argue that some of the same theological interests we find in certain letters of the Pauline corpus also are identifiable in redacting certain other letters in that same corpus.

Like detectives perusing the scene of a crime, New Testament scholars need to understand that multiple kinds of evidence are present. These different kinds of evidence present in the "scene" of the Pauline corpus and its letters require methodological sensitivity to the complexity of all the letters associated with Pauline congregations. Thus the path ahead of us is not a matter of dealing with texts analyzed in abstraction from their original contexts. We wish to discern what kinds of problems and what sorts of situations were faced in early Pauline communities, problems and situations that stood between the original texts by Paul we reconstruct and the edited texts we possess. For quite a few years now, Pauline scholars have been carefully investigating the situational character of each of the Pauline letters. What we do in this study is an extension of historical criticism beyond the canonical 1 or 2 Corinthians, moving to the analysis of each one of the components of an edited collection of Paul's letters. We are interested in how each of the original Corinthian letters as well as their redaction relate to the wider Pauline corpus and the history of Pauline congregations, as best we can reconstruct it.

NOTES

1. Hans Dieter Betz, "The Literary Composition and Function of Paul's Letter to the Galatians," *NTS* 21 (1975): 353–79. This article was originally delivered in 1974 at the general meeting of Studiorum Novi Testamenti Societas.

2. Frank W. Hughes, "George Kennedy's Contribution to Rhetorical Criticism of the Pauline Letters," in C. Clifton Black and Duane F. Watson, editors, *Words Well Spoken: George Kennedy's Rhetoric of the New Testament*, Studies in Rhetoric and Religion, 8 (Waco: Baylor University Press, 2008), 125–37; as well as Hughes, "Paul and Traditions of Graeco-Roman Rhetoric," in Stanley E. Porter and Brian R. Dyer, editors, *Paul and Ancient Rhetoric: Theory and Practice in the Hellenistic Context* (Cambridge: Cambridge University Press, 2016), 86–95. See also the essays in *Paul and Rhetoric*, edited by J. Paul Sampley and Peter Lampe (New York and London: T. & T. Clark, 2010). More recent is the fully documented book edited by Troy W. Martin, *Genealogies of New Testament Rhetorical Criticism* (Minneapolis: Fortress, 2014).

3. Raymond F. Collins, "'I Command That This Letter Be Read': Writing as a Manner of Speaking," in Karl P. Donfried and Johannes Beutler, editors, *The Thessalonians Debate: Methodological Discord or Methodological Synthesis?* (Grand Rapids: Eerdmans, 2000), 319–39.

4. Duane F. Watson and Alan J. Houser, editors, *Rhetorical Criticism of the Bible: A Comprehensive Bibliography with Notes on History and Method*, BibInt 4 (Leiden: E. J. Brill, 1994).

5. See Frank W. Hughes, "The Social Situations Implied by Rhetoric," in Donfried and Beutler, *The Thessalonians Debate*, 241–54.

6. John R. Donahue, "Redaction Criticism, New Testament," *DBI* 1.376-79.

7. See the especially clear discussion by Petr Pokorný, *Der Brief des Paulus an die Epheser*, 2nd, corrected edition, THKNT 10/II (Leipzig: Evangelische Verlagsanstalt, 2013), 3–21, in a section entitled "Die übernommenen Stoffe" ("materials taken over"). See also the fine discussion by Andrew T. Lincoln in *Ephesians*, WBC 42 (Dallas: Word Books, 1990), xlvii–lviii; as well as the classic treatment by C. Leslie Mitton in *The Epistle to the Ephesians: Its Authorship, Origin and Purpose* (Oxford: Clarendon Press, 1951), 55–81.

8. Bart D. Ehrman, *Forgery and Counter Forgery: The Use of Literary Deceit in Early Christian Polemics* (Oxford: Oxford University Press, 2013), writes of several criteria used in detecting forgeries in antiquity. These include "Style" (138–39), "Anachronisms and Other Historical Problems" (139–40), "Internal Inconsistencies and Implausibilities" (140–41), "Theological Sachkritik" (141–42), and "Established Patterns of Usage" (142–43). These subsections are part of his chapter 4, "Forgery in Antiquity: Motives, Techniques, Intentions, Justifications, and Criteria of Detection" (93–153). The problem of 1 Cor 11:18-19 in comparison with 1 Cor 1-4 would come under Ehrman's designation of an "internal inconsistency and implausibility."

Chapter 2

The Partition and Redaction of 2 Corinthians

In this chapter, we carry forward the consensus among critical scholars that 2 Corinthians contains more than one letter. As we noted in chapter 1, this is a very different situation from the critical appraisal of 1 Corinthians. The difference in scholarly assessment derives from the fact that the problematic transitions in 2 Corinthians are much more obvious and the changes in rhetorical situations are much more extreme.

EVIDENCE OF DISUNITY IN 2 CORINTHIANS

Since the work of Johann Salomo Semler in 1776,[1] scholars have noticed historical and literary discrepancies that indicate 2 Corinthians must contain more than a single letter. The reference in 2 Cor 2:4 to a "letter of tears" dispatched by Paul at an earlier point does not match the content or tone of 1 Corinthians, but it is a fair description of the last four chapters of the second letter. This indicates that chapter 2 must have been written later than these final chapters. A similar discrepancy is evident in the transition from 2 Cor 8:24 to 9:1. Paul's discussion of the Jerusalem Offering is concluded in 8:24 and then announced again in 9:1 as if it were a fresh topic. Obviously these two sections must have been part of two separate letters, as Maurice Goguel, Hans Dieter Betz, and others have shown.[2]

At the end of chapter 9, Paul concludes the discussion of the offering by praising the congregation's generosity, but in the very next verse, he begs them not to accept the allegation that he was "humble when face to face with you, but bold to you when I am away" (10:1) by writing powerful letters. These two sections obviously belong to different stages in Paul's troubled relation with the Corinthians. This insight was a decisive factor in the theory of a four-chapter letter (2 Cor 10-13), suggested by Semler[3] and developed by a number of other scholars in the nineteenth century.[4] Many subsequent scholars inferred from these details that chapters 1-9 and 10-13 belong to two or more separate letters.[5]

Second Corinthians is full of similarly awkward transitions and changes of relationships between Paul and his audience. The most obvious examples of rough transitions caused by the intrusion of extraneous material were identified and explained by Johannes Weiss in 1894,[6] which readers of this book can test by reading aloud the material in the left columns as if the material in the right columns were not there:

(2 Corinthians 2:12-13) "When I came to Troas to preach the gospel of Christ, a door was opened for me in the Lord; but my mind could not rest because I did not find my brother Titus there. So I took leave of them and went on to Macedonia."

(2 Corinthians 2:14–7:4) "But thanks be to God, who in Christ always leads us in triumph. . . . Such is the confidence that we have through Christ. . . . So we do lose heart. . . . I have great confidence in you; I have great pride in you; I am filled with comfort. With all our affliction, I am overjoyed.

(2 Corinthians 7:5) "And even when we came into Macedonia, our bodies had no rest but we were afflicted at every turn—fightings without and fear within."

The material on the left is a travelogue from Troas to Macedonia. Its mood is anxious and troubled, with no resolution in view. In contrast, the material on the right margin is triumphant and full of confidence. When one reads aloud the transitions between the left and right columns as they appear in 2 Corinthians, one moves back and forth between anxious travelogue and triumphant celebration. The shifts of mood, content, and style between the material on the left and right margins are so abrupt and unexpected that the very sanity of such a writer would seem to be questionable. If Paul was in fact sane, the material on the right and left margins must come from very different stages in Paul's relationship with the Corinthians.

A second widely cited example of an outrageously severe transition appears in 2 Cor 6-7; again we suggest you start by reading aloud the lines in the left column as if the material in the right column were not present:

(2 Cor 6:11-13) "Our mouth is open to you, Corinthians; our heart is wide. . . . In Return . . . widen your hearts also."

(2 Cor 6:14–7:1) "Do not be mismated with unbelievers. For what partnership have righteous and iniquity? . . . let us cleanse ourselves from every defilement of body and spirit, and make holiness perfect in the fear of God."

(2 Cor 7:2) "Open your hearts to us; We have wronged no one, we have corrupted no one, we have taken advantage of no one."

On the left margin, we encounter impassioned appeals for reconciliation along with personal defense concerning the fault of previous alienation that is now resolved. The material on the right margin shifts dramatically to severe moral exhortation. To read through the transitions between the left and right material is so shocking that anyone lacking a pious predisposition is forced to question how any sane person could be capable of such changes in content, style and mood. From the earliest days of literary-critical study of 2 Corinthians, it quickly seemed clear to sensitive interpreters that the material in the left columns is being interrupted by material that must originally have derived from other phases of the Corinthian controversy with Paul.[7] The Second Letter to the Corinthians must therefore contain material from several different letters that Paul originally wrote at different points in his relations with the congregation.

In addition to these awkward transitions that seem so uncharacteristic for the author of the coherent, well organized, and eloquent prose of Philemon, Galatians, 1 Thessalonians, and Romans, there are historical discrepancies in 2 Corinthians that cannot be explained away. In 8:16-23, Titus is recommended to the congregation as if he were unknown there. Titus "is going to you of his own accord" (8:17), after which Paul explains, "As for Titus, he is my partner and fellow worker in your service" (8:23). The Corinthians are obviously not acquainted with Titus at this point, because otherwise this introduction would have been both unnecessary and impolite. Yet earlier in canonical 2 Corinthians Titus is described as having come from Corinth to meet Paul in Macedonia; Paul reports his relief at the success of Titus's mission:

> We rejoiced still more at the joy of Titus, because his mind has been set at rest by you all. For if I have expressed to him some pride in you, I was not put to shame; but just as everything we said to you was true, so our boasting before Titus has proved true. And his heart goes out all the more to you, as he remembers the obedience of you all, and the fear and trembling with which you received him. (7:13-15)

This material in chapter 7 reflects a relationship between Titus and the Corinthians at a time after Paul's introduction of the forthcoming visit in chapter 8. Something is clearly out of sequence in 2 Corinthians.

A similar historical discrepancy relates to Paul's own travel plans. In chapter 1, Paul apologizes for failing to carry through with his plan to revisit Corinth. "I wanted to visit you on my way to Macedonia, and to come back to you from Macedonia and have you send me on my way to Judea" (2 Cor 1:16). He answers the accusation that the cancelled plan was an instance of "vacillating" (2 Cor 1:17) and explains that "it was to spare you that I refrained from coming to Corinth. . . . For I made up my mind not to make you another painful visit" (2 Cor 1:24-2:2). So at this point at the beginning of 2 Corinthians, there were canceled second and third visits, counting Paul's founding visit to Corinth as number one, followed by a painful visit—the actual visit number 2—that Paul has decided not to repeat. However, toward the end of 2 Corinthians, there is a changed situation. Paul announces a forthcoming visit that he had earlier been reluctant to make: "Here for the third time I am ready to come to you" (2 Cor 12:14). His concern was that "when I come again my God may humble me before you, and I may have to mourn over many of those who sinned before and have not repented of the impurity, immorality, and licentiousness which they have practiced. This is the third time I am coming to you" (2 Cor 12:21–13:1). Something must have occurred between the beginning and the end of 2 Corinthians that changed Paul's mind about revisiting Corinth after his second "painful visit." This means that the material at the end of the letter must have been written at a different time than the material at the beginning.[8]

Finally, as visible in the aforementioned illustration, in 2 Cor 2:14–6:13 + 7:2-4, Paul makes a powerful appeal for reconciliation with the congregation, but in 2 Cor 1:1–2:13 + 7:5–8:24, he recapitulates a reconciliation already achieved. Since such an appeal must precede the achievement of reconciliation, and would have evoked outrage after such an achievement, it is logical to infer that the material in the opening verses of 2 Corinthians was written later than the material beginning with 2 Cor 2:14. The sequence in canonical 2 Corinthians at this and many other points is simply untenable. This is not just a matter of rough transitions; in the instances described earlier, the passages in question shift back and forth between completely different rhetorical situations.[9] As Lloyd Bitzer showed, a unique and unrepeatable exigence lies behind each rhetorical action. In his words, "a rhetorical response fits a situation"[10] shaped by a specific "historical context."[11] Different stages in the troubled relationship between Paul and his congregation are reflected in these abrupt transitions. The contradictions in historical detail also reflect different stages of Paul's relations with the Corinthians. Moreover, these drastic shifts from situation to situation entail seemingly arbitrary shifts between the three basic rhetorical genres. As Duane Watson observes, Paul's letters are usually either predominantly judicial, deliberative, or epideictic.[12] In all of the letters other than 1 and 2 Corinthians, this is the case. 1 Thessalonians and Romans are epideictic;[13] Galatians is judicial;[14] Philemon is deliberative;[15] Philippians is primarily deliberative;[16] 2 Thessalonians, whether authentically Pauline or not, is deliberative.[17] Watson goes on to state the widely accepted generalization concerning the function of rhetorical *genera*:

> To some extent identification of the species of the rhetoric of a Pauline epistle is a partial identification of its purpose. The predominant species indicates the rhetorical situation and purpose(s) of a Pauline epistle. If judicial, Paul may be defending himself against the charges of opponents and/or leveling his own charges against them. If deliberative, Paul may be advising and dissuading his audiences against taking certain courses of action. If epideictic, he is trying to increase audience adherence to values it already holds through praise, or to decrease its adherence to values he disdains through blame.[18]

Each of the three *genera* involves a different role on the part of the speaker or writer: from judge or defender, to advisor, or to celebrator or detractor of communal values. To shift back and forth between these three *genera* therefore entails fundamental alterations of the relations between Paul and his audience.

Although he was writing three-quarters of a century before the concept of a rhetorical situation or the extensive discussion of rhetorical *genera* emerged, Johannes Weiss appropriately observed that to suppose 2 Corinthians is a unified letter reflecting a single moment in time is a "nachgerade kühnen Hypothese";[19] it constitutes an "absolutely audacious hypothesis" that is far less probable than the literary-critical and historical theories devised to account for the stitching together of 2 Corinthians. As an illustration of this audacious challenge, Laurence Welborn[20] has commented on Johannes Weiss's description of the transition between 2 Cor 2:13 and 7:5 as fitting together "as neatly as the broken pieces of a ring." From a literary point of view, the separation of these verses was "unheard of and intolerable,"[21] in Weiss's view. Welborn showed that the language and parallel structure of 2:12-13 and 7:5 as well as the mood of Paul's account of his anxious journey require that these verses follow one another without interruption. He provides a clinching argument that the words καὶ γάρ in 7:5 should be translated "*yes, and* even when we came into Macedonia, our bodies had no rest." These words confirm the truth of what he says, which Welborn shows is the function of καὶ γάρ in classical and biblical usage.[22] The coherence between 2:14 and 7:5 conforms to the highest standards of ancient literary theory that stressed the need for "connection . . . continuity . . . and symmetry."[23]

A similar case could be made about the transition between 2 Cor 6:13 and 7:2 and the lack of adequate transitions between 2 Cor 9:15 and 10:1 or between 2 Cor 7:16 and 8:1. We are convinced that these details are the literary equivalent of archaeologists piecing together clay pots from broken potsherds. Scholars have learned to accept the evidentiary force of such reconstructions, because the odds against an accidental matching of the fragments are astronomical. If innumerable, identical clay pots are shattered, only the sherds from uniquely broken pots will fit together exactly. It is a sad reality that so many of our academic colleagues disregard the evidentiary force of such probabilities and continue to believe in the unity of 2 Corinthians. In the next section, we turn to the remarkable resurgence of such improbabilities.

RECENT DENIALS OF DISUNITY IN 2 CORINTHIANS

Until rather recently the opponents of the disunity hypothesis concentrated on clearing away, as they see it, the alleged contradictions within 2 Corinthians. A. M. G. Stephenson affirmed the unity of the letter on the grounds that the contradictions can be resolved and that the advocates of division disagree on details.[24] Niels Hyldahl contended that by eliminating the theory of an intermediate visit to Corinth and identifying the "letter of tears" with 1 Corinthians, the premises of partition theories are eliminated.[25] However, this does not remove the rough transitions and the strange shifts from one rhetorical *genus* to another. Michael Goulder tried to resolve the tension between "unbeliever" in 6:14 and 4:15 by defining both as referring to faithless Jesus-believers,[26] but this does not relieve the transition problems on both sides of 6:14–7:1. Margaret Thrall rejected the theory that this passage was interpolated because "no adequate reason has so far been given why an editor should insert this passage where it seems to interrupt the argument and to leave us with a difficult sequence of thought."[27] The redactional theory that we shall advance in this chapter, pursuing the path paved by Günther Bornkamm, provides such a reason.

David deSilva argues that the theory of 2:14–7:4 interrupting the discourse ending at 2:13 and beginning again at 7:5 "creates as many problems as it purports to solve."[28] For instance, "the καὶ γάρ ('and even') would be out of place if 7:5 followed directly upon 2:13," but compare this with the transition from 7:4, in which the explanatory 'for' with regard to Paul's affliction in 7:5 provides the reason why he is 'overjoyed' (7:4)."[29] DeSilva claims that the partition theory makes no sense of the joyful tone of 7:4,[30] but it is perfectly consistent with 2:14–7:3 with its thanksgiving and confidence "through Christ." The travel details have a "purely transitional" function in Paul's argument in deSilva's opinion, an extraordinary claim in view of the fact that they are interrupted by completely disparate material in 2:14–7:4. The travel details in 2:13 and 7:5 are in fact non-transitions, comprising parts of the roughest movements between sentences in the Pauline corpus, indeed in the entire New Testament. DeSilva's argument that 2 Cor 1-7 comprises a single rhetorical unit rests on the fact that 7:4-16 recapitulates 1:15–2:11,[31] but this is exactly what advocates of partition maintain by identifying 2 Cor 1:1–2:13 + 7:5-16 as a separate letter. The recapitulation he perceives in 7:5-8:24 does not include the extraneous material of 2 Cor 2:14–6:13, 7:2-4, or 6:14–7:1, and deSilva makes no effort to include these chapters in his analysis. This competent but incomplete rhetorical analysis ends up providing additional grounds for partitioning 2 Corinthians.

The penetrating study by J. D. H. Amador continues the effort to eliminate the contradictions that provide a basis for partitioning 2 Corinthians. He rejects the separation between chapters 9 and 10 and the theory of an interpolation of 6:14–7:1 while maintaining that in partition theories, "it is the referential and informational function of the letter(s) that drives historical–critical reconstruction, not an appreciation of the letter as an act of communication and persuasion."[32] We concur with this emphasis on persuasion but regret that so weak a case is made for the effectiveness of moving from congratulating the congregation ("because of the surpassing grace of God in you. Thanks be to God for his inexpressible gift!" [9:14-15]) to the defensive tone of 10:1ff. ("I, Paul, myself entreat you, by the meekness and gentleness of Christ, I who am humble when face to face with you, but bold to you when I am away! I beg of you that when I am present I may not have to show boldness with such confidence as I count on showing against some who suspect us of acting in worldly fashion.") This is a complete about-face,[33] including a shift from the deliberative *genus* of 2 Cor 9 and the judicial *genus* of the apology in chapter 10. Amador tries to explain this by showing thematic links between chapters 10–13 and 1–9, but this does not require such an extreme change of tone, which any competent rhetorician would avoid if he or she really wanted to persuade an audience. Bashing an audience in the face immediately after complimenting them is hardly the art of persuasion taught in any of the ancient rhetorical handbooks. As for introducing the matter of the offering in chapter 9 as if Paul had forgotten the extensive discussion of the same topic in chapter 8, Amador asserts this is a case of *paraleipsis* by which a speaker refrains from mentioning a sensitive topic.[34] Having searched these two chapters in vain to find such restraint, we conclude that Betz's hypothesis is more likely, namely, that the differing details suggest these chapters were sent to two different audiences.[35] That 6:14–7:1 is a peroration rather than an interpolation[36] is advocated by Amador on the basis of alleged parallels in argumentative development elsewhere in the Pauline letters, but this sidesteps the issue of whether summing up an argument with extraneous material after repeatedly making abrupt changes of topic and rhetorical *genus* from 6:13 to 6:14 and 7:1 to 7:2 constitutes an effective peroration. No rhetorical teacher or practitioner in the Greek or Latin traditions would view this as persuasive. Amador goes on to argue that 2:14 is not an ordinary epistolary thanksgiving,[37] but that does not explain the dramatic change in tone and *genus* from 2:13. He concludes his study by asking, "What was the exigence that would have motivated any other redactor than Paul to do so?"[38] This is the very question that our study of the redaction and rhetoric of the Corinthian correspondence seeks to answer.

There is a significant decline in the quality of rhetorical study from deSilva and Amador to the book-length defenses of the integrity of 2 Corinthians by David Hall and Frederick Long. The latter contends that "Paul composed 2 Corinthians as a rhetorically unified apology drawing on the well-known Greco-Roman forensic tradition."[39] To make this case, Long presses the deliberative material in what we call Letters F and G and the material of 6:14–7:1 into his forensic model, which actually fits well only with the material in the letter of tears that is actually judicial sections.[40] But Long denies all of the difficult transitions in 2 Corinthians and, although repeatedly making sweeping claims that all of the letter fits his judicial *genus* of apology, he lamely admits on p. 233 that chapters 8–9 are deliberative. Long's rhetorical analysis is superficial and misleading. He overlooks 1:12-14, which looks and functions like a partitio, and calls 1:17-24 a "divisio and partitio"[41] although it lacks features of either. He names 2:12-13 a "narrative transition"[42] despite the fact that there is a complete break between verses 13 and 14, including a shift from deliberative rhetoric in 1:1–2:13 and judicial rhetoric in 2:14ff. He names 7:2-16 another "narrative transition" despite the clear break between verses 4 and 5, again moving from the judicial to the deliberative *genus*. The category of a "narrative blockage" would be more appropriate. Long calls 5:11–7:1 the fourth proof although it contains an apology from 5:11–6:13 followed by material on a completely different topic from 6:14–7:1. In a tortured exegesis based on the use of "spare" in the Old Testament, Long contends that the content of this section was announced in 1:23 when Paul says, "It was to spare you that I refrained from coming to Corinth."[43] This entitles him to overlook the abrupt transitions and changes of rhetorical *genus* between 6:13 and

14 and between 7:1 and 2, which are baptized by the category of "narrative transition," an expression that can be found in no rhetorical handbook. Although his book provides appropriate rhetorical terminology to describe the forensic material in 2 Cor 10-13, Long fails to show that the entirety of the letter should be identified as an apology. As for the awkward transitions and historical discrepancies evident throughout 2 Corinthians, Long believes that they can be removed by renaming them with pseudo-rhetorical terms and paraphrases.

Ivor Jones provides an extensive evaluation of Long's work.[44] He shows that there is more than a single epilogue in 2 Corinthians, which tends to support the theory of multiple letters. Jones draws from Aristotle the rule that "forensic speech" may contain an epilogue while "deliberative speech will only require an epilogue if a division of opinion regarding future action requires it; epideictic speech should not need one at all."[45] This rule would seem to support Long's assessment that there is a form of epilogue at the end of chapter 13, but Jones is skeptical of identifying the entirety of 12:11–13:10 as a peroration.[46] He concludes that the letter closing begins in 12:19 and is modeled on "the Jewish hortatory tradition rather than the rhetoric of classical oration," and thus that the identification of the genre as forensic is mistaken.[47] We feel that Long makes a stronger case that chapters 10–13 should be identified as forensic, but believe that the peculiar style of a fool's discourse needs to be taken into account. Jones moves on to identify 9:15 as a "climax" that "suggests that chs. 10–13 may belong to a context and time different from that of ch. 9,"[48] which is certainly correct. The conclusion of Jones's essay has a skeptical tone that contrasts with the certainty of Fredrick Long, that "chs. 10–13 could belong to a different time and a different context from chs. 1–9."[49] Indeed, without the coordinated use of more sophisticated methods such as redaction criticism, historical reconstruction, rhetorical situation, and a reading of these texts in the light of specific audiences, no advance beyond general skepticism is likely to be made.

David Hall avoids reliance on rhetorical critical methods in attempting to show that both 1 and 2 Corinthians are integral letters in their current canonical form.[50] It contains no new arguments against disunity. Friedrich Wilhelm Horn's survey of 2004 indicates that the recent trend in Germany follows this conservative direction in dealing with Paul's letters. He names Thomas Söding,[51] Andreas Lindemann,[52] Udo Schnelle,[53] Martin Meiser,[54] and Helmut Merklein[55] as representatives of this reluctance to employ literary-critical and redactional methods.[56] The extensive studies by Reimund Bieringer and Jan Lambrecht from Belgium conform to this trend.[57] Among many others, one could add Paul Barnett,[58] David Garland,[59] James Scott,[60] Jan Lambrecht,[61] Simon Kistemaker,[62] Scott Hafeman,[63] Murray Harris,[64] Thomas Stegman,[65] and Thomas Schmeller,[66] as advocates of unity. The main strategy employed in most of these studies of 2 Corinthians is to deny or explain away the contradictions and difficult transitions. But the evidence will not disappear, despite the enormous efforts expended.[67] A more constructive contribution was made by Stephen Hultgren, that 2 Cor 6:14–7:1 "originated in a Jewish Jesus-believing circle in Ephesus, whose work is also detectable in Revelation 21.3–8 and Ephesians 5, and that was interpolated by an Ephesian redactor of 2 Corinthians."[68] The case is made on the basis of linguistic parallels between Revelation, Ephesians, and 2 Cor 6:14–7:1, which are undeniable, but this does not mean that these texts derived from a single like-minded group. The parallels reveal a typical rationale for sectarian groups in competition with each other rather than an ideological affinity between these groups. A similar worldview is visible in the Qumran community, with many parallels to 2 Cor 6:14–7:1, as Fitzmyer, Gnilka, and Hultgren demonstrate.[69] In the light of studies by Meeks,[70] Esler,[71] and others, all of the early groups of Jesus-believers had sectarian tendencies; the Hermeneia commentary on Romans traces the conflicts between congregations in Rome to confirm this assessment.[72] That a group of Jewish Jesus-believers would have been involved in the publication of 2 Corinthians or the Pauline letter corpus is highly unlikely in view of Paul's opposition to Jewish legalism in Galatians and Romans as well as the hostile rejection of Judaism in the Pastoral Epistles. Why would a group of Jewish Jesus-believers publicize the work of its prime adversary? The promotion and distribution of Pauline material presupposes a theological and organizational affinity with some branch of the Pauline movement, which for several centuries stood in tension with Jewish groups who believed in Jesus.

Like Hultgren, Thomas Schmeller is certain that 2 Cor 6:14–7:1 is out of place in its current location.[73] He also accepts the longstanding insight that there is an unbridgeable gap between chapters 1–9 and 10–13.[74] He seeks to solve both problems by suggesting that 6:14–7:1 originated as a transition between these sections and that it was later removed. Paul placed this material after discussing the Jerusalem offering to show his loyalty and thwart criticism by his opponents.[75] Unfortunately, despite a few thematic links, the discourse in 6:14–7:1 fits between chapters 9 and 10 even less smoothly than in its current location. After a sophisticated discussion of text-critical possibilities, Schmeller suggests that the editors of 2 Corinthians found this section excessively pro-Judaism and removed it. A later editor, however, decided to restore it, and chose the wrong spot for its insertion,[76] which is hardly convincing as a redactional motivation. However, as a consideration of redactional possibilities in the context of early textual alterations and transmissions, this study prepares the way for the extension of Günther Bornkamm's hypothesis.

PURSUING THE PATH LAID OUT BY GÜNTHER BORNKAMM

In Günther Bornkamm's study of 2 Corinthians, there is an exemplary fusion of historical and literary criticism, followed by redaction criticism that keeps the historical developments in the early church in view. There is a clarity about Bornkamm's work that stands in contrast with the turgid defensiveness of most recent studies. He bestrides the path leading from Johannes Weiss through Rudolf Bultmann to a compelling resolution of the main problems in 2 Corinthians. Bornkamm's analysis begins with a detailed analysis of the congregational situation, the identity of Paul's opponents, and the sequence of events from Paul's initial visit to the letter of reconciliation that allegedly closed the correspondence.[77] He then turns to the integrity question and concludes there are four originally separate letters or fragments as well as one non-Pauline interpolation embedded in 2 Corinthians. The first letter was an apology of Paul's apostolic office (2 Cor 2:14–6:13 + 2 Cor 7:2-4); the next was the letter of tears (2 Cor 10:1–13:13); then Paul wrote the instructions concerning the offering for the saints (2 Cor 9:1-15); the letter of reconciliation followed (2 Cor 1:1–2:13 + 2 Cor 7:5–8:24); finally there is the apocalyptic discourse that Bornkamm thought was of non-Pauline origin (2 Cor 6:14–7:1).

At approximately the same time that Bornkamm's study was published, several other scholars provided independent confirmation that 2 Corinthians contains four or five distinct components that reflect different phases of communication with the congregation. The Schmithals essay of 1956, based on his dissertation of 1954, identified the same components and differed from Bornkamm only in the identification of 2 Cor 6:14–7:1 as originally Pauline rather than a non-Pauline interpolation. The results are congruent with the Schmithals hypothesis of 1956 except for the identification of this interpolation. Also in contrast to Bornkamm, Schmithals was convinced that Paul's opponents in 2 Corinthians were as gnostic as opponents in 1 Corinthians, an assessment that has not proved adequate.[78] The work of Wolfgang Schenk provides a similar redactional theory.[79] J.-F. Collange's detailed analysis of 2 Cor 2:14–7:4 in *Énigmes* provides substantial confirmation of Bornkamm's results, except that he views 2 Cor 6:14–7:1 as an extended Pauline parenesis. There are more recent variants by G. Dautzenberg (1987),[80] Maria Margareta Gruber (1998),[81] Eve-Marie Becker (2002),[82] and Donald Walker (2002).[83] More recent contributions employing literary-critical and redactional methods stand within this critical consensus, include Betz, Dautzenberg, Becker, Baumert, Pesch, Donald Walker, and Welborn.

In his widely used commentary on the Corinthian correspondence, Heinz Dietrich Wendland (1972) sees three components joined in the second canonical epistle.[84] Philipp Vielhauer (1975)[85] comes to similar conclusions. Other scholars with a critical orientation such as Francis Watson (1984),[86] Victor Furnish (1984),[87] Edwin Freed (1991),[88] Margaret Thrall (1994),[89] Stephen Harris (1995),[90] Bart Ehrman (1997),[91] and Charles Wanamaker (2003)[92] treat 2 Corinthians as containing two letters: chapters 1–9 and 10–13.

The Bornkamm/Schmithals model of literary and redaction work on 2 Corinthians is reflected in a number of mainline studies. Among others, studies by Hans-Martin Schenke and Karl Martin Fischer (1978),[93] Willi Marxsen (1964/1968),[94] Helmut Koester (1987),[95] N. H. Taylor (1991),[96] Hans Dieter Betz (1992),[97] Dennis Duling and Norman Perrin (1994),[98] Steven Davies (1994),[99] David Barr (1995),[100] Erich Gräßer (2002),[101] Stephen Hultgren (2003),[102] Richard Pervo (2010),[103] and Lawrence Welborn (2011)[104] show the rise of the Bornkamm style of analysis to the level of a widely accepted premise among scholars committed to critical methods.

The result of this examination of literary-critical studies is that the framework developed by Bornkamm and Schmithals emerges as the most plausible basis for further refinement. The most influential development of this framework is provided by Margaret Mitchell and Calvin Roetzel.[105] They agree on a compelling hypothesis of five letters embedded in 2 Corinthians. While incorporating Betz's hypothesis of two administrative letters in 2 Cor 8 and 9, Mitchell infers from the references to Titus's journeys in 2 Cor 12:18 and 8:6, 18 that the references in the Letter of Tears refer back to arrangements in chapter 8. This indicates "quite clearly [that] 2 Corinthians 8 must have preceded 2 Corinthians 10-13."[106] She also observes that in Paul's initial instructions (1 Cor 16:3), he had indicated that the Corinthians would designate their own couriers to deliver the offering, while in 2 Cor 8:22, he takes it upon himself to appoint the credentialed couriers, which probably "led to their anger at him, suspicion about his motives, and doubt about his own credentials."[107] Since 2 Cor 2:14–6:13 + 7:2-4 appears to be "Paul's reply to the escalation of the Corinthian offense that Paul's letter of 2 Corinthians 8 had caused,"[108] she places the offering letter before the apology letter, which was viewed as an example of "arrogant overreaching of authority by Paul."[109]

Margaret Mitchell also attaches 13:11-13 to the end of the letter of reconciliation, but we cannot find her rationale. We accept Calvin Roetzel's argument that these verses fit "the conciliatory letter (2 Cor 1:1–2:13 + 2 Cor 7:5-16)," because παρακαλεῖσθε in 13:11 appears also in 1:4a and b, 1:6, and 2:7 and 8, as well as 7:6 and 13.[110] The conciliatory address "brothers" in 13:11 appears elsewhere in 2 Corinthians rationale only in 1:8. The tone of the closing admonitions and greetings in 13:11-13 fit more closely with this letter of reconciliation than with the fierce letter of chapters 10–13, including the "holy kiss" that had "special relevance in this fractured community,"[111] now that the conflict was over. Roetzel also makes a convincing case that the "tripartite benediction" in 13:14 resonates with the wording of 1:2 in the letter of reconciliation.[112] The references to "the love of God" and "the fellowship of the Holy Spirit" that are unique in this closing benediction reinforce the reconciliation that has been achieved. In summary, we accept their analysis with the addition of a few details[113]:

The fundraising letter = 2 Cor 8:1-24
The self-defense letter = 2 Cor 2:14–6:13 + 2 Cor 7:2-4
The letter of tears = 2 Cor 10:1–12:13 + [1 Cor 9:1-18] + 2 Cor 12:14–13:10
The reconciling letter = 2 Cor 1:1–2:13 + 2 Cor 7:5-16 + 2 Cor 13:11-13
The final fundraising letter = 2 Cor 9:1-15.

We feel compelled to alter this scheme in only minor regards. We are convinced that 2 Cor 6:14–7:1 is authentically Pauline material that originally appeared near the beginning of Letter B. It fits well with the other material in that letter and provides the explicit basis for Paul's subsequent comment in Letter C that he had written the Corinthians "not to associate with immoral people" (1 Cor 5:9). We also find that 1 Cor 9:1-18, which fits so poorly in its present location in canonical 1 Corinthians,[114] originally belonged in the Fool's Discourse, between 2 Cor 12:13 and 14. We agree with Bornkamm's conclusion that 2 Cor 9 is an independent letter sent to the Achaian churches after the crisis was over. Bultmann, Bornkamm, and others have shown that chapter 9 reflects a situation later than chapter 8.[115] Betz has provided a coherent analysis of these two chapters as administrative letters, one addressed to the church in the city of Corinth and the other to the congregations in the province of Achaia.[116]

The most significant shortcoming of the Mitchell / Roetzel refinement, however, is that they provide no redactional explanation of how these five documents came to be joined together to make canonical 2 Corinthians. They leave readers with the impression that the various papyrus leaves of the original letters fell together by accident to produce canonical 2 Corinthians. We are convinced that the method of redaction criticism can be employed to provide an answer to this puzzle.

DEVELOPING A COHERENT REDACTIONAL HYPOTHESIS

The route toward a plausible redactional hypothesis was traversed for the first time by Günther Bornkamm. Although the redactional process of joining these five pieces seems complicated at first glance, Bornkamm was able to visualize the process of editing papyrus scrolls, on which the Pauline letters were written. He proposed that 2 Corinthians was created by selecting the letter that needed correcting; that the redactor added two documents at the end of the framing letter and spliced two insertions in the middle. The redactor used the letter of reconciliation (1:1–2:13 + 7:5-8:24) as his frame and added the instruction for the Jerusalem offering (9:1-15) and the letter of tears (2 Cor 10:1–13:13) to the end. Then the apology (2 Cor 2:14–6:13 + 7:2-4) was inserted between 2 Cor 2:13 and 7:5 and the material of 2 Cor 6:14–7:1 was inserted in the middle of the apology.[117] The redactional process can be visualized as follows (figure 2.1).

Günther Bornkamm suggested plausible redactional motives for two of the four steps that were required to produce 2 Corinthians. The controversy with false teachers contained in the letter of tears (2 Cor 11:13-15) was placed at the end of the letter because of "a basic rule of early Christian edificatory literature . . . that the warning against false teachers is very often expressed at the end of certain writings and fragments."[118] He cites the parallels of 1 Cor 16:22, Gal 6:11-17 and Rom 16:17-20, but since the latter was probably added by a redactor,[119] it could not have served as a prior model.

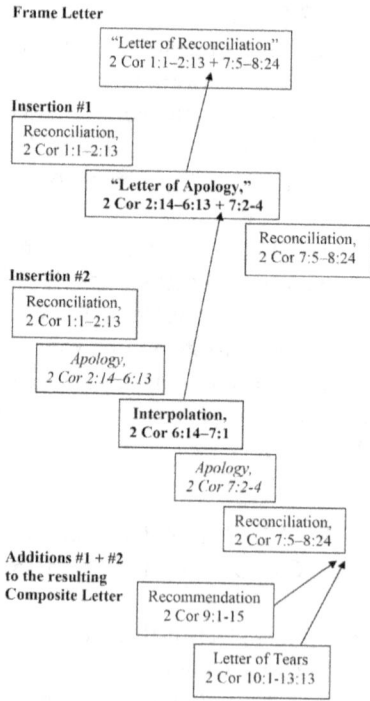

Figure 2.1 The Bornkamm Hypothesis.

The other examples Bornkamm cites are from works generally assigned to a period after the date he suggests for the redaction of 2 Corinthians: Jude 17ff.; 2 Peter 3:2ff.; Hebrews 13:9ff.; Revelation 22:11, 15, 18f.; Didache 16:3ff. The question of the placement of 2 Corinthians' redaction on the line of development between the original Pauline letters and the activities of the later Pauline school that created the Pastoral Epistles is therefore an issue raised by the critical examination of Bornkamm's study. It is entirely possible that the redactor of 2 Corinthians created or reinforced a precedent for later writers. The large number of parallels confirms the presence of a significant formal tradition, however, and Bornkamm's inference concerning the implications of early Catholicism is well taken. The redactor characterized Pauline opponents "as false prophets of the last times and put on the collection of letters the apocalyptic seal of inviolable validity. At the same time the apostle appears now in the role of the fully warranted messenger of God, warning and protecting his own congregation and the church at large from the fatal danger of heresy. Through this, our collection of letters assumes the character of an apostolic will and testament."[120]

Bornkamm also found a plausible motivation for the abrupt insertion of the apology at 2 Cor 2:13. Paul's account of the anxious journey from Troas to Macedonia is interrupted by the outburst of victorious thanksgiving. This has the effect of making the apostle's anxious travels into a "triumphal procession,"[121] depicted by the term θριαμβεύειν ("lead in triumph") which is associated with the Dionysian rites.[122] This countered the element of anxiety in the reconciliation letter, which was a serious contradiction to the heroic, stalwart image of Paul that was promoted at the end of the century in the Pastorals, Ephesians, and Acts.

The motivation for adding 2 Cor 9:1-15 at the end of the frame letter was less adequately explained by Bornkamm. Its thematic and temporal relationship with 2 Cor 8:1-24 were presumably such that the redactor could find no better place. This is not a compelling discernment of redactional motivation. Moreover, the connection of 2 Cor 9:1-15 to the Jerusalem offering, which seems so obvious to the modern historian,[123] is not stated explicitly. We offer a more cogent redactional suggestion here.

A more important area in which Bornkamm's hypothesis needs to be strengthened was suggested. Without taking up the complicated and ambivalent issue of the origin and authorship of this material,[124] its insertion at this particular location in 2 Corinthians appeared as baffling to Bornkamm as it did to other interpreters.[125] We return to this weakness in the next section of this chapter, where a redactional theory is developed for 2 Cor 6:14-7:1.

Finally, Bornkamm makes some suggestions about the place and time of the redaction of 2 Corinthians. Since the first clear reference to this letter is by Marcion, Bornkamm suggests it was assembled after the distribution of 1

Corinthians, around the turn of the century.[126] Although Bornkamm suspects it was not widely distributed at the beginning, it appears to belong to the period of the writing of Acts and the Pastorals. Since the redactor used only portions of the Corinthian letters, disregarding the origin of 2 Cor 6:14–7:1, Bornkamm insists that only Corinth can be considered as a place of origin.[127] This is hardly conclusive, however, because the gathering of Pauline letters could well have been the consequence of a half century of exchanging apostolic materials, or else the specific work of the redactor himself. Nevertheless, Bornkamm's study is a model worth refining. The fact that each of the redactional steps visible in 2 Corinthians reflects a motivation to align Paul more closely with the viewpoints of the Pastoral Epistles and Acts helps to provide a benchmark for measuring the trajectory through 1 Corinthians, which appears to have been published earlier in its canonical form. In its methodological and historical clarity and plausibility, this work by Bornkamm provides a model for our study. We feel that this is the most promising track to follow in seeking a resolution of the dilemmas in 2 Corinthians.

With regard to the addition of the Letter of Tears at the end of canonical 2 Corinthians, the redactional suggestions by Günther Bornkamm can be accepted as the starting point for our analysis. He explained why the powerful critique of false teachers contained in Letter F, the Letter of Tears / Fool's Discourse, was placed at the end of 2 Corinthians. Since the end of a letter contains the point of emphasis, this has the effect of emphasizing Pauline authority in the conflict with heresy. Although Bornkamm sought to ground this redactional decision in a general pattern for early Jesus-believing literature, this grounding proved to be less than compelling. We feel that a stronger case can be made that the redactional decision to place Letter F at the point of emphasis at the end correlates with the Pastorals. The reason they stress Pauline authority in the conflict with adversaries is to justify their strategy of excluding heretics. For example, by standing up against "Alexander the coppersmith" (2 Tim 4:14), Paul provides a model for Timothy's strategy of being on guard against such adversaries of the gospel (2 Tim 4:16). Although no one stood up for Paul in his "first defense" in the trial before a Roman authority, "the Lord stood by me and gave me strength to proclaim the message fully" (2 Tim 4:15, 17). This confirms Paul's role "to further the faith of God's elect and their knowledge of the truth which accords with godliness" (Tit 1:1). His authenticated followers are called to stand up against "insubordinate men, empty talkers and deceivers" who "must be silenced" (Tit 1:10-11). Titus is ordered to "rebuke them sharply . . . instead of giving heed to Jewish myths or to commands of men who reject the truth" (Tit 1:13-14). Exclusion is the proper policy for dissenters: "As for a man who is factious, after admonishing him once or twice, have nothing more to do with him, knowing that such a person is perverted and sinful; he is self-condemned"

(Tit 3:10-11). Timothy is ordered to "avoid such godless chatter, for it will lead people into more and more ungodliness, and their talk will eat its way like gangrene" (2 Tim 2:16-17).

As in the Pastoral Epistles, Paul's authority in Letter F contains "divine power to destroy strongholds. We destroy arguments and every proud obstacle to the knowledge of God, and take every thought captive to obey Christ, being ready to punish every disobedience, when your obedience is complete" (2 Cor 10:4-6). This theme of obedience plays an important role for Titus, who is commanded to "exhort and reprove with all authority. Let no one disregard you. Remind them to be submissive to rulers and authorities, to be obedient" (Tit 2:15-3:1). If Timothy is faithful to the "charge" of apostolic service, he will "wage the good warfare, holding faith and a good conscience. By rejecting conscience, certain persons have made shipwreck of their faith, among them Hymenaeus and Alexander, whom I have delivered to Satan that they may learn not to blaspheme" (1 Tim 1:18-20). The struggle against what Letter F called "every proud obstacle to the knowledge of God" (2 Cor 10:5) is carried out in 1 Timothy by castigating the motives of those who disagree:

> If anyone teaches otherwise and does not agree with the sound words of our Lord Jesus Christ and the teaching which accords with godliness, he is puffed up with conceit, he knows nothing; he has a morbid craving for controversy and for disputes about words, which produce envy, dissension, slander, base suspicions, and wrangling among men who are depraved in mind and bereft of the truth, imagining that godliness is a means of gain. (1 Tim 6:3-5)

In the Pastorals, the ultimate source of such bad conscience and impure motives is demonic, which also carries forward a theme in Letter F. Paul suspects that "as the serpent deceived Eve by his cunning, your thoughts will be led astray from a sincere and pure devotion to Christ" (2 Cor 11:3). In 1 Timothy, this satanic campaign continues to be effective against women: "For Adam was formed first, then Eve; and Adam was not deceived, but the woman was deceived and became a transgressor" (1 Tim 2:13-14). In 2 Timothy, the author hopes that by submitting to the authority of Paul's legitimate successors, "God may perhaps grant that they [i.e. the opponents] will repent and come to know the truth, and they may escape from the snare of the devil, after being captured by him to do his will" (2 Tim 2:25-26).

For the polemical orientation of the Pastorals, there would also have been a welcome resource in 2 Cor 11:4, which criticizes anyone who "comes and preaches another Jesus than the one we preached." Letter F challenges the audience to "examine yourselves, to see whether you are holding to your faith. Test yourselves. Do you not realize that Jesus Christ is in you?

unless indeed you fail to meet the test!" (2 Cor 13:5). This theme in Letter F is picked up in 2 Tim 2:8, which lists fragments of Paul's Christology that constitute traditional doctrine: "Remember Jesus Christ, risen from the dead, descended from David, as preached in my gospel." Timothy is urged to "be strong in the grace that is in Christ Jesus, and what you have heard from me before many witnesses entrust to faithful men who will be able to teach others also" (2 Tim 2:1-2). This traditional faith is to be maintained against those who preach, in effect, a very different Jesus: "For the time is coming when people will not endure sound teaching, but having itching ears they will accumulate for themselves teachers to suit their own likings, and will turn away from listening to the truth and wander into myths" (2 Tim 4:3-4).

Letter F contains a strong emphasis on the need to sustain responsible moral behavior within the congregation, which is an important theme throughout the Pastorals. Paul fears that he "may have to mourn over many of those who sinned before and have not repented of the impurity, immorality, and licentiousness which they have practiced" (2 Cor 12:21). This is linked with adherence to the law in 1 Timothy:

> Now we know that the law is good, if any one uses it lawfully, understanding this, that the law is not laid down for the just but for the lawless and disobedient, for the ungodly and sinners, for the unholy and profane, for murderers of fathers and murderers of mothers, for manslayers, immoral persons, sodomites, kidnapers, liars, perjurers, and whatever else is contrary to sound doctrine. (1 Tim 1:8-10)

Titus is urged to provide "in all respects a model of good deeds" (Tit 2:7), so his followers will learn to "apply themselves to good deeds; these are excellent and profitable to men" (Tit 3:8). Hence, the mark of the followers of the Pastoral Epistles is their conformity to the rule: "Let everyone who names the name of the Lord depart from iniquity" (2 Tim 2:19).

In summary, there are echoes throughout the Pastoral Epistles for the authoritative image of Paul in the conflict with heresy that is conveyed by the redactional decision to place Letter F at the end of canonical 2 Corinthians. This congruity confirms our thesis that the authors of the Pastorals were responsible for the redaction of 2 Corinthians.

As noted earlier, Bornkamm provided a compelling rationale for inserting the material from Letter E (2 Cor 2:14–6:13 + 7:2-4) into the travelogue of Letter G whose tone of anxiety was so troubling. After the beginnings of imperial persecution under the emperors Nero, Domitian, and Trajan, there was a need to celebrate models of courageous martyrdom.[128] For a community needing a model of unbending, fanatical courage in the face of death to follow, Letter G stood in urgent need of correction. The resultant triumphalism is reminiscent of the reasons for generosity in the book of Acts, noted by Helmut Koester.[129] By placing Paul on the pedestal of a super apostle, the abrupt changes of mood and subject in 2:13-14; 6:13-14; 7:1-2; and 7:4-5 are rendered plausible, since normal standards of behavior and mentality no longer apply.

1 and 2 Timothy create a similar image of the courageous, triumphant Paul. In 1 Tim 1:12, Paul thanks God for giving him "strength" for the ministry of spreading "sound doctrine" (1 Tim 1:10). In 2 Timothy, the stories in the "book of acts" seem to be alluded in references to "my persecutions, my sufferings, what befell me at Antioch, at Iconium, and at Lystra, what persecutions I endured; yet from them all the Lord rescued me" (2 Tim 3:11). In all the adversities recounted in Acts, "the Lord stood by me and gave me strength to proclaim the message fully, that all the Gentiles might hear it. So I was rescued from the lion's mouth. The Lord will rescue me from every evil and save me for his heavenly kingdom" (2 Tim 4:17-18). Although Paul has been made to "suffer as I do," this does not make him "ashamed, for I know whom I have believed, and I am sure that he is able to guard until that Day what has been entrusted to me" (2 Tim 1:12). Although Paul is "suffering and wearing fetters like a criminal," he remains triumphant because "the word of God is not fettered" (2 Tim 2:9). This triumph will be shared by Paul and his devoted followers, because "if we endure, we shall also reign with him" (2 Tim 2:12). This leads to the famous recapitulation of Paul's stalwart courage and its sure reward:

> For I am already on the point of being sacrificed; the time of my departure has come. I have fought the good fight, I have finished the race, I have kept the faith. Henceforth there is laid up for me the crown of righteousness, which the Lord, the righteous judge, will award to me on that Day, and not only to me but also to all who have loved his appearing. (2 Tim 4:6-8)

Paul urges Timothy to share in this battle by fighting "the good fight of the faith" (1 Tim 6:12), because "God did not give us a spirit of timidity but a spirit of power." (2 Tim 1:7). Timothy is admonished to "be strong in the grace that is in Christ Jesus" (2 Tim 2:1) and to "share in [Paul's] suffering as a good soldier of Christ Jesus" (2 Tim 2:3). Timothy is urged to "always be steady" and to "endure suffering," following Paul's stalwart example (2 Tim 4:5). In 2 Tim 1:4, it is the young man rather than the stalwart Paul who is remembered for his "tears," and Paul confesses, "I long night and day to see you, that I may be filled with joy," which reformulates the anxiety of Letter F followed by joyful triumph of Letter G in less problematic terms.[130] In summary, the redactional insertion of Letter E into the most problematic point in the travelogue of Letter G is closely paralleled by the details in the Pastorals, which confirms once again our hypothesis that the same hands were involved in both creations.

Returning now to the material in 2 Cor 9:1-15, Letter H, which Bornkamm was unable fully to explain, the appropriate redactional question is what purpose it would serve at the end of the first century when the editing likely took place. Compared with the specific instructions about the completion of the offering in 2 Cor 8:1-24, including travel details for Titus and other unnamed representatives (8:18-24), which would have been hard for a later generation to follow, 2 Cor 9:6-15 provides pious reasons for generosity within a context that goes beyond a specific offering in the mid-fifties. 2 Cor 9:13 speaks of "your contribution for them and for all others." This would be highly useful for justifying financial support for clergy, which was a major issue at the end of the century. The proximity to the Pastoral Epistles is particularly palpable in verse 13, whose combination of ὑποταγή ("subordination, obedience") and ὁμολογία ("confession") is compatible with the thought of the Pastorals.[131] 2 Cor 9:1-15 appears to place apostolic authority behind the effort to institutionalize charity and the support of ordained clergy, shifting both "gospel" and "service" in the direction of submission to ecclesiastical norms.

Just as in 2 Cor 9:9, there is biblical warrant for the remuneration of leaders in 1 Timothy: "Let the elders who rule well be considered worthy of double honor, especially those who labor in preaching and teaching; for the scripture says, 'You shall not muzzle an ox when it is treading out the grain,' and, 'The laborer deserves his wages' " (1 Tim 5:17-18). Titus is admonished, "Do your best to speed Zenas the lawyer and Apollos on their way; see that they lack nothing. And let our people learn to apply themselves to good deeds, so as to help cases of urgent need, and not to be unfruitful" (Tit 3:13-14). The provision of travel resources for Zenas and Apollos is similar to the reference at the end of Romans. Like the matter of helping "cases of urgent need," it involves meeting needs for specific occasions rather than undertaking an ongoing financial obligation.

We noted earlier that Bornkamm was unable to suggest a redactional rationale for the insertion of 2 Cor 6:14–7:1. This section was inserted into Letter E immediately after the exhortation, "Be broadened also" in 6:13. The verb πλατύνω ("be enlarged") in the passive was used by Epictetus to depict tolerant breadth.[132] It is similar to the modern expression, "be broad minded." In the context of Paul's original controversy with the Corinthians, which is the point of concentration for commentators, the meaning is clear. But what would it have implied half a century later, in the context of competing groups of Jesus-believers castigating each other as heretical? Now it becomes a call to tolerance, a suitable guideline from the apostle himself to reject the trend toward separation from groups holding disparate opinions and toward resultant institutional rigidity. This is the precise opposite of the admonition typical of the Pastorals, "Avoid such people" (2 Timothy 3:5) and echoed in the interpolation of Romans 16:17, "avoid them."[133] This strategy of excluding some people from the community is implied in Titus 3:10-11, "as for a man who is factious, after admonishing him once or twice, have nothing more to do with him, knowing that such a person is perverted and sinful; he is self-condemned." Hymenaeus and Alexander are named in 1 Tim 1:20 as persons whom Paul excluded from the church, thus providing a model for later excommunications. A method of excluding contact with insubordinate people who remain inside a community is implied by the command in Titus 1:11 that "they must be silenced."

Given the openness of the gnostic opponents of the Pastorals to Hellenistic philosophy and astrology, a motto like πλατύνθητε καὶ ὑμεῖς ("broaden yourselves also") in the frame letter G would tend to imply a broad-minded attitude toward paganism. In this kind of context, the insertion of 2 Cor 6:14–7:1 by conservatives associated with the creation of the Pastoral Epistles would have been highly useful. It sharply delimits the scope of tolerance, forbidding close associations with "unbelievers." In a similar manner, the interpolation in Romans 16:17-20 delimits the scope of the holy kiss, which Paul urged in 16:16 should be extended to one another.[134]

This redactional hypothesis is not damaged by suggestions about the possibly non-Pauline origin of 2 Cor 6:14–7:1.[135] As Betz concludes, this "carefully constructed parenesis . . . is undoubtedly Christian: Christ is the decisive divine force opposing Beliar both cosmically and upon earth. The Christian people are under Christ's protection, as long as they stand firmly in the Sinai covenant. The purpose of the Christian life is to achieve the state of holiness and thus to become acceptable to God in the final judgment. This is done through purification from all defilement brought about by Beliar and his forces. Because of this goal, any contact with people outside of the covenant must be eliminated."[136] Whether or not Betz is correct in assigning the original of this material to the Judaizer movement of the fifties, it serves perfectly around 100 to place the weight of apostolic authority behind the anti-heretical barricades of the Pastoral Epistles.

An important unfinished task resulting from the conviction that 2 Cor 8:1-24 is part of a separate letter addressed to the Corinthian church is to develop a hypothesis about why the redactor appended it after the portion of the letter of consolation ending with 7:16. So far as we can tell, no such hypothesis has ever been developed. In contrast to the earlier insertions in 2 Corinthians, there are no indications that the ending of chapter 7 posed an issue that the addition of chapter 8 could resolve. While no antithesis is visible, the transition between these two chapters is not particularly smooth, with a shift from first person singular discourse in 7:12-16 into first-person plural discourse in 8:1-3 and an even more abrupt shift in style and content from celebration in chapter 7 to business in chapter 8.[137] Paul's complete confidence in the reconciled Corinthians in 7:16 moves without transition into praise of the Macedonians in 8:1-5. There is no doubt about these two chapters reflecting two completely different rhetorical situations. What they share, as Margaret Thrall points out, are "two points of connection . . . in both chapters Paul refers to the situation in Macedonia, and in both he speaks of visits to Corinth by Titus."[138] In view of the similarities in other aspects of the redaction that we have identified,[139] it is likely that the references to Titus were more significant. He is an agent of the "obedience of all" the Corinthians in 7:15, a theme of importance in the letter to Titus.[140] His name is mentioned three times in 2 Cor 7:6, 13, 14, while there are allusions to him in 7:7, 14, and 15. In Letter D, Titus is mentioned by name in 2 Cor 8:6, 16 and 23, in addition to allusions to him in 8:17, 18, and 22-23. In contrast, although 2 Cor 9 also deals with the Jerusalem offering, there is no reference to Titus. In chapter 8, Titus is entrusted with the organization of the Corinthian fundraising (8:6); his eagerness to serve in this connection is extolled in 8:16-17; and in 8:23, he is authorized as Paul's "partner and co-worker in your service," referring to the Corinthian participation in the offering.[141] This resonates with the climactic advice at the end of the letter to Titus that he should see to it that Zenas and Apollos have travel funds for their mission and that church members should be taught to perform such "good works" (Tit 3:13-14). Since it is likely that the Pastoral Epistles were created by the same hands that edited the Corinthian letters, the references in chapter 8 provide an authorization for Titus's leadership in subsequent philanthropy. This may explain why Letter D was added to the frame letter of 2 Corinthians in the position immediately after the references to Titus in chapter 7 and immediately before the insertion of Letter H, 2 Cor 9:1-15 (figure 2.2).

The redactional motive for selecting the ending of the letter of consolation (2 Cor 13:11-13) must be inferred from the context, since we cannot compare it with the other four endings of the letters embedded in canonical 2 Corinthians, which the redactor discarded. There is a direct verbal link between καταρτίζω ("restore" or "make complete") in 13:11 and κατάρτισις ("restoration") in 13:9, which probably supported the redactor's choice of this particular ending. 1 Cor 13:10 ends by clarifying the God-given ἐξουσία ("authority") conveyed in Paul's letter. In contrast to the original context of 13:11-13 that avoided the idea of authority while stressing mutual vulnerability and injuries on both sides that needed to be assuaged by divine comfort (1:4-6), the new context at the end of the canonical letter redefines everything as an expression of Paul's authority. The address "brothers" in 13:11 now has the connotation of persons willing to submit to apostolic authority, which definitely excludes those involved in "strife, envy, outbursts of anger, disputes, slanders, whispers, self-inflations, disturbances" (12:20). The admonition καταρτίζεστε no longer has the connotation of achieving perfection under the comfort of Christ[142] but now means "pull yourselves together,"[143] "put things in order" or "put to rights"[144] by submitting to Pauline authority under the threat of severe punishment (13:2-4, 10). The admonition παρακαλεῖσθε in 13:11 no longer has the sense of consolation[145] but of submitting to authoritative admonition, reflected in translations like "be exhorted,"[146] "be admonished,"[147] "heed my appeal,"[148] "accept correction,"[149] or "pay attention to my appeals."[150] The admonition τὸ αὐτὸ φρονεῖτε, which in the original context of the letter of consolation, implied the solidarity of believers whose mode of affliction differed but whose comfort in Christ was the same. Now "be of one mind"[151] implies doctrinal and ethical uniformity enforced by the authority of Paul that silences dissenters involved in "strife . . . disputes, slanders, [and] disturbances" (2 Cor 12:25).[152] To "be at peace" in this canonical context is the result of eliminating such dissent. The "God of peace" achieves such unification not by reconciling adversaries as in the letter of consolation but by stamping out heretics under the feet of the orthodox, to use the language of the interpolation in Romans 16:20.[153]

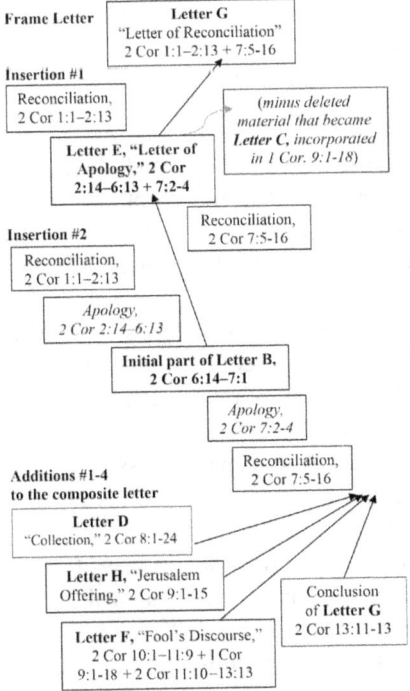

Figure 2.2 Our Hypothesis about the Redactional Composition of 2 Corinthians.

1:1–2:13	2:14–6:13	6:14–7:1	7:2-4	7:5-16
From **Letter G,** the Letter of Reconciliation	From **Letter E,** the Letter of Apology	From **Letter B,** the Letter of Bodily Relations	From **Letter E,** the Letter of Apology	From **Letter G,** the Letter of Reconciliation

8:1-24	9:1-15	10:1–11:9 + 11:10–13:13	13:11-13
From **Letter D,** the first Offering Letter	From **Letter H,** the Jerusalem Offering Letter	From **Letter F,** the Fool's Discourse	Conclusion of **Letter G**

Figure 2.3 The Result: Canonical 2 Corinthians.

In contrast to the impartial love of God in the authentic letters of Paul, the context at the end of the canonical letter implies that only those submitting to Paul's authority receive "the love of God." Only they are to be given the "holy kiss" and receive the threefold blessing that Calvin Roetzel discerned in 13:13.[154]

In the context of canonical 2 Corinthians, the final appeal matches the spirit of the Pastorals: "Finally, brethren, farewell, mend your ways, heed my appeal" (2 Cor 13:11). 1 Timothy makes clear that one of the "ways" to be mended included the threat of proto-gnostic heresy: "O Timothy, guard what has been entrusted to you. Avoid the godless chatter and contradictions of what is falsely called knowledge, for by professing it some have missed the mark as regards the faith" (1 Tim 6:20-21). Throughout the Pastorals, this call to heed Paul's "appeal" is continued in ways that matched the perceived needs of their communities. The apostle's appeal in 2 Timothy is to "follow the pattern of the sound words which you have heard from me, in the faith and love which are in Christ Jesus; guard the truth that has been entrusted to you by the Holy Spirit who dwells within us" (2 Tim 1:13-14). Titus is enjoined

2 Cor. 1:1–2:13
from **Letter G,** the Letter of Reconciliation

2 Cor. 2:14–6:13
from **Letter E**, the Letter of Apology

2 Cor. 6:14–7:1
from **Letter B,** the Letter of Bodily Relations

2 Cor. 7:2-4
from **Letter E,** the Letter of Apology

2 Cor. 7:5-16
from **Letter G,** the Letter of Reconciliation

2 Cor 8:1-24
Letter D, the first Offering Letter

2 Cor 9:1-15
from **Letter F**, the Jerusalem Offering Letter

2 Cor 10:1–11:9 + 11:10–13:13
From **Letter E,** the Fool's Discourse

2 Cor. 13:11-13
Conclusion of **Letter G**

Figure 2.4 The Result: Canonical 2 Corinthians, Showing the Order of Composition of Materials.

"but as for you, teach what befits sound doctrine," (Tit 2:1) which consists of behaviorial guidelines for various categories of congregational members. He is urged to "declare these things; exhort and reprove with all authority" (Tit 2:15).

We therefore propose the following redactional scheme for 2 Corinthians, which correlates in almost every detail with the viewpoint of the Pastoral Epistles (see figure 2.4).

NOTES

1. Johann Salomo Semler, *Paraphrasis II. Epistolae ad Corinthios* (Halae Magdeburgicae: Hemmerde, 1776).

2. Hans Dieter Betz, *2 Corinthians 8 and 9: A Commentary on Two Administrative Letters of the Apostle Paul*, Hermeneia (Philadelphia: Fortress, 1985), 37–128; Maurice Goguel, *Introduction au Nouveau Testament. Les épitres pauliniennes* (Paris: Editions Ernest Leroux, 1926), 4.32, 69–72.

3. Noted by Wolfgang Schenk, "Korintherbriefe," *Theologische Realenzyklopädie* 19 (1990): 620–40; 624. This is described in detail by Betz, *2 Corinthians 8 and 9*, 3–4.

4. See the detailed account of this research in Betz, *2 Corinthians 8 and 9*, 10–18.

5. Reimund Bieringer, "Teilungshypothesen zum 2. Korintherbrief," pp. 67–105 in Reimund Bieringer and Jan Lambrecht. *Studies on 2 Corinthians*, BETL 112 (Leuven: University Press and Peeters, 1994), 96–97, provides a comprehensive list of scholars advocating the major hypotheses.

6. Johannes Weiss, Review of Anton Halme, *Der Vierkapitelbrief im zweiten Korintherbrief des Apostels Paulus* (Essen: Baedeker, 1894), in *Theologische Literaturzeitung* 17 (1894): 512–14. Weiss' literary-critical insights were accepted by Halmel in *Der zweite Korintherbrief des Apostels Paulus* (Halle: Niemeyer, 1904). According to Walter Schmithals in "Die Korintherbriefe als Briefsammlung," *Zeitschrift für die neutestamentliche Wissenschaft* 64 (1973): 263–88 (275), Christian August Gottfried Emmerling, *Epistula Pauli ad Corinthios posterior graece perpetuo commentario illustrata* (Leipzig: J. A. Barth, 1823), was actually the first to identify 6:14-7:1 as an insert into 2:14-7:4, but it was Weiss's work that influenced the future. For an English language version of Weiss' insight, see Weiss, *Earliest Christianity: A History of the Period A. D. 30-150, Books I-II*, edited by F. C. Grant (New York: Harper and Row, 1959), 345–53.

7. Among early advocates of Weiss' view were Albert Loisy, "Les épîtres de S. Paul," *Revue d'histoire et de literature religieuses* 7 (1921): 213–50; Loisy, *Les Livres du Nouveau Testament* (Paris: Émile Nourry, 1923), 39–47; Paul-Louis Couchoud, "Reconstitution et Classement des Lettres de Saint Paul, *RHR* 87 (1923): 8–31; Herbert Preisker, "Zur Komposition des zweiten Korintherbriefes," *TBl* 5 (1926) 154–57; Hans Windisch, *Der zweite Korintherbrief*, KEK 6 (Göttingen: Vandenhoeck & Ruprecht, 1970), 19; and the influential lectures by Rudolf Bultmann that were later edited and published by Erich Dinkler, available in English translation as *Second Letter to the Corinthians* (Minneapolis: Augsburg, 1985), 16–18. For a discussion of later advocates of Weiss' viewpoint, see the notes below.

8. Margaret Mitchell in her treatment of 2 Cor 8:6 and 18 refers to the plan of sending Titus, while 1 Cor 12:18 looks back on this journey. See the discussion in Mitchell, "Paul's Letters to Corinth: The Interpretive Intertwining of Literary and Historical Reconstruction," in Daniel N. Schowalter and Steven J. Friesen, editors, *Urban Religion in Roman Corinth: Interdisciplinary Approaches*, HTS 53 (Cambridge: Harvard University Press, 2005), 307–38; 326. She cites C. K. Barrett, *The Second Epistle to the Corinthians*, HNTC (New York: Harper & Row, 1973), 325.

9. This concept derives from Lloyd F. Bitzer, "The Rhetorical Situation," *Philosophy and Rhetoric* 1 (1968): 1–14; see also Bitzer's refinement in "Functional Communication: A Situational Perspective," in E. E. White, editor, *Rhetoric in Transition: Studies in the Nature and Uses of Rhetoric* (University Park: Pennsylvania State University Press, 1980), 21–39. See also Robert Jewett, *Romans: A Commentary*, Hermeneia (Minneapolis: Fortress, 2007), 41–42; Albert Brendle, *Im Prozeß*

der Konfliktüberwendung. Eine exegetische Studie zur Kommunikationssituation zwischen Paulus und den Korinthern in 2 Kor 1,1-2,13; 7,4-16, European University Studies, Series XXIII, Theology, 533 (Frankfurt: Peter Lang, 1995), as well as David A. deSilva, "Meeting the Exigency of a Complex Rhetorical Situation: Paul's Strategy in 2 Corinthians 1 through 7," *AUSS* 34 (1996): 5–22; Elisabeth Schüssler Fiorenza, "Rhetorical Situation and Historical Reconstruction in 1 Corinthians," *NTS* 33 (1987): 386–403; Dennis L. Stamps, "Rethinking the Rhetorical Situation: The Entextualization of the Situation in New Testament Epistles," in Stanley E. Porter and Thomas H. Olbricht, editors, *Rhetoric and the New Testament: Essays from the 1992 Heidelberg Conference*, JSNTSup 90 (Sheffield: JSOT, 1993), 193–210; Duane F. Watson, "The Contributions and Limitations of Greco-Roman Rhetorical Theory for Constructing the Rhetorical and Historical Situations of a Pauline Epistle," in Stanley E. Porter and Dennis L. Stamps, editors, *The Rhetorical Interpretation of Scripture: Essays from the 1996 Malibu Conference*, JSNTSup 180 (Sheffield: Sheffield Academic Press, 1999), 125–51.

10. Bitzer, "Rhetorical Situation," 10.

11. Bitzer, "Rhetorical Situation," 6.

12. Watson, "Contributions," 133.

13. Jewett, *The Thessalonian Correspondence: Pauline Rhetoric and Millenarian Piety*, FF (Minneapolis: Fortress Press, 1986), 71–78; *Romans*, 42–46.

14. Hans Dieter Betz, *Galatians: A Commentary on Paul's Letter to the Churches in Galatia*, Hermeneia (Philadelphia: Fortress, 1979), 14–25.

15. Church, "Rhetorical Structure," 17–33.

16. L. Gregory Bloomquist, *The Function of Suffering in Philippians*, JSNTSup 78 (Sheffield: JSOT Press, 1993), 119–38; John Reumann, *Philippians: A New Translation with Introduction and Commentary*, AB 33B (New Haven and London: Yale University Press, 2008), 10 n. 2.

17. Jewett, *Thessalonian Correspondence*, 81–87; Frank W. Hughes, *Early Christian Rhetoric and 2 Thessalonians*, JSNTSup 30 (Sheffield: JSOT Press, 1989), 51–74.

18. Watson, "Contributions," 133.

19. Weiss, Review of Halmel, 513.

20. L. L. Welborn, "Like Broken Pieces of a Ring: 2 Cor 1,1-2,13; 7,5-16 and Ancient Theories of Literary Unity." *NTS* 42 (1996): 559–83; reprinted pp. 95–131 in L. L. Welborn, *Politics and Rhetoric in the Corinthian Epistles* (Macon: Mercer University Press, 1997), 95, providing the translations of Weiss that follow.

21. Weiss, *History I-II*, 1.349.

22. Welborn, "Literary Unity," 119–24.

23. Welborn, "Literary Unity," 131.

24. Alan M. G. Stephenson, "A Defence of the Integrity of II Corinthians," in Kurt Aland, editor, *The Authorship and Integrity of the New Testament*, Theological Collections, 4 (London: SPCK, 1965), 82–97; "Partition Theories on II Corinthians," in F. L. Cross, editor, *Studia Evangelica* II, TU 87(Berlin: Akademie Verlag, 1964), 639–46.

25. Niels Hyldahl, "Die Frage nach der literarischen Einheit des Zweiten Korintherbriefes," *ZNW* 64 (1973): 289–306.

26. Michael Goulder, "2 Cor 6:14-7:1 as an Integral Part of 2 Corinthians," *NovT* 36 (1994): 47–57; 54–47.

27. Margaret E. Thrall, "The Problem of II Cor. vi. 14 - vii. 1 in Some Recent Discussion," *NTS* 24 (1977–78): 132–48; 139.

28. David A. deSilva, "Meeting the Exigency of a Complex Rhetorical Situation: Paul's Strategy in 2 Corinthians 1 through 7," *AUSS* 34 (1996): 5–22; 9. See also his articles, "Measuring Penultimate Against Ultimate Reality: An Investigation of the Integrity and Argumentation of 2 Corinthians," *JSNT* 52 (1993): 41–70; and "Recasting the Moment of Decision: 2 Corinthians 6:14-7:1 in Its Literary Context." *AUSS* 31 (1993): 3–16.

29. See Welborn, "Broken Pieces," 562–66 for a demonstration of the appropriately rhetorical transition between 2:13 and 7:5.

30. deSilva, "Meeting the Exigency," 9.

31. deSilva, "Meeting the Exigency," 10–14.

32. J. D. H. Amador, "Revisiting 2 Corinthians: Rhetoric and the Case for Unity," *NTS* 46 (2000): 92–111; 93–94.

33. Amador admits this on p. 98, that "it is difficult not to admit an abrupt change in intonation and modality when chapters 10–13 are read after the volitional appeals of chapters 8–9. Tones of defensiveness, irony (sometimes playful, sometimes serious) and a shift in the position of authority (*ethos*) of Paul vis-à-vis his audience enter into the discourse in a way that seems abrupt, if not altogether risky in its potential to alienate the community."

34. Amador, "Revisiting 2 Corinthians," 107–8.

35. Betz, *2 Corinthians 8 and 9*, especially 129–40.

36. Amador, "Revisiting 2 Corinthians," 101–5.

37. Amador, "Revisiting 2 Corinthians," 105–6.

38. Amador, "Revisiting 2 Corinthians," 111.

39. Fredrick J. Long, *Ancient Rhetoric and Paul's Apology: The Compositional Unity of 2 Corinthians*, SNTSMS 131 (Cambridge: Cambridge University Press, 2004), 1.

40. See the studies by Belleville, Danker, Fitzgerald, Gruber, Hafemann, Heckel, Holland, Oliveira, Stockhausen, and Sundermann.

41. Long, *Paul's Apology*, 144.

42. Long, *Paul's Apology*, 144.

43. Long, *Paul's Apology*, 170–71.

44. Ivor H. Jones, "Rhetorical Criticism and the Unity of 2 Corinthians: One 'Epilogue', or More?" *NTS* 54 (2008): 496–524.

45. Jones, "Rhetorical Criticism," 499.

46. Jones, "Rhetorical Criticism," 502–12, evaluating Long, *Paul's Apology*, 190–97.

47. Jones, "Rhetorical Criticism," 511–12.

48. Jones, "Rhetorical Criticism," 516; on the next page Jones declares that 9:15 is "most certainly" an epilogue.

49. Jones, "Rhetorical Criticism," 523.
50. David R. Hall, *The Unity of the Corinthian Correspondence*, JSNTSup 251 (London and New York: T & T Clark, 2003).
51. Söding, *Wege der Schriftauslegung*, 191.
52. Lindemann, *erste Korintherbrief*, 3–6.
53. Schnelle, *Einführung*, 93–94.
54. Meiser and Kühneweg et al, *Proseminar II*, 61.
55. Merklein, "Einheitlichkeit," 345–75.
56. Horn, "Literarkritik," 748–49.
57. Bieringer and Lambrecht, *Studies*, 67–180; 531–70.
58. Barnett, *Second Epistle*, 17–25.
59. Garland, *2 Corinthians*, 38–45.
60. Scott, *2 Corinthians*, 4–7.
61. Lambrecht, *Second Corinthians*, 8–12.
62. Kistemaker, *Second Epistle*, 11–15.
63. Hafemann, *2 Corinthians*, 37–39.
64. Harris, *Second Epistle*, 8–51.
65. Stegman, *Second Corinthians*, 23–24.
66. Schmeller, *zweite Brief*, 19–38.
67. See the excellent and recent analysis of partition theories of 2 Corinthians and the positive statement of the need for them in Jay Twomey, *2 Corinthians: Crisis and Conflict*, Phoenix Guides to the New Testament, 8 (Sheffield: Sheffield Phoenix Press, 2013), 8–20.
68. Hultgren, "Ephesian Redaction," 39.
69. Hultgren, "Ephesian Redaction," 41–43; Fitzmyer, "Qumran," 271–80; Gnilka, '2 Corinthians 6:14–7:1," 48–68.
70. Meeks, *Urban Christians*, 84–103; Horsley, "Alternative Society," 392–95.
71. Esler, *The First Christians in their Social Worlds*, especially pp. 52–91.
72. Jewett, *Romans*, 61, 72–74, 225, 710, 836.
73. Schmeller, "2 Kor 6.14-7.1," 220–24.
74. Schmeller, "2 Kor 6.14-7.1," 224–26.
75. Schmeller, "2 Kor 6.14-7.1," 231.
76. Schmeller, "2 Kor 6.14-7.1," 236–37.
77. Bornkamm, "Vorgeschichte," 4–36.
78. See Georgi, *Opponents*, passim.
79. Schenk, "Korintherbriefe," 620–40.
80. Gerhard Dautzenburg, "Der zweite Korintherbrief als Briefsammlung. Zur Frage der literarischen Einheitlichkeit und des theologischen Gefüges 2 Kor 1–8," in *Aufstieg und Niedergang der römischen Welt* 25, no. 4 (1987): 3045–66.
81. Gruber, *Herrlichkeit*, 23–25.
82. Becker, *Letter Hermeneutics in 2 Corinthians*, 65–71.
83. Walker, *Letter Fragment*, 1–9.
84. Heinz-Dietrich Wendland, *Die Briefe an die Korinther*, NTD 7 (Göttingen: Vandenhoeck & Ruprecht, 1968), 7–9.
85. Vielhauer, *Geschichte*, 150–55.

86. Watson, "Painful Letter," 324–46.
87. Furnish, *II Corinthians*, 35–47.
88. Freed, *Critical Introduction*, 263–65.
89. Margaret E. Thrall, *A Critical and Exegetical Commentary on the Second Epistle to the Corinthians*, 2 volumes, ICC (Edinburgh: T. & T. Clark, 1994, 2000), 3–43.
90. Harris, *Introduction*, 260–62.
91. Ehrman, *Historical Introduction*, 280–85.
92. Wanamaker, "Power of God," 202–3.
93. Schenke and Fischer, *Einleitung*, 1.108-123.
94. Marxsen, *Introduction*, 77–91.
95. Koester, *Introduction*, 53–54.
96. Taylor, "Composition," 70–71.
97. Betz, "Corinthians," 1148–54.
98. Duling and Perrin, *Myth & History*, 178–83.
99. Davies, *Fundamentals*, 89.
100. Barr, *New Testament Story*, 115–17.
101. Gräßer, *zweite Brief*, 1.29-33.
102. Hultgren, "Ephesian Redaction," 39–56.
103. Richard I. Pervo, *The Making of Paul*, 38–43.
104. Welborn, *End to Enmity*, 23–25, 445–46.
105. Mitchell, "Letters to Corinth," 307–38; Mitchell, "Corinthian Correspondence," 22–36; Calvin J. Roetzel, *2 Corinthians*, ANTC (Nashville: Abingdon Press, 2007), 30–36.
106. Mitchell, "Letters to Corinth," 326; this was also argued by Barrett, *Second Epistle*, 325.
107. Mitchell, "Letters to Corinth," 328.
108. Mitchell, "Letters to Corinth," 331.
109. Mitchell, "Letters to Corinth," 332.
110. Roetzel, *2 Corinthians*, 144.
111. Roetzel, *2 Corinthians*, 145.
112. Roetzel, *2 Corinthians*, 145–46.
113. Mitchell, "Paul's Letters to Corinth," 324; Roetzel, *2 Corinthians*, 32–33.
114. For an analysis of this problem, see the next chapter.
115. Bultmann, *zweite Brief*, 258; Bornkamm, "History," 260–61; Klein, "2Kor 8 und 9," 122–24.
116. Betz, *2 Corinthians 8 and 9*, 37–128.
117. Vielhauer advocates a similar redactional scheme in *Geschichte*, 153–54.
118. Bornkamm, "History," 261.
119. See Jewett, *Romans*, 985–96.
120. Bornkamm, "History," 262.
121. Bornkamm, "History," 262.
122. Bornkamm, "Vorgeschichte," 30. For an extensive investigation of Paul's meaning in using the verb θριαμβεύειν, see Christoph Heilig, *Paul's Triumph: Reassessing 2 Corinthians 2:14 in its Literary and Historical Context*, BTS 27 (Leuven: Peeters, 2017).

123. Georgi, *Geschichte der Kollekte*, 67–78.

124. Betz, "2 Corinthians 6:14-7:1," 88–108, supplies the basic argument against Pauline authorship. His key premise is that ἑτεροζυγεῖν ("unequally yoked") in 2 Corinthians 6:14 implies the yoke of the law. This is problematic because the relationship is elaborated in the following verses with relational terms such as "share . . . fellowship . . . agreement". Without reading the entire Judaistic program of assuming the yoke of the law into this term, the passage could be understood more naturally as admonishing the avoidance of relationships with pagans. The issue of the authenticity of this passage remains open.

125. See, for example, Barrett, *Second Epistle*, 23–25.

126. Bornkamm, "Vorgeschichte," 33–34.

127. Bornkamm, "Vorgeschichte," 33.

128. See Frend, *Martyrdom and Persecution*, 79–235; Castelli, *Martyrdom and Memory*, 39–68, 104–33, 197–203; Moss, "Martyrdom," 24–25. See also Gruber, *Herrlichkeit in Schwachheit*, 97–124.

129. James M. Robinson and Helmut Koester, *Trajectories through Early Christianity* (Philadelphia: Fortress, 1971), 153.

130. Norbert Brox in *Die Pastoralbriefe*, RNT (Regensburg: Friedrich Pustet, 1969), 226, relates the tears of 2 Timothy 1:4 to Paul's taking his leave of the Ephesian presbyters in Acts 20:37, as well as the contrast between pain and joy. He also suggests that this passage is, like many other passages in 2 Timothy, an imitation of an authentic Pauline image rather than a direct quotation from a Pauline letter. Raymond F. Collins in his *1 & 2 Timothy and Titus*, NTL (Louisville and London: Westminster John Knox Press, 2002), 192, points out that there is no indication in the New Testament as to when Paul would have witnessed the weeping of Timothy. "The mention of Timothy's tears may perhaps result from the fact that in his desire to eulogize Paul the Pastor [i.e., the author of the Pastoral Epistles] did not want to present his hero as someone who was concerned only with his own personal well-being." See also A. T. Hanson, *The Pastoral Epistles*, NCB (Grand Rapids: William B. Eerdmans Publishing, 1982), 119–20.

131. Cf. Bauer, 1957:855; *TDNT* 8:46; 5:215-17.

132. See Moulton and Milligan, *Vocabulary*, 516, for a "partial parallel" from the sixth century; Liddell and Scott, *Lexicon*, note a "metaphorical use" of "widen" from *Inscriptiones Graecae* 5 (2), 268, 12.

133. See Jewett, *Romans*, 990–91.

134. See Jewett, *Romans*, 988–96.

135. Fitzmyer, "Qumran," 271–80.

136. Betz, "2 Corinthians 6:14-7:1,"108.

137. See Windisch, *zweite Brief*, 309–10.

138. Thrall, *Second Epistle*, 2.521.

139. See the earlier parts of this chapter and the discussions in chapters 5–7.

140. Titus 3:1 is the only explicit admonition to obedience that Titus is authorized to deliver; critiques of disobedience are found in Tit 1:6; 3:3; 1 Tim 1:9; 2 Tim 3:2.

141. Furnish, *II Corinthians*, 425.

142. See Plummer, *Second Epistle*, 378, 380; Windisch, *zweite Korintherbrief*, 424, 426; Filson, *Second Epistle*, 421 423.

143. Barrett, *Second Epistle*, 341.
144. Thrall, *2 Corinthians*, 2.906-07.
145. See Furnish, *II Corinthians*, 110–11 on 1:4a-b and 1;6; other references are in 2:7-8,7:6 and 13.
146. Robertson and Plummer, *Second Epistle*, 380; Barnett, *Second Epistle*, 616.
147. Thrall, *2 Corinthians*, 2.904.
148. Hughes, *Second Epistle*, 486.
149. Harris, *Second Epistle*, 933.
150. Furnish, *II Corinthians*, 582.
151. Furnish, *II Corinthians*, 581.
152. See Thrall, *2 Corinthians*, 907.
153. See Jewett, *Romans*, 994–96.
154. Roetzel, *2 Corinthians*, 145–46.

Chapter 3

The Need to Partition 1 Corinthians

The first scholars to raise questions about the unity of the canonical 1 Corinthians employed the methods of literary criticism. Along with other scholars, starting in the late eighteenth and nineteenth centuries, who were identifying strands in the Pentateuch and theories about the synoptic gospels, they searched for sections of Paul's letter that displayed characteristics that differed from other sections. In the field of literary criticism, attention is devoted to the beginnings and ends of particular sections of discourse, the content and style of those sections, and the transitions that provide a sense of their relation to each other. These details are often correlated with historical evidence about the situation and provenance of the literary text.

Because of the peculiar nature of the literary evidence within 1 Corinthians, we begin our analysis with the transitions between sections of the letter. The nature of such transitions, or the lack thereof, provides clues about the origin and argumentative function of particular literary units. In view of the enormous disparity in the frequency of awkward transitions in 1 and 2 Corinthians as compared with the rest of the Pauline letters, this is a logical place to begin our analysis. Whereas Galatians, Philemon, and 1 and 2 Thessalonians are marked by smooth transitions between every section, and Paul's longest letter, Romans, displays rough transitions only in proximity to the interpolations of 16:17–20 and 16:25–27, 1 Corinthians contains no less than seventeen problematic transitions. Further, 2 Corinthians has seven rough transitions, some so egregious and obvious that most scholars are forced to acknowledge them. Since recent scholars are far less inclined to recognize the transitional problems in 1 Corinthians, we begin with this evidence.

THE EVIDENCE OF ROUGH TRANSITIONS IN 1 CORINTHIANS

We begin each section with insights about the transitions developed by literary critics and commentators using critical methods, including the most insightful of them all, Johannes Weiss. Wherever possible, we compare these literary-critical observations with Margaret Mitchell's rejection of such evidence for the sake of maintaining 1 Corinthians as an integral letter.

Transition #1 from 6:11 to 6:12

> And such were some of you. But you were washed, you were sanctified, you were justified in the name of the Lord Jesus Christ and in the Spirit of our God.
> [. . .]
> "All things are lawful for me," but not all things are helpful. "All things are lawful for me," but I will not be enslaved by anything.

Johannes Weiss pointed to the abruptness of 6:12 after the rounded conclusion of 6:11.[1] After the affirmation in 6:11, "You were justified in the name of the Lord Jesus Christ and in the Spirit of our God," there is a complete change of mood and topic as Paul cites a motto in 6:12: " 'All things are lawful for me,' but. . . ."[2] Suddenly the basis of theological and ethical confidence is a matter of debate. In the preceding argument, there was no question about the total unacceptability of sin within the community; the sinner in 5:13 was to be excluded without further consideration. In the discussion beginning with 6:12, in contrast, temptation is a constant danger to be resisted and Paul enters into discussion with believers claiming to derive a problematic level of ethical freedom from Christ himself.[3] All in all, Weiss concluded, "in 6:12-20, we do not have a tone of sharply shaming faultfinding that began in chapter 3 but rather a tone of instructional interaction with strongly charismatic viewpoints in Corinth."[4] This actually reflects a change of rhetorical *genus*, from judicial accusation to deliberative argumentation. Mitchell notes that "the first instance of the appeal to advantage is in 1 Cor 6:12,"[5] but she overlooks the decisive shift from the foregoing discourse, which reflects this decisive change in the rhetorical situation. The material up to 6:11 reflects different phase of Paul's controversy with the Corinthians than the material in 6:12-20.

Transition #2 from 6:20 to 7:1

> You were bought with a price. So glorify God in your body.
> [. . .]

> Now concerning the matters about which you wrote. It is well for a man not to touch a woman.

Johannes Weiss pointed to the significant change of situation between 6:12-20 and 7:1-7. The former responds to an issue of libertinism and the latter to a question about sexual asceticism. If this extreme asceticism was a reaction against Paul's total prohibition of adultery in 6:12-20, it follows that the prohibition must have been written earlier.[6] Richard Horsley refers to the "dramatic change in tone" at 7:1.[7] The formula "now concerning" clearly indicates a question the Corinthians posed to Paul, which further differentiates the subject matter of these two paragraphs. The Nestle-Aland 28th edition inserts a double space between 6:20 and 7:1, reflecting the editors' sense of a rough transition. Margaret Mitchell skips over these distinctions by subordinating both arguments to the issue of social unity. Thus, the mystical union between believers and Christ that excludes joining believers with prostitutes is reduced to the threat of being "factionalized"[8] and the question of the acceptability of sexual relations been marital partners is generalized under the rubric of social "concord."[9]

Transition #3 from 8:13 to 9:1

> Therefore, if food is a cause of my brother's falling, I will never eat meat, lest I cause my brother to fall.
> [. . .]
> Am I not free? Am I not an apostle? Have I not seen Jesus our Lord? Are not you my workmanship in the Lord?

The "choppy transition"[10] or "sudden digression"[11] between 8:13 and 9:1 has provoked extensive discussion. Johannes Weiss observed that this transition "does not appear to grow organically out of the thinking of an author but was inserted by a redactor."[12] Nothing in chapter 9 relates to the question of idolatry and the definition of freedom in 9:1 is totally unclear from the context. If one comes from chapter 8, it is a question of the freedom to eat food offered to idols, and if one defines the matter in chapter 9, it is a question of the legitimacy of congregational support. Weiss therefore identified 9:1–18 as one of the remarkable "abschweifenden Einlagen" ("extraneous insertions") that characterize 1 Corinthians.[13] While Wolfgang Schrage attempts to explain this section as an *exemplum* of renunciation,[14] on the assumption that first Corinthians is an integral letter, Joseph Fitzmyer more appropriately refers to this section as a "digression."[15] Richard Horsley provides an apt description of the extraneous aspects of this transition to 9:1-18:

In the structure of the argument of chapters 8–10 as a whole, chapter 9 is an autobiographical illustration of the principle set forth in 8:13, that, for the sake of others, one should not make use of one's liberty/authority. Yet Paul is far more defensive and goes to far greater lengths to justify his rights than would be necessary simply for a personal illustration. His posing of one rhetorical question after another (nineteen in all) indicates a clearly defensive strategy. The heavy concentration of explanatory clauses, particularly in 9:15-25, further intensifies the defensive tone. His explanation in 9:15 – 18 of why he does not make use of his rights is too emotionally charged to be very functional as an illustration of the principle in 8:13. As he indicated in 9:3, this is as much or more his *defense* written to those who are examining and judging him as it is an illustration from his own practice of how the Corinthian should act with regard to food sacrificed to idols.[16]

In Margaret Mitchell's view, the issue in 8:7-13 is "factional disputes" in a political sense because Polybius employs the term προσκόπτειν ("causing stumbling") in such a context.[17] This confuses the argumentative means selected by Paul with the congregational issue itself, which is far from Polybius who has no interest in food offered to idols. It is self-evident that the same categories can be employed in an almost infinite variety of situations. Moreover, by defining 9:1-18 as a "mock defense speech,"[18] Mitchell hopes to avoid the transitional issue of the insertion of judicial discourse in the middle of a deliberative argument, once again sidestepping the actual issue, in this case, the legitimacy of Paul's renunciation of congregational remuneration. In her opinion, the issue is the now-familiar matter of social harmony: "Factionalism can be stopped only by compromise."[19] Thus, one of the most egregious transitions in the entire Pauline corpus is explained away.

Transition #4 from 9:18 to 9:19

What then is my reward? Just this: that in my preaching I may make the gospel free of charge, not making full use of my right in the gospel.
[. . .]
For though I am free from all men, I have made myself a slave to all, that I might win the more.

In his earlier study of Pauline rhetoric,[20] Johannes Weiss viewed 9:19-22 as a masterpiece of Pauline rhetoric with "an unusually sophisticated feeling for rhythm, measure, resonance and displaying an extraordinary compositional ability."[21] He argued that this eloquent statement of renunciation for the sake of mission belonged thematically with chapter 8, which concludes with "if food is a cause of my brother's falling, I will never eat meat, lest

I cause my brother to fall."[22] Hans Lietzmann also supported the idea that verse 19 connects back to 8:13.[23] The argumentative "for" in verse 19 does not provide an explanation or rationale for the renunciation of wages in 9:1-18. It leads rather to an account of the "accommodations" Paul makes for the sake of a successful mission.[24] In Mitchell's view, there is no change of subject here because Paul's self-denial "for the sake of the greater good" in 9:1-18 is continued in 9:19-23, which "shows how this kind of behavior extends into social relations."[25] The shift from judicial discourse in 9:18 back to discourse in the deliberative *genus* in 9:19 can thus be rendered irrelevant.

Transition #5 from 9:23 to 9:24

> I do it all for the sake of the gospel, that I may share in its blessings.
> [. . .]
> Do you not know that in a race all the runners compete, but only one receives the prize? So run that you may obtain it.

Johannes Weiss saw a double problem with this transition, first and foremost that the subject of accommodation in 9:19-22 does not correlate with the "personal, bodily experienced renunciation" of 9:24-27, which undermines the theological rationale of Paul's missionary strategy. This transition is "extremely bad," whereas 9:24-27 would fit more smoothly with 10:1-23 and 6:1-20.[26] The second issue is that 9:23 breaks out of the poetic structure of 9:19-22 and shifts abruptly into a subjective motivation of Paul's own salvation. This verse struck Weiss as a rather clumsy effort by a later redactor to make a transition to the next paragraph.[27] For Mitchell, however, there is nothing problematic with this transition. She acknowledges a "shift to an eschatological frame of reference" in 9:24-27,[28] but contends that this paragraph "is the fitting culmination" of Paul's appeal of renunciation for the sake of social harmony.[29] The fuzzy shift to Paul's individual salvation in 9:23 is not discussed. The shift to the style of diatribe in the rhetorical question of verse 24 and the change of focus from the collective context of mission to the individual achievement of a prize in athletic competition remain unexplained.

Transition #6 from 10:22 to 10:23

> What! Shall we provoke the Lord to jealousy? Are we stronger than he?
> [. . .]
> "All things are lawful," but not all things are helpful. "All things are lawful," but not all things build up.

Although Johannes Weiss did not discuss this transition explicitly, it is both harsh and abrupt. On the basis of Deut 32:21, the audience is expected to give a negative answer to the rhetorical questions in 10:22 about provoking the Lord to zealous anger on the presumption of being "stronger than He." Weiss asserted that these sarcastic questions are directed to those we would today identify as the proto-gnostics.[30] This is followed in 10:23 with a seemingly unrelated motto, "All things are lawful," which reformulates the question in 6:12.[31] Weiss suggested that these mottos originally appeared in separate letters,[32] which clearly implies that material written for different occasions surfaces in the rough transition between 10:22 and 23. Conzelmann states the problem bluntly: "there is no connection [in 10:23 – 11:1] with the preceding section."[33] When Mitchell discusses this issue, she does not refer to the rhetorical questions in 10:22 while following her theme of "social unity."[34] She refers to 10:23–11:1 as a "sub-argument" that calls the audience to seek the advantage of the many.[35] Paul uses this language in 10:33, bringing this τόπος to an end while discussing the ethical issue of eating food offered to idols. But there is nothing in Mitchell's analysis to explain the rough transition between 10:22 and 23.

Transition #7 from 11:1 to 11:2

> Be imitators of me, as I am of Christ.
> [. . .]
> I commend you because you remember me in everything and maintain the traditions even as I have delivered them to you.

Johannes Weiss observed that the reference to imitating Christ in 11:1 remains somewhat undefined and that imitating Paul seems to require a specification of his missionary strategy such as we find in 1 Cor 9:19-23. This verse therefore calls out for discourse that differs from what follows in the canonical text.[36] Conzelmann states the transitional problem in blunt terms: "the new topic is introduced entirely out of the blue."[37] What Weiss found particularly disturbing, however, was the fulsome praise of 11:2 after Paul was forced to defend his authority against attacks in chapters 1–4, and reestablishing his moral authority in chapters 7–10. After such extended controversy, how could Paul possibly say that "you remember me in everything and maintain the traditions even as I have delivered them to you"?[38] In the context of canonical 1 Corinthians, this verse cannot possibly function as a *captatio benevolentiae* because it follows ten chapters of criticism. No one would have believed that Paul was sincere in congratulating the audience for having followed him in "everything." This verse would be more suitably located toward the beginning of a letter written before the congregation's conflicts with Paul had so fully developed.[39] On these grounds, rather than on the lack of a graceful transition, Weiss concluded that these two verses must have originally belonged in separate letters. The editors of Nestle-Aland[28] must have been impressed with some of these observations because they separated 11:1 from 11:2 with a double space. None of these penetrating exegetical observations is taken into account by Margaret Mitchell, who fails to mention the open-endedness of 11:1 or the contradictions in 11:2. She simply moves on to contend that the question of hairstyles in chapter 11 was an issue of "factionalism."[40]

Transition #8 from 11:2 to 11:3

> I commend you because you remember me in everything and maintain the traditions even as I have delivered them to you.
> [. . .]
> But I want you to understand that the head of every man is Christ, the head of a woman is her husband, and the head of Christ is God.

Richard Horsley shows that the discussion of hairstyles in 11:3-16 interrupts the flow of the argument about banqueting in pagan temples in 8:1–11:2, which moves smoothly into the discussion of the Lord's Supper in 11:17-34.[41] The transition between 11:2 and 3 is so rough that William Walker and G. W. Trompf have inferred that the entirety of 11:3-16 must be an interpolation.[42] Horsley observes that what "Paul recites in 11:23-25. . . and discusses in 17-34 is precisely such a tradition mentioned 11:2, whereas the custom or practice discussed in 11:3-16 is not."[43] Moreover "the term 'to begin with' in 11:18 suggests that what follows in 11:18-34 is the first instance he has in mind among the 'traditions' in 11:2."[44] Finally, there is a strange shift between first-person plural discourse in 11:16 and the first-person singular discourse in 11:2 and 11:17. These observations suggest that 11:2 was originally followed by 11:18–34 and that the material concerning hairstyles in 11:3-16 is out of place.

Transition #9 from 11:34 to 12:1

> If anyone is hungry, let him eat at home, lest you come together to be condemned. About the other things I will give directions when I come.
> [. . .]
> Now concerning spiritual gifts, brethren, I do not want you to be uninformed.

Johannes Weiss did not discuss this transition, noting only that Paul begins the discussion of spiritual gifts in 12:1 with "now concerning" in response to the congregation's query.⁴⁵ Perhaps he considered the rough transition to 11:34 too obvious for comment, because Paul completes his discourse therein with the words, "About the other things I will give directions when I come." This comment obviously belongs near the end of a letter,⁴⁶ and for it to be followed by an additional six chapters of discussing congregational issues would have been perceived as totally inappropriate. Although this transition is one of the clearest indications that separate letters are contained in 1 Corinthians,⁴⁷ we find no discussion of these details in Mitchell's study.

Transition #10 from 12:31 to 13:1

> But earnestly desire the higher gifts. And I will show you a still more excellent way.
> [. . .]
> If I speak in the tongues of men and of angels, but have not love, I am a noisy gong or a clanging cymbal.

Johannes Weiss provided an extensive and penetrating analysis of the problematic transition between chapters 12 and 13.⁴⁸ He showed that Paul's admonition to strive for higher gifts in 1 Cor 12:31a is out of place so soon after he had rejected all striving for the higher charismata in 1 Cor 12:29-30. In fact the entire argument from 12:4-30 aims at dispelling the competition between those claiming to possess superior gifts that would justify their domination of others. Moreover, a further case can be made that 12:31a would lead much more directly into 14:1, "Make love your aim, and earnestly desire the spiritual gifts, especially that you may prophesy." In any event, Weiss observed that the δὲ in 12:31a does not adequately prepare one for a major transition such as that between chapters 12 and 13, and thus seems inappropriate for the function it must serve in this spot. Furthermore, the plural "gifts" in 12:31a is problematic since Paul goes on to recommend prophecy as the single, higher gift in chapter 14. The transition between 1 Cor 12:31a and 31b is so abrupt that one must assume a dictation pause and an unexpected change of plan, as if Paul suddenly decided after a sleepless night to insert the love chapter before turning to chapter 14. Furthermore, 1 Cor 12:31b fits loosely with the foregoing material in chapter 12 because the point of comparison in the "higher way" is unclear. The clumsiness of this muddled transition is extraordinary enough for a writer of Paul's competence, but it rises to the level of unbelievability next to the supreme rhetorical sophistication of chapter 13. However, there is no discussion of these details in Margaret Mitchell's study, which moves predictably forward to contend that the message of chapter 13 is "Love as the Antidote to Factionalism."⁴⁹ Modern generalizations are thereby employed to obscure the problematic details in the Greek text.

Transition #11 from 13:13 to 14:1

So faith, hope, love abide, these three; but the greatest of these is love.
[. . .]
Make love your aim, and earnestly desire the spiritual gifts, especially that you may prophesy.

Johannes Weiss showed that the content of 1 Cor 13 does not really prepare the way for the discussion of congregational arrangements in 1 Cor 14, despite the numerous suggestions by commentators to the contrary.[50] Except for 1 Cor 14:1a, the word ἀγάπη does not even appear in chapter 14. The transition between 1 Cor 13 and 14 is "harsh," in the view of Hans Conzelmann.[51] It is even more illogical than the transition between chapters 12 and 13, because if "the greatest of these is love" in 13:13, how can prophecy, which is a contributor to both faith and love, be prioritized in 14:1? Did Paul not argue in 13:2 that prophecy without love is "nothing"? Furthermore, the admonition to "aim at love" is unbearably flat after the completion of the great peroration about ἀγάπη in chapter 13, and, one might add, the formulation of the admonition reveals that the internal dynamic of the charismatic ethic is no longer understood. Finally, there is no logical connection between aiming at love and desiring the spiritual gifts in 1 Cor 14:1a and b. "Is this not, to be honest," asked Weiss, "a more artificial and even sloppier return to the transition of 12:31a" concerning seeking the "higher gifts"?[52] As in the examples discussed earlier, there is no discussion of this problematic transition in Mitchell's study.

Transition #12 from 14:33a to 14:33b-34

For God is not a God of confusion but of peace.
[. . .]
As in all the churches of the saints, the women should keep silence in the churches. For they are not permitted to speak, but should be subordinate, as even the law says.

An abrupt change of subject is introduced in verse 33b, the silencing of women, that is separate from the foregoing discussion of prophecy in congregational meetings. Weiss suggested that the contradiction with 11:5 where women prophets are accepted, in addition to the textual variants in the placement of verses 34-35, indicate that this material must have been inserted by a later hand.[53] The employment of non-Pauline vocabulary and argumentative style in verses 33b-36 expresses a contempt for the public function of women that is out of step with the rest of 1 Corinthians and the usual practice of

Paul toward women. However, the abrupt transition between 33a and 33b is unproblematic for Mitchell because the subordination of women coheres with the priority of avoiding factionalism. She argues as follows:

> 14:33 contains an implicit appeal by Paul to the Corinthians to turn from faction and instability towards peace and unity, in imitation of the deity (cf. 11:1). Concrete advice in 14:34-35 once again appeals to the *status quo* social conservatism which accompanies the appeal for unity as the primary goal, where Paul urges submission and silence of women for the sake of peace.[54]

Even if one were prepared to accept this view of Paul as a social conservative, disregarding all of the evidence of Paul's female colleagues as well as his explicit principle in Galatians 3:28, this statement does nothing to explain the rough literary transition between 14:33a to 14:33b.[55]

Transition #13 from 14:36 to 14:37

> What! Did the word of God originate with you, or are you the only ones it has reached?
> [...]
> If anyone thinks that he is a prophet, or spiritual, he should acknowledge that what I am writing to you is a command of the Lord.

The rhetorical questions in verse 36 directed to "you" are followed rather awkwardly by third-person discourse in verse 37, "If anyone thinks he is a prophet." The subject is abruptly shifted from the role of women back to the theme of prophecy that dominates the rest of chapter 14. In fact, as Weiss observed, 14:37-40 provides an energetic conclusion for the discourse of 14:1-33a.[56] Moreover, if 33b-36 were removed, there would be a smooth transition from 14:32 and 33a to 14:37: "the spirits of prophets are subject to prophets. For God is not a God of confusion but of peace . . . . If anyone thinks that he is a prophet, or spiritual, he should acknowledge that what I am writing to you is a command of the Lord."[57] Mitchell does not discuss this awkward transition between 14:36 and 37.[58]

Transition #14 from 14:40 to 15:1-2

> But all things should be done decently and in order.
> [...]
> Now I would remind you, brethren, in what terms I preached to you the gospel, which you received, in which you stand, by which you are saved, if you hold it fast unless you believed in vain.

In contrast to the "now concerning" formula that introduces 7:1, 8:1, and 12:1 as questions posed by the Corinthians, Weiss observed that 15:1 announces a fresh topic unrelated to congregational questions or the previous discussion. There is a significant shift in perspective from the current issues of congregational life being discussed in chapters 12–14 to the previous doctrinal teachings imparted in Paul's first visit to Corinth. The content of chapter 15 therefore seems to belong to an earlier letter.[59] After the finality of Paul's admonition in 14:40, "all things should be done decently and in order," there is no smooth transition to the new topic of the resurrection in 15:1-58 that begins with the words, "Now I would remind you, brethren." Hans Conzelmann concurs: "Paul introduces the new theme [15:1–11] without a transition."[60] Margaret Mitchell does not touch on the question of the missing transition but concentrates on explaining how the issue of resurrection involves factionalism in that different groups are disputing over this doctrine.[61]

Transition #15 from 15:58 to 16:1

> Always give yourselves to the work of the Lord, because you know that your labor in the Lord is not in vain.
> [. . .]
> Now concerning the collection for God's people. Do what I told the Galatian churches to do.

The exultant exhortation of 15:58 serves as a climax of the preceding argument.[62] It concludes with assurance based on the eschatological certainty reflected in 1 Cor 15:32.[63] After this high point, there is an insufferable return to business in the final "now concerning" trope of the letter. The transition from 15:58 to 16:1 is abrupt.[64] The business details concerning gathering contributions for the Jerusalem offering, designating authorized representatives to accompany the funds, and arrangements for Paul's future visit obviously belong in an earlier part of a Pauline letter, prior to its concluding admonitions and greetings. The reference to the instructions Paul had given the Galatians on his recent visit requires that this paragraph be placed in a very early stage of the Corinthian correspondence. Alfred Suhl shows that this paragraph must have been written before the Judaizer crisis arose in Galatia, since the reference in 16:1 reflects an unproblematic view of Galatian participation in the offering.[65] We shall return to this detail in our final assessment of the provenance of 16:1-4.

Transition #16 from 16:4 to 16:5

> If it seems advisable for me to go also, they will accompany me.

[. . .]
> After I go through Macedonia, I will come to you.

After stating his travel plans in no uncertain terms to visit Corinth on his way to deliver the Jerusalem offering, so that it will be ready "when I come" in 16:2,[66] Paul announces a completely different travel plan to visit Corinth in 16:5-8. This time he plans to visit Corinth after seeing the Macedonians, and rather than proceeding directly to deliver the offering, Paul hopes to spend the winter in Corinth, and in any case, he expects to remain in Ephesus "until Pentecost" (16:8) because of challenging opportunities there (16:9). The two travel plans follow one another without any explanation, resulting in an awkward double reference. Furthermore, in view of the likelihood that the initial plan in 16:1-4 reflects an early stage in the development of the offering project,[67] the revised plan in 16:5-12 reflects a later development. It follows that 16:4 and 16:5 could not have been dictated at the same time. Mitchell does not deal with these details in denying that there is any reason to partition 16:1-24.[68]

Transition #17 from 16:12 to 16:13

> As for our brother Apollos, I strongly urged him to visit you with the other brethren, but it was not at all his will to come now. He will come when he has opportunity.
> [. . .]
> Be watchful, stand firm in your faith, be courageous, be strong.

The discussion of travel details that begins in 16:5 comes to a conclusion in 16:12 with the disclosure of Apollos's decision to delay visiting Corinth. These practical details are abruptly followed by five admonitions that return to the style of 15:58.[69] Unlike 15:58, however, there is no transitional introduction in 16:13.[70] In Joseph Fitzmyer's words, "The transition to this paragraph [16:13-18] is abrupt. . . ."[71] As Weiss observed, the content of 16:13-14 fits the matter of doctrinal uncertainty rather than issues of morality such as one finds in chapters 12-14.[72] In fact, if these two verses followed 15:58 with its graceful transition, they would fit perfectly:[73]

> But thanks be to God, who gives us the victory through our Lord Jesus Christ. Therefore, my beloved brethren, be steadfast, immovable, always abounding in the work of the Lord, knowing that in the Lord your labor is not in vain. Be watchful, stand firm in your faith, be courageous, be strong. Let all that you do be done in love.

The abrupt transition between 16:12 and 13 is not discussed by Mitchell, but she responds indirectly to the situation by associating verses 13-14 with "the argument for unity in the body of the letter"[74] rather than with the immediately preceding verses.

In conclusion, the evidence of this, the seventeenth awkward transition allegedly created by one of the most skilfully persuasive and influential writers in world history, continues to undermine efforts to maintain the currently orthodox opinion that 1 Corinthians is an integral letter. This evidence contributes to the literary-critical problem of 1 Corinthians, which was felt to be much more urgent by the scholars from the 1880s through the 1950s than by contemporary specialists.

LOGICAL AND HISTORICAL CONTRADICTIONS

1. The most significant contradiction is that Paul knows less about the situation in Corinth in 1 Corinthians 11 than he does in chapters 1 through 4,[75] so that the question of how one can "unknow" something needs to be confronted. Why is it that a basic rule of investigation is never applied to 1 Corinthians? This rule of historical investigation is best expressed in this question: "What did Paul know and when did he know it?"

2. The praise of the congregation in 11:2 is out of place after 10 chapters of criticism. Johannes Weiss pointed out the contradiction between saying "I praise you because you remember me in respect of everything" after criticizing them in chapters 1–4 for misunderstanding his gospel as supporting partisanship.[76] He observed that this kind of compliment might be appropriate at the beginning of a letter but not in the middle, after discussing misbehavior in chapters 5–6.

3. The reference to dealing with the other issues "when I come" occurs in the middle of discourse (11:34) rather than at the end of a letter, where such travel references appear in other Pauline letters.

4. There is a shift in rhetorical *genus* to judicial in chapter 9, whereas the rest of 1 Corinthians is deliberative. We note Mitchell's effort to make what she perceives as exceptions into general rules, which skews the definitions and distinctions between the three *genera*; the classical handbooks recommend employing discourse consistent with a particular *genus*.

5. In 1 Cor 9:1-18, Paul defends himself against attacks concerning his apostolic behavior, whereas in chapters 1–8, there are no hints of such conflicts.[77] This contradiction is enhanced by the confusion of rhetorical *genera*, which reflect the relation of the writer to the audience. In 9:1-18, Paul employs judicial rhetoric in defending himself against charges of behavior that his critics deem to be inappropriate for an apostle. The arena for such rhetoric is some sort of a court. In the rest of 1 Corinthians, Paul employs deliberative rhetoric with arguments based on honor and advantage; the arena

for such rhetoric is the decision-making assembly. Classical rhetorical theory did not encourage confusing these *genera*, and nowhere else in Paul's letters do we find such confusion.

6. The failure of the *exordium* in 1:1–9, or of the thesis statement in 1:10, to account for all of the topics in 1 Corinthians is a decisive contradiction of Paul's usual practice. There is no allusion here to the maintenance of exclusive bodily relations (6:12-20), to bodily discipline (9:24–10:22), or to the denial of the bodily element in resurrection (15:1-58). There is no hint in these opening verses of 1 Corinthians that Paul will be forced to defend his right to receive financial support from the congregation (9:1-18).

7. The claim of unity confuses no less than four rhetorical situations, each of which reflects a distinctive stage in the developing controversy between Paul and the Corinthians. This violates a fundamental rule of historical research: to place events and writings in their proper chronological sequence. Therefore we postulate that Letter A is a letter-fragment which presupposes that Paul thinks the situation of disunity in Corinth is not serious. Letter B is a letter against πορνεία being practiced by people in the Corinthian church. By the time of Letter C, Paul has received the detailed report from "those of Chloë" which he thoroughly believed and because of which he corrected the Corinthians at length for their disunity. 1 Cor 9:1-18 was originally part of Letter F, the bombastic letter in which Paul attacks his opponents with a huge amount of sarcasm.

8. There are several separate endings in 1 Cor 16, which logically reflect at least three separate letters. In 16:1-4, Paul suggests the same arrangements in collecting funds for the Jerusalem offering that he had arranged in Galatia, which reflects a time shortly after revisiting North Galatia on the so-called Third Missionary Journey in the first half of 52.[78] The next section of chapter 16, verses 5-12, reflects a period in the summer of 54 toward the end of the Ephesian ministry when Paul is making plans to spend the winter Corinth before proceeding to Jerusalem with the offering. Paul states that he now plans to "remain in Ephesus until Pentecost" (16:8).[79] In the final section, 16:13-24, Paul writes an extended commendation of Stephanus and his colleagues in support of urging the congregation to "be subject to such people" (16:16). This admonition to follow authoritative leaders reflects the situation before Paul hears of the emergence of partisan groups in Corinth, so it must be placed before the writing of 1 Cor 1-4. We therefore assign this material to Letter B, written in the fall of 53.

9. There are contradictions in travel plans: in 4:19, Paul says that he will come quickly from Ephesus, and in 16:2-3, he refers with similar certainty to an impending visit, but in 16:5-8, he plans to remain in Ephesus until Pentecost and travel to Corinth by way of Macedonia.[80] These changes in travel plans reflect different stages in the conflict between Paul and the Corinthians and must have been written on separate occasions.

10. The presence of doublets reflects the fusion of materials from separate letters; the rule drawn from literary criticism about doublets deriving from separate sources is still valid. The examples in 1 Corinthians are the discussion of the formula "all things are lawful" in 6:12 and 10:23, the two discussions of food offered to idols in 8:1-13 and 10:1-22, the two discussions of the Lord's Supper in 11:17-34 and 10:14-22. These doubled discussions of issues create discrepancies such as Paul's criticism of sharing pagan meals in 10:1-22, in contradistinction to his acceptance of such meals in 8:1-13 and 10:23–11:1.

11. There is a contradiction between 10:1-22, where there is an exclusive antithesis between the Lord's Supper and pagan meals, and 8:1-13 and 10:23–11:1, where Paul allows eating meat offered to idols so long as it does not violate the conscience of the weak.[81]

12. The elegant discourse on love in chapter 13 interrupts the discussion of the spiritual gifts in chapters 12 and 14.[82] This produces a series of contradictions. The call to strive for higher gifts in 1 Cor 12:31a contradicts the argument in 1 Cor 12:29-30 that opposes a hierarchy of gifts.[83] Paul argues that the gifts are equally valuable and in 12:7 declares that each believer has been given a spiritual gift "for the common good." The plural "gifts" in 12:31a and 14:1 contradicts the recommendation of prophecy as the single higher gift in 14:24. Moreover, the celebrative material in 1 Cor 13 does not really prepare the way for the discussion in 1 Cor 14; except for the clumsy 1 Cor 14.1a, the word ἀγάπη does not even appear in chapter 14. Finally, there is no logical connection between aiming at love and desiring the spiritual gifts in 1 Cor 14:1a and b.

13. The formula "now concerning" introduces six topics in 1 Corinthians, probably reflecting questions posed by the Corinthians to Paul. These include questions about marriage and divorce (7:1-24), the unmarried (7:25-40), food offered to idols (8:1-13), and the spiritual gifts (12:1–14:40). In contrast to these four topics that are extensively developed with theological argumentation, two short sections deal with administrative arrangements and travel plans: the Jerusalem offering (16:1-4) and the visit by Apollos (16:12), both of which appear to belong in an earlier letter, as shown in item 8 earlier. However, some of the most important topics in 1 Corinthians, nine in all, are not introduced with this formula: namely, the sexual purity of the body (6:12-20); subduing the body (9:24-27); the warning about falling (10:1-13); the worship of idols (10:14–11:1); hairstyles in worship (11:3-16); the Lord's Supper (11:17-34); resurrection (15:1-58); the travel plans of Paul and his colleagues (16:5-11); and the recommendation that the Corinthians submit to the authority of Stephanus (16:15-18). Margaret Mitchell has constructed an elaborate case that this formula does not always refer to questions being answered, which opens the door to other items that are included in 1 Corinthians, but this seems to be a case of special pleading.[84]

Chapter 3

THEORIES OF LITERARY PARTITION

By taking account of transitions, logical and illogical development, styles of discourse and conflicting historical details, literary critics proposed a series of theories about how the various parts of 1 Corinthians originally functioned. John C. Hurd, Jr., provides a revealing tabulation of literary-critical hypotheses by Weiss, Loisy, Couchoud, Goguel, de Zwaan, Schmithals, and Dinkler, indicating large areas of agreement between these critical scholars.[85] Hurd opts for the integrity of 1 Corinthians[86] without taking up the detailed exegetical arguments developed by Weiss and Schmithals, the most substantial efforts made prior to his publication date. We begin with a brief summary of the 1956 hypothesis by Walter Schmithals. Throughout this discussion, the exegetical observations of Johannes Weiss and the insights from earlier critics will be taken into account.

Walter Schmithals's *gnosticism in Corinth*, translated into English in 1971, divides the material of 1 Corinthians into two letters of roughly equal length. Since 1 Cor 11:2-34 refers to the threat of schisms as trivial, whereas 1 Cor 1-4 deals with them as a serious problem on the basis of information from "Chloe's people," the first four chapters must have been written later. The sections beginning with περὶ δὲ ("now concerning") are joined to 1 Cor 1-4, producing the original answer letter. Each of the remaining sections in 1 Corinthians reflects an earlier stage in the development of the controversy and is thus assigned by Schmithals to Letter A. The results are as "shown in figure 3.1.

Despite the fact that Schmithals provided no explanation of the redactional motivation in joining these letters into the canonical 1 Corinthians, and the fact that his conclusions have not been widely accepted, the resultant letters lend themselves well to the tasks of literary-critical and historical reconstruction. With the help of a few minor revisions, to be discussed earlier, this partition theory can provide the basis for a viable redaction-critical analysis, to be taken up in our next chapter.

A thorough and appreciative critique of the Schmithals hypothesis was published by Wolfgang Schenk in 1969.[87] After examining all of the arguments, he concludes that it makes the best sense out of the evidence to

Table 3.1 Schmithals's Earlier Partition of 1 Corinthians

Letter A	Letter B
1 Cor 9:24–10:22	1 Cor 1:1–6:11
1 Cor 6:12-20	1 Cor 7:1–9:23
1 Cor 11:2-34	1 Cor 10:23–11:1
1 Cor 15:1-58	1 Cor 12:1–14:40
1 Cor 16:13-24	1 Cor 16:1-12

consider 1 Corinthians a redactional composition.[88] In particular, he provides new evidence to sustain the assignment of 2 Cor 6:14–7:1, 1 Cor 11:2-34 and 1 Cor 15:1-58 to Letter A, but he departs from Schmithals's analysis of chapters 6, 9, and 10. Although agreeing with Schmithals and Weiss that 1 Cor 10:1-22 flows most naturally into 1 Cor 6:12-20, Schenk does not want to assign them both to Letter A because of Bornkamm's suggestion that 1 Cor 6:9f. is a correction of 1 Cor 5:9-13.[89] However, there is no hint of a changed situation or new information to require a separation of these two passages, and it seems preferable to follow Conzelmann who sees both passages as part of a single, well-developed argument.[90] Even less convincing is Schenk's argument that Paul would not have repeated himself in Letter A by using the temple image in 1 Cor 6:19 that was first articulated in 2 Cor 6:16. This aesthetically grounded judgment is not compelling, and there are other instances where Paul uses the same image or concept repeatedly in a single letter. Hence the major reasons for reassigning portions of 1 Cor 6 appear untenable.

Schenk moves next to 1 Cor 5:1-13, which begins with Ὅλως ("actually"), relying on Bachmann's commentary[91] in concluding that the topic of immorality must have been discussed in the immediately preceding section. This leads him to link 1 Cor 6:12-20 and 1 Cor 5:1-13 as adjoining portions of Letter B. But the relationship alluded to by ὅλως could easily have been the arrogance of proto-gnostic libertinists (cf. 1 Cor 5:13f.), which is picked in 1 Cor 6:2, and which stands in ironic contrast to the report about incest in 1 Cor 6:1. Whether one translates this with "actually"[92] or "universally,"[93] the thematic and logical connections between 1 Cor 4:1-21 and 1 Cor 5:1-13 are so close that Schenk's argument proves unconvincing. To place 1 Cor 5:1-13 after 1 Cor 6:12-20 produces a series of jarring and confusing new connotations of σῶμα and σάρξ immediately after the notable discussion of somatic relations in 1 Cor 6:12-20. It raises unanswerable problems while seeming to resolve a trivial puzzle about the translation of ὅλως.

The questions Schenk raises about the travel details in 1 Cor 4:17-21 as compared with 1 Cor 16:3-11 are more worthy of consideration. It is not that his observation, that travel details are ordinarily discussed only at the conclusion of a letter, is binding. Phil 2:19ff. and 1 Thess 3:1-10 are exceptions for everyone who views those letters as integral. It is clear that 1 Cor 16:10-11 provides a more elaborate defense and recommendation of Timothy than 1 Cor 4:17ff., but this may be precisely suited to the complex and risky plan Paul announced with trepidation in 1 Cor 5:17-21 to send him as a replacement for himself when there were already criticisms of Paul's absenting himself from a troubled situation (1 Cor 4:18). Those who have worked most conscientiously with the travel details find the references consistent with Timothy's mission to stop back through Corinth on his way from Macedonia.[94]

Schenk's discussion of the information presupposed in the Corinthian letters leads him to the answer letter material from the report on schisms brought by Chloe's people (1 Cor 1:11). There is admittedly no indication in this verse that they had brought a letter for Paul to answer, but on the other hand, there is nothing to exclude it. Schenk finds it strange that such a letter included nothing about the schism question proper, overlooking that each of the topics Paul takes up in the answer letter touches on aspects of the controversy. In issues like food offered to idols, it is clear from 1 Cor 8 and 10 that Paul takes up separate questions posed by competing sides.[95] To separate the περὶ δὲ sections from 1 Cor 1:11ff. is to assume an unwarranted omniscience on the part of scholarship about precisely what Chloe's people reported and why Paul chose to answer the basic question of divisions before coming to specific questions posed by the Corinthian factions.

The most effective arguments in Schenk's article relate to the disposition of 1 Cor 9:1-18 and the material on either side of it. He follows Weiss in observing that 1 Cor 9:19-23 carries out the accommodation strategy of 1 Cor 8:1-13, and that it is seriously interrupted by 1 Cor 9:1-18. Schenk's placement of Paul's defense of his apostolic privilege in 1 Cor 9:1-18 is unsatisfactory, however, because linking it with 9:24-27 forces him to the strained conclusion that the sports image deals with the right to ministerial support.[96] In fact, this passage speaks of self-discipline in a moral sense[97] and stands more naturally in close proximity to 2 Cor 6:14–7:1 and 1 Cor 6:12-20.

The Schenk hypothesis of a fourfold division of 1 Corinthians, illustrated in Appendix III, needs to be examined in terms of whether it results in coherent, smoothly flowing, and historically consistent letters. On these counts, the difficulties are manifold. A series of rough transitions emerge, of which the most problematic are from 2 Cor 7:1 to 1 Cor 6:1, from 1 Cor 9:18 to 1 Cor 9:24, and from 1 Cor 6:20 to 1 Cor 5:1. In contrast to the usual function of a Pauline thanksgiving to contain a kind of table of contents of the letter that follows, Schenk's placement of 1 Cor 1:4-9 at the beginning of Letter A eliminates any meaningful relationship to the rest of the material assigned to that letter. When one tries to reconstruct the course of Paul's conflict with the Corinthians, 1 Cor 1:10–4:21 appears to comprise an impossible anticlimax as the fourth letter in the sequence. It is particularly difficult to imagine the reference to suddenly "hearing" of difficulties this late in the controversy (1 Cor 1:11).

The most difficult obstacle of all, from the perspective of redaction criticism, is the large number of seemingly unmotivated steps that Schenk's thesis requires to produce 1 Corinthians. As the "Schluß" (conclusion) of Schenk's article indicates, Frame Letter A requires twelve insertions from three separate letters in addition to a deletion. In one location (between 1 Cor 6:1-11 + 1 Cor 11:2-34), six different insertions are required, forcing one to assume that several of them were not joined to any section of the frame letter before being joined to other floating pages from other locations. Despite Schenk's claim that a simple process of repeated insertions was involved,[98] such complex handling of scroll or codex materials is hard to imagine. If redactional motivations were adduced, one might be inclined to consider the price of extreme complication, but Schenk does not make any suggestions. Without developing some redactional theory as Bornkamm did with 2 Corinthians, there is no way to move the Schenk hypothesis past the "flying pages" level of nineteenth-century literary criticism.

Walter Schmithals refined his 1956 hypothesis in response to Schenk's suggestions, producing an even more complex redactional tangle.[99] He divides the material of 1 Corinthians into five separate letters, which compounds the problems of the Schenk hypothesis.[100] Now there are three locations where multiple insertions would have to be stitched together. Two insertions need to be placed prior to 1 Cor 6:1-11 in what we take to be the frame letter; three insertions are required after 1 Cor 6:20; and no less than five after 1 Cor 10:22. For redactional motivation, Schmithals relies on his earlier suggestion[101] that the redactor was aiming at the creation of seven letters designed for the universal church. He further observes that the fragments from historically sequential letters were linked, with the four earlier placed in 1 Corinthians and the five later in 2 Corinthians. This is inadequate since a portion of 2 Corinthians ended up in Letter B and a portion of 1 Corinthians in Letter F. That a redactor toward the end of the century could have reconstructed the original sequence of the Corinthian letters is about as improbable as the supposition that he would have allowed this to determine his redactional choices. Antiquarian concerns were not vital in the churches of the second generation, as far as one can tell.

To evaluate all of the suggestions Schmithals adapts from Schenk's study would be redundant in light of the discussion earlier. The most convincing part of the hypothesis is separating 1 Cor 11: 2-34 from the rest of Schenk's Letter A. He cites Weiss's observations that 11:2 fits badly with the foregoing and that it would serve nicely at the beginning of a letter.[102] The section concludes in 11:34b with a typical transition to final greetings. When one observes that it fits rather poorly in its assigned location in Schenk's or Schmithals's earlier hypotheses, the conclusion that it constitutes the initial phase of Paul's epistolary exchange with the Corinthians makes good sense. The reference to "hearing" and "partly believing" about factions in 1 Cor 11:18 would fit well at the beginning of such an exchange. Thus, Schmithals assigns 1 Cor 11:2-34 to the position of Letter A. Another significant component of the Schmithals's revision is the achievement of smooth transitions and thematic connections between 2 Cor 6:14–7:1 + 1 Cor 6:12-20 + 1 Cor 9:24–10:22, making the theme of the resultant Cor B into a warning against relapsing into paganism.[103] With the exception of placing 1 Cor 6:1-11 at the beginning of this letter, the reconstruction of Cor B as a whole is convincing. The exhortation not to join oneself to unbelievers in 2 Cor 6:14ff. fits very well with a subsequent discussion of temple prostitution in 1 Cor 6:12-20, but badly with a prohibition about the use of the civil court system in 1 Cor 6:11. Placing oneself under the jurisdiction of a court is not appropriately depicted by ἑτεροζυγοῦντες ("yoked"), μετοχή ("partnership"), κοινωνία ("fellowship"), συμφώνησις ("accord"), or μερίς ("share") in 2 Cor 6:14-15.

Schmithals's Letter C also holds together convincingly, with the exception of the leap from 1 Cor 5:13 to 7:1 and the problematic deletion of 1 Cor 9:23.[104] Finally, although it is not really decisive for our immediate task, Schmithals's placement of 1 Cor 9:1-18 with 2 Cor 6:3-13 and 2 Cor 7:2-4 as the components of Letter F opens up significant connections that we shall pursue in the analysis of the Letter of Tears, in our chapter 10.

Alfred Suhl's detailed study of the chronological relations between the Pauline letters contains a substantial discussion of the literary-critical problem of 1 Corinthians.[105] In the effort to reconstruct precise travel details and the development of Paul's controversies with his opponents, he finds it necessary to return to Schmithals's hypothesis of 1956. Having faulted the Schenk hypothesis for "arbitrarily subordinating history to literary criticism,"[106] he argues for two major letters in the same sequence as proposed by the original Schmithals study. The minor adjustments he makes in the Schmithals hypothesis, however, do little to enhance its effectiveness. Suhl shifts 1 Cor 5:1-8 to Letter A because he feels ἀκούεται in 5:1 too vague for information brought by Chloe's people, but as observed earlier, this presupposes we know precisely the form in which their reports were presented. Elements of hearsay may have been prominent, and in any case, it would have been more tactful to say "it is heard" than to say "I accuse you of the following." As Weiss observed, the verb fits perfectly with the preceding ὅλως,[107] also discussed earlier. Suhl also proposes that 1 Cor 6:12-20 be shifted into Letter B and placed next to 1 Cor 7:1-40. But this overlooks the substantial differences in the situation and issues dealt with by each. The former deals with libertinism, as Weiss's reconstruction of the motto partially cited in 1 Cor 6:13 reveals.[108] In contrast, 1 Cor 7:1-40 answers specific questions about asceticism and its opening citation takes up a motto cited by the congregation. If Suhl were correct in linking these two passages, 7:1 should clearly precede, not follow 6:12-20. Finally, the relative simplicity of Suhl's hypothesis is achieved at the price of solving neither the transitional problems with the canonical order of 1 Cor 12 + 13 + 14 nor the discrepancies in the content and argumentative style of 1 Cor 9:1-18 and 11:2-34.

One advantage of Suhl's hypothesis is that it allows the sections of Letter A to be inserted sequentially into Frame Letter B. He does not advance a

Table 3.2 Widman's Distribution of Materials in 1 and 2 Corinthians

Beginnings	A1	I 11:2-34; 16:7-9, 15-20
	A2	II 6:14–7:1; I 9:24–10:22; 6:1-11; I 5; 6:12-20
	A3	I 15:1-44a, 49-58; 16:1-7a, 11-14
Aggravation	B1	I 9:1-18; II 2:14–6:13; 7:2-4
	B2	I 1:1–2:5; 3:1–4:21; II 10–13
Clarification	C	I 7:1-35; 8:1-13; 9:19-22; 10:23–11:1; I 12:1-31a; 14:1c-40; 12:3lb-13:13; II 9
Relaxation	D	II 1:1–2:13; 7:5–8:24

theory concerning the motivation of the redactor but observes how significant it is for the plausibility of such a hypothesis to discover how the redactor proceeded. Suhl's conclusions are nevertheless relatively close to the ones advocated in this study.

Several other scholars have argued that 1 Corinthians contains elements of three original letters: H. Hagge,[109] Alfred Loisy,[110] and L. L. Welborn.[111] A much longer list of scholars have opted for a two-letter scheme.[112] Christophe Senft,[113] Rudolf Pesch,[114] Miguel de Burgos,[115] and Khiok-Khng Yeo[116] argue that parts of four letters make up 1 Corinthians. Paul-Louis Couchoud divided the letter into five parts.[117] Maurice Goguel divided the Corinthian letters into six original letters, while leaving out substantial portions of the canonical letters.[118] In 1978–1979, Martin Widmann wrote two articles proposing a seven-letter scheme for the Corinthian correspondence.[119] Inspired by Schenk and Schmithals, Widman distributes the material into four phases in Paul's relationship with the Corinthians (see Table 3.2).[120]

The beginnings of letters A1 and A2 make some sense, but there is little else to commend this scheme. The transitions between sections of these letters are frequently more problematic than in the canonical letters. His hypothesis is that Paul's proto-gnostic conversation partners wrote 1 Cor 2:6-12 in response to Paul's critique in 2:5 that their view was nothing but "worldly wisdom." This seems unlikely because of the Pauline style and vocabulary of 2:6-12.

Gerhard Sellin has written two extensive arguments in favor of partitioning 1 Corinthians into three parts,[121] following some methodological principles that warrant incorporation in any division hypothesis:

(1) It must prove that there are tensions in the canonical text that can only be resolved by an editor who created a new coherence at the level of communication.
(2) It must prove that the editor's alterations of the various sections of the letter are historically plausible (which involves, for example, naming the letter bearer and explaining temporal details).

(3) It must propose a plausible original sequence for the original sections of a letter. The reconstructed letter must be complete, or the missing sections should be explained.

(4) It must explain the reason for the editing, particularly the editor's motivation, while providing an explanation of the new sequence.[122]

These principles suggest a way to evaluate the detailed exegetical inferences that led Gerhard Sellin to his proposal of dividing the material in 1 Corinthians into three separate letters. We agree with his assignment of 11:2-34 as part of the "previous letter" mentioned in 5:9,[123] but it is implausible to suggest that four separate sections of the letter originally followed thereafter (5:1-8; 6:12-20; 9:24–10:22; 6:1-11). The wording of 11:34b clearly indicates that any additional issues will be discussed in Paul's forthcoming visit, which logically leads an audience to expect a letter closing rather than an extended discussion of additional topics. That 11:34b is immediately followed by 5:1 is not only extremely rough and contradictory, but it presupposes a more advanced level of information than is reflected in chapter 11. In 5:1-13, Paul is not only informed about the case of incest and also about the congregation's reaction as well as their response to his previous letter that recommended strenuous action. The link between 5:8 and 6:12 that Sellin proposes also entails a very rough transition and the level of information that Paul has about the congregational situation is more advanced in 5:1-8 than in 6:12-20. Chapter 5 deals with prostitution rather than incest, which was by far the more scandalous offense in the Greco-Roman environment. That incest was not mentioned in 6:12-20 remains inexplicable with this hypothesis.

Except for the fact that Paul's discussions in 6:12-20 and 9:24–10:22 reflect a stage in the controversy that was advanced over the situation reflected in 11:2-34, these two sections follow one another very smoothly. The stylistic links between the questions "do you not know?" in 6:19 and 9:24 draw these passages closely together. However, the transition between 10:22 and 6:1 is quite unbelievable. The strenuous warning in 10:21 against participating in pagan meals and the angry rhetorical questions in 10:22 are on a completely different ethical and emotional level than 6:1, "when one of you has a grievance against a brother."

Sellin's reconstruction of Letter B begins with 5:9-13, which does not reflect a further development in the congregational situation than 5:1-8. (No previous theory advocated dividing 5:1-8 from 5:9-13.) Sellin's proposed transition between 5:9 and 7:1 is strange since the general advice in 7:1-7 on sexual morality seems redundant after the severe condemnation of incest in 5:1-13. There is a serious problem, moreover, in believing that the entirety of 7:1–9:23 belongs together. In 1 Cor 8:1-13 and also in 1 Cor 9:19–10:22, Paul is in a sustained and continuous discussion of the propriety of Jesus-believers' eating foods from the market, which was almost certainly offered as part of pagan sacrifices. 1 Cor 9:1-18, however, deals with the completely different issue of Paul's rights as an apostle, including his rights to financial support. In addition, 1 Cor 9:1-18 uses judicial rhetoric, which contrasts greatly with the deliberative rhetoric of 1 Cor 8 and 10:1-22. On the other hand, the transition between 1 Cor 9:23 and 10:23 that Sellin proposes is very smooth. One reason it is smooth is because, in our view, 1 Cor 8:9-13 and 9:19-23, as well as 10:23–11:1, are dealing with the issue of the rights of fellow believers and the fact that both the Corinthians and Paul are called upon by God to relinquish their rights graciously for the sake of those who are not fully convinced of the non-existence of pagan deities. This is for the purpose of evangelism: "to win as many as possible" (1 Cor 9:19; cf. 10:24).

With the exception of 14:33b-36, which Sellin identifies as an interpolation, chapters 12–14 fit smoothly after 11:1. As in most of the other partition theories, 1 Cor 14:40 does not flow well into 15:1. In 1 Cor 12–14, the issues are spiritual gifts and congregational leadership. Chapter 15 is a totally different argument: Paul argues here against Corinthians who deny the resurrection of Christ and of their fellow believers. Paul presents the resurrection of Christ and of believers in Christ as a *sine qua non* of the faith; those who deny it turn the faith into falsehood. Whereas 16:1-12 has no connection with chapter 15 or the other material Sellin identifies as part of his Letter B, chapter 15 fits beautifully with 16:13, since both of them exhort the Corinthians to be steadfast in the resurrection faith.

Sellin's Letter C consists of 1 Cor 1:1–4:21 only. Sellin sees a probable, though not certain, ending to this letter at 4:21.[124] We do not favor 4:21 as an ending because of the careful rhetorical transition made by 4:19-21 in anticipation of the severe correction Paul must make to the case of incest and the congregation's prideful tolerance of this gross immorality. In 4:18, Paul introduces the dual topics of the arrogance of the congregation and Paul's impending second visit to Corinth. The transition in v. 19 is very effective because it mentions both of the dual topics in v. 18 (which will be picked up in 5:2) and expands this corrective warning by the use of a very old τόπος in Greek literature, the crucial connection in rhetoric between words and deeds, which virtually all users of rhetoric desire to employ. Those who only speak words but do not do deeds consistent with their words make rhetoric into the technology of words, which have no outcome in deeds.[125] Paul expands this comparison between words and deeds in v. 20 and connects it to a rare Pauline reference to the kingdom of God. Verse 21 heightens this transitional section further by raising it to the level of a threat, coupled with a strongly deliberative choice that is placed before the readers/hearers in question form. The heightened severity of v. 21 is the perfect transition to chapter 5 and its language of great severity toward the congregation, which has tolerated a level of immoral behavior, which Paul decries in 5:1, where he says this immorality exceeds any immorality that "pagans" (meaning "unbelievers" in this context) tolerate. 1 Cor 5:1-5 then fulfill the anticipation that Paul has skillfully built into 4:19-21.

Taken as a whole, there are some penetrating elements of Sellin's partition theory of 1 Corinthians. Yet all three of Sellin's reconstructions of the original letters embedded in 1 Corinthians fall short of full adherence to the four criteria for judging the coherence of reconstructed letters.

The analysis of efforts to improve upon the 1956 hypothesis worked out by Walter Schmithals has tended to confirm its basic usability. With the exception of 2 Cor 6:14–7:1, which does not serve thematically as an early section of Corinthians Letter A, the only substantial changes should be in the assignment of 1 Cor 9:1-18 and the placement of 1 Cor 11:2-34. We agree with Schenk and the Schmithals revised hypothesis of 1973 that the former cannot be left as part of Corinthians Letter B in the original 1956 assignment. The defense of Paul's apostolicity (9:1-2) fits perfectly with the so-called letter of tears, and the rebuttal of charges that his refusal to accept financial remuneration was a sign of his lack of authority is congruent with the situation Georgi so convincingly reconstructs from evidence in 2 Corinthians.[126] The theme of boasting (1 Cor. 9:16) is congruent with the extensive development in 2 Cor 10-13, and seems isolated and unmotivated in the context of 1 Corinthians. Our suggestion is that 1 Cor 9:1-18 fits most naturally between 2 Cor 12:13 and 14 and thus originally belonged to the letter of tears. The sarcastic apology in 2 Cor 12:13 that Paul had not "burdened" the Corinthians with monetary demands is comprehensible only on the assumption that his opponents claimed this was an inalienable mark of apostolicity. In this context, Paul's peculiar "defense" in 1 Cor 9:3ff. proves that his nonburdening modus operandi implied neither that he was not ἐλεύθερος nor that he suffered from a lack of ἐξουσία, the latter being particularly significant in the Letter of Tears.[127] The reference in 1 Cor 9:12 to others who claim the right of apostolic payment leads smoothly into 2 Cor 12:14ff., where Paul states he seeks "not what is yours but you." The rhetorical question, "If I loved you the more, am I to be loved the less?" (2 Cor 12:15), is very close in theme and mood to 1 Cor 9:11. Finally, the 1 Cor 9:17f. discussion of Paul's "commission" as an apostle leads very smoothly into 2 Cor 12:14ff., where Paul discusses his forthcoming third trip to Corinth. In both places, he insists that his failing to place a financial burden on the congregation is no sign of illegitimacy.

Finally, we agree with Schmithals's 1973 revision in assigning 1 Cor 11:2-34 as a separate letter, to be placed at the beginning of the Corinthian exchange. The contextual evidence Walker gathers to suggest 1 Cor 11:2ff. is an interpolation[128] would be accounted for by such an assignment, although we are convinced that this is authentic Pauline discourse.

SUMMARY OF OUR PARTITION HYPOTHESIS

Taking the literary-critical studies since the latter part of the nineteenth century into account, we suggest the following hypothesis about the original components of 1 Corinthians. This hypothesis removes all seventeen of the problematic transitions in the letter as well as all of the contradictory details. As we shall show in subsequent chapters, these reconstructed letters conform to the high standards of literary and rhetorical coherence in the rest of Paul's correspondence.

Corinthian Letter A: 1 Cor 11:2, 17-34a + 11:3-16 + 11:34b ("Troubles in Worship")

We believe that this chapter is part of the first letter Paul sent to Corinth, responding to hearsay reports about the congregational situation that Paul received in his first weeks of ministry in Ephesus in the fall of 52. Since Paul refers to his information about the Corinthian situation as a matter of hearsay, which he only partially believes (11:18), the placement of chapter 11 as the first letter eliminates the contradictions with 1 Cor 1:10-12 where Paul responds to direct evidence from Chloe's people and now knows the slogans of the parties in conflict in Corinth. Whereas he accepts the divisions in 1 Cor 11:19 as a test of genuineness, he categorically rejects divisions in 1:13–3:23, so the placement of chapter 11 at the beginning of the correspondence removes the most egregious contradiction. This also removes the rough transitions between 1 Cor 11:1 and 11:2 and between 11:24 and 12:2.

The details in 16:1-4 fit the rhetorical situation of this earliest letter to the Corinthians. The offhand reference in 16:1 to the instructions Paul had given to the Galatians requires a dictation date within a few months of departing North Galatia in the early summer of 52. There is no indication in this reference to troubles in the Galatian congregations that are reflected in Paul's letter that was drafted in 53.[129] Since there is no further reference to Galatian contributions in Paul's letters or Acts, it is likely that they chose not to participate.[130] Since Paul mentions the instructions given to the Galatians as a motivation for the Corinthians,[131] this reference must have preceded the writing of the Galatian letter that responds to the crisis there, after which their involvement with the offering is passed over in silence. The travel plans and arrangements to select emissaries to bring the offering to Jerusalem (16:3-4) become items of controversy in 2 Corinthians, which confirms that these verses belong in an early phase of the offering project.

This hypothesis eliminates the rough transitions between 11:1 and 11:2 and between 11:34 and 12:1. It eliminates the highly significant contradiction between Paul's knowledge of and attitude toward partisanship in 11:18-19 and 1:10–4:21. It eliminates the awkward contradiction between ten chapters of criticism and the commendation in 11:2 that the Corinthians "remember me in everything and maintain the traditions as I have delivered them to you." This hypothesis eliminates the discrepancy between five chapters of additional discussion after announcing in 11:34 that Paul will give directions when he comes, which normally signals the close of a letter. It reduces the confusion between three separate endings in chapter 16 by identifying 16:1-4 as the only one that matches the rhetorical situation of chapter 11.

Corinthian Letter B: 2 Cor 6:14–7:1 + 1 Cor 6:12-20 + 1 Cor 9:24–10:22 + 1 Cor 15:1-58 + 1 Cor 16:13-24 ("The Body Matters")

We assign most of the material in 1 Corinthians that is not introduced by the "now concerning" formula to this second letter, probably written from Ephesus in the fall of 53. This is the letter that Paul describes in Letter C (1 Cor 5:9) as containing a warning "not to mingle with immoral people." Since this is precisely the theme of 2 Cor 6:14–7:1, not to be "unequally yoked with nonbelievers," we believe that these verses comprise the opening of the first proof that argues for separation from the pagan world. This provides the exegetical foundation for the second argument in 1 Cor 6:12-20 about avoiding sexual misyoking. The third argument in 1 Cor 9:24-27 makes a case for somatic discipline while 10:1-13 argues for bodily accountability. In 10:14-22, Paul applies these somatic insights to the issue of being misyoked with pagan worshippers, which is followed by 15:1-57, which argues against Corinthian skepticism of the bodily element in resurrection. A *peroratio* in 15:50-57 is followed by the epistolary conclusion in 15:58 + 16:15-24. This reveals that Stephanus and his colleagues have visited Paul in Ephesus (15:17), bringing a firsthand report about the situation in Corinth, to which Letter B responds. Since letter bearers in the Greco-Roman world were expected to fill in the implicit details in letters that were too delicate to put in writing, it is likely that Paul's admonitions to respect their leadership in 16:16, 18[132] indicate that Stephanus and his two colleagues are bringing the letter from Ephesus to Corinth. The postscript in Paul's own handwriting, "If anyone does not love the Lord, let him be cursed. Our Lord, come!" (16:22) reinforces their authority as well as the previous argument about the bodily element in the resurrection of Christ and of believers.

In recommending the authority of Stephanus and his colleagues, Paul obviously wishes to lend weight to his argument that the bodily aspects of theology and ethics must be respected. That they agree with Paul on these issues is indicated by the fulsome recommendation they receive in 16:15-18. However, in demanding that the Corinthians "be subject to such people," resolving complex issues by an appeal to authority, Paul encourages the emergence of factionalism that he must counter in the next letter. In view of this development, it is inconceivable that 16:13-23 could have been intended as the conclusion of Letter C. It also could not have been intended as the conclusion of Letter A because it reflects the receipt from Stephanus and his colleagues of too much firsthand evidence about the situation in Corinth.

This reconstruction of Letter B eliminates no less than ten rough transitions between 2 Cor 6:13 and 14; between 2 Cor 7:1 and 2; between 1 Cor 6:11 and 12; between 6:20 and 21; between 9:23 and 24; between 10:22 and 23; between 14:40 and 15:1; between 15:58 and 16:1; between 16:4 and 5; and between 16:12 and 13. In their stead, there are four smooth transitions in Letter B between thematically related sections of Paul's argument.

The hypothesis about Letter B as a unified letter arguing for the significance of bodily relations and the dangers of believers joining themselves inappropriately with non-covenanted partners eliminates several logical contradictions in canonical 1 Corinthians. The contradictions in travel plans in chapter 16 disappear, as does the conflict in rhetorical situations. The doublets are now gone, with the second reference to "all things are lawful" assigned to Letter C (1 Cor 10:23), the first of two discussions of food offered to idols now in Letter C (10:14-22), and the second discussion of the Lord's Supper (11:17-34) assigned to Letter A, which eliminates a doublet in Letter B (10:14-22). This also eliminates the contradiction between Paul's rejection of participating in pagan meals in Letter B (10:1-22) and his tolerance of such behavior in Letter C (1 Cor 8:1-13 and 10:23–11:1). Since all of the topics in canonical 1 Corinthians not introduced by the "now concerning" formula are now assigned to Letters A and C, no discrepancies in the use of this expression need to be explained. With these contradictions removed, Letter B emerges as a coherent, well-organized letter reflecting a single rhetorical situation.

Corinthian Letter C: 1 Cor 1:1–6:11 + 1 Cor 7:1–8:13 + 1 Cor 9:19-23 + 1 Cor 10:23–11:1 + 1 Cor 12:1-31a + 1 Cor 14:1c-40 + 1 Cor 12:31b–13:13 + 1 Cor 16:5-12 ("The Argument for Unity")

We propose the opening chapters of 1 Corinthians and all of the material that is introduced by the "now concerning" formula belong in Letter C. This letter responds to extensive information about the Corinthian situation brought by "Chloe's people" (1 Cor 1:11), and in the "now concerning" sections starting in 7:1, it replies to questions posed by the Corinthians in a letter to Paul. Since it is now clear that the congregation was seriously divided into sectarian groups, Letter C provides a coherent argument for unity and deals with serious ethical issues in the congregation.

The *exordium* in 1:1-9 contains an epistolary opening and a thanksgiving (1:4-9) that prepares for all of the topics in Letter C. The *propositio* of the letter is 1:10 that states the theme of unity both negatively and positively. This is followed by a *narratio* #1 in 1:11-17 that describes the situation of disunion while criticizing the congregation for violating the unity of Christ. This is the opening of the first proof in Letter C (1:11–4:21), which contains six arguments against factionalism. In the first argument (1:18-31) the message of the cross is shown to counter the competition in wisdom that lies at the heart of factionalism. The second argument also begins with a *narratio* in 2:1-5 that leads into the formal argumentation (2:6-16). Here Paul recalls that his preaching concentrated on Christ crucified rather than in human wisdom and that those who accept this message are the "spiritual persons." There is a third *narratio* in 3:1-3a that leads into the third argument (3:3b-17), showing that if the congregation had understood this gospel, they would not be competing but would display the unity and holiness of God's temple that they were intended to be. In the fourth argument (3:18–4:5), Paul challenges those who claim superiority in human wisdom, believing that their adherence to one of the apostolic groups will assure approval in the last judgment. The fifth argument in 4:6-13 is against groups being "puffed up" against each other, in contrast to the vulnerable status of the apostles. The sixth and final portion of this first proof (4:14-21) explains why Paul writes this letter and warns against the consequences of continuing to be "puffed up."

We identify the second proof as containing 5:1–6:11, which deals with what Paul views as even more problematic circumstances in the Corinthian congregation. There are three arguments in this proof. 1 Cor 5:1-8 deals with a case of incest that was outrageous even in the standards of the Greco-Roman world. In 5:9-13 Letter B says more on the question of mixing with immoral people, concluding with a demand to expel violators. The third argument in the second proof is 6:1-11, protesting against believers pursuing litigation against each other. It ends with the assertion that believers were made holy by their acceptance of the gospel, which means that such moral outrages should be a thing of the past.

The third proof in Letter C deals with the four issues raised by the Corinthians in their letter to Paul. The first is whether he really intended in Letter B to outlaw marriage (7:1-24). He turns next to the complicated issue of virginity in 7:25-40. In the third argument (8:1-13 + 9:19-23 + 10:23–11:1), Paul applies the insights from his first proof to show that "knowledge puffs up" when it leads believers to urge others to violate their conscience by eating food offered to idols. The final argument deals with the status of spiritual gifts (12:1-31a + 14:1c-33a + 14:37-40), maintaining that all believers have one gift or another and establishing guidelines for the constructive employment of such gifts in worship.

With the restoration of the original sequence of chapters 12, 14, and 13, the great climax of Letter C can be recognized as the *peroratio* of the letter. 1 Cor 12:31b–13:13 celebrates the kind of love that can unify the congregation, contrasting it with forms of religious knowledge that always remain partial. Genuine maturity is therefore the result of recognizing one's limitations, which means that the absolute knowledge being claimed in Corinth is actually available only at the end of time (13:12).

In 16:5-12, we have part of the letter closing that originally was part of Letter C. It contains reports of travel plans of Paul, Timothy and Apollos. These details match the situation in the summer of 54 when Paul expects to wrap up his Ephesian ministry and visit Corinth on the way to deliver the offering to Jerusalem in the following year. These plans were interrupted by the threat of an assassination (Acts 20:3) and by the worsening of the situation in Corinth. The epistolary postscript is missing.

This reconstruction of Letter C with a three-part *probatio* eliminates a total of sixteen rough transitions, including those between 1 Cor 6:11 and 6:12; between 6:20 to 7:1; between 8:13 and 9:1; between 9:18 and 19; between 9:23 and 24; between 10:22 and 23; and between 11:1 and 11:2. The reversal in the sequence of chapters 12, 13, and 14 eliminates rough transitions between 11:34 and 12:1; between 12:31 and 13:1; between 13:13 and 14:1; between 14:33a to 14:33b-34; between 14:36 and 37; and between 14:40 and 15:1-2. The assignment of 16:5-12 to Letter C eliminates the difficult transitions between 15:58 and 16:1; between 16:4 and 5; and between 16:12 and 16:13. As we shall demonstrate in the rhetorical analysis in chapter 8 of this book, these difficult transitions are replaced by smoothly flowing discourse that moves in a coherent manner between closely related topics.

The assignment of the material in the introduction and conclusion as well as in these three proofs to Letter C eliminates some of the most egregious contradictions in canonical 1 Corinthians. As we noted in discussing Letter B, Paul's knowledge of the situation in Corinth increases in each letter. Whereas in Letter A Paul has received hearsay reports about schisms in Corinth, and is not particularly disturbed, by the time of Letter C, he has received detailed reports from "Chloe's people" and categorically rejects schisms. Since Letter A reflects Paul's knowledge in the fall of 52, what he writes in the summer of 54 in Letter C reflects a changed situation and increased knowledge. It is not the contradiction; it would be if 1 Cor 11 were written at the same time as chapters 1-4. A second contradiction that this hypothesis removes is that there is no hint in these first four chapters of personal attacks against Paul, which are very much in evidence in chapter 9. His "defense" (9:3) is written in the judicial *genus* of rhetoric, which conflicts with the rest of 1 Corinthians written in the deliberative *genus*. The doublets detected by literary critics as signs of different original documents are also removed. There is now only one reference to "all things are lawful" in 10:23 and one discussion of food offered to idols in 8:1-13. The contradiction between Paul's categorical prohibition of participating in pagan meals in Letter B (10:1-22) and his tolerance on this point in Letter C (8:1-13 and 10:23–11:1) is removed. Restoring the original sequence of chapters 12, 14, and 13 eliminate the contradictions between calling for striving after "higher gifts" in 12:31a and the preceding argument that places all spiritual gifts on the same level (12:29-30). The contradiction between recommending prophecy as the single gift in 14:24 while referring to plural gifts in 12:31a and 14:1 is eliminated.

Letter C as reconstructed here is a coherent, rhetorically compelling, and logically organized letter that reflects the situation in the summer of 54 after Chloe's people brought a detailed report about partisan developments to Paul who was ministering in Corinth.

Corinthian Letter F: 2 Cor 10:1-11:9 + 1 Cor 9:1-18 + 2 Cor 11:10-13:13.

Much has been written about 2 Cor 10–13. Our reconstruction of Letter F includes 1 Cor 9:1-18 in between 2 Cor 11:9 and 11:10. This reconstruction of Letter F eliminates two rough transitions in canonical 1 Corinthians, between 8:13 and 9:1 and between 9:18 and 19. The most important contradiction removed by this hypothesis is that the self-defense in 9:1-18 protrudes like a sore thumb in the discourse of 1 Corinthians, which contains no other indications that Paul's apostolicity is under attack.[133] The shift to judicial discourse in this section is out of place with the deliberative *genus* of the rest of the letter.

With these problems removed, Letter F gives the impression of coherent discourse, reflecting the situation after Paul's "tearful visit" in the spring of 55.

THE PROVENANCE OF LETTERS A, B, AND C[134]

Paul's mission in Corinth probably began in the early spring of 50 CE, a date derived from the Gallio Inscription which establishes a tenure of July 1, 51, to July 1, 52, for the proconsul before whom Paul appeared (Acts 18:12-17). This correlates with the encounter with Prisca and Aquila, immigrants from Rome in 49, with whom Paul developed a tentmaking business (Acts 18:1-3). Several house churches were established in Corinth and its two harbor towns, whose patrons sponsored various traveling evangelists and came to favor competitive outlooks. The bulk of the converts were slaves and humble handworkers, led by patrons such as Gaius, Titius Justus, Chloe,

Phoebe, Stephanus, Erastus, Prisca, and Aquila. In the period between Paul's departure in 51 CE and his first return visit in 55, serious conflicts arose in the churches, eliciting Paul's letters. Apollos who missionized in Corinth during this period also played a prominent role in the development of the controversies.

In his first letter to the Corinthians (1 Cor 11:2 + 11:17-34a + 11:3-16 + 16:1-4 + 11:34b), Paul responds to hearsay information (11:18-19)[135] about agitation concerning male and female hairstyles[136] and disruptions of the Lord's Supper. This letter was probably written at the beginning of the mission to Ephesus in the fall of 52, which correlates with the fact that Paul's information about the Corinthian situation consisted of rumors about whose veracity he is skeptical (11:18). The letter was written before Paul had a chance to make further inquiries or to hear firsthand reports from members of the Corinthian congregations. The offhand reference in 16:1 to the instructions Paul had recently given to the Galatians also requires a provenance shortly after he had revisited the Galatian congregations. He urges the maintenance of traditional hairstyles while arguing both for the priority of males over females (11:3, 8) and interdependence between the sexes (11:11-12). There is no indication in this muddled argument that Paul suspects that prophetesses were probably adopting male hairstyles to express their reunification into the original, androgynous Adam.[137] Since some of the Corinthians viewed Christ as the First Adam, which Paul opposes at the end of his next letter (15:46-47), and since Paul was forced to counter their denigration of bodily responsibility in that letter (6:12-20; 9:24–10:22), it appears likely that the proto-gnostic viewpoint was already emerging in the congregation prior to the writing of Paul's first letter.[138] The women who adopted a male hairstyle were expressing their understanding of baptism along the lines of Gal 3:28 as incorporation in the original, bodiless Adam.

In the second half of Letter A Paul deals with distortions in the celebration of the Lord's Supper. The most likely reconstruction of the situation to which Paul responds in this passage is that the rich members of the Corinthian church had started to come early to the communal meals and were consuming all of the better food and all the wine before the slaves and handworkers arrived.[139] They were already drunk by the time the members who were obligated to work from dawn to dusk arrived to discover that only slave rations were left. In Paul's view, this destroyed the equality that was the essence of the meals that Jesus had established. The rich were violating this equality by "humiliating those who have nothing" (11:22). There is angry sarcasm in Paul's query to the rich about whether they didn't have houses where they could satisfy their hunger (11:22), having lain around all day while the other members of their congregation were laboring. In fact, only the rich had "houses" where their hunger could be satisfied,[140] while slaves and handworkers lived in tiny spaces in tenement buildings. Thus, the concluding admonition in 11:33 is to "wait for one another" so the meal can reflect genuine κοινωνία in the body of Christ. In this first letter to the Corinthians, Paul deals with the social dimension of the meal rather than opening up the theological issues as in his later letters.[141]

Letter B was written from Ephesus in the fall of 53 after Paul received a report about the situation in Corinth from Stephanus and his colleagues Fortunatus and Achaicus (16:15-18). It was probably brought to Corinth by Titus whose ministry there is described in Letter D, written about a year later (2 Cor 8:6).[142] Judging from the contents of this letter, their report must have included details about promiscuous relations between congregational members and inappropriate partners. In the next letter, Paul refers back to Letter B as a warning "not to mingle with sexually immoral people" (1 Cor 5:9). A series of terms closely related to this verb συναναμίγνυσθαι ("mingle") are strewn through Letter B: ἑτεροζυγοῦντες ("unequally yoked"), μετοχὴ ("sharing"), and κοινωνία ("fellowship") in 2 Cor 6:14; συμφώνησις ("agreement, harmony"), μερὶς ("portion"), and συγκατάθεσις ("concord") in 2 Cor 6:15-16; μέλη ("member") and κολλώμενος ("join together," twice) in 1 Cor 6:16-17; κοινωνία ("fellowship") in 1 Cor 10:16 (twice); and κοινωνοὺς ("partner") and μετέχειν ("sharing") in 1 Cor 10:20-21. Since the importance of bodily relations[143] carries through the entirety of Letter B, it is likely that the report by Stephanos and his colleagues contained details about the discrediting of such matters in the congregation. Several details from their report can be recovered from the wording of Paul's argument. The slogan πάντα μοι ἔξεστιν ("all things are lawful for me") is cited twice in 1 Cor 6:12 with the qualifications that not all things are advantageous and some things result in slavery. But aside from these qualifications, Paul presents the slogan as valid. In view of Paul's longstanding conflict with legalists on the question of requiring kosher food for Gentiles, it is likely that the slogan had been brought by Paul to Corinth and that now it is being misused as a rationale for sexual libertinism.[144] There is broader agreement that 6:13a is the first half of a Corinthian syllogism[145] that was probably completed as follows: "Foods are for the belly and the belly for food; so the body is for fornication and fornication for the body."[146] The prominent, twofold use of σῶμα ("body") in 6:13 indicates that the libertines in Corinth denied the moral dimension of bodily relations, a theme that resurfaces in 15:35 in the question of the kind of body Paul has in mind with the resurrection. Although formulated abstractly, this issue is clearly related to the denial of the significance of bodily relations countered elsewhere in Letter B.[147] This was probably related to the idea of an original spiritual and androgynous Adam that surfaced in Letter A, which led the proto-gnostics in Corinth to advocate the doctrine of a decline from the spiritual to the physical Adam that Paul counters in 15:45-46.[148] Paul flatly denies this sequence: "It is not the spiritual which is first, but the physical [Adam]" (15:46).

From the first proof to the last, the argument that "the body matters" is pursued throughout Letter B. In 2 Cor 6:14–7:1, Paul establishes his premise of the mutually exclusive spheres of Christ and paganism that requires purification of bodily pollution. This was followed by 1 Cor 6:12-20 that argues against prostitution in response to proto-gnostics who suggested that in Christ "everything is lawful." Here Paul develops the idea that the bodies of believers are "members of Christ," which eliminates the legitimacy of joining oneself with non-covenanted partners (6:15-18). In 1 Cor 9:24–10:22, Paul goes on to support bodily discipline and a recognition that Jesus-believers must not participate in pagan worship. In 1 Cor 15:1-58, Paul responds to contempt for the bodily component in the doctrine of resurrection. The letter concludes with the recommendation that the congregation "be subject" (1 Cor 16:16) to Stephanus and his coworkers who are bringing Letter B to Corinth.

Letter C was written in response to a precise report from Chloe's people (1 Cor 1:10-14) about intensified conflicts between Corinthian factions. It was sent from Ephesus in the summer of 54 when Paul was making plans to finish the ministry in Ephesus and spend the winter in Corinth (1 Cor 16:7-8) before heading off to Jerusalem with the offering. In contrast to the rumors to which he had responded in Letter A, Paul now has been informed even about the competitive mottos of the Corinthian factions: "I belong to Paul," "I belong to Apollos" and so on (1 Cor 1:12). In 1 Cor 1:1–4:21, Paul mounts a concerted attack on the worldly wisdom causing factionalism, arguing that the "foolishness of God is wiser than men" (1:26) and that the message of "Christ crucified" is the only true revelation of the power of God (2:2-5). Those who accept this message are the "spiritual ones" who have the "mind of Christ" (3:15-16). In 4:14-16, Paul explains that he writes this letter of unity to counsel his "beloved children" to become "imitators of me" in conforming to the gospel. If they do not, the Corinthians are inviting Paul to come with the "rod" of excommunication (4:21).

In 1 Cor 5:1-13, Paul demands discipline for a church member who was demonstrating his spiritual prowess by violating the incest taboo.[149] He then responds to the dismissal of his ethical demand in the previous letter as tantamount to the requirement to depart from this world (1 Cor 5:9-10).[150] He moves on to argue against worldly Jesus-believers settling their disputes in the courts (1 Cor 6:1-11).[151]

Beginning with 1 Cor 7, Paul responds to the first question raised in the Corinthians' letter, concerning a saying that was being misinterpreted as advocacy of Platonic marriage. Graydon F. Snyder showed that the words "it is better for a man not to touch a woman" (7:1) comprise the first half of a "better-than saying."[152] The first half of such a saying states the problem and the second half usually states the result or punishment. For example, in Mark 9:45, there is a "better-than" saying that fits this pattern: "it is better for you to enter life lame than with two feet to be thrown into hell." So with regard to the saying cited in 7:1, the question is "better than what?" Snyder showed that the word "woman" refers to the non-covenantal partner, a woman who is not one's wife. The original saying that Paul had apparently brought to Corinth probably had a similar second half, which we reconstruct as follows: "it is better for a man not to touch a[n uncovenanted] woman than to burn in hell." Paul apparently quotes this second half in 7:9, but the Corinthians had dropped it because they thought Paul advocated a complete rejection of sexual relations. In contrast, he urges married partners to fulfill sexual obligations in an egalitarian manner (7:3-4) but wishes that everyone were single as he was, while declaring that each person has a sexual gift that should be followed (7:7). This passage ends with the admonition for each "to remain in the state in which he or she was called" (7:20), except that if a slave has an opportunity of freedom, "it is better to take advantage of it" (7:21). He moves on in the next argument to deal with the Corinthians question about whether virgins should seek marriage, carrying forward the idea of each believer acting responsibly in the light of the sexual gift he or she has been given.

In 8:1-13 Paul takes up the question of eating food offered to idols, another matter on which "the community is divided."[153] He argues against violating the conscience of the weak and moves on in 9:19-23 to explain his own behavior in relation to groups of believers with differing views of the law. This continues in 10:23–11:1 that presents a strategy for the gradual education of the conscience of the weak. By seeking to "build up" others (10:23), Paul seeks to maintain the unity of the church by "pleasing all people in all things" (10:33).

In 1 Cor 12 and 14, Paul argues against the overvaluation of glossolalia and for a mutually edifying worship life based on the priority of love. These chapters are directly related to the thesis of 1:10 in countering divisiveness in the congregation.[154] There were controversies over the priority of specific gifts, particularly over speaking in tongues, and even whether it was legitimate to curse the bodily Jesus in order to highlight the spiritual Christ (12:3).[155] The proto-gnostic affirmation of the allegedly original spiritual Adam that surfaced in 1 Cor 15:46 likely motivated such cursing,[156] which Paul categorically rejects as an expression of the Spirit. The subsequent argument responds to the claim of some believers that glossolalia was "the spiritual reality *par excellence,* almost to the point of being the sole gift"[157] that marked practitioners as the spiritual elite. In 14:1-25, Paul restricts glossolalia to the private sphere and recommends prophecy as the gift best suited for public worship.

The magnificent celebration of love in 12:31b–13:13 serves as the *peroratio* of Letter C. It recapitulates the subordination of glossolalia to the requirements of love within the congregation and describes the limits of spiritual knowledge. Spiritual maturity is presented in 13:11-12 as overcoming the childish notion of having perfect knowledge. Love alone is capable of holding a congregation together despite all of the differences between its members (13:4-7). This chapter sums up all of the matters discussed in Letter C, but not those portions of 1 Corinthians that originated in Letter B; it celebrates love as the final cure of disunity.

With the remaining portions of the epistolary postscript (16:5-12), Paul sets forth his travel plans and announces movements of colleagues. By referring to Apollos as "the brother," Paul continues the cooperative attitude toward a colleague (3:6, 22; 4:6) who was being celebrated in Corinth in support of partisanship (1:12; 3:5). Thus, from beginning to end, Letter C comprises a coherent and unified argument for unity.

NOTES

1. Weiss, *Der erste Korintherbrief*, KEK, 9th edition (Göttingen: Vandenhoeck & Ruprecht, 1910; reprinted 1970 and 1977), 156; see also Gordon D. Fee, *The First Epistle to the Corinthians*, NICNT (Grand Rapids: Eerdmans, 1987), 250.

2. See also E. B. Allo, *Saint Paul: Première Épître aux Corinthiens*, 2nd edition, EBib (Paris: Gabalda, 1956), 141; Wendland, *Korinther*, 50.

3. Weiss, *erste Korintherbrief*, 156–57.

4. Weiss, *erste Korintherbrief*, 157.

5. Margaret M. Mitchell, *Paul and the Rhetoric of Reconciliation: An Exegetical Investigation of the Language and Composition of 1 Corinthians* (Louisville: Westminster John Knox, 1991), 33.

6. Weiss, *erste Korintherbrief*, 169.

7. Richard A. Horsley, *1 Corinthians*, ANTC (Nashville: Abingdon Press, 1998), 95.

8. Mitchell, *Reconciliation*, 120.

9. Mitchell, *Reconciliation*, 121.

10. David E. Garland, *1 Corinthians*, BECNT (Grand Rapids: Baker Academic, 2003), 396; David J. Lull, *1 Corinthians*, Chalice Commentaries for Today (St. Louis: Chalice, 2007), 81, refers to "an abrupt change of subject" in 9:1.

11. F. F. Bruce, *1 and 2 Corinthians*, NCB (Grand Rapids: Eerdmans; London: Marshall, Morgan & Scott, 1971), 82; see also Heinrich August Wilhelm Meyer, *Corinthians*, 195.

12. Weiss, *erste Korintherbrief*, 232.

13. Weiss, *erste Korintherbrief*, 231.

14. Wolfgang Schrage, *Der erste Brief an die Korinther*, 4 volumes, EKKNT 7 (Zürich and Düsseldorf: Benziger Verlag; Neukirchen-Vluyn: Neukirchener Verlag, 1991, 1995, 1999, 2001), 2.280-83.

15. Joseph A. Fitzmyer, *First Corinthians: A New Translation with Introduction and Commentary*, Anchor Yale Bible, 32 (New Haven: Yale University Press, 2008), 354–55; see also Hans Conzelmann, *1 Corinthians: A Commentary on the First Epistle to the Corinthians*, Hermeneia (Philadelphia: Fortress, 1975), 151; J. Paul Sampley, "The First Letter to the Corinthians," in *The New Interpreter's Bible* (Nashville: Abingdon, 2002) 10.771-1003, 902.

16. Horsley, *1 Corinthians*, 124.
17. Mitchell, *Reconciliation*, 128–29.
18. Mitchell, *Reconciliation*, 130; see also Sampley, *First Letter*, 904–6.
19. Mitchell, *Reconciliation*, 131.
20. Weiss, "Beiträge zur Paulinischen Rhetorik," 32.
21. Weiss, *erste Korintherbrief*, 242; this was confirmed by Hermann Probst, *Paulus und der Brief: Die Rhetorik des antiken Briefes als Form der paulinischen Korintherkorrespondenz (1 Kor 8 - 10)*, WUNT 2.45 (Tübingen: Mohr Siebeck, 1991), 212, which was accepted by Lindemann, *erste Korintherbrief*, 210.
22. See also Paul Wilhelm Schmiedel, *Die Briefe an die Thessalonicher und an die Korinther*, Hand-Commentar zum Neuen Testament, 2 (Freiburg: Mohr, 1891), 144.
23. Hans Lietzmann, *An die Korinther I/II*, 5th edition edited and expanded by Werner Georg Kümmel, HNT 9 (Tübingen: Mohr, 1949), 43.
24. Weiss, *erste Korintherbrief*, 242.
25. Mitchell, *Reconciliation*, 133.
26. Weiss, *erste Korintherbrief*, 246.
27. Weiss, *erste Korintherbrief*, 246.
28. Mitchell, *Reconciliation*, 136.
29. Mitchell, *Reconciliation*, 137.
30. Weiss, *erste Korintherbrief*, 262; see also Senft, *première Épître*, 136.
31. Fitzmyer, *First Corinthians*, 397: the material in 10:23 – 11:1 "is not directly connected with the topic of the preceding pericope . . . ."
32. Weiss, *erste Korintherbrief*, 263.
33. Conzelmann, *First Epistle*, 175.
34. Mitchell, *Reconciliation*, 142.
35. Mitchell, *Reconciliation*, 142–43.
36. Weiss, *erste Korintherbrief*, 267.
37. Conzelmann, *First Epistle*, 182.
38. See Fee, *First Epistle*, 500.
39. Weiss, *erste Korintherbrief*, 268.
40. Mitchell, *Reconciliation*, 150.
41. Horsley, *1 Corinthians*, 152.
42. William O. Walker, Jr., "The Vocabulary of 1 Corinthians 11:3-16: Pauline or Non-Pauline?" *JSNT* 35 (1989): 75–88; Walker, *Interpolations in the Pauline Letters*, JSNTSup 213 (Sheffield: Sheffield Academic Press, 2001), 91–126; G. W. Trompf, "On Attitudes toward Women in Paul and Paulinist Literature: 1 Cor 11:3 – 16 and Its Context," *CBQ* 42 (1980): 196–215.
43. Horsley, *1 Corinthians*, 152.

44. Horsley, *1 Corinthians*, 152.
45. Weiss, *erste Korintherbrief*, 294.
46. Conzelmann refers to 11:33-34 as "the final conclusion" in *1 Corinthians*, 203.
47. Here again the editors of the Nestle-Aland 28th edition place double spacing between 11:34 and 12:1, indicating a difficult transition.
48. Weiss, *erste Korintherbrief*, 309–11; in *First Epistle*, 217, Conzelmann refers to this transition as "ragged."
49. Mitchell, *Reconciliation*, 165.
50. Weiss, *erste Korintherbrief*, 310–11.
51. Conzelmann, *First Epistle*, 233.
52. Weiss, *erste Korintherbrief*, 311.
53. Weiss, *erste Korintherbrief*, 342.
54. Mitchell, *Reconciliation*, 174.
55. Nestle-Aland 28th edition places a fresh paragraph spacing between 14:33a and 33b, and another fresh paragraph spacing between 14:36 and 37.
56. Weiss, *erste Korintherbrief*, 343.
57. See Conzelmann, *First Epistle*, 246.
58. Mitchell, *Reconciliation*, 174.
59. Weiss, *erste Korintherbrief*, 343–44.
60. Conzelmann, *First Epistle*, 249; see also Lietzmann, *Korinther*, 76; Pheme Perkins, *First Corinthians*, Paideia Commentaries on the New Testament (Grand Rapids: Baker Academic, 2012), 171; Garland, *1 Corinthians*, 692 refers to this transition as "abrupt."
61. Mitchell, *Reconciliation*, 175–77.
62. See Conzelmann, *2 Corinthians*, 293; Collins, *First Corinthians*, 578.
63. See Clarence Tucker Craig, "The First Epistle to the Corinthians: Introduction and Exegesis," in George A. Buttrick et al., editors, *The Interpreter's Bible* (Nashville: Abingdon Press, 1953), 10.1-262; 254.
64. Schrage, *erste Brief*, 4.423.
65. Alfred Suhl, *Paulus und seine Briefe. Ein Beitrag zur paulinische Chronologie*, SNT 11 (Gütersloh: Gütersloher Verlagshaus, 1975), 222; Schrage, *Erste Brief*, 4.424-25.
66. See Dieter Georgi, *Remembering the Poor: The History of Paul's Collection for Jerusalem* (Nashville: Abingdon Press, 1992), 55–56.
67. In "First Epistle," 257, Craig observes that "Vs. 4 indicates that **at this early stage** in the enterprise the apostle was not certain that he would accompany them" (bold typeface added).
68. Mitchell, *Reconciliation*, 291–93.
69. Conzelmann, *First Epistle*, 297: "The paraenesis comes unexpectedly."
70. This was noted by Meyer, *Corinthians*, 400.
71. Fitzmyer, *First Corinthians*, 623; see also Perkins, *First Corinthians*, 201; Craig, "First Epistle," 259.
72. Weiss, *erste Korintherbrief*, 385.
73. See Weiss, *erste Korintherbrief*, 385.
74. Mitchell, *Reconciliation*, 178.

75. See Friedrich Lang, *Die Briefe an die Korinther*, NTD 7 (Göttingen: Vandenhoeck & Ruprecht, 1986), 7; Vielhauer, *Geschichte*, 141. In "1 Corinthians 11:3-16: Spirit Possession and Authority in a Non-Pauline Interpolation," *JBL* 124 (2005): 313–40, Christopher Mount observes that "the knowledge revealed in 1 Cor 11:3–16 suggests a situation and set of exigencies quite different from the situation in chs. 12 and 14" (336).

76. Weiss, *erste Korintherbrief*, 268.

77. Lang, *Korinther*, 7.

78. See Jewett, *A Chronology of Paul's Life* (Philadelphia: Fortress, 1979), 100, as well as the "Graph of Dates and Time Spans" on 161.

79. See Jewett, *Chronology*, 48–50, as well as the "Graph of Dates and Time Spans," 161.

80. Lang, *Korinther*, 7.

81. Lang, *Korinther*, 6.

82. Lang, *Korinther*, 7.

83. See Weiss, *erste Korintherbrief*, 309–11.

84. Margaret Mitchell, "Concerning περὶ δέ in 1 Corinthians," *Novum Testamentum* 31 (1989): 229–56.

85. John C. Hurd, Jr., *The Origin of I Corinthians*, new edition (Macon: Mercer University Press, 1983), 45.

86. Hurd, "Good News and the Integrity of 1 Corinthians," in *Gospel in Paul: Studies on Corinthians, Galatians and Romans for Richard N. Longenecker*, JSNTSup 108 (Sheffield: Sheffield Academic Press, 1994), 38–62.

87. Schenk, "Briefsammlung," 219–43.

88. Schenk, "Briefsammlung," 241.

89. Bornkamm, "Vorgeschichte," 34.

90. Conzelmann, *1 Corinthians*, 99–100, 106.

91. Philipp Bachmann, *Der erste Brief des Paulus an die Korinther*, 3rd edition, Kommentar zum Neuen Testament, 7 (Leipzig: Deichert, 1921), 201–13.

92. Barrett, *First Epistle*, 120; *BDAG*, 704.

93. Weiss, *Korintherbrief*, 124f.

94. See Barrett, *First Epistle*, 16; Suhl, *Chronologie*, 213–17.

95. Robert Jewett, *Paul's Anthropological Terms: A Study of Their Use in Conflict Settings*, AGJU 10 (Leiden: Brill, 1971), 421–30.

96. Schenk, "Briefsammlung," 239.

97. See Jewett, *Terms*, 254–63; Anthony C. Thiselton, *The First Epistle to the Corinthians: A Commentary on the Greek Text*, NIGTC (Grand Rapids: Eerdmans, 2000), 708–17.

98. Schenk, "Briefsammlung," 242f.

99. Walter Schmithals, "Die Korintherbriefe als Briefsammlung," *ZNW* 64 (1973): 263–88; 288.

100. See our diagram of the resultant redactional process in Appendix III.

101. Schmithals, *Paul and the Gnostics* (Nashville: Abingdon Press, 1972), 259–65.

102. Weiss, *erste Korintherbrief*, 268.
103. Schmithals, "Briefsammlung," 284f.
104. Schmithals, "Briefsammlung," 271.
105. Suhl, *Chronologie*, 203–12.
106. Suhl, *Chronologie*, 203.
107. Weiss, *erste Korintherbrief*, 124.
108. Weiss, *erste Korintherbrief*, 159–60; see also Thiselton, *First Epistle*, 462–63.
109. H. Hagge, "Die beiden Überlieferten Sendschreiben des Apostels Paulus an die Gemeinde zu Korinth," *Jahrbücher für protestantische Theologie* 2 (1876): 481–531; he was unable to fit 2 Cor 8 into his scheme.
110. Alfred Loisy, "Les épîtres de S. Paul," *Revue d'histoire et de literature religieuses* 7 (1921): 213–50.
111. L. L. Welborn, "The First Letter of Paul to the Corinthians," in Michael D. Coogan, editor, *The New Oxford Annotated Bible with the Apocrypha: New Revised Standard Version*, fully revised 4th edition (New York: Oxford University Press, 2010), 1000–1.
112. Raymond F. Collins, *First Corinthians*, SP (Collegeville: Liturgical Press, 1999),12, lists the following advocates of two letters in 1 Corinthians: Erich Dinkler, Johannes Müller-Bardorff, Hans-Martin Schenke, Karl Martin Fischer, Philipp Vielhauer, Günther Bornkamm, Willi Marxsen, Jean Héring. Hurd, *Origin*, 45 adds Johannes de Zwaan, *Inleidung tot het Nieuwe Testament. II. Brieven van Paulus en Hebreën* (Haarlem: Erven Bohn, 1948), 2.47, 57; see also Sellin, "Hauptprobleme," 2965–68.
113. Senft, *première Épître*, 19.
114. Rudolf Pesch, *Paulus ringt um die Lebensform der Kirche: Vier Briefe an die Gemeinde Gottes in Korinth. Paulus neu gesehen*, Herderbücherei, 1291 (Freiburg: Herder, 1986), especially 29–97, 247–53.
115. Miguel de Burgos Núñez, "La Correspondencia de Pablo con las Communidades de Corinto," *Communio* 26 (1993): 33–67.
116. Yeo, *Rhetorical Interaction*, especially 81–82.
117. Paul-Louis Couchoud, "Reconstitution et Classement des Lettres de Saint Paul." *RHR* 87 (1923): 8–31, especially 17–31.
118. Goguel, *Introduction*, 4. Part 2.86. He was unable to incorporate 1 Cor. 1:1-9; 16:13-14, 19-24; and 2 Cor. 13:11-13.
119. Martin Widman, "Die vier Phasen des Konflikts zwischen Paulus und den Korinthern: Eine Rekonstruktion der Korrespondenz insbesondere des Thesenbriefs der Korinther und des Antwortbriefs des Paulus," in Oswald Bayer and G. U. Wanzeck, editor, *Festgabe für Friedrich Lang zum 65. Geburtstag am 6. September 1978* (Tübingen: Evangelisch-Theologisches Seminar der Universität, typescript, 1978), 799–833; Widmann, "1 Kor 2,6-16: Ein Einspruch gegen Paulus," *ZNW* 70 (1979): 44–53.
120. The following diagram is derived from Jerome Murphy-O'Connor, "Interpolations in 1 Corinthians," *CBQ* 48 (1986): 81–94; the diagram is found on 84.
121. Gerhard Sellin, *Der Streit um die Auferstehung der Toten: Eine religionsgeschichtliche und exegetische Untersuchung von 1. Korinther 15*, FRLANT 138 (Göttingen: Vandenhoeck & Ruprecht, 1986), 49–62; "Hauptprobleme," 2964–86.

122. Sellin, "Hauptprobleme," 2968.
123. Sellin, "Hauptprobleme," 2974–75.
124. Sellin, "Hauptprobleme," 2978.
125. Homer, *Iliad* 9.443.
126. Dieter Georgi, "Second Letter to the Corinthians," in Keith Crim et al., editors, *The Interpreter's Dictionary of the Bible, Supplement Volume* (Nashville: Abingdon, 1976), 183–86, especially 184–85.
127. See Georgi, *Opponents*, 238–42.
128. William O. Walker, Jr., "1 Corinthians 11:2-16 and Paul's Views Regarding Women," *JBL* 94 (1975): 94–110; 97–100.
129. See Jewett, *Chronology*, 103.
130. Craig, *First Epistle*, 255, refers to "the defection of the Galatian churches;" see also the discussion in Georgi, *Remembering*, 49–50.
131. Schrage, *erste Brief*, 4.427.
132. On the roles of the envoys who carried Paul's letters to congregations, see M. Luther Stirewalt, *Paul, the Letter Writer* (Grand Rapids: William B. Eerdmans Publishing, 2003), 11–16; as well as Jewett, *Romans: A Commentary*, 90–91.
133. See Weiss, *erste Korintherbrief*, 231.
134. The material in this section is adapted from Jewett, "Corinth," 290–94.
135. Schrage, *erste Brief*, 3.19.
136. See Collins, *First Corinthians*, 396–404.
137. See Wayne A. Meeks, "The Image of the Androgyne: Some Uses of a Symbol in Earliest Christianity," *History of Religions* 13 (1974): 165–208; reprinted pp. 3–54 in *In Search of the Early Christians: Selected Essays*, edited by Allen R. Hilton and H. Gregory Snyder (New Haven: Yale University Press, 2002), 11–23; Dennis Ronald MacDonald, *There Is No Male and Female: The Fate of a Dominical Saying in Paul and Gnosticism*, HDR 20 (Philadelphia: Fortress, 1987), 72–111; Collins, *First Corinthians*, 408. In contrast, in *The Corinthian Women Prophets: A Reconstruction through Paul's Rhetoric* (Minneapolis: Fortress, 1990), 122–28, Antoinette C. Wire views the women prophets as arguing on the basis of Genesis that they embodied the divine image in Christ. Linda L. Belleville, "*Kephale* and the Thorny Issue of Headcovering in 1 Corinthians 11:2-16," in Trevor J. Burke and J. Keith Elliott, editors, *Paul and the Corinthians: Studies on a Community in Conflict. Essays in Honour of Margaret Thrall*, NovTSup 109 (Leiden: Brill, 2003), 230–31, argues that this chapter deals with "cross dressing" that opened the path to promiscuous behavior.
138. See Peter Lampe, "The Parties in Corinth (1 Corinthians 1-4)," in Lukas Vischer, Ulrich Luz, and Christian Link, editors, *Unity of the Church in the New Testament and Today* (Grand Rapids: Eerdmans, 2010), 85–86.
139. See Collins, *First Corinthians*, 417–19, following the research of Hans-Josef Klauck, *Herrenmahl und hellenistischer Kult. Eine religionsgeschichtliche Untersuchung zum ersten Korintherbrief*, NTAbh 15 (Münster: Aschendorff, 1982), 241ff., and Klauck, *1. Korintherbrief*, 4th edition, NEchtB 7 (Würzburg: Echter, 2000). See also Lampe, "The Corinthian Eucharistic Dinner Party: Exegesis of a Cultural Context (I Cor. 11:17-34)," *Affirmation* 4/2 (1991): 1–15.
140. Collins, *First Corinthians*, 423.

141. See Gerd Theissen, "Social Integration and Sacramental Activity: An Analysis of 1 Cor. 11:17-34," in John H. Schütz, editors, *The Social Setting of Pauline Christianity: Essays on Corinth* (Philadelphia: Fortress Press, 1982), 145–74, especially 153–5.

142. See Hans Dieter Betz's discussion of the date of Titus' earlier mission in *2 Corinthians 8 and 9*, 55.

143. See Collins, *First Corinthians*, 239: "The heart of Paul's argument is . . . the importance of bodily relations."

144. See Archibald Robertson and Alfred Plummer, *A Critical and Exegetical Commentary on the First Epistle of St. Paul to the Corinthians*, ICC (New York: Scribner, 1911), 121; Hans Lietzmann, *An die Korinther I/II*, edited and expanded by Werner Georg Kümmel, 5th edition, HNT 9 (Tübingen: Mohr, 1949), 27; for a version of this theory, see Brian J. Dodd, "Paul's Paradigmatic 'I' and 1 Corinthians 6.12," *JSNT* 59 (1995): 39–58.

145. Weiss, *erste Korintherbrief*, 159; Schrage, *erste Brief*, 2.10.

146. Fitzmyer, *First Corinthians*, 264: "What is implied in such a liberal slogan is that sexual intercourse is likewise for the human physical body, and the body for such intercourse."

147. See Fitzmyer, *First Corinthians*, 586; Schrage, *erste Brief*, 4.270-72.

148. Schrage, *erste Brief*, 4.306-08, citing Schmithals, *Die Gnosis in Korinth: Eine Untersuchung zu den Korintherbriefen*, 3rd edition, FRLANT 66 (Göttingen: Vandenhoeck & Ruprecht, 1969), 159f.; see also Fitzmyer, *First Corinthians*, 598.

149. See L. L. Welborn, *An End to Enmity: Paul and the "Wrongdoer" of Second Corinthians*, BZNW 185 (Berlin: de Gruyter, 2011); on the history of the identification of the "wrongdoer" of 1 Corinthians 5, see especially pp. 3–22. Mitchell, *Reconciliation*, 225, shows that this is one of the issues that "divide the Corinthian church."

150. See Schrage, *erste Brief*, 1.388-89.

151. Mitchell, *Reconciliation*, 230–31, makes a good case that this issue "endangers the unity of the Corinthian church."

152. Graydon E. Snyder, "The Tobspruch in the New Testament," *NTS* 23 (1976–77): 117–20; Snyder, *First Corinthians*, Faith Community Commentary (Macon: Mercer University Press, 1993), 91–92. Ecclesiastes 7:5 is an example of a typical *Tobspruch*: "it is better for a man to hear the rebuke of the wise than to hear the song of fools."

153. Mitchell, *Reconciliation*, 237.

154. See Mitchell, *Reconciliation*, 267.

155. See Schrage, *erste Brief*, 3.114-16.

156. Schmithals, *Gnosticism*, 124–30; Norbert Brox, "ΑΝΑΘΗΜΑ ΙΗΣΟΥΣ [1 Kor 12,3]," *BZ* 12 (1968): 103–11, 103–11; Ulrich Wilckens, *Weisheit und Torheit: Eine exegetisch-religionsgeschichtliche Untersuchung zu 1. Kor. 1 und 2*, BHT 26 (Tübingen: Mohr Siebeck, 1959), 121; Kurt Rudolf, *Gnosis: The Nature and History of Gnosticism* (San Francisco: Harper & Row, 1983), 166.

157. Collins, *First Corinthians*, 461.

Chapter 4

The Redaction of 1 Corinthians

Our identification of Letters A, B, C, and a part of F within the boundaries of canonical 1 Corinthians in a previous chapter makes it possible to reconstruct the redactional process in precise detail.

THE METHOD OF REDACTING 1 CORINTHIANS

Our hypothesis is that Letter C served as the frame letter into which portions of Letters A, B, and F were inserted. When one visualizes the redactional process on scrolls, the steps were relatively simple, and far from the "flying fragments" envisioned by earlier opponents of division hypotheses. Four sections from Letter B, the body of Letter A, and one section from Letter F were inserted into discrete locations of the frame letter, with no more than one insertion at any one location. It is probable that the redactor began the insertion process by severing Cor B into segments from back to front. The first piece (1 Cor 16:13-24) was placed at the conclusion of the frame letter and the second piece was put in next, in front of 1 Cor 16:1. The reversal of chapters 14 and 13 was probably accomplished next. Then the third (1 Cor 9:24–10:22) and the fourth (1 Cor 6:12-20) pieces of Letter B were inserted. This left 2 Cor 6:14–7:1, which was originally a part of Letter B, to be deleted and ultimately to become part of canonical 2 Corinthians. If Bornkamm is right in suggesting that 2 Corinthians was edited sometime after 1 Corinthians, 2 Cor 6:14–7:1 would not have been designated yet as appropriate for 2 Corinthians, and it is hard to conceive of the redactor making a choice to delete it at the beginning of the process for 1 Corinthians. It seems more likely to have simply been left over from the intentional severing of Corinthian Letter B into portions to fit specific needs related to the redaction of Letter C. Hence, the suggestion that Letter B was more likely to have been cut apart starting at the end of the scroll. The fifth and sixth insertions, which completed the basic redaction of 1 Corinthians, placed 1 Cor 11:2-34 in its present spot, reversing the sequence of the two proofs. The redactor then inserted 1 Cor 9:1-18 after removing it from its original location in Letter F. A schematic illustration of the literary-critical hypothesis is provided in appendix I.

With the exception of Suhl's hypothesis, whose weaknesses were noted earlier, this is the simplest redactional scheme currently being offered to account for the literary-critical tangle of 1 Corinthians. The plausibility of the scheme depends, of course, on a variety of historical and literary assessments. In chapters - 13, we provide a rhetorical, epistolographic, and exegetical documentation that the eight letters are formally comprehensible, revealing body openings and closings that hitherto appeared out of place in the longer, canonical Corinthian letters. They also appear to be historically comprehensible, revealing progressive stages of the Corinthians controversy. This leads us to the decisive question: What were the redactional motives of the six insertions and the reversal of material in Letters A and C? How do they relate to the content and motives of the interpolations?

THE BEARING OF THE ORIGINAL CORINTHIAN LETTERS ON THE TRAJECTORIES OF ECCLESIASTICAL CONFLICT

To provide a context for understanding the redaction of 1 Corinthians, it is essential to consider the bearing of Paul's original letters on the controversies developing in the half-century after they were written. It is correctly assumed that such letters would have circulated among other churches. The well-known reference in Col 4:16 explicitly recommends the exchange of Pauline letters among neighboring churches and may well constitute, according to Eduard Schweizer, "the first impulse for a Pauline letter collection."[1] If the factions in churches possessed copies of the several letters that Paul had addressed to Corinth, what role would they have played in the conflicts between competitive factions?[2] Georg Strecker has shown that the Pastoral Epistles served to incorporate the authentic letters into an ecclesiastical framework in order to prevent their use by proto-gnostics and charismatic enthusiasts.[3] It is widely recognized that the Pastorals opposed forms of Jesus-belief with Jewish and gnostic tendencies.[4]

A survey of the contents of Letters A, B, and C will suggest they contained ready weapons in the hands of opposing factions in the conflicts between factions of the Pauline churches that developed after his death. To conceptualize this process, we rely on the trajectory theory developed by Helmut Koester and James Robinson: "At one stage of a movement a document may function in a specific way, have a certain meaning or influence on the movement; at a subsequent stage on the trajectory that document, unaltered, may function or cut in a different way, may mean in effect something different, may influence the movement differently."[5] When one follows the trajectory of Pauline material into the latter part of the first century or early second century of the Common Era, it is likely that Corinthian Letter A (1 Cor 11:2, 17-34a + 3-16 + 16:1-4 + 11:34b) would have been particularly useful to those advocating the institutions of ecclesiastical authority. Here Paul explicitly commends those who retain the *paradosis* ("tradition") of the apostolic era (1 Cor 11:2, 23). The hierarchy of Christ / husband / wife and the insistence on the retention of traditional feminine roles are reminiscent of themes in the Pastorals and would have been offensive to any faction attempting to retain the more egalitarian relationships that had been present in the earlier Pauline congregations. What Paul originally intended as a balance between equality and sexual differentiation could have sounded like chauvinism in the situation at the end of the century. The emphasis on the traditional words of institution (1 Cor 11:23-25) would be useful for the advocates of pastoral authority, and the stress on "discerning the body" (1 Cor 11:29) in the bread and wine of the Lord's Supper would have remained as offensive to gnostically inclined Jesus-believers as it was likely to have been during Paul's lifetime.

All of the material in Corinthian Letter B would be useful on the same side of the conflict. The first extant section of Letter B, assuming that 2 Cor 6:14–7:1 is authentic Pauline material, would confirm the exclusivist position and provide no comfort at all for gnostically inclined intellectuals seeking to accommodate the faith to Hellenistic culture. The discussion of marriage in 1 Cor 6:12-20 glorifies the sanctity of bodily relations in a manner guaranteed to be odious to gnostics; its opening delimitation of believers' freedom, "All things are lawful . . . but not are helpful," would be serviceable in support of the prudential ethic developing in the circle that produced the Pastoral Letters. The following section, 1 Cor 9:24–10:22, carries out the theme of moral self-control and demands a separation between the table of the Lord and the table of demons. This section would certainly provide no support for gnostic assimilationists around the end of the century. Similarly, the exhortation in 1 Cor 15:1-8 to hold fast the received traditions of the bodily resurrection would have been useful in developing the orthodox position and offensive to a group like the one condemned by 2 Tim 2:18. The rejection of gnostic speculation about the first and second Adams in 1 Cor 15:46-47 would remain serviceable in the hands of traditionalists.[6]

The discussion of the resurrection in Corinthian Letter B closes with the admonition to be "steadfast and immovable" (1 Cor 15:58), themes that become crucial for the mindset of the later Shepherd of Hermas (2:7) and are related to 1 Tim 3:15's reference to the "steadfast foundation of truth." The opening admonition of the final section in the reconstructed Cor B (1 Cor 16:13-24), sets the tone of watchfulness and standing firm in the faith that is close to the exhortations at the end of the Pastorals (2 Tim 3:10, 4:1-5; 1 Tim 6:11-20; Titus 2:2) where "steadfast" is virtually a watchword. The call to "recognition" and "subordination" in relation to established church leaders (1 Cor 16:16, 18b) would be a welcome aid to the advocates of a paid clergy in the apostolic succession. The anathema in 16:22 would be interpreted in the late first-century context as support for excommunication of those who resisted the emerging orthodox definitions of the faith. As a whole, therefore, Letters A and B would appeal exclusively to the conservative groups in the late first century. In a number of instances they would supply potent weapons in the campaign to reinforce the legitimacy of conservative institutions.

The picture is completely reversed when one surveys the contents of Letter C in view of the late first-century context. Here apostolicity is not a matter of human tradition at all, but of the unmediated will of God (1 Cor 1:1); here *gnosis* is explicitly affirmed as congruent with the "testimony of Christ" (1 Cor 1:5-6); here the *charismata* so valued by gnostically inclined Jesus-believers and enthusiasts are afforded a central place in the definition of the church (1 Cor 1:7). These themes are elaborated throughout Letter C to make it into a virtual manifesto for the kind of radicalism that stood opposed to conservative trends in places like Ephesus. The list of useful themes for the assimilationist, proto-gnostic side of the controversy is extensive. The downplaying of baptism in 1 Cor 1:14-17 would appeal to those resisting the bodily components in the sacraments. The identification of Christ with *sophia* in 1 Cor 1: 30 and the reference to "the secret and hidden wisdom of God" given to the church in 1 Cor 2:7 would be useful in arguing for the propriety of philosophical speculations, while the original, polemical bite of Paul's argument could well have been dulled by the simple assumption that the proto-gnostic enclave shared Paul's definition of saving wisdom. The claim that the "spiritual man" judges all and is subject to none (1 Cor 2:15), and that such persons have the "mind of Christ" (1 Cor 2:16) would have provided powerful support for gnostic theologizing, despite Paul's original intent. These verses certainly would have sustained resistance against subordination to any established leaders. In fact, the entire concept of an authoritative apostolic tradition is undercut by the way 1 Cor 3:5-7 would have sounded toward the end of the century, for it downplays the role of authority figures and ascribes power exclusively to God. It is a vivid expression of the principle of charismatic authority as an interpretation of widely shared charismatic experience in the first generation, but it verges on the "heretical" in the context of the second and third generations. From this perspective, it is possible to take 1 Cor 4:8-13 as an admission of the superiority of gnostically inclined Jesus-believers even over the apostles themselves; the bitterly ironic tone heard by modern exegetes reconstructing the original audience situation[7] would not necessarily have been caught at the end of the first century by proto-gnostic readers who assumed that Paul was on their side of the argument. The true church, according to this opening section of Letter C, consists of *pneumatikoi*, as the temple image of 3:16 implies. The idea of the church being wherever the spirit "dwells" is far removed from the systems of legitimation being developed by the groups we later think of as "orthodox." Furthermore, the critique of gnostic arrogance in 1 Cor 5:1-8 would have been less challenging to an audience far removed from the original Corinthian conflict than for the original participants; Paul's radical disciples toward the end of the century may well have felt that the incest question was unrelated to themselves.

There is little in Paul's discussion of lawsuits that would likely have been relevant in the controversies between liberals and conservatives toward the end of the century. This section ends with a catalog of moral offenders (1 Cor 6:9-11), which cannot have been congenial for libertinists. But when one reads its conclusions from the perspective of the end of the century, a generous loophole emerges for proto-gnostic intellectuals: if one is cleansed from all such defilements (6:11), it might be possible to conclude that henceforth one's bodily relations were inconsequential. The grounds for 1 Timothy's frustration with believers whose conscience was "seared" (1 Tim 4:2) may well have been the use—or one might say, misuse—of this material from Letter C.

The discussion of marriage in the next section of Corinthian Letter C would provide some support for gnostic ascetics (1 Cor 7:1, 7, 38), because it provides space for individual ethical discretion in matters of marriage and the clergy; here Paul refrains from issuing hard and fast rules that would have appealed to the Pastoral writers toward the end of the first century. The discussion of food offered to idols would have been highly appealing to late first-century radicals because it appeals specifically to those who have the proper *gnosis* (1 Cor 8:7). The original anti-gnostic implications of the discussion about conscience would have been less controversial in the second generation because increasing numbers of members from original Jesus-believing families would not have been raised in homes "accustomed to idols" (1 Cor 8:7). Paul's concern that the proto-gnostic freedom of his era might "destroy" the weak was understandable in the 50s, but given the rise of bigotry in place of uneasy conscience in the era of emerging orthodoxy, it is doubtful that Paul's argument in 1 Cor 8 and 10 would have been taken to be critical of those advocating the freedom position. In fact, Paul's rhetorical questions about freedom not being limited by the scruples of the narrow minded in 1 Cor 10:29b-30 would be perfectly suited for proto-gnostic controversialists.

Despite the fact that the next section of Letter C (1 Cor 12 + 14) was originally intended to counter proto-gnostic overreliance on glossolalia and disdain for the community, its bearing in the later controversy over hierarchical church leadership would shift dramatically in the opposite direction. The church is defined in these chapters in a charismatic rather than an authoritarian manner, particularly in 1 Cor 12:7 and 14; the emphasis in the body metaphor is on equality rather than subordination. When Paul lists the charismatic offices in a kind of hierarchical sequence (1 Cor 12:28), the "administrators" and "bishops" are not in a place of prominence demanded by the polity of the Pastorals.[8] Paul's suggestions for the exercise of charismatic gifts in 1 Cor 14:26-33a do not involve a single leader or dominant elders determining who should participate and when. Rather, in a radical doctrine of the democracy of Jesus-believers, the ordering principle is clearly within each spirit-filled member of the congregation. That every prophetic utterance was to be weighed and evaluated by the congregation as a whole (1 Cor 14:29) was sharply opposed to a rule by bishops or elders; thus what would have been taken as a criticism of proto-gnostic arrogance in the 50s becomes a criticism of ecclesiastical authority in the 90s. To say "the spirits of prophets are subject to prophets" (1 Cor 14:31) could easily have been taken as a declaration of independence from ecclesiastical control, the new argumentative context having altered its bearing from the original insistence on prophetic self-control and mutual criticism.

Finally, if the original sequence of these chapters was 1 Cor 12 + 14 + 13, the principle of love rather than of authority was in the position of emphasis as the supreme guideline for a charismatic congregation. The originally intended jibes against the excesses of gnostic *glossolalia* (1 Cor 13:1, 11) and of gnostic certitude (1 Cor 13:2, 12) could well have faded into the familiar rhythms of exalted poetry by the end of the first century. In comparison with the authoritarian ethic later embodied in the Pastorals, the basic theme of chapter 13 is congenial to those favoring freedom in the spirit. The calls for tolerant love and broadmindedness (1 Cor 13:7) would clearly have been more comfortably cited by gnostics than by advocates of the Pastoral Epistles.

Taken as a whole, Corinthian Letter C would have provided a paralyzing series of weapons against any effort to use the authority of the Apostle Paul to support the institutions, the theology, or the emerging ethos of orthodoxy at the end of the century. It contained enough explosive material to discredit the conservative reaction in the name of Paul through the Aegean region. These inferences about the bearing of Letters A, B, and C on the situation some forty to fifty years after their composition not only confirms a key principle of trajectory analysis but it also provides the most significant clues to decipher the redaction of 1 Corinthians.

THE GENERAL REDACTIONAL HYPOTHESIS

We reconstruct the situation as follows. A generation after the death of Paul, a series of ecclesiastical developments reflected in the deutero-Pauline writings and Acts came into conflict with proto-gnostic developments in various centers around the Aegean Sea. As Egbert Schlarb has shown, these conflicts reflected competitive strands of the Pauline legacy, in which the opponents targeted by the Pastoral Epistles were charismatics whose sense of current salvation led them to oppose traditional ethical norms.[9] By examining the polemic in these epistles, scholars have also detected some elements of early Jewish gnosticism.[10] In the Pastoral Epistles, Paul's authority was adduced in support of a traditional, socially conforming type of church organization and leadership. Some of Paul's letters, including Corinthian Letters A and B and those making up canonical 2 Corinthians, were undoubtedly advanced as arguments in support of this conservative system. The difficulty was that the opposition factions also claimed loyalty to the Pauline legacy, and they had an undoubtedly genuine Corinthian Letter C to counter every argument in favor of the conservative program. The shock waves from this frustrating situation reach through the Pastoral Epistles, which attempt to set the Pauline legacy straight, to the creation of 1 and 2 Peter as pseudonymous efforts to provide an apostolic counterbalance in the name of someone who did not pen letters usable by the enemy.[11] The remarkable reference in 2 Pet 3:15f. to the problematic letters of "our beloved brother Paul" has its clearest foil in Corinthian Letter C: "There are some things in them hard to understand, which the ignorant and unstable twist to their own destruction, as they do the other scriptures." The trajectory of the gnostic use of Paul can be traced through the second century and beyond, as Elaine Pagels has done in *The Gnostic Paul*.[12]

Our thesis is that sometime around the end of the first century the people who created the Pastoral Epistles[13] decided to cope with the frustrating impasse over the interpretation of Paul's letters by co-opting the chief weapon from their opponent's arsenal. They took a copy of the offensive Letter C and fused it with their own most valuable resources, Letters A, B, and F, distributing the resultant canonical 1 Corinthians as widely as their resources would permit in order to crowd out and replace the scattered copies of the original letters. The superior usability of what came to be accepted as the canonical letter for the congregations of anti-gnostic persuasion accounts for its wide circulation and hence its survival when the shorter autographs and their copies disappeared.

To confirm this hypothesis, it would be necessary to show that each step in the redaction of 1 Corinthians was plausibly motivated by the desire to ward off undesirable interpretations of Corinthian Letter C and to bend the trajectory of its interpretation in the direction of the Pastoral Epistles and Acts. Additional confirmation would be provided if unequivocal redactional signatures in the form of non-Pauline interpolations and transitional emendations could be shown to point in the same direction. As we shall see in the sections that follow, both kinds of evidence point with abundant clarity toward the same conclusion.

PHASE ONE: THE REVERSAL OF 1 COR 13 AND 14

Two forms of evidence support the hypothesis that the redaction of 1 Corinthians proceeded in two stages. (1) As noted at the end of the preceding chapter, the location of nine of the ten interpolations and emendations in the same letter C indicates that these changes were made prior to the insertion of material from Letters A, B, and F. If these changes were made after these extensive insertions were made, it is difficult to explain why they were concentrated in a single earlier letter. (2) The redactional rationale of the reversal only makes sense prior to the insertion of chapter 15 at the climactic point of the redacted letter. These two forms of evidence are independent of each other, and their pointing in the same direction provides mutually supportive evidence that the redaction proceeded in two phases. We begin with the redaction critical evidence concerning the reversal.

We accept Wolfgang Schenk's detailed substantiation of earlier suggestions by Johannes Weiss, Walter Schmithals, and others that 1 Cor 13 originally stood after 1 Cor 14 in Letter C.[14] If the original ending of 1 Cor 12 + 14 + 13 in Letter C was the climactic, "the greatest of these is love," the reversal is comprehensible. Ἀγάπη as the supreme mark of the life of a believer was feasible only so long as charismatic experience was a widely shared premise, so that persons gained the inner motivation to meet the needs of their neighbors. The difficulty in providing objective criteria for love becomes acute in times of conflict between ethical norms, and it is interesting that the Pastorals never use ἀγάπη in isolation or present it as the ultimate norm. It is combined with piety, righteousness, patience, promise, and most frequently, with πιστός, the standard of correct belief in the usage of the Pastorals. Furthermore, there are indications of the misdirection of love at the end of the NT era: Jude 12 speaks of carousing at the love feasts while 2 Tim 3:6 castigated those who exploit "weak women." The suspicion has occasionally been voiced by commentators that Paul's qualification of the greeting as a "holy" kiss indicates that problems had arisen already. By the time of the Apostolic Constitutions, abuses had led to a prohibition of such kissing between the sexes.[15] In addition to the potential sexual dangers, ἀγάπη as defined in 1 Cor 13:7 implied far too much tolerance to suit the program of the Pastorals. To bear and endure "all things" is unproblematic, but what would have been the significance of hoping and believing πάντα when conservatives were seeking to limit the range of speculative theologizing toward the end of the first century?[16]

Johannes Weiss's suggestion that 1 Cor 13 belongs somewhere close to 1 Cor 8 has not gained the acceptance that his basic arguments for the rejoining of 1 Cor 12 and 14 have deserved. Schmithals suggests that the placement of 1 Cor 13 was due to a careless copyist.[17] This is certainly implausible since every copy of 1 Corinthians in our possession presents the chapters in the canonical sequence. Schenk's suggestion is much more congruent with the redaction-critical method, namely that with the insertion of 1 Cor 15:1-58 the original conclusion of the preceding section in the frame letter (1 Cor 13:13) produced an extremely difficult transition. It would have moved from "the greatest of these is love" to the reminder about the content of the "faith."[18] By placing the redactional question more firmly in the context of the controversy between the movement of the Pastorals and early gnosticism at the end of the first century, we are able to advance Schenk's view to even more solid ground. When 1 Cor 13 is placed between chapters 12 and 14, it is no longer the ἀγάπη each charismatic shares with Paul and Christ that is definitive, but rather the apostolic command of 1 Cor 14:37. At century's end, its wording would seem even more denigrating to pneumatics than it was during Paul's time: "if anyone thinks that he is a prophet, or spiritual, he should acknowledge that what I am writing to you is command of the Lord." Paul's argument about "peace" in the congregation (1 Cor 14:33) and above all, his demand for "decency and order" (1 Cor 14:40), replace love as the decisive criterion of community life. The consequence of this is that ἀγάπη is reduced to an ethical virtue whose presence or absence could become an accusation in heretical controversy, and whose basis along with faith and hope is the apostolic παράδοσις ("tradition"). Love can no longer function as the decisive guide for the community. With the rearrangement of 1 Cor 12-14, love is neatly replaced by the apostolic command that is safely in the possession of those who guard the παράδοσις.

The redactional method of reversing the location of chapters 13 and 14 was simple. Since chapter 13 formed the peroration of Letter C, it was cut out and inserted after chapter 12. The textual emendations analyzed in chapter 4 earlier were added to smooth over the transitions at both ends of the new location of 1 Cor 13. The original ending of Letter C was then appended to the end of 1 Cor 14. When the seven interpolations were added, the initial redaction of Letter C was complete. But when the redactors looked over what they had accomplished, they were apparently dissatisfied. There still remained too many passages that would have been useful for their proto-gnostic opponents, and there was an important aspect of their program that remained untouched.

The Shortcomings of the Initial Redaction of Letter C

Taking the viewpoint of the conservative redactors into account, we detect seven important flaws in this initial redaction of Letter C. The first three pertained to the conclusion of the redacted letter, which was the new climax achieved by reversing chapters 13 and 14.

1. The letter ended with 1 Cor 16:12 which refers to Apollos rather than to Paul or his co-workers, whose authority stood at the center of the program of the Pastoral Epistles.
2. There was a strong affirmation of charismatic activities in 14:39 that countered the program of the Pastoral Epistles.
3. The definition of "decency and order" in 14:40 was dangerously compromised by the affirmation of the legitimacy of charismatic activities in the preceding verse.
4. The encouragement of dangerous levels of freedom encouraged by 1 Cor 10:21-29 still remained.
5. The "loophole" in 1 Cor 6:11 as well as the potentially ascetic implications of 1 Cor 7:1 still remained dangerous.
7. There was a need for an unambiguous reference to the financial remuneration of church leaders, which could be resolved by the insertion of 1 Cor 9:1-18 from Letter F.

PHASE TWO IN THE REDACTION OF 1 CORINTHIANS

In response to the shortcomings of the initial redaction of 1 Corinthians, the decision was made to insert the formidable material from Letters A, B, and F. For the sake of simplicity, we will follow the sequence the redactor appears to have selected in fusing segments of Corinthian Letters A, B, and F into frame letter C. We conceptualize the redactional process as a matter of working with scrolls, which were the original form of the Pauline letters. Our hypothesis is that the first of these redactional insertions occurred at the end of the frame letter.

Insertion #1

Part of the original ending of Letter C was retained by the redactor, the travel details in 16:5-12, which contained the troubling reference to Apollo, who was not a hero to the faction that created the Pastoral Epistles. This unpromising conclusion was improved by inserting material from Letters A and B that resonated with key aspects of the conservative consolidation. Part of the ending of Letter A (16:1-4) was inserted before this, the instructions about the weekly collection "for the saints" by congregational members. That this vague allusion originally referred to the Jerusalem offering was likely to have been long forgotten fifty years later, especially since it turned out so badly that the Book of Acts would avoid mentioning the outcome. But the reference would have been useful in encouraging financial support of the clergy and of the church's philanthropy (1 Tim 5:18; 2 Tim 2:6; Titus 3:13-14).

The addition of the ending of Corinthian Letter B in 16:13-24 resulted in some obvious advantages. One of these is the anathema in 1 Cor 16:22 against any who do not have "love for the Lord." The word "φιλεῖν," used only one other time in the authentic Pauline letters, has the sense of "the adoration and religious consecration of the believer to his God," as Barrett summarizes the study by C. Spicq.[19] It connotes the kind of cultic and legal obligation favored by the later Pastorals, and it is worth observing that the closest parallel to this use is Titus 3:15. Spicq shows that 1 Cor 16:22 is translated from the Aramaic, and that it suggests the basis for communal approbation.[20] In the late first-century setting, it could provide justification for extending disciplinary procedures to controversialists.

The affirmation of Stephanus and his people in 1 Cor 16:15 would be useful in establishing a succession of legitimate leaders whose predecessors were appointed by Paul. The following sentence speaks of being "subject" to such leaders; if Conzelmann is correct, the original connotation of ὑποτάσσω ("subordinate") in this context was "voluntary subordination,"[21] but in the context of the program of the Pastoral Letters, its clear implication is institutional subordination. Once again the clearest parallels are in the Pastorals (Titus 2:5, 9 and 3:1). It is noteworthy that 1 Cor 16:16 generalizes the example of Stephanus in a very convenient manner from the perspective of those advocating the polity of the Pastorals: the congregation should be "subject to such men and to every fellow worker and laborer." 1 Cor 16:18 pushes in the same direction: "Give recognition to such men," which would have been very useful for the group promoting the ideals of the Pastoral Epistles.

Insertion #2

The insertion of 1 Cor 15:1-58 is comprehensible when the problems of the initial editing of Letter C are noted. "Be eager to prophesy" and "do not forbid speaking in tongues" in 1 Cor 14:39 provides too much support for dangerous charismatics at the end of the century. Moreover, the guidelines for conducting affairs "in decency and order" are unclear, especially when the

Pastorals would prefer to eliminate this dangerous activity altogether. These troublesome questions are effectively downplayed by the redactor's insertion of 1 Cor 15:1-58 to replace the problematic chapter 14 as the climactic argumentative section in what we now call 1 Corinthians. The item of "first importance" as far as 1 Cor 15:3 is concerned is not prophecy or glossoalia but the impartation of the traditional faith. As the argument of 1 Cor 15:3-7 makes clear, the apostolic witness to the resurrection is absolutely essential, for without it the faith becomes ludicrous (15:19) and erroneous (15:15). The climactic location of 1 Cor 15 at the place of final emphasis in the canonical letter therefore embodies a shift from a charismatic faith acting itself out in spontaneous love to a traditional faith legitimized by apostolic witnesses. Finally, as far as the apparent interest of the redactor was concerned, 1 Cor 15 could not have concluded more helpfully than it does in verse 58: "be steadfast, unmovable, always abounding in the work of the Lord."

Insertion #3

The next section of Corinthian Letter B to be inserted into the frame letter was 1 Cor 9:24–10:22. When one reflects on the bearing of the original argument of Letter C that was interrupted by the redactor's knife, his motivation becomes transparent. Paul was discussing his accommodation strategy of becoming a Greek to the Greeks and a Jew to the Jews, and in the original sequence of Letter C, this led directly into the radical statement of freedom from the law in 10:23-29. In the conflict between gnostically inclined assimilationists and conservative moralists at the end of the century, this passage from Corinthian Letter C must have been the most inflammatory in the entire perplexing letter. Although Paul undoubtedly meant "Gentile" when referring to *hoi anomoi* ("the lawless") in 1 Cor 9:21,[22] the flat statement that he became ὡς ἄνομος ("as a lawless one") would have placed him on the side of the antinomians by the end of the century. Paul's compressed attempt to cover himself in 1 Cor 9:21b was so ambiguous[23] that it could easily have sustained the gnostic position. They would have been very comfortable with the proviso to be ἔννομος Χριστοῦ ("subject to the law of Christ"), for they claimed to possess the mind of Christ in their spiritual knowledge.

The problem this passage would pose to the originators of the movement of conservative consolidation is explicitly dealt with in the Pastorals. 1 Tim 1:6ff. inveighs against "teachers of the law" who fail to understand that the law was intended to guard against "lawlessness." Such teachers thereby misunderstand the apostolic truth. Titus 2:14 adapts the entire atonement doctrine to the problem of ἀνομία ("lawlessness"): "Christ gave himself for us to redeem us from all lawlessness." It is clear that these writers no longer understood Paul's complex doctrine of the law,[24] and in their muddled efforts to be true to their model, they arrived at virtually the opposite conclusion than the one he would have favored. E. F. Scott remarked that the writer of 1 Timothy "laid himself open to his own stricture on the false teachers that 'they do not understand the things on which they insist.' "[25] But the problem was a formidable one, how to rescue Pauline thought from the hands of intellectuals who were committed to his accommodation strategy and sought to be ἄνομοι ("lawless") like their mentor.

The redactors found a wedge for the moralistic insertion they wanted to make at the end of 1 Cor 9:23 where Paul speaks of doing everything for the sake of the gospel in order to become a συγκοινωνὸς ("partner"). The succeeding verses in Letter B show that this end can be achieved by uniting freedom with what is "helpful" and what "builds up" the congregation. At this point, the redactor inserted the strict statements about moral self-discipline in 1 Cor 9:24-27, thus redefining the requirement for being a participant in the gospel. To gain the "imperishable wreath" (1 Cor 9:25) now requires "self-control," a concept used otherwise only in the products of the Pastoral movement like Titus 1:8 and 2 Pet 1:6. The passage then goes on in 1 Cor 10:1-22 to prohibit accommodation to paganism. The sentences that stand out as congruent with the purpose of the redactor are 10:7, "Do not be idolaters"; 10:8, "We must not indulge in immorality"; 10:12, "Therefore let anyone who thinks that he stands take heed lest he fall"; 10:14, "Shun the worship of idols"; 10:21b, "You cannot partake of the table of the Lord and the table of demons." The concept of "sharing" in this final verse is closely related to the coparticipation cited in 1 Cor 9:23. Thus, a series of moralistic restraints define the genuine participant of the church, marking the true followers of the apostle's will. With this insertion, the accommodation ethic fades into a more sharply defined distinction between the church and the world. In place of the self-limitation of freedom for the sake of love, stressed in Letter C, there emerges a series of prohibitions defining what any true disciple is to avoid. With this, perhaps the most brilliant coup in the redaction of 1 Corinthians, Paul's authority is rescued from the brink of freedom and the way is smoothed for the moralistic trends of the future.

Insertion #4

The redactor's decision to insert 1 Cor 6:12-20 from Corinthian Letter B into the discussion of the sexual ethic in Letter C relates to the possible gnostic misuse of the "loophole" in 1 Cor 6:11 as well as the potentially ascetic implications of 1 Cor 7:1. The marriage ethic of 1 Cor 7, as seen by recent studies, stresses the autonomy of individual believers within a framework of mutual subordination in the body. When 7:1 is understood as one half of a *Tobspruch*,[26] its rhetorical purpose is clarified and it becomes clear that Paul was not setting a legalistic norm. But there is every likelihood that churches several decades later would have lost touch with the precise motto being cited in Corinth, and that the ascetic interpretation that has dominated exegesis ever since had already begun. The presence of ascetic tendencies among the gnostics opposed by the Pastorals make such an inference likely. That such an approach to sexuality was allowed by the charismatic premise of Letter C is undeniable: the "spirit of our God" in 1 Cor 6:11 leads directly to the sex ethic in 1 Cor 7:1-40 whose guiding principle seems to be following one's own best judgment in view of the eschatological urgency. Paul refrains from a "command" (1 Cor 7:6) because each person has his own sexual charisma (1 Cor 7:7). Given the tendencies toward either asceticism or libertinism in Gnosticism, 1 Cor 7:17 and 24 would have offered a substantial basis for gnostics to follow their previous inclinations, assuming of course that they had been cleansed by spiritual knowledge (1 Cor 6:11): if everyone was to remain in the state in which he was called, why should one not remain ascetic or promiscuous, particularly if this was Paul's "rule in all the churches" (1 Cor 7:17). The entire program of creating an apostolic rule as a defense against immorality and disorder, as well as the concern to develop a universally applicable norm, was threatened by the gnostic possibilities latent in this passage.

An effective hedge against a dangerously charismatic sex ethic was provided by the insertion of 1 Cor 6:12-20. This passage contains an absolute prohibition against temple prostitution or promiscuous fornication (6:15, 18). It warns about the possibility of sexual excesses leading to enslavement (6:12). By placing this before 1 Cor 7, the scope of the charismatic sex ethic is radically limited. Certain kinds of sexual charismata (1 Cor 7:7) are eliminated, such as the inclination toward promiscuity or even toward extreme asceticism. Paul's incorporation of the traditional marriage concept (1 Cor 7:16) would serve in the late first-century context to ward off the radical implications of 1 Cor 7:1.

Insertion #5

The insertion of Letter A provides a superior thematic link to chapters 12, 13, and 14, where the charismatic view of the church was stated, which the insertion of letter A sought to replace. On literary-critical grounds, there is a smooth transition between the discussions of church life in 11:18-34 and 12:1-30 + 14:1-40. As Fee observes, "It is not simply by coincidence that Paul begins his corrective on spiritual gifts in the next section [12:1–30] by placing that once again in the context of the unity of the body, all members being equally concerned for each other."[27]

To comprehend the ideological significance of inserting the second proof of Cor A (1 Cor 11:2-34) between 1 Cor 11:1 and chapters 12-14, it is first necessary to recapitulate the definition of charismatic faith implied by the original sequence in Letter C. The imitation of the apostle, and consequently of Christ himself (1 Cor 11:1), is developed by the succeeding discussion of charismatic gifts in 1 Cor 12:1ff. Those who wish to be Paul's genuine disciples must clearly possess spiritual gifts of some kind. Paul himself exercises the gift of glossolalia (1 Cor 14:18) and explicitly states he would like the entire congregation to follow him in this (1 Cor 14:5). To be a Paulinist was to be a charismatic, and the emphasis on the democratic dispersion of the gifts in 1 Cor 12:7 places everyone on a fundamentally equal level. This approach undermined the effort by conservative Paulinists to redefine the imitation of the apostle in terms of accepting the authorities he appointed and the traditions he promulgated.

The problem was beautifully solved by inserting 1 Cor 11:2-34 between the exhortation to imitate Paul and the discussion of the charismatic gifts. This redefined Paulinism in terms of recollecting and maintaining the παράδοσις that Paul originally delivered to his churches. 1 Cor 11:2 sets the tone of the dramatic new definition of what it means to imitate Paul: "I praise you because you remember me in everything and maintain the traditions even as I delivered them to you." This is a giant leap in the direction of the Pastoral Letters, and commentators have displayed uneasiness about the resultant shift in the direction of imitation.[28]

A series of advantages accrue to the redactor's side of the conflict over the proper imitation of the Apostle Paul by the insertion of 1 Cor 11:2-34. Whereas the original charismatic rationale developed in Letter C had clearly egalitarian tones (1 Cor 12:7) consistent with Paul's encouragement of female leadership in the church, the insistence on the subordination of women in 1 Cor 11:3-16 pushes in the opposite direction. This editing certainly would have had that connotation in the minds of chauvinistic circles that later produced the Pastorals. A subordinate role for women is emphasized in two of the Pastorals, and, as we suggested in the discussion of the interpolation 1 Cor 14:33b-36, it was clearly an important issue for the redactor. In addition, the discussion of the sacrament in 1 Cor 11:23-26 is opened by the stress on the authoritative tradition delivered by the apostle to the church. The terminology is close to that used in 1 Cor 11:2 and proved highly adaptable for the development of orthodox controls against charismatics and proto-gnostics, as the Pastoral Letters reveal. The inserted passage from Cor A ends with a reference to Paul's forthcoming oral instructions, thus offering a programmatic basis for the materials later embodied in the Pastorals. It lends support to the effort at the close of the century to replace the radical arrangements for a charismatic democracy in congregational worship (1 Cor 12-14) with authoritative regulations in legal style that purport to come from Paul's emissaries.

The sensitive issue of feminine roles in the church is dealt with by means of the authority of the Pauline tradition, which is explicitly mentioned at the end of verse 2. The theme of conforming to the tradition of the early church is reiterated in verse 16. By linking the tradition of feminine subordination so directly with Pauline authority, the ground is laid for the interpolation of 14:33b–36. The priority of this issue is clearly indicated by the insertion of the two proofs in Cor. A.

Insertion #6

The final redactional step in creating the sequence of our canonical 1 Corinthians was the insertion of 1 Cor 9:1-18 from Letter F. The context of this choice was Paul's discussion of missionary strategy, which, as the foregoing analysis showed, was an item of central significance for the redactor. The frame letter C had moved directly from the discussion of Paul's refraining from food offered to idols in 1 Cor 8:18 to his presentation of the accommodation strategy in 1 Cor 9:19-23. The prior insertion of 1 Cor 9:24–10:22 had eliminated the antinomian possibilities implicit in this missionary method. From the perspective of the ecclesiastic conservatives, there remained a final organizational concern that no portion of the now-lengthy composite had articulated, namely, the payment of church leaders. The desired material lay ready at hand, embedded in the argument of Corinthian Letter E, which, because of its many anti-heretical traits, would have been well-used material in the hands of the opponents of gnostic assimilation. Annette Merz has shown how this material was taken up in the Pastorals to counter the use of some Pauline texts that seemed to undermine the legitimacy of such payments.[29]

The choice of where to insert 1 Cor 9:1-18 appears to have been thematic rather than argumentative. Since the words in Letter C that originally followed 1 Cor 8:18 were Ἐλεύθερος γὰρ ὢν ἐκ πάντων ("for though being free from all," 1 Cor 9:19), the opening words of the desired insertion seemed virtually interchangeable: Οὐκ εἰμὶ ἐλεύθερος; ("am I not free?"). Thematically, it was the best choice available, and only a few exegetes even in the modern period of historical research have observed the transitional discrepancies that resulted.[30] The transition that resulted at the end of the splice, between 1 Cor 9:18 and 9:19 is even smoother stylistically, though the discrepancies in substance are still apparent.[31]

From the perspective of those who created the Pastoral Epistles, a great deal was accomplished by this final insertion. 1 Cor 9:4 states a general apostolic "right to food and drink" and 9:14 places the authority of Jesus himself behind the desired goal of a paid clergy. The arguments Paul develops in support of this *exousia* ("right") possessed by all who serve in the apostolic work became the model for similar discussions in 1 and 2 Timothy. The citation from Deut 25:4 that Paul used in 1 Cor 9:9 is appropriated for the support of a ministerial stipend in 1 Tim 5:18.[32] Even more striking is the use of all three metaphors for ministerial support and discipline in the resultant 1 Cor 9 by the writer of 2 Tim 2:3-7. The church leader as a good soldier is derived from 1 Cor 9:7; the athlete whose reward comes from keeping the rules is lifted from 1 Cor 9:24-27; and the farmer whose labor earns a right to a share of the crop is derived from 1 Cor 9:7, 10.[33] Such detailed paraphrasing, probably the most concentrated on a single chapter of any of the borrowed materials in the Pastorals, reveals the continued interest in the themes that coalesced in the redaction of 1 Cor 9. The decisive nexus, of (1) a responsible missionary strategy that refrains from extending accommodation into immorality; (2) a right of full-time workers to be paid by the congregation; and (3) an insistence that all who are paid should live by the rules, constitutes the distinctive program of the Pastoral Letters. Although each theme was available in Pauline writings, each was originally attached to a different context and related to Paul's more charismatic concept of ministry. Therefore, the drawing together of all three ministerial metaphors in a single location had wide-ranging effects. The redactor of 1 Corinthians thereby created a new, non-charismatic context in which each theme was to be understood. This completes the transition from Paul's original interpretation of charismatic authority of believers "in Christ" to the institutionalized program of control by the authorized representatives of the apostolic tradition.

THE RESULT OF THE REDACTION

The creation of the canonical 1 Corinthians provided a radical alteration of Letter C, which had been drafted by Paul to interact in a critical manner with proto-gnostic groups in Corinth, but had subsequently provided decisive support for similar groups around the end of the first century CE. This undoubtedly authentic Pauline letter contained support for the proto-gnostic position on a number of issues that were contested by the creators of the Pastoral Letters. The redaction resulted in a radical transformation of Letter C in the direction of the authoritarian letters to Timothy and Titus. The lines of demarcation between the historical Paul and the Paul of the Pastorals were permanently fudged. Paul's theology, his ethics, his argumentative methods and rhetorical finesse, and his image were thereby transformed and confused, presenting subsequent interpreters with irresolvable conflicts. Since the redacted Letter C became the canonical 1 Corinthians that was passed on to subsequent generations while the original letters perished, this redaction poses an ongoing challenge to scholars.

NOTES

1. Eduard Schweizer, *The Letter to the Colossians: A Commentary* (Minneapolis: Augsburg, 1982), 242.
2. Barrett's discussion in "Pauline Controversies in the Post-Pauline Period," *NTS* 20 (1973–74): 229–45, traces the impact of Pauline ideas on the period after his death, but passes over the redaction-critical possibilities without comment.
3. Georg Strecker, "Paulus in nachpaulinischer Zeit," *Kairos* 12 (1960): 208–16, particularly 215.
4. For example, see Norbert Brox, *Die Pastoralbriefe*, 4th revised edition, RNT 7.2 (Regensburg: Pustet, 1969), 33–40; Helmut Koester, *Introduction to the New Testament*, two volumes (Berlin: Walter de Gruyter, 1987), 2.305-06.
5. Robinson and Koester, *Trajectories*, 16.
6. See Schmithals, *Gnosticism*, 169–70; Jewett, *Terms*, 352–54.
7. See Thiselton, *First Epistle*, 357–79; Horsley, *1 Corinthians*, 69–72; Schrage, *erste Brief*, 1.338-51.
8. See Brox, *Pastoralbriefe*, 42–46.
9. See particularly Egbert Schlarb, *Die gesunde Lehre: Häresie und Wahrheit im Spiegel der Pastoralbriefe*, Marburger theologische Studien, 28 (Marburg: Elwert, 1990), 132–41. For a slightly earlier discussion of competing strands of the Pauline legacy, see Hughes, *Early Christian Rhetoric*, 91–104.
10. In his article, "Pastoralbriefe," in Hans Dieter Betz et al., editors, *Religion in Geschichte und Gegenwart*, 4th edition (Tübingen: Mohr Siebeck, 2003), 6.988-91, and his commentary, *1 and 2 Timothy and Titus*, NTL (Louisville: Westminster John Knox, 2002), Raymond F. Collins argues that conservative views of doctrine, church leadership and the role of women are central, but that it is not possible to precisely identify the opponents. Michael Wolter, *Die Pastoralbriefe als Paulustradition*, FRLANT 146 (Göttingen: Vandenhoeck & Ruprecht, 1988), 256–67, makes a compelling case that the adversaries targeted by the Pastorals were proto-gnostics of a Jewish-Jesus-believing type. This is supported by Pietersen, *Polemic*, 134.
11. See Raymond E. Brown, "Peter," in Keith Crim, V. P. Furnish, L. R. Bailey and E. S. Bucke, editors, *Interpreter's Dictionary of the Bible, Supplement Volume* (Nashville: Abingdon, 1976), 654–57; 657.
12. Elaine Pagels, *The Gnostic Paul: Gnostic Exegesis of the Pauline Letters* (Philadelphia: Fortress, 1975; reprinted, Philadelphia: Trinity Press International), *passim* but especially 53–100, 157–66.
13. The dating of the Pastorals is notoriously difficult, but Annette Merz has made a convincing case that the use of these letters by Polycarp and Ignatius requires a provenance no later than the last decade of the first century; see her *Die fiktive Selbstauslegung des Paulus. Intertextuelle Studien zur Intention und Rezeption der Pastoralbriefe*, NTOA 52 (Göttingen: Vandenhoeck & Ruprecht; Fribourg: Academic Press, 2004), 195.
14. Schenk, "Briefsammlung," 225–26.
15. Héring, *First Epistle*, 186.

16. Robinson and Koester, *Trajectories*, 156–57.
17. Schmithals, *Gnosticism*, 95.
18. Schenk, "Briefsammlung," 226.
19. Barrett, *First Epistle*, 397, summarizing Spicq's analysis in "1 Cor. xvi, 22," 200–4.
20. Spicq, "1 Cor. xvi, 22," 204.
21. Conzelmann, *1 Corinthians*, Hermeneia (Philadelphia: Fortress, 1975), 298.
22. Lietzmann, *Korinther*, 43.
23. Weiss, *erste Korintherbrief*, 244–45.
24. See Jewett, *Romans: A Commentary*, 344–554.
25. Ernest Findlay Scott, *The Pastoral Epistles* (New York: Harper, 1936), 11.
26. See the discussion of Snyder, "Tobspruch,"120 in our chapter 10.
27. Fee, *First Epistle*, 569.
28. See Barrett, *First Epistle*, 245–46; Betz, *Nachfolge*, 153ff.
29. Merz, *fiktive Selbstauslegung*, 232–33.
30. See Weiss, *erste Korintherbrief*, 231–32; Conzelmann, *1 Corinthians*, 151; most other commentaries pass over the rough spot between 1 Cor 8:13 and 1 Cor 9:1 without pointing out the difficulties.
31. See Weiss, *erste Korintherbrief*, 242.
32. Barrett, *Pastoral Epistles*, 79.
33. Jeremias, *Timotheus and Titus*, 53.

Part Two

THE PROVENANCE AND RHETORIC OF THE ORIGINAL LETTERS

Chapter 5

Letter A

Troubles in Worship (1 Cor 11:2, 17-34a + 11:3-16 + 16:1-4 + 11:34b)

INTRODUCTION

There is nothing in the extant portions of Letter A that either introduces Paul to his audience as an apostle or someone whose ἦθος qualifies him as one who should be listened to or read. No introduction of the topics of the two-part *probatio* is found other than the two statements which introduce each of the parts of the *probatio* in 11:3 and 11:17. Since the *exordium* of Letter A is missing, our analysis must begin with 11:2, which most scholars identify as a *captatio benevolentiae*.[1] In view of the discrepancy between complimenting the Corinthians for remembering Paul's teachings "in respect of everything," while in subsequent verses strongly criticizing their behavior, John Hurd has made a case for an ironic interpretation.[2] However, his theory depends on confusing what we identify as Letters A and C by assuming that in the former letter Paul replies to a letter the Corinthians wrote describing their adherence to his instructions about worship. Paul responds to such a message in our Letter C, but in Letter A, he is relying on hearsay evidence (11:18) rather than in any direct communication. Gordon Fee clarifies the rhetorical situation somewhat more plausibly, that "even though they remember him in everything, there are some areas with regard to the 'traditions' where praise is not in order."[3] But whether this particular *captatio benevolentiae* could have functioned effectively to elicit the good will of the audience seems doubtful when the content of the subsequent argument is taken into account.

Chapter 5

THE FIRST PROOF

The first proof of Letter A begins with a thesis statement in verse 17. Gordon Fee observes that this verse serves to "set the stage for what follows by announcing at the outset that their 'gatherings' do 'more harm than good.'"[4] Andreas Lindemann refers to verse 17 as the *Überschrift* ("caption, heading") of the argument.[5] The reference to Paul's refusal to "praise" the congregation in this matter forms an antithesis to 11:2, thus introducing the new topic.[6] As in the thesis of the second proof, this one is marked by *paronomasia* in the use of συνέρχεσθαι ("come together") in verse 17, which is repeated in 11:18, 20, 33, 34. This term appears to be an emerging technical term for the early church.[7]

The first argument in 11:18–22 is introduced by reference to what Paul has "heard" but not fully believe, that there are "divisions (σχίσματα) among you" (11:18). In the rhetoric of this letter, these divisions seem considerably less serious than the issues discussed in 1 Cor 1:10-17 and more generally in chapters 1–4. In 1 Cor 1:13, the divisions are so serious that Paul can launch a short *interrogatio* in which he asks, "Is Christ divided? Was Paul crucified for you? Or were you baptized in the name of Paul?" which certainly seems more serious than what Paul says about the divisions in 11:17: the Corinthians' assemblies, apparently for worship, are "not for the better but for the worse."

Bruce W. Winter has a novel interpretation of καὶ μέρος τι πιστεύων in 11:18, taking μέρος τι as "a certain report."[8] He then can argue that Paul certainly did believe the report referred to in 11:18, so that the preferred translation should be "I am convinced of a certain matter" or "I am convinced of a certain report."[9] The translation of μέρος τι as "a certain report" might seem to remove the problem of the inconsistency of 11:18 with 1 Cor 1-4. Two problems make it difficult for us to adopt this interpretation. The first is the lack of the definite article before μέρος, which seems to be more common when it means "report" and when the word is used substantively. The other problem is that 11:19 shows Paul making a kind of concession that, after all, divisions are necessary. This verse confirms the difficulty of accepting Winter's interpretation, since it also stands in very significant tension with what Paul has already written about divisions in 1 Cor 1-4, if it is true that 1 Corinthians was an integral letter. However, we can confirm Winter's diagnosis of the problem when he writes, "It is usually translated either as 'and I partly believe it' or 'and in part I believe it.' If this is what Paul were really saying, then it is astonishing that he should have written as he did in 1:10–4:21 and 11:17-34."[10] The astonishment can be best removed if Paul has a more extensive level of knowledge (or a different level of belief in the information he has received) about the situation in Corinth when he wrote 1:10ff. than when he wrote 11:18-19. To deny this insight, as the defenders of unity must do, entails believing that it is possible for someone to "unknow" matters that he or she already knows.

It is interesting to note that within 11:18-34, there are two arguments. First, the σχίσματα are dealt with in 11:18-22. Paul, having stated the argument in 11:18 and then having given a significant qualification of the severity of what he says about σχίσματα in 11:19 then gives *exempla* of the behavior of those who are acting wrongly. Their behavior is so bad, Paul says, that it is not the Lord's Supper that is being eaten but those people's own supper. Paul's response consists of several questions which are very sharply stated in 11:22; perhaps the worst offense of all is that "you show contempt for the church of God and you shame those who do not have anything." The last of the five rhetorical questions, "Shall I praise you? In this I will not praise you!" reminds the reader or hearer of the topic of praise at the beginning of this part of the *probatio* (11:17) as also at the beginning of the first part (11:2). It forms a kind of *inclusio*.

Paul seems to be thinking more charitably of the Corinthians in 11:23ff. than in 1 Cor 1-4, because there, especially in 1:18-31, Paul thinks the divisions have nothing to do with a lack of knowledge. Indeed, in what we identify as Letter C, we are told that "knowledge puffs up but love builds up" (8:1). The knowledge of God is radically different from human knowledge (2:1-9) and it is able to be transmitted only to spiritual people (2:10-3:4). What is being argued in 11:23-33 reflects a completely different rhetorical strategy than in chapters 1-3. In the early chapters of 1 Corinthians, knowledge is something that only spiritual people truly have. In chapter 11, however, Paul makes a quite rational argument for the behavior that should be practiced during the celebration of the Lord's Supper. If Paul when writing chapters 1-4 thought that human reason would fail the believer who would contemplate the things of God, he has abandoned that line of argument in chapter 11. Starting at 11:23, he gives the origin of the tradition about the Lord's Supper, including a *narratio* of the institution of the Eucharist in 11:23b-25 and a statement of the theological significance of the Eucharist in 11:26.

After Paul completed his historical and theological review of the traditions about the Lord's Supper, in the third argument, he launches into dissuasion against the abuses that had been occurring during the Lord's Supper in Corinth (1 Cor 11:27-32). He gives advice on the worthy reception of the Lord's Supper, specifying that people who receive the Lord's Supper unworthily are those "not discerning the body" (meaning the body of Christ, 11:29). In 11:30, he advises that illness and death have happened to those who have eaten the Lord's Supper unworthily.

The conclusion of the argument about the Lord's Supper is stated in 11:33-34a, having to do with the practical matters of eating at home and waiting for one another before beginning the Eucharistic meal. The use of Ὥστε ("so then") signals the consequences to be drawn from the preceding argument.[11] This exhortation provides a healthy antithesis to 11:21, recapitulates συνέρχεσθαι ("come together") in 11:17, 18, and 20, recapitulates 11:21-22 with εἰς τὸ φαγεῖν ("[come together] to eat") and 11:25 with ἐν οἴκῳ ἐσθιέτω ("eat at home").[12] Moreover, as Raymond Collins observes, the "apostrophic vocative of v. 33" conveys a kinship in "my" brothers [and sisters],[13] whom Paul does not wish to see falling under judgment (11:34a). The advice about eating "at home" if hunger becomes unbearable is surely directed at the rich,[14] because only they had homes in this sense while slaves and handworkers lived in crowded tenement buildings without dining rooms. The hunger of the rich would not ordinarily reach the intensity of that of other congregational members who had been engaged in hard labor since sun-up. The ironic implications are obvious as Paul urges the congregation in Richard Horsley's words, to "break with those hierarchical patterns" and adopt "more egalitarian relations as members of the body" of Christ.[15]

THE SECOND PROOF

The Apostle states the thesis of 11:3-15 in 11:3. The antithetical formulation of verse 3, translating δὲ as "but" or "yet," signals the change of subject from the close of the first proof. It indicates that the new topic is one in which Paul is dissatisfied with the situation in Corinth.[16] The statement that follows is "the fundamental theological principle that will govern Paul's discussion in this pericope, a principal of headship" based on the hierarchy of God / Christ / men / women.[17] This is stated in a formal manner[18] that provides the thesis for the second proof. The term "κεφαλή" ("head") is emphasized by *paronomasia*,[19] appearing three times in the thesis and five times in the subsequent argument of the second proof, while the idea of woman deriving from man is repeated in 11:8 and 12. The related theme of male and female hairstyles that reflect this hierarchy is pursued throughout the entire proof. While many commentators and translators continue to assume that the issue in this proof is the veiling of women, it is in fact more likely that hairstyles are in view.[20]

After stating the thesis of the second proof in 11:3, namely the cosmic order established by Christ, Paul goes on to state the first argument in 11:4-6. A man who prays or prophesies with his head covered with long hair like a woman's does a shameful thing. This would be also a violation of a tradition, the keeping of which Paul has already praised (11:2). In his view, the proper style for men was for short hair that comes downward from the head, whereas women in public were expected to wear their hair coiled on the tops of their heads. Any Corinthian woman violating this tradition about women's hairstyle during prayer or prophecy in the worship assembly acted shamefully: "It is one and the same as if her head were shaved." Paul then provides an "expanded rhetorical repetition"[21] in two applications of this principle of shameful violation of the norm in the exempla of 11:6. In the first example, a woman who refuses to conform to the female custom should enter an even deeper level of shame by having her hair entirely cut off. In the second example, a woman wishing to avoid such shame should conform to the cultural custom.

The second argument is introduced in 11:7: "man is the image and glory of God whereas woman is the glory of man." This argument is based on the premise of a cosmic order introduced in 11:3. Paul alternates negative and positive statements drawn from the creation stories in Genesis in 11:8-9 to show that the first man preceded the first woman. This carries forward the theme in verse 3, that the man "is the source of her life. . . . The woman was created for the man's sake."[22] A final argument is stated in 11:10, that "the woman ought to have ἐξουσία on her head because of the angels." Raymond Collins argues that the "natural meaning of Paul's phrase is that a woman has authority or power over her head. She presumably exercises [proper] control over her head when she wears her hair appropriately, that is, as is fitting in the context of worship."[23] This authority probably also pertains to what was previously prohibited for women, namely the right to pray and prophesy along with men.[24] This helps us to understand verse 10 as the climax of the second argument and paves the way to a compelling interpretation of the "angels." Joseph Fitzmyer identifies seven different theories about this reference to angels, concluding that the most likely alternative is that good angels were thought to be present in worship, serving as cosmic guardians of the order of creation,[25] which was acknowledged by male and female hairstyles. In the words of Joël Delobel, "The behavior of women in worship has to respect the order of creation symbolized by the angels who are indeed present in worship and watching the observance of this order."[26]

In 11:11-12, Paul develops his third argument, which is founded upon two presuppositions that the Corinthian believers were likely to affirm. In 11:11, Paul argues that men and women are mutually subordinated to each other because of their unity in the Lord. As Gordon Fee observes, the argument is in the form of a "perfect double chiasm":

Perhaps this is based on baptism, and perhaps this is also connected with Paul's argument about the Corinthians' celebrations of the Eucharist in 11:17-34. It is interesting to note that Paul does not here bring in the analogy of the church as the body of christ, as we see elsewhere in Paul, for example, 1 Cor 12:12 and Romans 12:4-5. The analogy of the body would have been quite *a propos* here, but Paul chose not to use it in this case. This is yet another indicator that 1 Cor 11 reflects a prior congregational situation compared with what we see in 1 Cor 1-4. Paul does not argue here in 1 Cor 11:3-16 in such

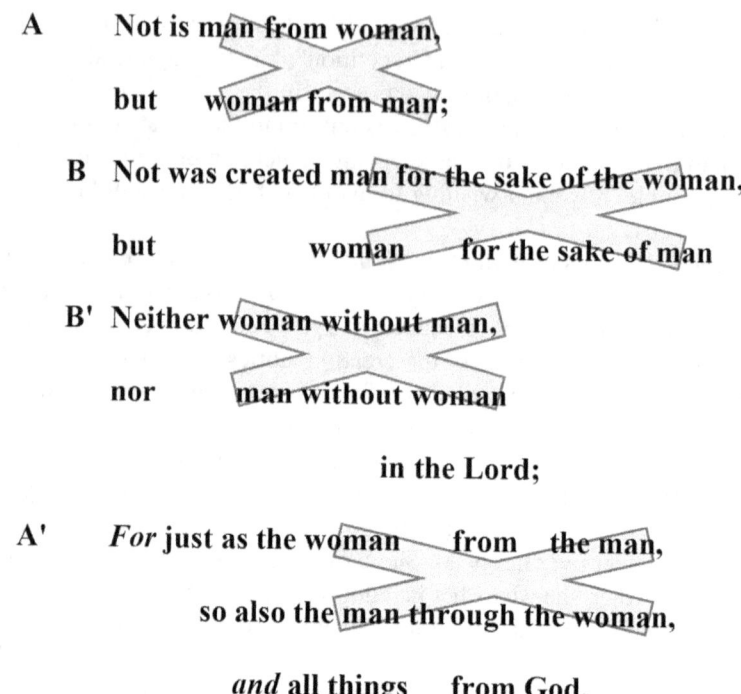

Figure 5.1 The Double Chiasm Argument in 1 Cor 11:11-12.[27]

a way that this text presupposes divisions that Paul believes to be extremely serious. Paul can simply state in 11:11 that "in the Lord, women is not independent of man nor man of women," and then he can move on to another statement in 11:12a. In the context of the argumentation about divisions (σχίσματα) in the letter which includes 1 Cor 1-4 and 12-14, we believe that it is striking that he not only says in 1 Cor 11 different things about the seriousness of the divisions but also in 11:10 seems to have understood that no further argumentation was needed about unity when he has simply *mentioned* the topic of unity of men and women "in the Lord." This is a rhetorical move that is quite different from what we see in 1 Cor 1-4 and 12-14.

Paul makes a fourth argument in 11:13-15, appealing to nature and human custom. He states his argument as *interrogatio* in 11:13 to the effect that "it is not proper" for a woman to pray to God without an appropriate hairstyle. This statement is then supported by two reasons, which are also stated as *interrogatio* in 11:14-15a. This argument is also based on a combination of human and theological argumentation: in 11:14 "nature itself" teaches that a man dishonors himself by wearing (long) hair. Theology reemerges in 11:15

where Paul states that a woman's hair "was given to her as a covering," a use of the "divine passive."

The conclusion of this tangled argument in verse 16 reveals that Paul "is aware that his complicated arguments about this problem may not be convincing to everyone."[28] As Elisabeth Schüssler Fiorenza observes, Paul closes his argument with "an authoritarian appeal."[29] Abandoning his earlier arguments about the new being "in Christ," about the creation stories in Genesis and about human custom, he reverts in the end to appeals from ἦθος, his own personal authority and that of his colleagues expressed by the pronoun "we," and the example of the "churches of God."[30] The rhetorical and argumentative differences between this passage and the rest of 1 Corinthians is accurately discerned by Richard Horsley:

> In contrast with every other section of the letter, where Paul refers to the imminence of final events and the continuation of the historical circumstances of life, or both, this paragraph has no eschatological perspective. The argument in 11:3 – 16 differs strikingly from that of chapter 7, which also deals with central issues in relation between men and women. There, clearly convinced that men's and women's sex roles have been relativized and are about to change decisively with the "end," he works around that carefully, in gender-balanced rhetoric addressed to both men and women. In chapter 7, moreover, he does not advocate any hard and fast general norm, but adjusts to particular people's circumstances. On the much less central issue of hair arrangement, however, the paragraph of 11:3-16 presents an established practice or custom grounded in creation and nature.[31]

In our opinion, these differences are explained by the hypothesis that Letter A reflects a situation in the earliest stage of Paul's efforts to cope with developments in Corinth. He is responding to hearsay evidence without appearing to understand the challenge of emerging radicalism that entailed a repudiation of traditional sexual roles.

EPISTOLARY CONCLUSION

The abrupt manner in which Paul addresses the topic of the Jerusalem offering in 1 Cor 16:1-4 indicates that the Corinthians had already been informed about the agreement made at the Apostolic Conference. As Joseph Fitzmyer observes, "If Paul were making this request for the first time, he would undoubtedly be giving more of a background for his requests than he now supplies in vv. 2-4."[32] But if Letter A was Paul's first communication with the Corinthians, written in the autumn of 52, a little more than a year after the conference in Antioch, how could Paul have been so sure that the Corinthians were already informed about the agreement he made in behalf of the Gentile churches? The clue is in 2 Cor 8:6 where Paul announces that he had urged Titus "as he had already made a beginning, so he should also complete this generous undertaking among you." This reference in Letter D, written in the fall of 54, clearly indicates that Titus had traveled to Corinth in order to start the process of collecting the Jerusalem offering. While it is clear from Galatians 2:3 that Titus had been with Paul at the Apostolic Conference, it is not until the redaction of the Corinthian correspondence is untangled that it becomes possible to coordinate these details in a coherent chronological sequence. Titus must have been sent to Corinth in the spring or summer of 52, the traveling season after the Apostolic Conference that occurred in October 51. He had started the process of raising the money in Corinth, which Paul carries forward in his instructions in 1 Cor 16:1-4. Since Paul writes these instructions shortly after departing from North Galatia, it was natural for him to refer to those instructions: "just as I directed churches of Galatia, so you should do as well." Collecting the contributions on "the first day of the week," the typically Jewish reference to Sunday, evoked the resurrection of Jesus, which would undergird the motivation for generosity.[33] Since most of the early congregations had special celebrations on Sundays, this reference brings the topic of the offering within the context of "meeting together" in 11:17. The imperative verbs in 16:1 and 2 make it clear that Paul's "appeal is not an incidental matter . . . it also suggests the mandatory nature of his appeal on behalf of the Jerusalem community," and expresses Paul's "authority" in the estimate of Raymond Collins.[34] In addition to his authority as the founder of Gentile churches, however, a second consideration is mentioned in verse 2: "so that the collections do not take place when I come." Various motivations for this remarkable comment have been suggested: that Paul desired a larger contribution that could only be gathered over a longer period;[35] that Paul had more important tasks than "to go round begging";[36] that Paul wishes to avoid putting pressure on the congregation;[37] or as C. K. Barrett more plausibly suggests, that he wanted "to avoid the possibility of accusations with regard to misappropriation, and perhaps to avoid misappropriation itself."[38] This last suggestion appears related to the arrangements in verses three and four, that the Corinthians themselves would select representatives to convey the funds to Jerusalem, that Paul would authorize such representatives with official letters, and that the question of whether Paul himself be to go to Jerusalem remained open. In any event, Paul has decided to set the offering in motion so it will be ready when he arrives, which fits the pattern of changed arrangements for the offering that led to accusations in Corinth as reconstructed from other evidence by Margaret Mitchell.[39]

In 11:34b, Paul signaled that the letter was nearing its end: the other matters (τὰ δὲ λοιπὰ) Paul proposes to set in order (διατάξομαι) when he arrives. This detail belongs at the end of a letter and is utterly out of place when followed by five chapters of further argument as in the canonical first Corinthians.

THE PROVENANCE OF LETTER A[40]

The materials in the Corinthian letters were written in response to exigencies that arose from Paul's mission in Corinth. This mission probably began in the early spring of 50 CE, a date derived from the Gallio inscription that establishes a tenure from July 1, 51, to July 1, 52, for the proconsul before whom Paul appeared (Acts 18:12-17).[41] This correlates with the encounter with Prisca and Aquila, refugees from Rome in 49, with whom Paul developed a tentmaking business (Acts 18:1-3). Several congregations were established in Corinth and its two harbor towns, whose patrons sponsored various traveling evangelists and came to favor competitive outlooks. The bulk of the converts were slaves and humble handworkers, led by patrons such as Gaius, Titius Justus, Chloë, Phoebe, Stephanus, Erastus, Prisca, and Aquila. In the period between Paul's departure in CE 51 and his first return visit in 55, serious conflicts arose in the churches, eliciting Paul's letters. Apollos also missionized in Corinth during this period and played a prominent role in the development of the controversies.

In his first letter to the Corinthians (which we reconstruct as 1 Cor 11:2, 27-34a + 11:3-16 + 16:1-4 + 11:34b), Paul responds to hearsay information (1 Cor 11:18-19)[42] about agitation concerning male and female hair styles[43] and disruptions of the Lord's Supper. This letter was probably written at the beginning of the mission to Ephesus in the fall of 52, which correlates with the fact that Paul's information about the Corinthian situation consisted of rumors about whose veracity he is skeptical (1 Cor 11:18). The letter was written before Paul had a chance to make further inquiries or to hear firsthand reports from members of the Corinthian congregations. The offhand reference in 1 Cor 16:1 to the instructions Paul had recently given to the Galatians also requires a provenance shortly after he had revisited the Galatian congregations. He urges the maintenance of traditional hairstyles while arguing both for the priority of males over females (1 Cor 11:3, 8) and interdependence between the sexes (1 Cor 11:11-12). There is no indication in this muddled argument that Paul suspects that prophetesses were probably adopting male hairstyles to express their reunification into the original, androgynous Adam.[44] Since some of the Corinthians viewed Christ as the First Adam, which Paul opposes at the end of his next letter (1 Cor 15:46-47), and since Paul was forced to counter their denigration of bodily responsibility in that letter (1 Cor 6:12-20; 9:24–10:22), it appears likely that the proto-gnostic viewpoint was already emerging in the congregation prior to the writing of Paul's first letter.[45] The women who adopted a male hairstyle were probably expressing their understanding of baptism along the lines of Gal 3:28 as incorporation in the original, bodiless Adam.

In the second half of Letter A, Paul deals with distortions in the celebration of the Lord's Supper. The most likely reconstruction of the situation to which

Paul responds in this passage is that the rich members of the Corinthian church had started to come early to the communal meals and were consuming all of the better food and all the wine before the slaves and handworkers arrived.[46] They were already drunk by the time the members who were obligated to work from dawn to dusk arrived to discover that only slave rations were left. In Paul's view, this destroyed the equality and κοινωνία that was the essence of the meals that Jesus had established. The rich were violating this equality by "humiliating those who have nothing" (1 Cor 11:22). There is angry sarcasm in Paul's query to the rich about whether they didn't have houses where they could satisfy their hunger (1 Cor 11:22), having lain around all day while the other members of their congregation were laboring. In fact, only the rich had "houses" where their hunger could be satisfied,[47] while slaves and handworkers lived in tiny spaces in tenement buildings. Thus, the concluding admonition in 1 Cor 11:33 is to "wait for one another" so the meal can reflect genuine κοινωνία in the body of Christ. In this chronologically earliest letter to the Corinthians, Paul deals with the social dimension of the meal rather than opening up the theological issues as in his later letters.[48]

In the light of the disruptions in the worship of the congregation caused by the rejection of culturally accepted hairstyles and the violation of social equality in the shared meals, the rhetorical situation of Letter A required Paul to clarify and reassert the "teachings" (1 Cor 11:2) that he had brought in his initial mission to Corinth.

Since both the opening and closing of letter A were deleted by the redactor, we have no way of knowing how or precisely when Paul's letter was brought to Corinth. However, in view of the intense interaction between congregations around the Aegean Sea, it seems likely that Paul dispatched the letter soon after arriving in Ephesus. In the light of details in 11:2 and 11:17, it appears likely that the original sequence of Letter A began with a proof concerning the Lord's Supper (11:17-34 a) and ended with a proof concerning hairstyles in congregational worship (11:3-16). We therefore identify the theme of Letter A as "troubles in worship."

The Rhetorical Arrangement of Letter A

(Missing)	(I. *Exordium*)
11:2	II. Introduction: *captatio benevolentiae*: "I commend you . . ."
	III. *Probatio* (in two parts)
11:17	A. *Propositio*
11:18-34a	B. The First Part
11:18-22	1. First argument: cliques in the congregation
11:18	a. Statement of argument: "First, I am hearing that when you assemble as a congregation there are divisions among you, and I partly believe it."

Letter A

11:19	b. Qualification of argument: the necessity of divisions: "so that those who are *dokimoi* may be made manifest."
11:20-21	c. *Exempla* of cliques
11:22	d. Paul's response to the abuses at the Lord's Supper, stated as *interrogatio*
11:23-26	2. Second argument: The tradition of the Lord's Supper
11:23a	a. Identification of the source of the tradition: "the Lord"
11:23b-25	b. *Narratio* of the institution of the Lord's Supper
11:26	c. *Narratio* of the theological significance of the Lord's Supper
11:27-32	3. Third argument: concerning abuses at the Lord's Supper
11:27	a. Statement of argument
11:28	b. Paul's advice concerning the worthy reception of the Lord's Supper
11:29-30	c. Reason for advice: judgment because of unworthy reception of the Lord's Supper
11:29	i. Statement of reason
	ii. Specification of unworthy reception: "not discerning the body"
11:30	iii. *Exempla* of unworthy reception: "This is why some of you are sick and some have died"
11:31-32	d. Reiteration of advice
11:31	i. Statement of reiteration
11:32	ii. Purpose of judgment: discipline for future salvation
11:33-34a	4. Exhortation to apply teaching about the Lord's Supper
11:33	a. Stated positively
11.34a	b. Stated as a threat
11:3-16	B. The Second Part: Hairstyles in worship
11:3	1. Thesis: the cosmic order of God, Christ, man, woman
11:4-7	2. First argument: male and female hair styles should conform to the cosmic order
11:4	a. Men incur shame when violating the cosmic order with regard to hair style
11:5	b. Women incur shame when violating the cosmic order with regard to hair style
11:6	c. *Exempla* of application of principle
	i. First *exemplum*: the case of a woman not wishing to veil herself: "she should have her hair cut off"
	ii. Second *exemplum*: the case of a woman not wishing to have her hair cut or shaved: "she should wear a veil"
11:7	d. The creation establishes a hierarchy of glory between men and women
11:8-12	3. Second argument: the order of creation supports different hairstyles for men and women
11:8-9	a. Inferences from the Genesis account of creation
11:8	i. Stated negatively: "for man did not come from woman"
	ii. Stated positively: "but woman came from man"
11:9	iii. Stated negatively: "For indeed man was not created by means of woman"
	iv. Stated positively: "but woman was created by means of man"

11:10	c. Consequences for the obligation of women to retain the proper hairstyle as her "authority" and protection from "the angels"
11:11-12	d. Clarification of mutuality between men and women
11:11	i. Negatively, by reference to mutuality of men and women in Christ
11:12a	ii. Positively, with reference to the acts of creation and birth
11:12b	iii. Positively, with reference to God as origin of all things
11:13-15	4. Third argument from nature and custom
11:13	a. Statement of argument as *interrogatio*: "Judge among yourselves: is it proper for a woman to prophesy with her head uncovered to God?" (understood answer: no)
11:14-15	b. Reasons for argument (stated as *interrogatio*)
11:14	i. The question for men
11:15	ii. The question for women
11:16	5. Exhortation to conform to tradition
16:1-4 + 11:34b	IV. Epistolary Conclusion
16:1-4	A. Instructions for the Jerusalem Offering
16:1	1. The command to emulate the Galatians
16:2	2. Collection on Sundays to complete the offering before Paul arrives
16:3-4	3. Arrangements for delivering the offering
11:34b	B. Plan to deal with "other matters" when Paul comes
(Missing)	C. (Concluding Benediction)

THE *GENUS* OF LETTER A

The employment of the classical topics of persuasion in epideictic rhetoric, praise and blame, needs to be taken into account. In 11:2, 17, 22, the term "praise" is employed and blameworthy behavior is described in 11:4-6, 13, 16, 18, 21, 29. The topic of praise is, however, close to the standard deliberative the topic of honor. These arguments are employed to support Paul's argument against women adopting male hairstyles in public worship and his command to celebrate the Lord's Supper in a way that honors the weak. This clearly is advice being given by Paul as to the congregation's policy for the future of the Corinthian congregation. The argument for advantage that is typical for deliberative rhetoric is employed in 11:10, 27–31 and 34, in the form of avoiding divine judgment. The encouragement of honorable behavior and the appeal to avoid dishonorable behavior appears in 11:6-7, 13, 21-22, 29, 33–34; 16:2-3. This has led Richard Horsley,[49] Wolfgang Schrage, and others to identify chapter 11 as deliberative.[50] We conclude that this chapter is deliberative.

NOTES

1. See Fee, *First Epistle*, 500; Collins, *First Corinthians*, 395; Schrage, *erste Brief*, 2. 499, cites Conzelmann, Barrett, Senft, Bouman, and Sandt as supporting this view.
2. Hurd, *Origin*, 182–85, following Evans, *Corinthians*, 117.
3. Fee, *First Epistle*, 500.
4. Fee, *First Epistle*, 536; see also Lietzmann, *Korinther I/II*, 55.
5. Lindemann, *erste Korintherbrief*, 248.
6. Lietzmann, *Korinther I/II*, 55; Hays, *First Corinthians*, 194.
7. See Schrage, *erste Brief*, 3.18-19.
8. Winter, *After Paul Left Corinth*, 159–63.
9. Winter, *After Paul Left Corinth*, 163.
10. Winter, *After Paul Left Corinth*, 159.
11. Weiss, *erste Korintherbrief*, 292; E. B. Allo, *Saint Paul: Première Épître aux Corinthiens*, 2nd ed., *EBib* (Paris: Gabalda, 1956), 284; Lietzmann, *Korinther I/II*, 60.
12. See Schrage, *erste Brief*, 3.56.
13. Collins, *First Corinthians*, 437.
14. See Fee, *First Epistle*, 568; Schrage, *erste Brief*, 3.57.
15. Horsley, *1 Corinthians*, 165.
16. See Fee, *First Epistle*, 501: "The 'but' with which this argument begins suggests that things are not quite" right with the Corinthians.
17. Fitzmyer, *First Corinthians*, 409.
18. See Schrage, *erste Brief*, 2. 500, citing Godet, *First Epistle*, 2.69.
19. See Collins, *First Corinthians*, 405.
20. Schrage, *erste Brief*, 2.492; Collins, *First Corinthians*, 401.
21. Thiselton, *First Epistle*, 833.
22. Fee, *First Epistle*, 517; see also Schrage, *erste Brief*, 2.509.
23. Collins, *First Corinthians*, 411.
24. See Morna D. Hooker, "Authority on Her Head: An Examination of 1 Cor. 11:10," *NTS* 10 (1964): 410–16; 415–16; Fiorenza, *Memory*, 228; McGinn, "Authority of Women," 98–99.
25. Fitzmyer, *First Corinthians*, 418–19.
26. Delobel, "1 Cor 11," 386, cited by Collins, *First Corinthians*, 412.
27. Fee, *First Epistle*, 523.
28. Fitzmyer, *First Corinthians*, 421; Moffatt, *First Epistle*, 155: "to turn a social convention, which was far from universal, into a moral obligation binding upon all, is doubtfully wise, however well-meaning its motive may be."
29. Fiorenza, *Memory*, 229.
30. Collins, *First Corinthians*, 414.
31. Horsley, *1 Corinthians*, 157.
32. Fitzmyer, *First Corinthians*, 611; see also Schrage, *erste Brief*, 4.424.
33. See Schrage, *erste Brief*, 4.428.
34. Collins, *First Corinthians*, 588.
35. Fee, *First Epistle*, 814; Collins, *First Corinthians*, 589; Lindemann, *erste Korintherbrief*, 377.

36. Robertson and Plummer, *First Epistle*, 385.
37. Kistemaker, *1 Corinthians*, 595; Morris, *1 Corinthians*, 233; Talbert, *Reading Corinthians*, 132.
38. Barrett, *First Epistle*, 387.
39. Mitchell, "Paul's Letters to Corinth," 331–35.
40. The material in this section is adapted from Jewett, "Corinth," 290–94.
41. See Jewett, *Chronology*, 36–38.
42. Schrage, *erste Brief*, 3.19.
43. See Collins, *First Corinthians*, 396–404.
44. See Meeks, "Image of the Androgyne," 11–23; MacDonald, *No Male and Female*, 72–111; Collins, *First Corinthians*, 408. In contrast, in *Corinthian Women Prophets*, 122–28, Wire views the women prophets as arguing on the basis of Genesis that they embodied the divine image in Christ. Linda L. Belleville, "*Kephale* and the Thorny Issue of Headcovering in 1 Corinthians 11:2-16," in Trevor J. Burke and J. Keith Elliott, editors, *Paul and the Corinthians: Studies on a Community in Conflict. Essays in Honour of Margaret Thrall*, NovTSup 109 (Leiden and Boston: Brill, 2003), 215–32, especially 230–31, argues that this chapter deals with "cross dressing" that opened the path to promiscuous behavior.
45. See Lampe, "Parties," 85–86.
46. See Collins, *First Corinthians*, 417–19, following the research of Hans-Josef Klauck, *Herrenmahl und hellenistischer Kult. Eine religionsgeschichtliche Untersuchung zum ersten Korintherbrief*, NTAbh 15 (Münster: Aschendorff, 1982), 241ff., as well as his commentary: *1. Korintherbrief*, 4th edition, NEchtB 7 (Würzburg: Echter Verlag, 2000). See also Peter Lampe, "The Corinthian Eucharistic Dinner Party: Exegesis of a Cultural Context (I Cor. 11:17-34)," *Affirmation* 4/2 (1991): 1–15.
47. Collins, *First Corinthians*, 423.
48. See Theissen, "Social Integration," 145–74.
49. Horsley, *1 Corinthians*, 157–58.
50. Schrage, *erste Brief*, 1.490; he cites van der Sandt, "eenheid," 411, and Berger, *Formgeschichte*, 93 in support of this assessment. Although he views 1 Cor 11 as part of an integral letter, Collins comes close to the epideictic genus by viewing this chapter as a "rhetorical demonstration" in *First Corinthians*, 392–414.

Chapter 6

Letter B

The Body Matters (2 Cor 6:14–7:1 + 1 Cor 6:12-20 + 1 Cor 9:24–10:22 + 1 Cor 15:1-58 + 1 Cor 16:13-24)

THE RHETORICAL SITUATION AND PROVENANCE OF LETTER B

Letter B was probably written from Ephesus in the fall of 53 after Paul received a report about the situation in Corinth from Stephanus and his colleagues Fortunatus and Achaicus (16:15-18). Judging from the contents of this letter, their report must have included details about promiscuous relations between congregational members and inappropriate partners. In the next letter, Paul refers back to Letter B as a warning "not to mingle with sexually immoral people" (1 Cor 5:9). A series of terms closely related to this verb συναναμίγνυμι ("mingle") are strewn through Letter B: ἑτεροζυγοῦντες ("unequally yoked"), μετοχή ("sharing"), and κοινωνία ("fellowship" / "communion") in 2 Cor 6:14; συμφώνησις ("agreement, harmony"), μερίς ("portion"), and συγκατάθεσις ("concord") in 2 Cor 6:15-16; μέλος ("member") and κολλάω ("join together," twice) in 1 Cor 6:15-17; κοινωνία ("fellowship" / "communion") in 1 Cor 10:16 (twice); and κοινωνός ("partner") and μετέχειν ("share") in 1 Cor 10:20-21. Since the importance of bodily relations[1] carries through the entirety of Letter B, it is likely that the report by Stephanus and his colleagues provided the exigency of this letter by reporting details about the violation of bodily relationships by members of the congregation.

Several details from the report of Stephanus can be recovered from the wording of Paul's argument. The slogan πάντα μοι ἔξεστιν ("all things are lawful for me") is cited twice in 1 Cor 6:12, with the qualifications that all things are advantageous and some things result in slavery. But aside from these qualifications, Paul presents the slogan as valid. In view of Paul's longstanding conflict with legalists on the question of requiring kosher food for Gentiles, it is likely that the slogan had been brought by Paul to Corinth. The problem was that the slogan was now being misused as a rationale for sexual libertinism.[2] There is broader agreement that 6:13a is the first half of a Corinthian syllogism[3] that was probably completed as follows: "Foods are for the belly and the belly for food; so the body is for fornication and fornication for the body."[4] The prominent, twofold use of σῶμα ("body") in 6:13 indicates that the libertines in Corinth denied the moral dimension of bodily relations, a theme that resurfaces in 1 Cor 15:35 in the question of the kind of body Paul has in mind with the resurrection. Although formulated abstractly, this issue is clearly related to the denial of the significance of bodily relations countered elsewhere in Letter B.[5] This was probably related to the idea of an original spiritual and androgynous Adam that surfaced in Letter A, which led the proto-gnostics in Corinth to advocate the doctrine of a decline from the spiritual to the physical Adam that Paul counters in 1 Cor 15:45-46.[6] Paul flatly denies this sequence: "It is not the spiritual which is first, but the physical [Adam]" (15:46).

From the first proof to the last, the argument that "the body matters" is pursued throughout Letter B. In 2 Cor 6:14–7:1, Paul established his premise of the mutually exclusive spheres of Christ and paganism that required purification of bodily pollution. This was followed by 1 Cor 6:12-20 that argues against prostitution in response to proto-gnostics who suggested that in Christ "everything is lawful." Here Paul develops the idea that the bodies of believers are "members of Christ," which eliminates the legitimacy of joining oneself with non-covenanted partners (1 Cor 6:15-18). In 1 Cor 9:24–10:22, Paul goes on to support bodily discipline with a recognition that believers in Christ cannot participate in pagan worship. In 1 Cor 15:1-58, Paul responds to contempt for the bodily component in the doctrine of resurrection. The letter concludes with the recommendation that the congregation "be subject" (1 Cor 16:16) to Stephanus and his coworkers who are probably bringing Letter B to Corinth.

In summary, the rhetorical situation of Letter B was to cope with the rejection of the ethical relevance of bodily relations by radical advocates of spiritual salvation in Corinth. Paul responds to this challenge by clarifying the bodily substance of life "in Christ" and in the doctrine of resurrection. He hopes that "recognition" of leaders like Stephanus (1 Cor 16:18) will reinforce the boundaries between "believers and non-believers" (2 Cor 6:15; cf. 1 Cor 6:15; 10:14, 21) and preserve the holiness of the church (1 Cor 6:19; 10:8, 14).

Earlier in this book the thorny literary problem of 2 Cor 6:14–7:1 within the odd pastiche known as 2 Corinthians was discussed. Without a doubt 2 Cor 6:14–7:1 has appeared to be the oddest piece of 2 Corinthians of all, so odd that a number of distinguished scholars even reject it as a non-Pauline interpolation.[7] It was, in fact, surprising to us that it fits so well within the rhetorical argumentation of Letter B.

The report brought by Stephanus and his colleagues apparently also involved some form of denying the resurrection. In 1 Cor 15:12, Paul asks how "some of you can say there is no resurrection of the dead." From the extensive discussion of this detail, the most plausible suggestions are that it reflects a dualistic understanding of human nature that downplays the significance of the body[8] and a skepticism about apocalyptic judgment.[9] As Wolfgang Schrage observes, it is likely that some Corinthians denied the somatic and futuristic components of the faith.[10] Dale Martin has argued persuasively that the Corinthian radicals did not reject all forms of resurrection; "what they question is the idea that human's *bodies* can survive after death and be raised to immortality."[11] This appears to be related to Paul's rejection of the idea that the "spiritual Adam" preceded the physical Adam (1 Cor 15:46), which was apparently being taught by the same Corinthians who rejected the bodily resurrection. They interpreted the first creation story as the establishment of the original spiritual man who was both male and female in bearing the "image of God" (Genesis 1:26-27), while the second creation story in Genesis 2 described the physical Adam who was created out of dust without a divine image and consequently was doomed to be driven from the garden.[12] This reading of Genesis sustained the idea that humans were divided between spiritual and physical sides and that salvation was a matter of recovering one's original divine image. This viewpoint was closely related to Corinthian tendencies to violate somatic relationships and to reject moral accountability, because such matters were not thought to be relevant for the redeemed who had recovered their lost spiritual identity.

When we take this Adam speculation into account, it is possible to discern a single rhetorical situation that evoked the writing of Letter B, which contains the basic argument that the body matters. Neither the rhetorical situation of the material in what we identify as Letter B nor the burden of the argument therein can be fit into the theme of unity that Margaret Mitchell claims to find throughout the entirety of 1 Corinthians as an integral letter.

THE FIRST PART OF THE *PROBATIO* (2 COR 6:14–7:1 + 1 COR 6:12-20 + 1 COR 9:24–10:22)

As mentioned earlier, we have neither an exordium nor a narratio nor a partitio. Thus, we do not know what topics would have been introduced in the sections of the letter preceding the probatio. In the peroratio of 1 Cor 16:13-24, we can identify the topics and themes that are recapitulated. We can easily identify the two-part probatio. In our reconstruction, the first part of the probatio includes 2 Cor 6:14–7:1 + 1 Cor 6:12-20 + 1 Cor 9:24–10:22 and the second part is 1 Cor 15:1-58. The first part of the probatio is about being "misjoined" or "misyoked."

This probatio begins with a command that provides the thesis for the first proof,[13] "do not be misyoked with unbelievers" (2 Cor 6:14). To be misjoined in some way with some part of the pagan world was to impugn one's "joining" with God, which was accomplished mystically by becoming a member of the body of Christ. In Romans 6, we learn that to be baptized is to be joined with Christ in a death similar to his in baptism. Christ's resurrection signifies to believers their ability and the responsibility to walk—joined to the risen Christ—in newness of life. The believer in Jesus is not just another person walking on the street. Such a believer is, in Paul's theology, a member of the body of Christ. Thus, to be misjoined to nonbelievers is to bring into serious question the reality of one's joining with Christ. One cannot be joined both to Christ and to any form of paganism, in Paul's view. After the command not to be misjoined with nonbelievers (2 Cor 6:14), Paul gives *exempla* of misjoining that are amplified through repetition.[14] One cannot join a thing with its opposite. Righteousness and lawlessness cannot be joined, nor light and darkness, nor Christ with Beliar, nor faith with unbelief, nor God's temple with idols. The five rhetorical questions in 2 Cor 6:14b-16a all require a negative responses from Paul's audience.[15] This is followed by an inferential confession formulated in first person plural style, "for we are the temple of the living God" (2 Cor 6:16b).[16]

After a citation formula referring to "God's own words," Paul provides *testimonia* drawn from eight biblical passages that describe the promise of relationship with God and demand separation from idolatry, thus carrying forward the theme of avoiding misyoking.[17] This set of testimonia (2 Cor 6:16b-18) provides passages from the Old Testament, including the Torah (Leviticus 26:12), the former prophets (2 Samuel 7:8, 14), and the latter prophets (Jeremiah 32:38; Ezekiel 37:27; Isaiah 52:11; Ezekiel 20:34, 41; Isaiah 43:6, and Jeremiah 31:9). The text of the final citation is altered with the addition of "and daughters," thus extending the promise of covenantal relationship to women as well as men.[18] In 2 Cor 7:1, Paul refers to these "promises" provided by the voice of God.

The proper response to the divine promises is stated in 2 Cor 7:1: "Having therefore these promises, beloved, let us cleanse ourselves from all defilement of flesh and spirit, fulfilling holiness in the fear of God." This is what it means to be properly yoked to God. Once the believer is joined to God, holiness of flesh and spirit is needed: holiness of the spirit alone is not enough. The exhortation to spiritual and fleshly cleanliness is also an appeal to the topic of honor. It is not honorable to be defiled in either flesh or spirit. The argument makes clear what will happen to the congregation's relationship with God if they follow the Corinthians who are advocating various forms of misyoking.[19] Therefore, both the topics of honor and advantage typical for deliberative rhetoric surface here.

The first proof flows very smoothly from 2 Cor 7:1 to 1 Cor 6:12. After Paul has stated his general principle about what it means to be joined with God, he then cites two exempla of the Corinthians' misjoining (1 Cor 6:12-13). These two *exempla* are slogans that were current in the Corinthian church.[20] The first slogan in 1 Cor 6:12 is "All things are allowed me," which Paul himself may well have brought to Corinth as an expression of freedom from the Jewish kosher regulations.[21] However in the context of sexual ethics, Paul quotes the Corinthian motto in order to criticize it. Paul limits the scope of the motto by countering that "not all things are advantageous." This is a direct use of the most important topic of deliberative rhetoric, the topic of advantage.[22] In the same verse, 1 Cor 6:12, he quotes the slogan "all things are allowed me" a second time, but then responds in a way which again uses the topic of advantage along with the other standard deliberative topic, the topic of honor. "I will not be made a slave by anything" suggests both advantage and honor. It is disadvantageous to lose one's freedom, and in all societies, it was a dishonorable thing to be a slave. So in a single verse, Paul has used both the topics of advantage and honor to critique the way that some Corinthians were behaving. It is not too much to say that already in this first part of the proof Paul has made a unique fusion of Old Testament law and prophecy with Greek rhetoric. He quotes the Bible to relate immorality to dishonor. He then quotes the Corinthians' slogans to relate their immoral behavior first to disadvantage and then again with dishonor in 1 Cor 6:12.

In 1 Cor 6:13, there is a second Corinthian slogan that Paul quotes: "food is for the belly and the belly is for food." This was the premise of an implicit syllogism whose conclusion was "so also fornication is for the body and the body is for fornication." These terms are cited in Paul's refutation in 6:13b, and even if this reconstruction is rejected, there is a scholarly consensus that such libertinism is implied by the slogan.[23] This slogan strongly suggests that some Corinthians thought that any sexual activity whatsoever was allowed, because there was an appetite for it. The choice of sexual partners allegedly had no more moral relevance than the choice of foods. Paul responds, "God, however, will destroy both the one and the other" (meaning both the belly and food). If God, in the eschaton, is going to destroy both the belly and food, then of what advantage would it be to continue to live human lives merely as the satisfaction of appetites? It would be only a short-term advantage at best. In the long term, it would be advantageous to act in a way which God would approve. A second advantage is stated in 6:14, "God who raised the Lord [Jesus] will also raise us through his power." In the resurrection life, the temporal concerns of appetites for either food or sex will be no more. So living the resurrected life with Christ is, among other things, the ultimate advantage and the ultimate honor.[24]

In 1 Cor 6:15-20 Paul responds to the problem of πορνεία in Corinth, and one of the most striking features in this paragraph is that the traditional legal arguments do not appear. Rather than demanding obedience to the law, Paul makes his case on the basis of the union between believers and Christ, which had been established in baptism. His basic insight is stated in 6:15-16, that since believers are now members of the body of Christ, they are not allowed to join with the bodies of prostitutes, because "he who unites with a prostitute is one body with her."[25] In *The Mysticism of Paul the Apostle*, Albert Schweitzer pointed to the significance of using the verb "cleave," drawn from Genesis 2:24, to describe both the "bodily union between man and woman and union with Christ. . . . He represents the two connections as of so much the same character that the one may be either included in the other, or may exclude it."[26] This mystical concept of physical union with Christ implies that "sexual intercourse . . . creates a mysterious but real and enduring union between man and woman." Richard Hays goes on to explain that the "union of a member of the church with a prostitute is disastrous for the Christian community, precisely because it creates a real bonding with her; therefore, it creates an unholy bond between the Lord's members and the sinful world. The result is both defilement and confusion."[27] The third, fourth, fifth, sixth, and seventh responses Paul makes in 6:17-20 are all appeals to the topic of honor, concluding with the advice to "glorify God in your own body" in 6:20. As Fitzmyer concludes, "In light of the foregoing context, it suggests that all Corinthian Jesus-believers should see to it that God is honored in the individual conduct of their bodily lives. Rather than using the physical 'body' for fornication, they should use it to honor and praise God . . . even the human body can enter such service of God."[28] There are elements of diatribe in this argument, with four rhetorical questions in 1 Cor 6:15 (2 x), 16, 19.[29]

The rhetorical question "do you not know?" at the beginning of 9:24 links the succeeding material closely with the rhetorical questions in 6:15-20. The theme of bodily discipline is continued in the exemplum[30] of athletes in 1 Cor 9:24-27. As Pfitzner has shown, the details in this paragraph focus on the need for "self-control" (ἐγκράτεια, verse 25).[31] That athletic discipline included sexual renunciation[32] links this passage closely with 6:12-20. Paul uses the example of "all" athletes running in a race, yet only "one" athlete wins the prize (9:24). It is honorable to win the prize, and dishonorable to lose. The topic of advantage is stated in 9:25. Every contestant disciplines himself or herself in every respect; yet contestants in a race compete for a perishable crown while believers compete to obtain an imperishable crown. The imperishability of the crown evokes the prize of eternal life.[33] Not only is it honorable to receive any crown, it is more honorable to receive an imperishable crown. Yet more importantly, it is advantageous to receive eternal life, a gift only God can give. Finally in 1 Cor 9:26-27, Paul turns to himself as an example of disciplined control over his body. This continues the theme of bodily discipline in 6:12-20. Paul does not run aimlessly, nor is he merely shadow-boxing. In 9:27, he tells us that he disciplines his own body to attain ἐγκράτεια ("self-control"),[34] so that after preaching to others, he may not be found unworthy. This *exemplum* of somatic self-discipline thus serves the argument developed from the thesis in 2 Cor 6:14, of avoiding misyoking and holding fast to the new relationship established by Christ. Taking this argument from 6:14 onward into account, we affirm Anthony Thiselton's summary: *"The whole of everyday life* must be held captive to the purpose of the gospel."[35]

In 1 Cor 10:1-13, the fourth argument in his first proof,[36] Paul continues his warnings against violating covenantal boundaries by citing exempla from the Old Testament. After a disclosure formula in 10:1, he introduces a series of five[37] exempla from the biblical accounts of the exodus of the Israelites from Egypt. The activities of "our fathers" included travel under the cloud, passing through the sea, baptism "into Moses," eating of spiritual food and the drinking of spiritual drink. Yet even after baptism, the eating of spiritual food, and drinking of spiritual drink, "our fathers" were "overthrown in the wilderness." The lesson of the exemplum for the Corinthians[38] is stated in 10:6a: "these things have become models for us, in order for us not to be those who long for evil things, just as those people did." This is the first of five warnings that "loosely parallel" the five biblical exempla.[39] The Old Testament example of the people who came out of Egypt with Moses shows that even after baptism and receiving spiritual food and drink, disobedience is possible, and those disobedient to God will be overthrown.

In 10:7-13, the expectations drawn from these Old Testament examples are stated as exhortations against longing for "the evil thing," participation in idolatry or πορνεία, putting the Lord to the test, and grumbling against God. The consequence of doing any of these is disaster, so the primary rhetorical function of this argument is "warning."[40] Thus, the conclusions drawn from this Old Testament exemplum relate quite directly to the problem of inappropriate yoking in the Corinthian church. The reference to "grumbling" in 10:10 probably alludes to Numbers 14, where those complaining against Moses say they wish to return to Egypt and are punished by the "Destroyer."[41] This reference therefore relates to violating the relationship with God through idolatry. Those Jesus-believers who are participating in similarly distorted relationships in Corinth in Paul's time should expect punishment. In 10:11, Paul explicitly says that the scriptural examples were there for the purpose of warning, and warnings are also repeated in 10:12-13.

Further, 10:14-22 begins a new section concerning idolatry, with the Eucharist providing the exemplum for communion with Christ that excludes communion with demons. Here Paul returns to the theme of exclusive bodily relationships that was introduced at the beginning of 2 Cor 6:14–7:1. In 1 Cor 10:16, Paul contends that the sacramental cup and bread shared by believers establishes a mystical κοινωνία[42] with Christ that excludes participation in the "table of demons" (1 Cor 10:21). The argument concludes with rhetorical questions in 10:22 about the wisdom of challenging the exclusive claim of Christ, referring back to the episode of Israel's downfall described in 10:1-8. To deny that bodily relationships are exclusive as the Corinthians have done is to engage in a contest in which no mere human can prevail.

A TRANSITIONAL PASSAGE IN THE *PROBATIO* (1 COR 15:1-2)

These two verses provide a transition to the second proof of 1 Cor 15:3-57 by reminding the Corinthians that they had already answered the rhetorical questions posed at the end of the first proof. Rather than provoking God on the false premise that they were stronger than He, ensuring that they would "fall" (1 Cor 10:12); rather than rejecting κοινωνία with Christ by joining themselves with "Belial" (2 Cor 6:15) and prostitutes (1 Cor 6:15), they had taken "their stand" (1 Cor 15:1) in accepting the gospel by which they were "being saved" (1 Cor 15:2). These two verses serve as an introduction to the second proof,[43] which reviews what the Corinthian converts had believed (15:11) and insists that without the resurrection, their faith would be in vain (15:14, 17-19). The advantage of being "saved" by believing "the gospel" is in danger of being lost. Holding fast to this faith (15:2) is reiterated in the exhortation of 15:58.

THE SECOND PART OF THE *PROBATIO* (1 COR 15:3-49)

In 15:3-11, Paul provides a narration of the resurrection faith that Paul had brought to Corinth. As Duane Watson shows, this "narration of the past facts underlying the traditional moorings of the doctrine of the resurrection facilitates Paul's argumentation about the future resurrection."[44] The traditional formulation of Christ's death and resurrection in verses 3 and 4 is followed by the list of witnesses in verses 5-8. This listing of eyewitnesses has the argumentative function of confirming the resurrection faith that was being denied in Corinth. The last of these eyewitnesses was Paul himself, who refers to himself as an "abortion" in verse 8,[45] a misfit whose witness was widely discredited and cast aside,[46] in part because he was a turncoat who had persecuted the church. He responds in verses 10-11 to those who have discredited his ministry, showing that "by the grace of God" his proclamation of the resurrected Lord had been effective in converting the Corinthians.[47] As in 15:2, the redemptive impact of the resurrection message had been confirmed in their own experience of salvation as mystical union with Christ.

In the first of five arguments that follow the narration, 1 Cor 15:12-19, Paul shows that belief in the resurrection of Christ is logically joined to a belief in the future resurrection of believers. The point of this *refutatio*[48] is that to deny the one is to reject the other. In the words of Joseph Fitzmyer, the Corinthian denial "is illogical, baseless, and a contradiction of the most crucial Christian belief."[49] Paul begins in verse 12 by describing the logical contradiction between the resurrection faith proclaimed and accepted in Corinth and the denial of the resurrection. In verses 13-15, he shows that such a denial invalidates faith in Christ, and makes Paul into a con artist. In effect, Paul and the other apostles, "have foisted upon you and all those whom we have evangelized a hoax of notable proportion."[50] Such a hoax would be far from harmless, because thereby "Christianity is completely destroyed."[51] To deny the resurrection is therefore to deny the truthfulness of Christ's resurrection, to invalidate the Corinthian's faith and their new life of freedom from sin, and to consider that those who had died "in Christ" were lost forever. "They have simply been destroyed by death and consigned to eternal oblivion," as Richard Hays observes.[52] He goes on to explain why these contradictions turn believers into objects of pity:

> First, if Christ has not been raised, we Christians mock ourselves with falsehood. We preach a message that turns out to be an illusion. We offer for the world's ills a pious lie that veils from ourselves the terrifying truth that we are powerless and alone. Second... Christians—in Paul's view—are called to a life of "embracing death," suffering through selfless service of others..., not seeking their own advantage or pleasure. If there is no resurrection, the self-denying style of life makes no sense; those who follow the example of Jesus and Paul are chumps missing out on their fair share of life's rewards.[53]

In the second argument of 15:20-28, Paul turns to the positive implications of the resurrection faith. This logical turn in the direction of Paul's argument is described by Anthony Thiselton: "After refuting the counteraxiom of the denial by ruthlessly exposing its unacceptable logical consequences Paul reverses the direction of argument to establish the remarkable consequences for which the axiom of the resurrection, and in particular, the resurrection of Jesus Christ, stands as the foundation."[54] The first of these consequences in 15:20b is that Christ's resurrection inaugurates the era of resurrection for his followers. The use of the term "first fruits" to describe the resurrection of Jesus implies that he was "not only the 'first 'to be raised from the dead, and likewise the 'pledge' or 'guarantee' of the resurrection of all the Christian dead."[55] This is followed in verses 21 and 22 by a carefully formulated *ratio*, an inductive proof that uses historical examples such as in this case, Adam and Christ.[56] With an eloquent use of double parallelism,[57] Paul shows the influence of these two characters that supports the claim that Christ's brought resurrection life:

Since as by a man came death,
by man came also the resurrection of the dead (v. 20);
for as in Adam all die,
so also in Christ shall all be brought to life (v. 21).

The logical force of this *ratio* derives from the double parallelism between "man . . . man / Adam . . . Christ" and "death . . . resurrection / die . . . brought to life." While Adam brought sin into the world, the second Adam provides its resolution. Moreover, the effect of Adam on "all" is paralleled in a climactic manner with the second Adam's achievement of bringing life to "all" who are "in Christ."

Before returning to the Adam-Christ paradigm in 15:45- 49, Paul elaborates the sequence of the resurrection events in verses 23-28. These verses are in contrast to the Corinthian radicals who in the next letter are chided for behaving as if the resurrection had already occurred: "Already you are filled! Already you have become rich! Without us you have become kings! And would that you did reign, so that we might share the rule with you!" (1 Cor 4:8). Paul insists that the resurrection occurrences will follow the divinely ordained sequence: at first Christ will be raised; then those who "belong to Christ" will be raised; and finally the "end" will come. This is elaborated in detail in verses 24-28, with the subjugation of alien powers, and the destruction of death itself. The climax of this sequence of events is the willing submission by Christ to God (15:28), which eliminates the last hierarchical dimension of Christ's sovereignty while preserving the unity of God.[58] The purpose clause in verse 28, "in order that God may be all in all," challenged the radicals in Corinth who were inclined to think that they were superior spiritual beings,[59] while affirming divine sovereignty over life and death.[60]

In 15:29-34, Paul fashions his third argument to show that "Christian existence can be fully understood only in terms of the future. He argues on the basis of Christian institutions, Christian suffering, and Christian ethics."[61] Two examples are employed to make this case, beginning with baptism on behalf of the dead. The most widely accepted explanation of this curious reference concerns proxy baptism in behalf of persons who had died without being baptized, thus giving them access to life after death.[62] Since this was being performed in Corinth, Paul asks what sense it makes if there is no resurrection. The second example in 15:30–32 concerns the risks Paul takes in preaching the gospel. How would he have the courage to face "peril every hour" without the promise of resurrection? The boast to which he refers in verse 31 is that these risks resulted in the conversion of the Corinthians.[63] The final example of risking Paul's life in spreading the gospel was fighting "the beasts at Ephesus." Although the exact circumstances cannot be reconstructed today, this event was well known in Corinth, because Paul asks the rhetorical question about what he would gain by taking such a risk if there were no resurrection. Johannes Weiss correctly insists that the rhetoric of this verse requires life-threatening circumstances, which renders a purely symbolic interpretation implausible.[64]

In 15:32b-33 Paul provides two citations that describe the ethical consequences of denying the resurrection. The first is an exact citation of Isaiah 22:13, "let us eat and drink, for tomorrow we die." The implication is that a rejection of the resurrection encourages a libertinistic lifestyle. Eriksson concludes his analysis of the citation as follows: "Paul uses it to point to the utter futility of a life without the motivation given by the resurrection of Christ."[65] Paul's second citation points in the same direction: "bad company ruins good morals." This citation from Menander's lost comedy *Thaïs* implies, in Barrett's view, that "the Christian behavior of the Corinthians will be ruined if they mix much with those who, not sharing the resurrection hope, live as they please."[66] In the context of letter B, which argues against sexual libertinism that was being practiced in Corinth, these two citations expose the ethical deceit that arises out of the denial of the resurrection. The warning in verse 33a, μὴ πλανᾶσθε, has the sense of "do not continue being seduced,"[67] which refers explicitly to the danger of remaining under the influence of the radical skeptics in the Corinthian congregation.[68]

The first three arguments in the second proof are drawn to a conclusion by the exhortations in 15:34. The first is a succinct, two-word formula, ἐκνήψατε δικαίως, "come to your right mind," which evokes waking up from a destructive fantasy. Richard Horsley relates this expression to "awakening from dreams" of transcendence through the possession of divine wisdom.[69] Wolfgang Schrage interprets this as a warning against spiritual enthusiasm and charismatic illusions.[70] The following exhortation in the present tense, μὴ ἁμαρτάνετε, should be translated "sin no more,"[71] which clearly implies that Paul's audience in Corinth was currently involved in serious violations of the faith.

The serious nature of the issues in letter B is confirmed by the remarkable charge that some Corinthians "have ignorance of God." Paul's choice of the term "ἀγνωσία" ("unknowledge, ignorance") is the first hint we have of a major theme in his next letter to the Corinthians, that all believers have "knowledge" (1 Cor 8:1), but that some lack certain "knowledge" (1 Cor 8:7). This controversy arose from the claim of the radicals in Corinth that their knowledge made them into divine beings.[72] In the context of this letter, however, the knowledge in question concerns the apocalyptic scenario laid out in 15:20–28. To deny the resurrection is to lack knowledge of God the sovereign, who in the end shall be revealed as "all in all." Paul's final jab was the most damaging of all, in the context of an honor and shame society like Corinth: "I say this to your shame." As J. Paul Sampley observes, Paul is trying to push his "hearers to the limits . . . to shock them back into their (better) senses,"[73] and there was no lower blow than to expose them as shamed, lacking in any form of honor, and revealing themselves to be unworthy of participating in any decent society. This was an awful thing to say to the Corinthian radicals who prided themselves in having transcended the ordinary limits of honor, believing that their knowledge had lifted them to a super status.

After devoting the first three arguments in this second proof of letter B to show the logical absurdity and the deplorable moral consequences of denying the resurrection, the fourth argument in the form of a *refutatio*[74] begins with 15:35 to explain the nature of resurrection itself. The questions "how are the dead raised? With what sort of body do they come?" may well be direct quotations of the Corinthian radicals who called themselves the "strong."[75] The questions are introduced by "but someone will say," which signals a contradictory viewpoint, which is typical for this kind of diatribe.[76] In the light of the previous discourse in letter B, the contrary views obviously concern the "body."[77] The two questions function as a formal *interrogatio* that introduces the explanatory reply that follows.[78] Paul's reply begins with a scornful rebuke: "fool!" As Fitzmyer observes,[79] this evokes the condemnation found in Psalm 14:1, "the fool says in his heart, 'there is no God.'" This continues the vituperative style of 15:32b–34, deriding those who claim to have divine knowledge[80] as grievously misguided.

Paul answers the questions with an analogy of seeds, which in ancient understanding required them to die before sprouting.[81] Roy Ciampa and Brian Rosner provide an explanation of the force of this analogy:

> The fact that the seed is buried in the ground like a dead body, but (like one resurrected from the grave) refuses to just lie there, but rather sends life rising up from the ground undoubtedly encourage the analogy.[82]

In verse 37, the analogy is extended to the issue of the body by showing that a seed appears to be nothing like the plant that will grow from it. In Fitzmyer's formulation, "There has to be some kind of change or transformation, despite the sameness or continuity of life that persists."[83] Verses 38–41 draw three inferences from this agricultural analogy concerning the divinely ordained differentiation of bodies. The first is that in the resurrection, God will provide each person with a unique resurrection "body." Its shape will come "from the determination of the Creator,"[84] which means that the "body does not bear continuity within itself, but will be given by God to each as the basis of communication and relationship."[85] The second inference in verse 39 is that the "flesh" of humans, animals, birds, and fish is inherently different. The word "σάρξ" ("flesh") is employed here in a traditional Jewish manner as synonymous with "body" in the preceding verse.[86] "The point is that since there are so many different kinds of bodies in the world, the skeptical Corinthians should not assume that a resurrection body is just like our present bodies. It may be quite different."[87] The third inference in 15:40-41 is that different forms of glory are given to earthly and heavenly bodies, probably referring in the latter to "stars and planets."[88]

FIRST ADAM *VS.* SECOND ADAM (1 COR 15:42-49)

The point of Paul's analogy is introduced by Οὕτως καὶ ("thus, so it is also") in 15:42, which occurs frequently in the interpretation of parables.[89] The discontinuity between earthly and heavenly bodies transformed by the resurrection involves perishability versus imperishability, dishonor versus glory, weakness versus strength (15:42-43), and Paul's innovative antithesis between the spiritual and the physical body (15:44).[90] The word "σῶμα" ("body") is used in the context as "the divinely given basis of relationship," for without it a person is "merely a naked seed (1 Cor 15:37), buried in the ground and isolated from relationship with God" or fellow humans.[91] He supports this with a citation from Genesis 2:7, that "the first man Adam became a living being" (ψυχὴν ζῶσαν), to which the antithesis is added, that Christ as the "last Adam became a life-giving spirit" (πνεῦμα ζῳοποιοῦν). This distinction between ψυχὴν ζῶσαν and πνεῦμα ζῳοποιοῦν provides an analogous support for Paul's distinction between physical and spiritual bodies.

The denial in verse 46 makes it clear that some Corinthians were in fact maintaining that the first Adam was spiritual while the second Adam was physical, as we noted in section one earlier. The significance of this background is frequently downplayed for theological reasons, but the rhetoric of denial undermines the credibility of the speaker if the point being denied is in fact advocated by no one. There are significant parallels that support the teaching that Paul opposes, including Philo, *De Abrahamo* 56, which describes the Adam of the first creation story as bearing the divine image (Genesis 1:26), while the Adam in the second creation story was created from clay (Genesis 2:7) and was thus fated to fall into corruption. Egon Brandenberger's survey of early gnostic material showed that this distinction between a spiritual first Adam and a fleshly second Adam was widely prevalent.[92] Kurt Rudolf synthesized a wide variety of gnostic sources to explain their speculations on the two Adam stories.[93] Elaine Pagels has shown that the

Gospel of Thomas reflects the various gnostic texts that interpret the image of God in the original Adam as the divine legacy that the enlightened should recover.[94] This Corinthian speculation about the sequence of the first and second Adams was problematic because it supported the denial of the bodily resurrection and of the ethical obligations that derive from bodily union with Christ. Paul therefore insists that the first Adam was a "man of dust," the single earthly figure in both creation stories, while the second Adam, Christ, "is from heaven" (15:48), which refers to "the realm where God and the risen Christ dwell and are active."[95] The climax of the argument in verse 49 calls the Corinthians to abandon their speculation about Adam and to make the choice of bearing "the image of the man of heaven" (15:49). The subjunctive reading of the verb "φορέσωμεν" ("let us bear") is not only overwhelmingly supported by the textual evidence,[96] but it also fits the context of Paul's argument that the congregation should turn away from the image of an allegedly original spiritual Adam, with its divinizing illusions, and turn toward the image of Christ whose resurrection granted believers the promise of a future bodily resurrection.[97]

THE *PERORATIO* (1 COR 15:50-57)

In classical rhetoric, a *peroratio* serves as the climax of an oration by means of recapitulation and emotional appeal. The classical handbooks recommend that this section should be particularly eloquent.[98] This *peroratio*[99] begins with a *propositio* that no one can enter the kingdom of God "without the resurrection body."[100] This opening sentence is in the form of synonymous parallelism[101] in which the Semitic categories of "flesh and blood" are restated in the second half with categories drawn from the Greco-Roman environment[102] that he had employed in 15:42.[103] The "mystery" that Paul reveals in verse 51 is that "the coming transformation of all Christians, whether they die before or are still alive at the parousia of the risen Lord, is assured."[104] That all humans will be changed at the end of time reiterates the theme of 15:37–42. The elegant threefold repetition in the first part of verse 52 reaches its climax with "the last trumpet," the traditional biblical signal for the "day of the Lord."[105] At that moment, "the dead will be raised imperishable, and we shall be changed" (15:52), which restates the themes of the preceding proof (15:22, 22-24, 49). The distinction between the perishable and the imperishable in verse 50 is then recapitulated in verses 53-54, which eliminates any possibility of continuity between earthly and heavenly existence,[106] which the Adam speculation and the denial of the physical resurrection implied. Paul insists that believers are not spiritual beings that can pass smoothly from this life to the next; their bodies must be transformed into "spiritual bodies" when the trumpet sounds. The urgent call in verse 29 to "bear the image" of Christ is reinforced by the necessity of being clothed with a new "imperishable" nature and with a form of "immortality" that only Christ can provide.[107]

The scriptural citations in verses 54c-55 are introduced with an apocalyptic formula, "then shall come to pass, the saying that is written."[108] Paul alters the wording of Isaiah 25:8 to proclaim that death will be overcome by the victory announced by the last trumpet. He also alters the wording of Hosea 13:14 to produce the rhetorical questions in verse 55, "O death, where is thy victory? O death, where is thy sting?"[109] The parallelism between these two citations gives an eloquent celebration of Christ's triumph over death.[110] In verse 26, Paul explains the details in these citations. That Adam's sin led to death was a theme in the creation story (Genesis 2:17; 3:14, 19) that Paul shared with Judaism[111] and stated explicitly in 15:22.[112] That "the power of sin is the law" (15:56) was an insight that Paul derived from the Judaizer crisis, that boasting in legal conformity resulted in rejecting impartial grace. This had led the Judaizers to demand circumcision for Gentiles, thus opposing freedom from the law in Christ.[113]

In contrast to the burdens of sin, death, and the law, Paul thanks God for the "victory through our Lord Jesus Christ" (15:57). Although this victory will not be finalized until the last trumpet, it is already guaranteed by the resurrection of Christ. As Thiselton explains, "The present reality is that the sting of death has been drawn out by Christ's victory. Believers already in some measure share in this victory, even though the final appropriation of all that this entails has yet to be appropriated and experienced fully at the last day."[114] With this exultant thanksgiving, the second proof of Letter B is drawn to an inspiring conclusion.

THE EPISTOLARY CONCLUSION (1 COR 15:58 + 16:13-24)

The exhortation near to the end of Letter B reflects themes throughout the letter.[115] To be "steadfast and immovable" involves conforming to the community's behavior on the divine promises (2 Cor 7:1), shunning immorality (1 Cor 6:18), maintaining self-control (1 Cor 9:25), avoiding the temptations that led the desert generation to fall (1 Cor 10:6-13), continuing their stand in the gospel (1 Cor 15:1-2),[116] and avoiding the lure of the "bad company" (1 Cor 15:33) of those who deny the resurrection (1 Cor 15:35-36). The admonition to "abound in the work of the Lord, knowing that in the Lord your labor is not in vain" recapitulates the warnings that denying the resurrection renders the entire faith vain (1 Cor 15:2, 14, 17, 19).[117] The mystical theme of the community residing "in the Lord" resonates with 1 Cor 6:13-20.

The exhortations in 16:13-14 are closely allied with 15:58. The first, "be on your guard," otherwise translated "be watchful," relates both to the warning about joining "bad company" (1 Cor 15:32b-34) and to the apocalyptic scenario in 1 Cor 15:22-28,[118] in which believers are expected to be intimately involved. The second admonition, "stand firm in your faith," resonates with the passages that we associated here with the wording of 15:58 concerning steadfastness. The preceding discussion of sexual discipline and maintenance of the resurrection faith is picked up in this formulation. The admonition to "be courageous" resonates with the reference in 15:58 to "knowing that in the Lord your labor is not in vain," because the ecclesiastical labor involves elements of risk that Paul described in eloquent detail in 15:30-32.[119] It is unclear thus far how the admonition, "Be strong," fits into letter B, although there is a reference to the congregation's strength in 10:13.[120] Perhaps the resistance against absorption into Greco-Roman culture in the first part of letter B could fit this admonition.

The recommendation of Stephanas and his colleagues in verse 15 is a typical reference to the letter bearer. There was no postal service in the ancient world, except for governmental service, so the usual method was to entrust a traveler with one's letter. In the ancient custom, more was involved than merely delivering a letter; the letter bearer was ordinarily entrusted with the presentation and explanation of the letter as well as negotiating its outcome. Since Stephanas and his colleagues were visiting Paul in Ephesus at the time, Paul expresses the impact of their presence and says that they "made up for your absence" and "refreshed my spirit." (1 Cor 16:17-18). Since Stephanas was a prominent member of the Corinthian church, it seems curious that his status would be described in such fulsome terms in verse 15. Paul's reminder that his household was the "first fruits" of the mission in Corinth therefore must have been intended to establish his authority. This is confirmed by the curious formulation in the latter part of verse 15, that Stephanas and his colleagues "appointed themselves to the service of the saints." Since they were not appointed by Paul or the church, their authority must have come from God, which places them in an authoritative relationship to the rest of the Corinthian church. This authority is strongly enforced in verse 16, where Paul urges the congregation to "be subject to such men." Paul returns to this theme that the end of verse 18: "give recognition to such men."

In view of the content of letter B, it seems clear that Stephanas and his colleagues were not only the bearers of the report on the emerging crisis in Corinth, which inspired Paul's letter, but that they were being authorized to carry out the disciplinary program implied by the letter. Since it is probable that letter B failed to resolve the Corinthian conflict, requiring Paul to write letter C, it is likely that Stephanas and his people were unable to settle matters. In fact their intervention may well have been a factor in the development of parties in Corinth. They surely would have been prime candidates for the group that said, "I belong to Paul," a comment preserved in 1 Cor 1:12.

In verse 19, Paul sends greetings from the churches of Asia, whose capital was Ephesus where Paul was residing at the time of writing letter B. He sends particular greetings from Aquila and Prisca along with the "church in their house"; according to the book of Acts. They had earlier resided in Corinth, having been exiled from Rome by the edict of Claudius in 49 CE. When Paul reports that "all the brethren send greetings," this refers to all of the members of the various congregations in Ephesus and its surrounding territory. The admonition, "greet one another with a holy kiss," is the family greeting that church members have for each other when they met for love feasts, signaling that each was a bona fide member of the new covenant.

Paul signs the letter with his own hand, as indicated in verse 21, and then adds, "if anyone has no love for the Lord, let him be accursed. Our Lord, come!" (1 Cor 16:22). This intense apocalyptic acclamation serves to summarize both proofs of Letter B. The mystical relation between Christ and believers was the dominant theme in the first proof, and the fierce apology for the resurrection of Christ and the expectation of an early fulfillment of the end-time schedule formed the second proof. Since the Aramaic expression *marana tha* ("our Lord, come!")[121] appears here without a Greek translation, it has the force of a traditional formula from the earliest church.[122] The intense eschatological expectation resonates with the second proof of letter B, while the pronoun "our" reinforces the boundary between believers and nonbelievers in the first proof.[123] The "grace of the Lord Jesus" sustains each believer in the midst of these trials and tribulations, while Paul's love is extended to "you all in Christ Jesus." With the "amen" at the end of verse 24, Paul employs the traditional "so be it!" to close his letter.

The Rhetorical Arrangement of Letter B

(Missing)	(I. Exordium)
	II. Probatio
II 6:14–7:1; I 6:12-20; I 9:24–10:22	A. The First Proof: Separation from the Pagan World

II 6:14–7:1
II 6:14
	1. The first argument: introduction
	   a. Admonitory thesis: "Do not be misyoked with unbelievers"
	   b. Exempla of misyoking, stated as questions
	      i. Righteousness with lawlessness?

138   Chapter 6

	ii. Light with darkness?
II 6:15	iii. Christ with Beliar?
	iv. Faith with unfaith?
	v. God's temple and idols?
II 6:16a	c. Inference: "We are the temple of the living God"
II 6:16b	d. Testimonia confirming separation from the pagan world
	i. Leviticus 26:12
	ii. Jeremiah 32:38
	iii. Ezekiel 20:34, 41
II 6:17	iv. Isaiah 52:11
	v. Ezekiel 20:34, 41
II 6:18	vi. 2 Samuel 7:8, 14
	vii. Isaiah 43:6
	viii. Jeremiah 31:9
II 7:1	e. Concluding admonitions
	i. The basis of the appeal: "these promises"
	ii. The admonition to: "cleanse ourselves"
	iii. The result of the admonition: "fulfilling holiness"
I 6:12-20	2. The second argument: avoiding sexual misyoking
I 6:12-14	a. Exempla of Corinthian "misyoking" in sexual relations
I 6:12	i. The first slogan, and Paul's responses
	(A) "All things are allowed me"
	(B) First response: "not all things are advantageous"
	(C) Repetition of the first slogan
	(D) Second response: "not be made a slave"
I 6:13	ii. The second slogan, and Paul's responses
	(A) "Food is for the belly"
	(B) First response: God judges both food and belly
	(C) Second response: belly is for the Lord
I 6:14	(D) Third response: the hope of resurrection
I 6:15-20	b. The sexual relevance of participation in Christ
I 6:15	i. The premise: believers are parts of Christ's body
	ii. The argument of exclusive relationship
	(A) The inferential question: "shall I join the members of Christ with whores?"
I 6:16	(B) The rationale: "he who unites with a whore is one body with her"
	(C) Proof text from Genesis 2:24
I 6:17	(D) Inference: "He who unites with the Lord is one Spirit with him"
I 6:18	iii. The ethical admonition: shun immorality because of somatic union with Christ
	(A) The explanation: immorality is a sin against one's own body
I 6:19	(B) The believer's body is the temple of the Spirit
	(C) Believers belong to God
I 6:20	(D) Since you were "bought" by God, God should be glorified "in your bodies"
I 9:24-27	3. The third argument: the need for somatic self-discipline explained by an athletic exemplum

Letter B

9:24	a. Comparatio about winners
9:25	b. Contestants discipline themselves for a perishable prize; believers for an imperishable one
9:26-27	c. Paul as an exemplum of somatic self-discipline
10:1-13	4. The fourth argument: scriptural exempla of somatic accountability
10:1	a. Disclosure formula
	b. Address to "brothers"
	c. The disclosure concerning "our fathers"
	i. Travel under the cloud and through the sea
10:2	ii. Baptism "into Moses"
10:3	iii. Eating manna as "spiritual food"
10:4	iv. Drinking from the rock that "was Christ"
10:5	d. Divine judgment on "our fathers"
10:6-13	e. Exhortations drawn from Scriptural exempla
10:6	i. The first exhortation
	(A) The Israelites are "models for us"
	(B) The exhortation not to "long for the evil thing"
10:7	ii. Te second exhortation
	(A) The exhortation against misyoking with idols
	(B) The citation of Exodus 32:4, 6
10:8	iii. The third exhortation
	(A) The exhortation against sexual misyoking
	(B) The exemplum of punishment from Numbers 25:1-18
10:9	iv. The fourth exhortation
	(A) The exhortation not to test the Lord
	(B) The exemplum of punishment from Numbers 21:5-6
10:10	v. The fifth exhortation
	(A) The exhortation not to grumble against God
	(B) The exemplum of punishment
10:11	vi. The purpose of biblical exempla as warnings to believers
10:12-13	vii. Warnings about accountability
10:12	(A) The warning about overconfidence in yoking
10:13	(B) The assurance that God limits the scale of testing
10:14-22	5. The fifth argument: advice concerning the Eucharist and being misyoked with idolatry
10:14-15	a. The warning to shun idolatry as "sensible people"
10:16-17	b. The Eucharist as exclusive participation in Christ
	i. The rhetorical question about the cup as "sharing in the blood of Christ"
	ii. The rhetorical question about the bread as sharing in the body of Christ"
	iii. Sacramental sharing in "one body"
10:18-22	c. Sacramental meals establish exclusive relationships
10:18	i. The exemplum about worship derived from "Israel according to the flesh"
10:19-20a	ii. The question about whether idols are "anything more than idols," which Paul denies

I 10:20b-22		iii. The warning about respecting the exclusive sacramental relationship with the Lord
I 10:20b		(A) Paul's warning against partnership with demons
I 10:21		(B) Participation in the Eucharist rules out being yoked with idols
I 10:22		(C) The warning not to provoke God by violating exclusive sacramental relationships
I 15:1-57	B.	Second proof: a refutation of those who deny the resurrection of Christ and believers

15:1		1. Introduction of the second proof: presuppositions about the resurrection
		   a. Identification of the resurrection as the same teaching as before
		      i. Paul preached it previously
		      ii. Corinthians believed it
		   b. Statement of the general topic: the advantage of salvation

15:2		c. Requirement to receive the advantage salvation: "if you hold firmly to the message I preached to you"
		      i. Stated positively
		      ii. Stated negatively

15:3-11		2. Narratio: rehearsal of historical details about the certainty of belief in the resurrection of Christ
15:3		a. First stage: Paul's transmission of the tradition of the death and resurrection of Christ

15:3-4		b. Content of the tradition Paul handed on
		   c. A listing of eyewitnesses to the resurrection in historical order
		      i. Cephas
		      ii. The twelve
		      iii. More than five hundred
		      iv. To James and then to all the apostles
		      v. To Paul himself, finally

15:9-11		d. A listing of Paul's qualifications as an apostle and eyewitness

15:9		i. Paul's past as a persecutor of the church
		      ii. Paul's present office(as an apostle): "By the grace of God I am what I am"
		         (A) Statement of present office
		         (B) Description of God's grace as the source of Paul's office
		      iii. Paul's past: Paul "worked harder than any of them(other apostles)"
		         (A) Statement of Paul's hard work
		         (B) Description of God's grace as the true worker
		      iv. Paul's past: Paul's ministry and the ministries of others
		         (A) Statement about ministries
		         (B) Result of ministries: "so you have come to believe"

Letter B 141

15:12-19	3. First *refutatio*: the linking of the resurrection of Jesus-believers to the certainty of the resurrection of Christ
15:12	a. Statement of argument(as an *interrogatio*): Paul chides those who deny the resurrection of believers
15:13	b. First false inference: Christ has not been resurrected
15:14	c. Second false inference: Paul's proclamation has been in vain
	d. Third false inference: Corinthian believers' faith has been in vain
15:15	e. Fourth false inference: "We are even found to be false witnesses about God" because of Paul's proclamation of the resurrection of Christ
15:16-19	f. The religious consequences of the denial of the resurrection:
15:16	i. The non-resurrection of believers impugns the truthfulness of the resurrection of Christ.
15:17	ii. The non-resurrection of Christ impugns "your [the Corinthians'] faith."
15:18	iii. The non-resurrection of Jesus-believers and of Christ means that the dead in Christ are lost forever.
15:19	iv. Final conclusion: the denial of resurrection means that "we [believers]" are "the most pitiable people of all."
15:20-28	4. Second argument: the meaning of the death and resurrection of Christ for the death and resurrection of Jesus-believers
15:20	a. Transition from second argument: Christ as the first fruit
15:21-22	b. A *ratio* concerning parallels between Adam and Christ
15:21	i. Adam brought death and Christ brought resurrection.
15:22	ii. Adam brought death for all while Christ brought life for all.
15:23-28	c. The order of the general resurrection
15:23	i. First Christ
	ii. Then those who belong to Christ at his(second) coming
15:24-28	iii. Then the end
15:24	(A) Statement of this segment of the order
15:24-28	(B) Events related to the resurrection
15:24	(1) Subjugation of all powers other than God
	(a) Statement of event
15:25	(b) Quotation of Psalm 110:1
15:26	(2) Destruction of death
15:26	(a) Statement of event
15:27	(b) Quotation of Psalm 8:7
15:28	(3) Final subordination of "all things"
	(a) "All things" subordinated to Christ
	(b) Christ subordinated to God
	(c) Result: "that God may be all in all"
15:29-34	5. Third argument showing the contradiction between congregational practice and denial of the resurrection
15:29-32a	a. Exempla of necessity of the resurrection

15:29	i. First exemplum: proxy baptism makes no sense without the resurrection of Jesus-believers.
15:30-31a	ii. Second exemplum: Paul's heroic ministry makes no sense without the resurrection of Jesus-believers.
15:30	(A) Paul's putting himself in danger
15:31a	(B) Paul's hyperbolic description of the level of danger to himself
15:31b	iii. Third exemplum: Paul's boast of the Corinthian congregation (which would not exist without Paul's hard and dangerous work among the Corinthians)
15:32a	iv. Fourth exemplum: Paul's fighting wild beasts at Ephesus
15:32b-34	b. Vituperation: Two sarcastic quotations and a corrective exhortation
15:32b	i. Quotation from Isaiah 22:13
15:33	ii. Quotation from Menander
15:34	iii. A corrective exhortation: "Sober up as you justly should, and do not sin. For certain people possess only ignorance of God. I say this to your shame!"
15:35-41	6. Fourth argument in the form of a *refutatio*: bodies in other parts of God's creation are not the same as mortal human bodies
15:35	a. Introduction to the argument, stated as an *interrogatio*
	i. The *interrogatio*
	(A) First question: "How are the dead raised?"
	(B) Second question: "With what kind of body do they come?"
15:36-41	ii. Paul's response
15:36	(A) Paul's exclamation: "Fool!"
15:36-37	(B) Analogy of the death and resurrection of human beings with planting seeds
15:38-41	(C) Conclusions concerning God's activity in giving bodies to different parts of creation
15:38	(1) First conclusion: God gives to each seed a body of God's choosing
15:39	(2) Second conclusion: Not all flesh is alike
15:40	(3) Third conclusion: Bodies in creation include both heavenly bodies and earthly bodies
15:41	(4) Fourth conclusion: Heavenly bodies differ in glory
15:42-49	7. Fifth argument: application of previous arguments to the resurrection of the dead
15:42a	a. Statement of relation of this argument to the previous arguments
15:42b-44a	b. Antitheses concerning sowing of seeds and resurrection
15:42b	i. Sown perishable / raised imperishable
15:43	ii. Sown in dishonor / raised in glory
	iii. Sown in weakness / raised in power
15:44a	iv. Sown a physical body / raised a spiritual body
15:44b-49	c. Comparisons of the physical body with the spiritual body

15:44b		i. Statement of proposition: "If there is a physical body, there is also a spiritual body."
15:45		ii. Application of this proposition to Adam and Christ
		(A) Quotation from Genesis 2:7(Septuagint) concerning "the first Adam"
		(B) Conclusion about "the last Adam"(Christ): "a lifegiving Spirit"
15:46		(C) A series of comparisons of the first and last ἄνθρωποι
		(1) The first man was not the spiritual one but the physical one; the spiritual man came later.
15:47		(2) The first man was from the earth; the second man was from heaven.
15:48		(3) The earthly man is like such earthly people; the heavenly is like such heavenly people.
15:49		(4) Just as we have borne the image of the earthly man, so also shall we bear the image of the heavenly man.

15:50-57   III. Peroratio

15:50   A. Introduction to peroratio: "Now I say this . . ."

B. Recapitulation of probatio: "flesh and blood cannot inherit the kingdom of God"

15:51   C. An apocalyptic timetable

1. General remark about eschatological events: not all will "sleep"(die), but all will be changed
15:52   2. Time of change: "in the twinkling of an eye," "at the last trumpet.
3. Details of eschatological change
   a. sound of trumpet
   b. resurrection of the dead
   c. "we shall be changed"
15:53   d. necessity of change: corruptible and mortal must be replaced by incorruptible and immortal
4. Significance of change: when the change from corruptible and mortal happens, then scripture will be fulfilled.
   a. Statement of significance
   b. Quotation of Isaiah 25:8
   c. Quotation of Hosea 13:14
   d. Response to scriptures quoted: "The sting of death is sin, and the power of sin is the Law."
   e. Thanksgiving to God for victory over death and sin
      i. Statement of thanksgiving
      ii. Person prayed to: God

	iii. Mediator of prayer: Jesus Christ
15:58 + 16:13-24	IV. Epistolary Conclusion
15:58+	A. Exhortation to steadfastness
16:13-14	1. Statement of exhortation 2. Reason for steadfastness: knowledge that in the Lord the addressees' labor is not in vain 3. Admonition to be strong in the faith 4. Admonition to do everything in love
16:15-16	B. Exhortation to submit to Stephanas

16:15	1. Statement of exhortation
	2. Identification of Stephanas
	   a. as the first Asian convert
	   b. as a well-known diaconal minister

16:16	3. Exhortation to be subordinated
	   a. to "such as those"
	   b. to "all fellow workers and laborers"

16:17-18	C. News about fellow workers: the arrival of Stephanas, Fortunatus, and Achaïcus
16:17	1. Statement of news 2. Comment about fellow workers: "they make up for your absence" 3. Comment about fellow workers and the Corinthians: "For my spirit and yours have been refreshed."
16:18	4. Request: "Therefore give recognition to such persons."
16:19-24	D. Final greetings and blessings
16:19	1. Greetings from the churches of Asia 2. Greetings from Prisca and Aquila and the church, which meets in their house
16:20	3. Greetings from "all the brothers and sisters" 4. Request: "Greet each other with a holy kiss."
16:21	5. Greeting from Paul "in my own hand"
16:22	6. Warning: "If anyone does not love the Lord, let that person be accursed." 7. Eschatological Prayer: "Our Lord, come!"
16:23	8. Blessing from Jesus: "The grace of our Lord Jesus be with you."
16:24	9. Blessing from Paul: "My love be with all of you in Christ Jesus."

THE *GENUS* OF LETTER B

In view of the consistent use of deliberative rhetoric, with appeals to honor and advantage throughout, it is clear that Letter B should be identified as deliberative.

NOTES

1. See Collins, *First Corinthians*, 239: "The heart of Paul's argument is . . . the importance of bodily relations."
2. See Robertson and Plummer, *1 Corinthians*, 121; Hans Lietzmann, *Korinther*, 27; for a version of this theory, see Brian J. Dodd, "Paul's Paradigmatic 'I' and 1 Corinthians 6.12," *JSNT* 59 (1995): 39–58.
3. Weiss, *erste Korintherbrief*, 159; Schrage, *erste Brief*, 2.10.
4. Fitzmyer, *First Corinthians*, 264: "What is implied in such a liberal slogan is that sexual intercourse is likewise for the human physical body, and the body for such intercourse."
5. See Fitzmyer, *First Corinthians*, 586; Schrage, *erste Brief*, 4.270-72.
6. Schrage, *erste Brief*, 4.306-08, citing Schmithals, *Gnosis in Korinth*, 159f.; see also Fitzmyer, *First Corinthians*, 598.
7. Hans Dieter Betz, "2 Corinthians 6:14–7:1: An Anti-Pauline Fragment?" *JBL* 92 (1973): 88–108. For an excellent survey of opinions on 6:14–7:1, see Bieringer, "2 Korinther 6,14-7,1 im Kontext des 2. Korintherbriefes," in Bieringer and Lambrecht, *Studies on 2 Corinthians*, 551–70, especially 551, note 2.
8. See Gerhard Sellin, *Der Streit um die Auferstehung der Toten: Eine religionsgeschichtliche und exegetische Untersuchung von 1. Korinther 15*, FRLANT 138 (Göttingen: Vandenhoeck & Ruprecht, 1986), 79–189; Dale B. Martin, *The Corinthian Body* (New Haven: Yale University Press, 1995), 104–36.
9. Thiselton, *1 Corinthians*, 1176.
10. Schrage, *erste Brief*, 4.113.
11. Martin, *Corinthian Body*, 122.
12. For the evidence of this interpretation in early gnosticism and other speculative forms of Judaism, see Egon Brandenburger, *Adam und Christus: Exegetisch-religionsgeschichtliche Untersuchung zu Rom. 5, 12-21 (1. Kor. 15)*, WMANT 7 (Neukirchen: Neukirchener Verlag, 1962), 73–75; Rudolf, *Gnosis*, 91–95; Barrett, *First Epistle*, 373–77; Jewett, *Terms*, 265–67.
13. See Franz Zeilinger, *Krieg und Friede in Korinth: Kommentar zum 2. Korintherbrief des Apostels Paulus*, 2 volumes (Vienna: Böhlau, 1992–97), 400.
14. See Zeilinger, *Krieg*, 401.
15. Zeilinger, *Krieg*, 400; J. Paul Sampley, "The Second Letter to the Corinthians," in L. E. Keck, editor, *The New Interpreter's Bible* (Nashville: Abingdon, 2000), 11.1-180; 103.
16. Zeilinger, *Krieg*, 400.

17. Sampley, "Second Letter," 103.

18. See Zeilinger, *Krieg*, 414–15; this detail cannot be accommodated with the Betz hypothesis that 2 Cor 6:14–7:1 derives from a conservative Jewish circle.

19. Zeilinger, *Krieg*, 403, cites studies by Bachmann and Oliveira on this point.

20. See Hurd, *Origin*, 68; Schrage, *erste Brief*, 2.10, 17; Collins, *First Corinthians*, 243; Thiselton, *1 Corinthians*, 460–61; Fitzmyer, *First Corinthians*, 263.

21. See Robertson and Plummer, *1 Corinthians*, 121; Allo, *Première Épître*, 142; Weiss, *1 Korintherbrief*, 157; Lietzmann, *Korinther*, 27.

22. This is noted by Mitchell, *Reconciliation*, 232, with the qualification on 234 based on 6:20 that "not individual advantage but God's glory should be the measuring-rod of Christian decision-making."

23. Fitzmyer, *First Corinthians*, 264: "What is implied in such a liberal slogan is that sexual intercourse is likewise for the human physical body, and the body for such intercourse." See also Schrage, *erste Brief*, 2.20; Thiselton, *Corinthians*, 458–59; Collins, *First Corinthians*, 245.

24. See Fitzmyer, *First Corinthians*, 266; Schrage, *erste Brief*, 2.25.

25. See Sampley, "First Letter," 862–63.

26. Albert Schweizer, *The Mysticism of Paul the Apostle*, translated by William Montgomery, foreword by Jaroslav Pelikan (Baltimore and London: Johns Hopkins University Press, 1998), 127.

27. Hays, *First Corinthians*, 105.

28. Fitzmyer, *First Corinthians*, 270.

29. Collins, *First Corinthians*, 242.

30. Schrage, *erste Brief*, 2.362.

31. V. C. Pfitzner, *Paul and the Agon Motif: Traditional Athletic Imagery in the Pauline Literature*, NovTSup 16 (Leiden: Brill, 1967), 87; Schrage, *erste Brief*, 2.362; Sampley, *First Letter*, 909.

32. Schrage, *erste Brief*, 2.365–66.

33. Fitzmyer, *First Corinthians*, 373; Schrage, *erste Brief*, 2.368.

34. See Thiselton, *1 Corinthians*, 711, citing Pfitzner and Gale.

35. Thiselton, *1 Corinthians*, 716; italics in the original.

36. Allo, *Première Épître*, 230–33, Barrett, *First Epistle*, 218–29, and Schrage, *erste Brief*, 2.380, treat verses 1-13 as a discreet unit.

37. See Fitzmyer, *First Corinthians*, 377.

38. See Barrett, *First Epistle*, 224; Schrage, *erste Brief*, 2.397.

39. Collins, *First Corinthians*, 366, noting also that the term "all" was repeated five times in the positive series of 10:1-4.

40. Anders Eriksson, *Traditions as Rhetorical Proof. Pauline Argumentation in 1 Corinthians*, ConBNT 29 (Stockholm: Almqvist & Wiksell, 1998), 167, citing Joop F. M. Smit, "'Do Not Be Idolaters': Paul's Rhetoric in First Corinthians 10:1-22," *NovT* 39 (1997): 40–53, citation from 45; see also Mitchell, *Reconciliation*, 250–51; J. Paul Sampley, "The First Letter to the Corinthians," in Leander E. Keck, editor, *The New Interpreter's Bible* (Nashville: Abingdon, 2002), 10.771-1003; 914.

41. See Collins, *First Corinthians*, 372; Thiselton, *1 Corinthians*, 742–43, referring to Richard B. Hays, *First Corinthians*, IBC (Louisville: Westminster / John Knox, 1997), 165.

42. Thiselton, *1 Corinthians*, 762–63 suggests "communal participation" as the proper translation of κοινωνία, but this appears to downplay the physical mysticism that we discerned in the earlier portions of Letter B. Schrage, *erste Brief*, 2.438-39, comes closer to the mark in referring to a real, bodily participation in Christ.

43. See Burton L. Mack, *Rhetoric and the New Testament*, GBS (Minneapolis: Fortress Press, 1990), 56–59; Duane F. Watson, "Paul's Rhetorical Strategy in I Corinthians 15," in Stanley E. Porter and Thomas H. Olbricht, editors, *Rhetoric and the New Testament: Essays from the 1992 Heidelberg Conference*, JSNTSup 90 (Sheffield: JSOT Press, 1993), 231–49; 235–36; Schrage, *erste Brief*, 4.17.

44. Watson, "I Corinthians 15," 237.

45. See Margaret M. Mitchell, "Re-examining the 'Aborted Apostle': An Exploration of Paul's Self-Description in First Corinthians 15.8," *JSNT* 25 (2002–03): 469–85; 484–85.

46. Weiss, *erste Korintherbrief*, 351–52; Schrage, *erste Brief*, 4.64.

47. See Schrage, *erste Brief*, 4.71.

48. Eriksson, *Traditions*, 255–61.

49. Fitzmyer, *First Corinthians*, 558.

50. Fitzmyer, *First Corinthians*, 563.

51. Barrett, *First Epistle*, 349.

52. Hays, *First Corinthians*, 261.

53. Hays, *First Corinthians*, 262; for an analysis of the radical equality of the resurrection faith that would be lost through this denial, see Schrage, *erste Brief*, 4.135-36.

54. Thiselton, *First Epistle*, 1223.

55. Fitzmyer, *First Corinthians*, 569.

56. Watson, "1 Corinthians 15," 241.

57. Barrett, *First Epistle*, 351.

58. Schrage, *erste Brief*, 4.184-85.

59. See Richard A. Horsley, *Wisdom and Spiritual Transcendence at Corinth: Studies in First Corinthians* (Eugene, OR: Cascade, 2008), 154: "these Corinthian are truly *wise, powerful, nobly born, filled, wealthy, kings*. They have reached the highest spiritual status. They are, through possession of Sophia, *perfect* and *spiritual*, and set themselves above those of lesser status, the *babes* and *psychics*—an attitude with obviously divisive implications for a religious community." Italics in the original.

60. See Schrage, *erste Brief*, 4.188; Hays, *First Corinthians*, 266.

61. Barrett, *First Epistle*, 362.

62. In *First Corinthians*, 578–79, Fitzmyer provides a list of commentators who follow this view. There are no other references in the writings of other Jesus-believing communities to this practice, but a wide variety of later gnostic groups are denounced by the church fathers for performing such rituals.

63. See Barrett, *First Epistle*, 365; Schrage, *erste Brief*, 4.242.

64. Weiss, *erste Korintherbrief*, 365–66.

65. Eriksson, *Traditions,* 266; Fitzmyer, *First Corinthians,* 583, concurs that Paul "realizes that the skepticism of some Corinthian Christians about the resurrection of the dead might be entailing other inadmissible attitudes or conduct." See also Schrage, *erste Brief,* 4.246-47.

66. Barrett, *First Epistle,* 367.

67. Thiselton, *First Epistle,* 1253.

68. See Hays, *First Corinthians,* 268–69, who cites Martin, *Corinthian Body,* 275 n. 79.

69. Horsley, *1 Corinthians,* 208.

70. Schrage, *erste Brief,* 4.249.

71. Fitzmyer, *First Corinthians,* 583. See also Barrett, *First Epistle,* 368.

72. See Barrett, *First Epistle,* 368: "this verse provides strong evidence for the existence of a Corinthian group claiming to have a special knowledge of God, and suggests that Paul believed that this *gnosis* would eventually have, if it had not already produced, regrettable moral consequences."

73. Sampley, "First Letter," 983.

74. Eriksson, *Traditions,* 267–72.

75. See Weiss, *erster Korintherbrief,* 367; Martin, *Corinthian Body,* 125; *cf.* Eriksson, *Traditions,* 267.

76. See Roy E. Ciampa and Brian S. Rosner, *The First Letter to the Corinthians,* Pillar New Testament Commentary (Grand Rapids: Eerdmans, 2010), 799.

77. See Fitzmyer, *First Corinthians,* 585.

78. In contrast Schrage, *erste Brief,* 4.272, identifies the opening questions as the *propositio*.

79. Fitzmyer, *First Corinthians,* 588.

80. Thiselton, *First Epistle,* 1259.

81. Fitzmyer, *First Corinthians,* 588.

82. Ciampa and Rosner, *First Letter,* 801.

83. Fitzmyer, *First Corinthians,* 588.

84. Fitzmyer, *First Corinthians,* 589; Thiselton, *First Epistle,* 1264–65.

85. Jewett, *Terms,* 267.

86. Jewett, *Terms,* 119; Fitzmyer, *First Corinthians,* 589.

87. Ciampa and Rosner, *First Letter,* 804.

88. Fitzmyer, *First Corinthians,* 589; Schrage, *erste Brief,* 4.292.

89. Schrage, *erste Brief,* 4.293 refers to Matthew 18:35; 23:28; 24:33, etc.

90. For a discussion of Paul's "striking innovation" in 15:44, see Jewett, *Terms,* 265 – 67; Schrage, *erste Brief,* 4.300 concurs that this is the only time the expression "spiritual body" is found in the entirety of ancient literature.

91. Jewett, *Terms,* 267.

92. Egon Brandenburger, *Adam und Christus: exegetisch-religionsgeschichtliche Untersuchung zu Rom. 5, 12-21 (1. Kor. 15),* WMANT 7 (Neukirchen: Neukirchener Verlag, 1962), 74ff.

93. Rudolf, *Gnosis,* 94–102.

94. Elaine H. Pagels, "Exegesis of Genesis 1 in the Gospels of Thomas and John," *JBL* 118 (1999): 477–96; see also her interpretation of 1 Corinthians 15 in *Gnostic Paul,* 80–86.

95. Fitzmyer, *First Corinthians*, 599.

96. Only two early manuscripts, Codex Vaticanus (B) and Codex Freerianus (I), from the fourth and fifth centuries CE, respectively, support the traditional translation as an indicative, while virtually all the other manuscripts support the subjunctive reading. The commentators who follow this evidence strictly include Fee, *First Epistle*, 787; Allo, *Première Épître*, 429–30; Wolff, *erste Brief*, 505–6; Collins, *First Corinthians*, 572; Heinrici, *erste Brief*, 500–1; Héring, *The First Epistle*, 149; Hays, *First Corinthians*, 273–74.

97. Raymond Collins, *First Corinthians*, 572, offers a significant rhetorical argument for the subjunctive reading, "that Paul concludes each of his proofs (vv. 34, 49) and his peroration (v. 58) with an exhortation."

98. See Eriksson, *Traditions*, 283.

99. See Michael Bünker, *Briefformular und rhetorische Disposition im 1. Korintherbrief*, GTA 28 (Göttingen: Vandenhoeck & Ruprecht, 1984), 71.

100. Eriksson, *Traditions*, 273.

101. Fitzmyer, *First Corinthians*, 603; Collins, *First Corinthians*, 579.

102. Collins, *First Corinthians*, 579.

103. Schrage, *erste Brief*, 4.368-69 shows that the "perishable" refers to the entire realm of life and death in the current age.

104. Fitzmyer, *First Corinthians*, 604.

105. Ciampa and Rosner, *First Corinthians*, 830, referred to Isaiah 27:13; Joel 2:1; Zephaniah 1:14–16.

106. See Schrage, *erste Brief*, 4.377-78.

107. Ciampa and Rosner, *First Corinthians*, 831, elaborate "the metaphor of clothing oneself in a new different set of qualities."

108. See Fitzmyer, *First Corinthians*, 606.

109. See Fitzmyer, *First Corinthians*, 606 for an analysis of these alterations.

110. Schrage, *erste Brief*, 4.380 explains the rhetorical effectiveness of the scornful expression of Christ's triumph.

111. Collins, *First Corinthians*, 582.

112. Fitzmyer, *First Corinthians*, 607, cites a series of studies on this point.

113. For an elaboration of Paul's view about law's perversion, see Jewett, *Romans: A Short Commentary* (Minneapolis: Fortress, 2013), 98–107.

114. Thiselton, *First Epistle*, 1304, citing Wolff, *erste Brief*, 419.

115. Fitzmyer, *First Corinthians*, 608 properly identifies verse 58 as an exhortation; so also Insawn Saw, *Paul's Rhetoric in First Corinthians 15: An Analysis Utilizing the Theories of Classical Rhetoric* (Lewiston: Mellen Biblical Press, 1995), 238. In contrast, Watson, "Paul's Rhetorical Strategy in I Corinthians 15," 247–48; Mitchell, *Paul and the Rhetoric of Reconciliation*, 290; Eriksson, *Traditions as Rhetorical Proof*, 275; and Thiselton, *First Epistle*, 1304, identify verse 58 as the peroration, which overlooks the more likely identification of 15:50-57 as the peroration of Paul's argument.

116. See Eriksson, *Traditions*, 275.

117. Watson, "1 Corinthians 15," 248.

118. Schrage, *erste Brief*, 4.450, points to the parallel in 1 Thess 5:6.

119. See Ciampa and Rosner, *First Letter*, 856.

120. See Schrage, *erste Brief*, 4.452.
121. For the translation of this Aramaic prayer, see Fitzmyer, *First Corinthians*, 630.
122. See Eriksson, *Traditions*, 117–19.
123. Eriksson, *Traditions,* 119 cites Schulz, "Maranatha," 140–41, in support of boundary setting.

Chapter 7

Letter C

Arguing for Unity (1 Cor 1:1–6:11 + 7:1–8:13 + 9:19-23 + 10:23–11:1 + 12:1-31a + 14:1c-33a + 12:31b–13:13 + 16:5-12)

THE EXORDIUM: 1:1-9

The exordium, 1 Cor 1:1-9, begins the letter. Paul mentions himself, with the honorific title of "apostle," and also "our brother Sosthenes." They are the senders of the letter. The addressees are "the assembly (ἐκκλησία) of God which is at Corinth." In Greek and Roman rhetorical theory, the exordium introduces the rhetor and the subjects of the discourse to the audience. Introducing the rhetor includes introducing the ἦθος of the rhetor, and usually includes an appeal, of varying degrees of directness, for the goodwill of the audience. Introducing the subject or subjects of the discourse (especially in Pauline letters) usually means giving, in a few words, glimpses of what will be argued in the probatio. The correlation between the subjects of the discourse found in the exordium and the probatio also extends to the peroratio and sometimes to a partitio. So, in accord with both the theory and practice of Greco-Roman rhetoric, rhetorical critics of Pauline letters generally expect subjects of the letter to be announced or alluded to in the exordium, with a selective amount of background information given in a narratio, sometimes enumerated in a partitio or propositio, developed in full particulars in the probatio, and recapitulated in the peroratio. In Greco-Roman rhetorical theory, everything before the probatio should lead up to the probatio; and everything after the probatio intensifies and reminds the audience of what was demonstrated in the probatio.

In the exordium of our reconstructed Letter C, in addition to the introduction of Paul and his ἦθος, several subjects argued later in the letter are introduced. These subjects are stated: Paul's thanksgiving for God's enrichment of the Corinthians with all λόγος and γνῶσις (1:5), which is a result of God's gracious bestowal of all spiritual gifts; thus no spiritual gifts are lacking in the Corinthian church (1:7). A note of judgment is sounded in 1:8 where Paul tells the Corinthian believers that they will be strengthened so as to be "blameless on the day of our Lord Jesus." This reference to their future innocence, as the readers will find out in chapter 3 and even more fully in chapters 5 and 6, is in marked contrast to the ways at least some of the Corinthians are living as Jesus-believers at the time of Paul's writing of Letter C. One of the Corinthians is involved in incest, and others are taking legal action against each other in courts. Others of the Corinthian church are aware of the incest that is going on and they are arrogant about it; they were perhaps involved in writing the letter to Paul to which he responds in Letter C, in which they lauded the richness of God's spiritual gifts to them. Thus, the Corinthians are a very long way away from being "blameless on the day of our Lord Jesus," as Paul hopes they will be. The theme of personal holiness and spirituality is alluded to in 1:9: God is faithful and the Corinthians have been called to communion with "Jesus our Lord." Yet, as we will see, it will be impossible for the Corinthian church truly to be in communion with Jesus Christ if the members of the church are practicing incest and taking public actions against each other in courts of law.

THE *PROPOSITIO*, 1:10

The *propositio* of Letter C is found in 1 Cor 1:10. This verse, which at first glance seems to be a rather repetitive exhortation to unity, is actually quite precise as to what it tells the reader about what will be argued in detail in Letter C. At first, there is the address to ἀδελφοι, meaning fellow Jesus-believers of both genders. The epistolary request is made for the ἀδελφοι in Corinth to live their lives as believers in ways that bespeak unity. This partitio is worded as an epistolary request, and the three phrases of the request tell a great deal about different aspects of the disunity in Corinth. The first part of the request is that all the Corinthians are asked to agree with each other, ἵνα τὸ αὐτὸ λέγητε πάντες. This agreement of which Paul speaks seems to be at the levels of doctrine and congregational policy. The Corinthians should do nothing as a church that causes division in the congregation. If the congregation follows policies or pursues actions that significant parts of the church cannot support, this will only result in more disunity than already exists in the Corinthian church. So Paul is adumbrating here in the exordium his advice much later in the letter that anything the congregation does should lead to the unity of the church, not lead to greater and greater division. This will be dealt with especially in 8:1-13 + 9:12-23 + 10:23–11:1, where Paul advises that the true issue in connection with eating meat previously offered in pagan worship was the way that it divided the Corinthian congregation.

The next phrase in the partitio that gives a clue to what will be argued in the probatio is the following: καὶ μὴ ᾖ ἐν ὑμῖν σχίσματα, "that there should be no divisions among you." The matter of the σχίσματα is dealt with in full in the first proof, 1 Cor 1:11-4:21. It is the major issue of Letter C.

The third phrase of the partitio that alludes to what Letter C will be about is ἦτε δὲ κατηρτισμένοι ἐν τῷ αὐτῷ νοΐ καὶ ἐν τῇ αὐτῇ γνώμῃ, "that you be established in the same way of thinking and hold the same opinion." This seems to us to relate to a restoration to the way of thinking about God and religion that Paul believed he left the congregation when he departed Corinth at the end of his founding visit. Perhaps Paul speaks a bit hyperbolically here about "the same mind and the same opinion," as if in a diverse group of people that were possible. Here he refers to the fact that the congregation is deeply divided, a matter that he will take up in 1:11-31. Paul wishes the Corinthians to be unified and not factionalized, as "those of Chloë" have reported to Paul concerning the Corinthians, in a report to which Paul gives full credence (in contradistinction to what Paul said in Letter A in 1 Cor 11:18-19). A congregation that is divided into factions cannot effectively act as a community of fellow believers. As we will see, despite what some members of the congregation believed about their congregation, as reflected in the letter to which Paul responded with this Letter C, the congregation was so divided that Paul believed that it could not survive without making significant changes. These needed changes Paul will specify in the probatio of this letter.

THE *PROBATIO*, 1:11–14:3

The long *probatio* in 1:11–14:39 (in the reconstructed Letter C) consists of several parts. Paul puts the more difficult and more theoretical arguments first, in 1:11–4:21. These three chapters deal with the more fundamental problems of the Corinthians' self-understanding (especially their σοφία, or more precisely their lack of it), and their understanding of apostleship. Only after these weightier and more theoretical problems have been dealt with in the probatio, does the probatio move (5:1–14:39) next to the moral issues that the Corinthians' behaviors have raised (5:1–6:11) and then to the practical matters that they have written Paul about. It is important to note the strong correlation between what is mentioned in the exordium and the parts of the probatio: the subject of wisdom, empowerment by spiritual gifts, and the right understanding of apostleship.

Often in rhetorical discourses there is a separate section of *narratio* that is located in the text between the exordium and the partitio. Rhetorical theory taught that a portion of narration could take place, however, within the probatio.[1] As we will see later, Paul did this in 2 Cor 1:15-16 and 1:23–2:4, in Letter G, the letter that uses topics of consolation.[2]

Here in Letter C, the probatio begins with a narratio of partisanship in the Corinthian church at 1 Cor 1:11-17, based on the detailed report from "those of Chloë" to which Paul very specifically refers (1:11). Paul adds severe sarcasm to this narratio in 1:13-15.

In 1:18-31, there is discussion of the fundamental flaw in the Corinthian church: the insistence by some of the church members on the high level of their wisdom. Paul counters this by relativizing human wisdom in comparison with God's wisdom.

Paul goes further to state that his ministry was characterized not by the success of his oral rhetoric; his ministry is described in more depth in the narratio, 2:1-5, where Paul again states the reality of his ministry in terms of his imparting of knowledge to the Corinthian church. Paul describes himself negatively in the narratio as not using an overabundance of λόγος or of σοφία (2:1), yet he "disclosed to you the mystery of God." His knowledge is highlighted again in the next verse, as he argues that he did not know anything except the crucified Jesus (2:2). Again he describes himself rhetorically as not using persuasive words of wisdom, but "with the demonstration (ἀποδείξις) of spirit and power" (2:4). Thus, Corinthians really did have knowledge of God imparted to them by Paul; yet it was not Paul's wisdom but the knowledge that God discloses. Thus, the Corinthians' faith should not derive from human wisdom—either Paul's or their own—but "in the power of God" (2:5).

After the brief section of narratio at 2:1-5, Paul argues in 2:6-15 about the meaning and extent of that knowledge which is referred to as wisdom. If there was a problem in the Corinthian believers receiving Paul's wisdom during his founding visit, Paul points out that wisdom can be given only to "the mature" (2:6). True spiritual wisdom is a γνῶσις that is given by the Spirit of God (2:10-12); Paul seems ostensibly to accept a perspective that Corinthian proto-gnostics shared or even argued. As far as the Corinthians are concerned, they "have been enriched in [Christ Jesus] ἐν παντὶ λόγῳ καὶ πάσῃ γνώσει" (1:5). Paul agrees that they have been indeed been so enriched, since Paul founded the church, but Paul will identify how the λόγος and γνῶσις have been put to use in the now deeply divided Corinthian church in his absence. Yet, despite the claims of the Corinthians to be spiritual, the knowledge, which Paul had conveyed to them, was of "spiritual things" and had been conveyed solely "to those who are spiritual" (2:13), which alludes to the issue, which Paul addresses in 3:1: the fact that the Corinthian believers are not actually spiritual. Indeed, to the person who is ψυχικός, spiritual matters are foolishness (2:14). Those who are not spiritual cannot receive the γνῶσις which is itself spiritual and comes from the Holy Spirit. Paul was actually refuting the Corinthian claims not only to be spiritual but also to have γνῶσις.

Paul opens what we know as chapter 3 of 1 Corinthians by identifying the problem in the Corinthian church as the church members' failure to be or to become spiritual (3:1). In 3:1-3a, he cites his experience with the Corinthians when he founded the church. He would have expected them to be immature at first, but the little *narratio* concludes in 3:3a by saying, "You are still fleshly." The actual argumentation of this part of the proof begins in 1:3b, where the Apostle reasons that the ζῆλος καὶ ἔρις still found among the Corinthian church members is proof that the Corinthians are fleshly. The fact that the Corinthians are not spiritual, both during Paul's founding visit and even as he wrote Letter C, coupled with the Corinthians' lack of growth into maturity, has meant that the Corinthians have focused on the wrong things: on the persons of the apostles Paul, Apollos, and Cephas themselves rather than on God whom the apostles represent. This is the reason that the slogans mentioned in 1:12 are repeated in 3:4. The focus on the persons of the apostles rather than God has caused the Corinthians to remain at the level of maturity that Paul argues is childish; he will recapitulate this argument in 1 Cor 13:11. Paul urges them to consider the eschatological outcomes of what any of the apostles either plant, water, or build (3:6-15): God will do the judging.

Paul returns to wisdom in the fourth argument, 3:18–4:5. In comparison with God's wisdom, all human wisdom is foolishness. Thus, the Corinthians should not attempt to judge Paul using their own wisdom, since God will judge at a time of his choosing (4:5). In the next argument in 4:6-13, Paul argues in favor of a proper understanding of apostleship, very much in response to the slogans about loyalty to particular apostles (1:12; 3:4). Paul contrasts the Corinthians with their "puffed up" attitude about themselves (4:6, 8) with the reality of what apostles are, namely those who are "in last place, as persons condemned to die" (4:9), those who are "fools for Christ," "weak," and "dishonored" (4:10), indeed "the refuse of the world, the off-scouring of all things" (4:13). The Corinthians, on the other hand, esteem themselves as "filled" (evidently with all the spiritual nourishment they needed), "rich," and "kings" (4:8). The contrast between what the Corinthians truly are—not possessed of wisdom, not spiritual, and not mature in Christ—and what they arrogate themselves to be could not be sharper or more ironic.[3]

In the sixth argument (4:14-21) of the first proof, Paul reveals his motives in writing, "not to make you ashamed, but to counsel you as my beloved children" (4:14). Paul continues the use of the motifs of family, including referring to himself as the father of the Corinthian church (4:15), so that he should be imitated by his children (4:16). Lest the Corinthians think they are too grown up for discipline, Paul gives them a choice of his coming with "with a rod or in a spirit of love and gentleness" (4:20).

The second proof, 5:1–6:11, opens with the report of immorality in the Corinthian church. A man is involved in a sexual relationship with his father's wife, which means that it is not merely an affair; it is incest. Worse, the Corinthians are "puffed up" about it (5:2). Paul prescribes an elaborate plan for dealing with this outrageous case of immorality in the Corinthian church (5:3-5). Paul recalls his previous letter against mixing with immoral people (5:9), and he orders the withdrawal of table fellowship with fellow believers who are denoted by various categories of immorality (5:11). The argument concludes with a pointed Old Testament quotation: "Throw the immoral one out from you" (5:13, quoting Deuteronomy 17:7 from the Septuagint).

The second proof is concluded by Paul's correction of believers who are taking legal disputes with each other to courts of law. Paul deals with this issue on the basis of his eschatological perspective. Since "the saints will judge the world," even including angels (6:2-3), could not some fellow Jesus-believers judge disputes that arise, in order to keep such cases out of court? If cases need to be decided, Paul advises the Corinthians to have a fellow member of the congregation decide them, rather than taking such cases to court. In 6:8, however, Paul gets at the root of the problem: "But you wrong and you defraud, and you do this to believers?" In other words, the problem is not merely that believers are taking each other to court over "trivial" matters, but that these disputes even arise at all. It is the Corinthians' foolish behavior—hardly befitting those who claim to have superior wisdom!—that causes such disputes in the first place. As far as that behavior is concerned, Paul ends this proof with a flourish in 6:9-11, with a warning about behaviors that will exclude anyone from inheriting the kingdom of God (6:9-10). In 6:11, Paul says bluntly, "And such were some of you," referring to the catalog of vicious people who will not inherit God's kingdom. This behavior stands in stark contradiction to the three changes of status, which have already happened to believers: being "washed," "sanctified," and "justified" "in the name of our Lord Jesus Christ and in the Spirit of our God." The rite of initiation, baptism, and the divine justification that has taken place should have led to a conversion away from pagan behavior and toward appropriate behavior for Jesus-believers. In the case of some of the Corinthians, however, it has not done so.

After Paul has dealt with the subjects that he had heard about from Chloë's people and which he probably read about in the Corinthians' self-congratulatory letter to him, Paul now moves to a new section of the peroration in order to deal with the problems about which the Corinthians had specifically written to him. He boldly signals in 1 Cor 7:1 a new part of the probatio with the words Περὶ δὲ ὧν ἐγράψατε ("Now concerning the matters about which you wrote"). Paul starts the argumentation in 1 Cor 7:1-24 by citing a general principle on sex and marriage, "It is well for a man not to touch a woman," and then goes on to expound this principle and apply it to several practical problems: the problems of the married, the unmarried, the widowed, and "the rest" (7:12). The next section of practical problems, which Paul addresses, is the section reconstructed as 8:1-13 + 9:19-23 + 10:23–11:1. Reconstructed in this way, without the editorial insertions of part of chapter 9 and one part of chapter 10, there is a completely coherent section, which in some ways follows the pattern in the earlier, more practical proof in chapter 7. Here too Paul states two general principles in 8:1 and further general principles in 8:4-6, and then in the rest of this reconstructed proof, Paul applies the general principles to the specific problem of food offered to idols. The observation that 9:1-18 disturbs the progression of the argument of 8:1-13 and 9:19-23 has been noted earlier, by such an observant commentator as Johannes Weiss.[4] What we note here is to point out the basic symmetry of argumentation between 7:1-24 and 8:1-13, if this argument continues at 9:19-23, because 9:19-23 is a perfect *exemplum* of what is argued in 8:1-18: Paul's behavior is not based solely on his own freedom, but on Paul's missional goal of bringing all persons to participation in the body of Christ. Thus, the Corinthians' imitation of Paul should mean that the solution to their problem about meat offered to idols does not chiefly lie in the intrinsic nature of the meat, but on what the practice does to and in the community of Jesus-believers. 1 Cor 10:23 ff. continues the same type of argumentation about meat offered to idols, applying the principle derived in 9:19-23, and answering objections to the application of the principle to specific cases.

The next section of the probatio is in 12:1-31a + 14:1c-40, concerning spiritual gifts. The type of argumentation is similar to that found in earlier proofs in this reconstructed letter. It consists of statements of general principles (12:2-3), and then applies these principles to specific cases, with a *congeries* of manifestations of the gifts: "gifts," "multiplicities," "ministries," "activities," with the repeated comparison of the multiple manifestations of the Spirit with the one God (12:6). A repetition of the same style of argumentation is seen in 12:7-11, which is full of *exempla* of the same principle: multiple manifestations of the one Spirit. A similar pattern of argumentation is seen in the introduction of the analogy of the body, with four *exempla* of the principle of the needed coherence of anatomical parts, and the chaos resulting if these anatomical parts declare themselves no longer part of the body (12:15-19; compare the factions, "I am of Paul," etc.). This is developed further, with special attention to ministries in the Body of Christ, in 12:27-30.

THE *PERORATIO*, 12:31B–13:13

The identification of the literary genre of chapter 13 of the canonical 1 Corinthians has been difficult. Many identifications have been made of the genre of this chapter, and as Garland points out, no consensus has been reached.[5] It has sometimes been called a "hymn to love," yet it lacks the literary characteristics of a hymn, since it is prose, not poetry.[6] One may indeed ask why Paul would want to write a hymn to the virtue or ideal of love. A major cause of the multiple genre identifications of 13:1-13 is the editing of the original Letter C into 1 Corinthians in the canonical New Testament, where chapters 13 and 14 were reversed from their original order, where what we now know as chapter 14 originally came before what we now know as chapter 13. By reading these chapters in what we reconstruct as their original order, chapter 13 follows chapters 12 and 14. Restoring the original order to Letter C helps the reader to identify 1 Cor 12:31b–13:13 as the peroratio of Letter C. It is a most memorable and extremely striking peroratio. Paul shows formidable rhetorical skill as he appeals to the emotions of the hearers and readers, and as he simultaneously recapitulates the probatio of Letter C. This is precisely what the peroratio was expected to do in Greco-Roman rhetorical speeches and in the surviving handbooks of rhetoric.[7] Perorations constituted both recapitulations of what was argued in the probatio, and they also appealed to the emotions of the hearers to decide in favor of what the discourse as a whole had argued.

The peroratio of Letter C begins in 12:31b. This phrase, coming after 12:31a, where the readers are exhorted to "earnestly seek the higher gifts," identifies love as the highest gift of all, higher even than speaking in tongues or the other spiritual gifts dealt with in chapters 12 and 14 of 1 Corinthians. It outranks glossolalia, prophecy, knowledge, faith, and even extreme examples of asceticism (13:1-3). Even the last mentioned extremely pious behavior does not gain the one who does it—even if it were the apostle Paul himself, since he wrote in the first person singular—any advantage (13:3). Then love is described according to its intrinsic nature: "patient," "kind," and "not jealous or boastful" (13:4). Even at this early stage of the peroratio, it is not hard to discern that Paul was describing love as the polar opposite of the divisive and "puffed up" behavior of the Corinthian church members. These first four verses of chapter 13 recapitulate the argument of significant earlier portions of Letter C. We mention here glossolalia (13:1, recapitulating 14:2-19, 21-23), prophecy (13:2, recapitulating 14:1c-5, 22-25, 37-40), knowledge (13:2, recapitulating 8:1-13 and 2:6-16; cf. 12:8), and faith (13:2, recapitulating 2:5, 12:9). Love in 13:4 is both patient and kind, and more importantly, it is not jealous or boastful; the last-mentioned term recapitulates 1:26-31; cf. 4:6-10; 5:1-2. These four verses of the peroratio recapitulate what was argued in the probatio in Letter C from 1:11 to 4:21. This first part of the probatio dealt with the Corinthians' lack of spiritual wisdom, and thus was in extreme contrast with the statement in 1:5, where Paul gave thanks that God had enriched the Corinthian believers with all kinds of λόγος and γνῶσις. As we find out in the latter part of chapter 1 and in chapter 2, the Corinthians' λόγος and γνῶσις may well be bogus. An underlying issue is: Just how could God's bestowal of gifts of the Holy Spirit produce factionalism and moral chaos in a congregation? Paul's sarcastic comment in 4:8 suggests that Paul's thanksgiving prayer in 1:5 for the Corinthians' spiritual gifts was extremely ironic. Yet, even if the Corinthians really did enjoy the presence of spiritual gifts, and even if the Corinthians had really received spiritual wisdom (which Paul argues against in chapters 2 and 3), the said spiritual gifts are outranked by the highest gift of all, love. Love, as Paul describes it, the Corinthians assuredly do not have. Everything that Paul says that love is, the Corinthians are not. The factionalism in the Corinthian church is all the proof that Paul needed to reach this negative conclusion. The members of the Corinthian church whom Paul has heard about from the detailed report of Chloë's people are exhibiting the behavior that makes their claim to higher spiritual knowledge false. They are neither patient nor kind, and their factionalism shows that they are jealous (13:4). They boast about immorality among the members of the church (13:4, cf. 5:1-2). Their factionalism encourages them to "insist on their own way" (13:5) and discourages them from "rejoicing together with the truth" (13:6).

There is more recapitulation in 13:5-6, where the readers are told that "love does not behave dishonorably" and also that love "does not rejoice in wrongdoing." This instruction about what love does not do recapitulates the dishonorable behavior in the Corinthian church, including some of the dishonorable behavior that some of them even boast about (5:1-8).

In 13:8-10, there is repeated recapitulation of three phenomena closely associated with the boasting of the Corinthian church: prophecies, speaking in tongues, and knowledge. Paul has said a great deal about each of these three phenomena, beginning with the exordium where Paul gave thanks that the Corinthians had been "enriched in [Christ] with every λόγος and all γνῶσις" (1:5); yet in 13:8-10, he emphasizes that even these phenomena will pass away at a time of God's choosing (13:8b). The Corinthian church, or a portion of it, is very proud of these phenomena, so that they already consider themselves "kings" along with their being "filled" (with wisdom) and "rich" (with spiritual gifts). Yet everything of which they are proud will eventually pass away. God will determine when and how this will come to pass, not the Corinthians and not Paul. When these gifts pass away, the Corinthians will be no more "filled" than anybody else. Paul counters the Corinthians' boasting with his eschatology. In the eschaton, only three things will remain: faith, hope, and love. The fact that, as Paul has argued in Letter C, the Corinthians are not spiritual but fleshly, together with the fact that there is a spiritual wisdom which "we" (Paul) have conveyed through his words, adds up to the conclusion that, despite their contentions, the Corinthians did not pay attention when Paul was teaching divine wisdom to them, during the time in which he was founding the church. Even worse, the Corinthians still had not received this wisdom at the time of his writing Letter C. In short, Paul has argued in Letter C several things: there is such a thing as a spiritual wisdom; Paul has taught it through his words; only spiritual people can receive this spiritual wisdom; and the Corinthian Jesus-believers who are doing divisive, fleshly things in that congregation did not and do not possess this wisdom. This accounts for the fact, Paul argues, that the Corinthian church is divided into factions.

To recapitulate, Paul was not sure about the divisions in the Corinthian church when he wrote 1 Cor 11:18-19 (Letter A). In Letter B, however, Paul responded to reports of immorality in 1 Cor 6:12-20, and he responded with an extended, formidable, tight argument in 1 Cor 15 to those who denied the resurrection of the body. Perhaps the tight argumentation of Letter B was a way of "one-upping" those Corinthian believers who claimed higher spiritual knowledge but denied the central doctrine of belief in Jesus: both the death and resurrection of Christ, which assuredly necessitated the existence of Christ's human body. Now, by the time of writing Letter C, Paul has received the detailed report of people associated with Chloë, as he acknowledged in 1 Cor 1:11-12. Thus, before he gets to answer the specific questions that he had been asked in the evidently self-congratulatory letter from the Corinthians to Paul, Paul chooses to deal with the much more fundamental questions that the Corinthians' lack of wisdom, fleshliness, division, and lawsuits among other church members have raised, not to mention the man living in an incestuous relation with his father's wife.

Letter C is certainly a letter in which Paul argues for unity in the church. Yet it is more than a plea for all the Corinthian church people to decide to tolerate each other and "get along." Letter C goes deeper than that. It is a plea for unity, but Paul is realistic enough to understand that there are significant causes of the disunity and factionalism. It is not just a matter of solving the factionalism associated with the names of Paul, Apollos, Cephas, and Christ. Letter C actually addresses the root causes of the disunity. It does so in a deeply Pauline way, given that Paul uses here his terminology of "flesh" versus "spirit." In the context of his letter to the Galatians, "flesh" had its roots in the circumcision controversy. Here in the Corinthian correspondence, the dichotomy of "flesh" versus "spirit" is not applied to any controversy over circumcision, but is applied to the issue of being spiritual versus being unspiritual. Circumcision was not an issue in Corinth, as far as there is evidence, but acting in a "fleshly" way is, as Paul argues. Paul argues, particularly in chapter 3 of 1 Corinthians that the Corinthians' behavior, both during the founding visit and even now, after he has received both the report of Chloë's people and the Corinthians' own letter, which lauded their being filled with wisdom and other spiritual gifts, that the Corinthians are anything but spiritual. And this is before Paul deals with sexual immorality in 1 Cor 5:1-13. The Corinthians' unspiritual behavior invalidates any and all of their claims to be spiritual, despite what their letter to Paul said or implied.

Hence, 1 Cor 13 is superficially about love. It is more fundamentally about disruptive behavior in the Corinthian church, the same church that has people who think they are "filled" and "rich" with spiritual gifts and even "kings" in their present circumstances, but which tolerates immorality and, as Paul argued in chapters 2 and 3, was never spiritual anyway—not when Paul was present as he founded and nurtured the church, and especially not when Chloë's people made their detailed report about disunity and immorality. This was the same church in which some members got drunk at the celebration of the Lord's Supper while other church members went hungry, and some members denied the death and resurrection of Christ, evidently because they thought that the body does not matter, neither Christ's nor their own, and the same church, which was divided up into four factions.

Finally we note that the peroratio of this letter recapitulates the arguments contained in Letter C. It does not recapitulate any part of 1 Corinthians that is not in Letter C. Thus, our rhetorical analysis of Letter C, which was done by one of the co-authors of this book in January 1982, independently confirms the partition theory of 1 Corinthians that the other coauthor published in 1978.[8]

1 Cor 12:31b-13:13 also fulfills the other traditional function of the peroratio, and this function is the appeal to the emotions. This was called *adfectus* in Latin rhetoric and πάθος in Greek rhetoric. Since the *genus* of this letter, as we will see here, is deliberative rather than judicial, there is not an attempt to arouse the emotions of the audience against opponents in a law court. Yet the peroratio here has the function of *adfectus*. It was designed to lift the emotions of the hearers, to cause the sympathies of the audience to be in favor of acting in a way that accords with love, not in the ways in which some members of the congregation have been acting out. In saying that love is "patient" and "kind" (13:4) the letter encourages the hearers to act in patient and kind ways, to act in ways that do not exhibit "puffed up" or "rude" or "self-seeking" behavior (13:4-5). Love also "does not rejoice in what is wrong" (13:6), as some members of the church have been doing (5:1-2). This encourages the congregation to eschew the gossipy delight that some church members have been taking in the sexual immorality of a man sleeping with his father's wife.

In 13:11, there is both *recapitulatio* and *adfectus*. Paul recapitulates the argument in 3:1-5, which argued in favor of maturity as Jesus-believers. Paul said in 3:2 that the Corinthian believers had been acting as children, based on the fact that the congregation was divided into factions, probably the most important of which were those following Paul and those following the other apostle who had visited Corinth, namely Apollos (3:5). In 1 Cor 3,

Paul relates the concern about maturity to oppose the factionalism into which the congregation had degenerated in his absence. This argument, based on the image of maturity, is also developed a bit further in 3:6-7 in that the role of the apostles who ministered in Corinth had done so in order to promote growth: Paul planted and Apollos came along later and watered. So the image of growth of the Corinthians into mature believers in Jesus is likened to the growth of plants in agriculture. Both Apollos' and Paul's ministries were done in order to promote the growth of the Corinthians into mature believers, a growth that, as Paul very pointedly indicates, had not happened either while Paul founded the congregation, or by the time of writing Letter C (3:2).

In 13:11, the argument in favor of growth is recapitulated, but now there is no mention of agriculture or harvest or any such thing. The type of growth of which Paul writes in the peroratio is the growth that children must make. As Paul writes the words, "When I was a child, I spoke as a child, I thought as a child, I reasoned as a child; when I became a man, I put aside childish things" (13:11). This both reinforces the argument of 1 Cor 3:1-4 and urges the hearers of this letter to give up behavior that belongs to childhood. The Corinthian addresses of this letter are doing such a wide variety of things that one would hope a group of Jesus-believers would not do. Their immature behavior, perhaps coupled with the differences in ministerial style between Paul and Apollos, as well as the immorality of some, along with the socioeconomic differences within the congregation, added to the belief by some that what one does with one's body does not matter, has caused the congregation in this boom town to fall into factionalism. Paul says in 1 Cor 13:11 both that he had been a child and that he grew up and "put aside childish things." This is a clear, though somewhat indirect, appeal to the congregation to give up the behavior that belongs on the playground and to move into behavior that befits adults who are Jesus-believers. This is an appeal to the emotions of the Corinthians to quit acting like children and thus to act like the adults they are. It is an appeal to the standard deliberative topic of honor. It is honorable to give up dishonorable behavior such as jealousy and boastfulness and arrogance (13:4) and rejoicing in what is wrong (13:6). And in 13:11, it is more honorable still to grow up and "put aside childish things." Thus, the bad behavior of the Corinthian church is derided as the behavior of children on a playground. That behavior is not a problem for those who are under the age of twelve years, but it is extremely out of place for those who are in Christ who have been taught about faith and practice by not one but two apostles! Their behavior has done damage to the image of the church in Corinth, especially the behavior of incest and lawsuits among Jesus-believers that Paul deals with in 1 Cor 5. Thus, this letter's final appeal in the peroratio includes the explicit use of the topics of advantage (13:3) and of honor (13:4-7, 11). Paul used Letter C to attempt to persuade the Corinthians to give up their bad behavior and to move into adulthood. Their factionalism is the presenting problem, Paul has been told. Paul now uses this letter to attempt to persuade the Corinthians to come together as a united congregation, to deal with their problems and their problem people, and, in short, to grow up into spiritual maturity.

THE RHETORICAL *GENUS* OF LETTER C

In this letter, Paul did not defend himself against charges, but he did advise the Corinthians to change their policies dealing with several issues. In the peroratio, there is no appeal to the hearers to incite their sympathies against opponents, but rather to give up disunity and other immature behavior. The appeals for the Corinthian congregation to change its policy for the future, together with its use of arguments that appeal to honor and promise advantage (as we see particularly in chapter 13, in the peroratio of the reconstructed letter) are fully consistent with the *genus* of deliberative rhetoric.

The Rhetorical Arrangement of Letter C

(1 Cor.)		
1:1-31	I.	*Exordium*
1:1-3		A. Epistolary prescript
1:4-9		B. Thanksgiving prayer
1:10	II.	*Propositio*
1:11–14:39	III.	*Probatio*
1:11–4:21		A. First part: Unity and spiritual wisdom
1:11-31		1. First argument
1:11-17		a. *Narratio*: Partisanship in Corinth
1:18-31		b. Rationale: Wisdom and the cross
1:1-16		2. Second argument
2:1-5		a. *Narratio*: Paul's preaching
2:6-16		b. Rationale: True wisdom
3:1-17		3. Third argument
3:1-3a		a. *Narratio*: Partisanship as immaturity
3:3b-17		b. Rationale: Apostolic cooperation
3:18–4:5		4. Fourth argument: The folly of worldly wisdom
4:6-13		5. Fifth argument: Lowly apostles and arrogant believers
4:14-21		6. Sixth argument: Paul's motive in writing

5:1–6:11	B. Second part: Moral issues
5:1-8	1. First argument: The case of incest
5:9-13	2. Second argument: Clarifying Letter B
6:1-11	3. Third argument: Lawsuits between believers
7:1–8:13 + 9:19-23 + 10:23–11:1 + 12:1–14:40	C. Third part: Questions from Corinth
7:1-24	1. First argument: Intercourse and marriage
7:25-40	2. Second argument: Virgins and marriage
8:1-13 + 9:19-23 + 10:23–11:1	3. Third argument: Idol meat and bodily discipline
12:1-31a + 14:1c-33a + 14:37-40	4. Fourth argument: Spiritual gifts
12:31b–13:13	IV. *Peroratio*: The highest spiritual gift of all: love
16:5-12	V. Epistolary Postscript
16:5-12	A. Travel plans
(Missing)	B. (Final greetings and blessings)

NOTES

1. Cicero, *De inventione* 1.30. There was some flexibility in the rhetorical tradition as to where and how to place the narratio since in the *Rhetorica ad Alexandrum* by Pseudo-Aristotle we learn that there are three ways to arrange narration. First, facts can be included in the exordium, when they are few and well known to the audience (1438b 15–17). Second, they can be connected to the probatio (1438b 17–20), which seems to mean that they are included in the probatio. Third, they can be placed in a separate section after the exordium (1438b 21–25). On the possibilities of breaking the narratio into portions (and placing it within the probatio), see Heinrich Lausberg, *Handbuch der literarischen Rhetorik*, 4th edition (Stuttgart: Steiner, 2008) §292, p. 167, where he refers to Quintilian as well as later rhetorical instruction.

2. Hughes, "The Rhetoric of Reconciliation," in Duane F. Watson, editor, *Persuasive Artistry: Studies in New Testament Rhetoric in Honor of George A. Kennedy*, JSNTSup 50 (Sheffield: JSOT Press, 1991), 246–61, especially 252–57.

3. Wolfgang Schrage, *erste Brief*, 1.338, puts it well: "An den bitteren Ironie ist in keinem Fall zu zweifeln."

4. Weiss, *erste Korintherbrief*, XL–XLII *et passim*; 232: "Für eine Ausscheidungs-Hypothese spricht vor allem auch die Unklarheit des Übergangs: V. 1 'Bin ich nicht frei?' Von was für Freiheit ist die Rede?"

5. David E. Garland, *1 Corinthians*, BECNT (Grand Rapids: Baker Academic, 2003), 606. He cites the encyclopedic work of Oda Wischmeyer, *Der höchste Weg: Das 13. Kapitel des 1. Korintherbriefes*, SNT 13 (Gütersloh: Mohn, 1981), 205; on the history of scholarship on 1 Cor 13, see also 11–26. See also the discussion of Wischmeyer's study in Mitchell, *Paul and the Rhetoric of Reconciliation*, 271–73.

6. C. K. Barrett, *First Epistle*, 299.

7. Aristotle, *Ars rhetorica* 3.19.1; Cicero, *De inventione* 1.98; Quintilian, *Institutio oratoria* 6.1.1; Pseudo-Cicero, *Rhetorica ad Herennium* 2.47. Further references are given in Lausberg, *Handbuch*, §§431–42, pp. 236–40.

8. Robert Jewett, "The Redaction of I Corinthians and the Trajectory of the Pauline School," *JAARSup* 46 (1978): 389–444.

Chapter 8

Letter D
Reorganizing the Offering (2 Cor. 8:1-24)

Among the many scholars who partition 2 Corinthians, there has not been agreement about 2 Cor 8. Some scholars have placed it at the end of what is often called the "Letter of Reconciliation," which would then be made up of 2 Cor 1:1–2:13 + 7:5–8:24. A compelling case, however, has been made recently by Hans Dieter Betz and Margaret Mitchell that 2 Cor 8 is a separate letter. It is not likely that 2 Cor 8 follows 2 Cor 7 in the original letter of Paul. Betz understands that 2 Cor 8 is an "administrative letter," namely a letter-fragment separate from any other Corinthian letter. Mitchell argues that 2 Cor 8 does not follow 2 Cor 7, but that it should be placed chronologically after the canonical 1 Corinthians and before the "Letter of Tears" mentioned in 2 Cor 2:4.[1]

THE PROVENANCE OF LETTER D

Letter D, of which we have only 2 Cor 8:1-24, was written in Ephesus in the late summer or fall of 54, after Paul gained the impression that his long argument in support of unity, Letter C, was sufficiently successful to restart the campaign for the Jerusalem offering. As Verlyn Verbrugge points out, however, Paul refrains from the commanding style he had employed in 1 Cor 16:1-2.[2] In 2 Cor 8, he employs the style of a "requesting letter" that avoids commands, while stressing the freedom of the audience to respond as they see fit.[3] This change in strategy reflects the conflict between Paul and the Corinthians.[4] Margaret Mitchell adds that Paul's defense against those who "might find fault with us" in administering the offering (8:20) indicates that he was aware of how his effort at bridge building was being received.[5] Mitchell appears to agree with Verbrugge when she explains that Paul "writes the letter in 2 Corinthians 8 to activate and justify a new plan for the completion of the collection, hoping that his persuasive tone of "opinion-giving" rather than commanding . . . joined with his deliberative appeal to advantage by reference to the Macedonians . . . will lead the Corinthians to do likewise."[6] The goal of the letter was to encourage the Corinthians to finish their part in the collection (8:11), whereby Paul slips back into the imperative style with ἐπιτελέσατε ("you should complete").[7] The same verb appeared in the description of Titus' mission to work with the Corinthians to complete the collection work he had encouraged on his earlier visit (8:6).[8] This had apparently occurred a year before the writing of Letter D, in view of the reference in 8:10.[9] As David Garland observes, "This verse [8:6] becomes a delicate admonition for the Corinthians to follow through on their initial commitments."[10]

Klaus Berger shows that giving "alms for Israel" had spiritual significance within Judaism, and that giving alms could be understood within Judaism as having the effect of providing the atonement for sins previously committed by those who gave alms.[11] Berger points out that the giving of alms by Gentile Jesus-believers to their Jewish counterparts in Jerusalem would have been understood in different ways by different groups among Jesus-believers.[12] It is nonetheless evident that Paul is making an appeal to honor. It was an honorable thing to help those who are in need, and probably it was very honorable indeed to help Jews in the land of Israel who were in need.

In a formal sense, Paul's first appeal is to the topic of honor in 8:1-9, indirectly urging the Corinthians to follow the example of the Macedonians' exemplary generosity (8:1-5).[13] He states explicitly that this appeal is not a command (8:8), thus respecting the freedom of the Corinthian audience.[14] It would be honorable to act with the generosity revealed in Christ (8:9). Acting in accordance with the principle of equality (8:13-14), a basic concept in Greco-Roman ethics and politics,[15] would be advantageous to the Corinthians if they needed help in the future from the Jerusalem church.[16]

Then, in 8:16-23, Paul provides a letter authorizing the delegates, including Titus who are coming to Corinth to collect and deliver the funds.[17] Hans Dieter Betz has shown that the formulation of 8:23a authorized Titus as Paul's "legal and administrative representative" in carrying forward the offering project.[18] The extant portion of Letter D ends with a peroration in 8:24 that recapitulates the themes of generous love from 8:7-8 and Paul's hope to be able to boast about the Corinthians as he had with the Macedonians (8:1-5).

THE RHETORICAL SITUATION

The offering arrangements in 1 Cor 16:1-4 need to be brought closer to the second visit to North Galatia because of the wording of 16:1. Galatia was revisited in summer 52, and we place Letter A in the fall of 52. This places the reference to what Paul had told the Galatians a year earlier than the writing of the Galatian letter, that is, before Paul knows of troubles in Galatia that will prevent their participation in the offering. This has always been an anomaly in studies of the Jerusalem offering, because the Galatians did not participate in the end. We date Paul's letter to the Galatian churches in the middle of 53.[19]

PAUL'S RHETORICAL RESPONSE

What we have of Letter D is stated as an exhortation to the Corinthians. We do not possess the entire letter, so we can only interpret the part of the original letter that we do have. The most straightforward way to view the rhetoric of 2 Cor 8 is to divide the exhortation into two basic parts. The first part, 8:1-15, is clearly concerned with fundraising. The second part, 8:16-23, is a recommendation of Titus, and the whole exhortation is summed up in 8:24.

The first part of the exhortation, 8:1-15, is based on appeals to two topics standard in deliberative rhetoric, honor, and advantage. In the first section, 8:1-9, Paul uses a variety of reasons based on the honor of the Corinthians to ask for their (continued) participation in the offering for the relief of fellow Jesus-believers in Judaea. First, he tells at some length of the generosity of the Macedonians in the midst of their proverbial poverty.[20] Precisely because of the unexpected extent of the Macedonians' financial generosity, they with their "deep poverty" made an excellent *exemplum* for Paul to use in order to persuade the Corinthians to give to the offering they had begun and that their strained relationship with Paul had interrupted. The Macedonians were poor in a financial sense; yet "their deep poverty abounded into the riches of their sincerity." The Thessalonians did not merely instruct their banker to write a modest check to the church; rather, as *The New English Bible* translates it, they "insistently begged us for the favor of participation in the ministry to the saints" (8:4)! Paul's language, exaggerated as it is, had a rhetorical purpose. The logic behind the *exemplum* of the poor Macedonians' giving "according to their means and beyond their means" (8:4) is to make the Corinthians consider their own honor, in having begun an offering and then having terminated it. Yet Paul also tempers his appeal to competitiveness with a theological interpretation of the Macedonians' activity: they "gave themselves first to the Lord and then, through the will of God, to us," which, in Paul's view, the Corinthians were only barely in the process of doing. Paul maintains that their giving to the offering for the saints depends not only on their civic pride but on their fundamental relationship with Paul and with God. If the Corinthians would be reconciled with both Paul and the one whom Paul represents, then their giving would become not be merely a financial matter, but a demonstration of their solidarity with Paul's apostolic ministry and mission. Paul even alludes to the "overflowing" or "abundance" of pain and consolation in connection with the Macedonians: they were experiencing "much testing of tribulation," yet "they were abundantly happy" (8:2), happy enough to "insistently beg" for the privilege of giving for the relief of fellow Jesus-believers, obviously unlike the Corinthians. After the *exemplum* of the poor Macedonians, Paul gives specific reasons for the Corinthians to give money: their own abundance in spiritual things such as faith, λόγος, knowledge, eagerness, and love (8:7; cf. 1 Cor. 1:5). Yet Paul is the sort of master of written λόγος himself that he need not "order" the Corinthians to give (8:8). As if the *exemplum* of the Macedonians and Paul's reminder of the Corinthians of their own abundance were not convincing enough, Paul concludes the appeal to honor by the ultimate *exemplum*, the example of Christ, who is characterized as having been originally rich, but later having become poor in order to bring blessings to sinners like the Corinthians (8:9).

The other topic standard to deliberative rhetoric is that of advantage, and Paul introduces it quite directly, using the verb form συμφέρει of the rhetorical term "σύμφερον" in 8:10. Paul argues in 8:10-15 that the Corinthians' giving need not be beyond their means (as indeed the Macedonians' giving was, 8:3) but according to their means, so that there will be equality in the Pauline churches. Paul's goal of equality is indeed a form of advantage, because it would be to the financial disadvantage of the Corinthians to be required to give beyond their means. While Paul specifically says he does not require sacrificial giving (8:13), it is clear that he shows his approval of it, referring to extraordinary generosity as "the grace of God given among the Macedonian churches" (8:1).

This letter fragment concludes in 8:16-23 with an honorific recommendation of Titus and two unnamed brothers who will receive and guard the collection to which Paul urges giving in 8:1-15.

THE *GENUS* OF LETTER D

The unmistakable use of the topics of honor and advantage, as well as the emphasis on the Corinthian congregation's policy for the future, shows that Letter D was written in the *genus* of deliberative rhetoric.

The Rhetorical Arrangement of Letter D

(Missing)	(I. *Exordium*)	
8:1-24	II. *Probatio*	
8:1-15		A. Concerning the collection for the saints

Letter D

8:1-9	1. The first proof: An appeal to the topic of honor
8:1	a) Narrative of the charity of the Macedonians
	i) Introduction to new section (disclosure formula): "Now we make known to you"
	ii) Address: "brothers"
	iii) Content of disclosure
	(A) Theological summary: "the grace of God given among the Macedonian churches"
8:2	(B) Statements of the generosity of the Macedonian churches (with repeated emphasis on the extraordinary circumstances of their generosity)
	(1) First statement: "in much testing of tribulation, they were abundantly happy."
	(2) Second statement: "their deep poverty abounded unto the riches of their sincerity."
8:3-4	(3) Third statement: "According to their means, and beyond their means, of their own accord they insistently begged us for the favor of participation in the ministry to the saints."
8:5	(4) Fourth statement: "And, more than we dared hope, they gave their very selves, first to the Lord, and, through the will of God, to us."
8:6	(C) Result of the Macedonian generosity: Paul's commissioning of Titus for the fundraising effort
	(1) Statement of result: "we have asked Titus"
	(2) Specification of activities of Titus
	(i) Past: "who began this work."
	(II) Future: "to thus complete it and do this favor for you."
8:7	b) Content of the request for funds: reasons related to honor why the Corinthians should give money
	i) First reason: the abundance of the Corinthians
	(A) In faith
	(B) In speech and knowledge
	(C) In all eagerness
	(D) In "love among you from us"
8:8	ii) Second reason: to test the love of the Corinthians
	(A) Stated negatively: "I am not ordering"
	(B) Stated positively: "but through (telling you of the eagerness of others, I am testing the genuineness of your love"
8:9	iii) Third reason: the exemplum of Christ
	(A) Identification of exemplum as Paul's past teaching: "you know"
	(B) Statement of reason: "though he was rich he became poor, in order that you might be enriched through his poverty"
8:10-15	2. An appeal to the topic of advantage
8:10a	a) Introduction: "I am giving my opinion of the matter"
	b) Statement of the topic: "this is to your own advantage"
8:10b-11	c) Statement of appeal

8:12-15		d) Reason for appeal: the goal of equality
8:12		i) First point (God's acceptance): "God accepts whatever someone has; he does not ask what that person has not"
8:13-14		ii) Second point (clarification of how much to give): "There is no question of relieving others at the cost of hardship to yourselves; it is a question of equality"
8:14		iii) Third point (someday the Corinthians might need money from others)
		iv) Fourth point (restatement of goal): "The aim is equality"
8:15		v) Fifth point (citation from Scripture)
		(a) Quotation formula
		(b) Quotation of Exodus 16:18
8:16-23	B. The second proof: commending the delegates	
8:16	1. The past attitude of Titus, stated as a thanksgiving prayer: "I thank God that he has given Titus so much eagerness in his heart for you"	
8:17	2. The present attitude of Titus	
	a) Transition from past activities: "Because he received this consolation"	
	b) Statement of attitude: "he is all the more ready to depart to come to you"	
8:18-22	3. The colleagues of Titus	
8:18-19	a) The first colleague	
8:18	i) His record	
8:19	ii) His authority from other congregations	
8:20-21	b) The reason for sending other colleagues	
8:20	i) Stated negatively: "We want to guard against any criticism . . ."	
8:21	ii) Stated positively: "our aims are entirely honorable, not only in the Lord's eyes, but also in the eyes of people"	
8:22	c) The second colleague	
8:23	4. Summary of recommendations	
	a) The status of Titus	
	i) Identification of Titus	
	ii) His titles	
	(A) "My partner"	
	(B) "fellow worker assigned to you"	
	b) The status of the other delegates	
	i) Identification of the delegates: "as for the brothers"	
	ii) Their titles	
	(A) With respect to office: "apostles of the churches"	
	(B) With respect to honor: "the glory of Christ"	
8:24	III. *Peroratio*: Show love to the delegates	

NOTES

1. Margaret M. Mitchell, "Paul's Letters to Corinth: The Interpretive Intertwining of Literary and Historical Reconstruction," in Daniel N. Schowalter and Steven J. Friesen, editors, *Urban Religion in Corinth*, HTS 53 (Cambridge: Harvard University Press), 306–88.
2. Verlyn D. Verbrugge, *Paul's Style of Church Leadership Illustrated by His Instructions to the Corinthians on the Collection: To Command or Not to Command* (San Francisco: Mellen Research University Press, 1992), 25–69.
3. Verbrugge, *Command*, 196–210.
4. Verbrugge, *Command*, 259.
5. Margaret M. Mitchell, "Letters to Corinth," 331.
6. Mitchell, "Letters to Corinth," 331.
7. Furnish, *II Corinthians*, 418, observes that this is the sole imperative form in chapter 8, revealing "the essence of Paul's appeal."
8. For the technical details about Titus' appointment, see Betz, *2 Corinthians 8 and 9*, 53–56.
9. See Collins, *Second Corinthians*, 169.
10. David E. Garland, *2 Corinthians*, NAC (Nashville: Broadman and Holman, 1999), 372.
11. Klaus Berger, "Almosen für Israel: Zum historischen Kontext der paulinischen Kollekte," *NTS* 23 (1977): 180–204, especially 180–92.
12. Berger, "Almosen," 203–4.
13. See Roetzel, *2 Corinthians*, 43.
14. See Garland, *2 Corinthians*, 375; Roetzel, *2 Corinthians*, 45. Stephan Joubert in *Paul as Benefactor: Reciprocity, Strategy and Theological Reflection in Paul's Collection*, WUNT 2.124 (Tübingen: Mohr Siebeck, 2000), especially 138–44, describes 2 Corinthians 8 in detail in social terms, within the framework of "benefit exchange," so that the equality between the Corinthian church and the Jerusalem church would be preserved by means of the reciprocity afforded by the mutual giving by the Corinthian and the Jerusalem Jesus-believers.
15. See Frederick W. Danker, *II Corinthians*, ACNT (Minneapolis: Augsburg, 1989), 128–29; Betz, *2 Corinthians 8 and 9*, 67–69.
16. Collins, *Second Corinthians*, 172; Ben Witherington, III, *Conflict and Community in Corinth: A Socio-Rhetorical Commentary on 1 and 2 Corinthians* (Grand Rapids: Eerdmans, 1995), 420.
17. See Betz, *2 Corinthians 8 and 9*, 70–79, for a discussion of the legal role they would play.
18. Betz, *2 Corinthians 8 and 9*, 79.
19. Jewett, *Chronology*, 103–4.
20. See the excursus in Betz, *2 Corinthians 8 and 9*, 49–53.

Chapter 9

Letter E

Apology for Paul's Apostleship (2 Cor 2:14–6:13 + 7:2-4)

THE PROVENANCE OF LETTER E

Letter E, the apology by means of unfavorable comparisons, was written in the spring of 55, after departing from Ephesus.[1] Having experienced a crisis that terminated the Ephesian ministry (2 Cor 1:8; Rom 16:3; Phil 1:12-14), Paul probably sent Letter E from somewhere else in Asia, perhaps from Colossae, which he was planning to visit after release from imprisonment (Philemon 22). In Letter E, Paul responds to charges about his conduct and the legitimacy of his apostolic role that have arisen in an already suspicious congregation, encouraged by the super-apostles who had arrived recently from Palestinian churches. They brought letters of recommendation (2 Cor 3:1) that affirmed their charismatic abilities and their theology of spiritual transcendence.[2] They denounced Paul because he seemed to lack apostolic "sufficiency" or "competence." He had no letters of recommendation; he had no valid hermeneutic compared with their inspired approach to scripture; he came with no validated pedigree in mainstream Judaism or Jesus-believing congregations; his career did not reflect a proper degree of divine "glory"; he failed to display appropriate "boldness" in leadership and proclamation, because he lacked personal charisma and authority; his career and personal appearance were too weak to be credible representatives of the power of Christ; and he failed to report ecstatic visions that could prove his spiritual capacity.

Letter E opens with Paul's response to these denunciations by thanking God for the triumph of his vulnerable ministry that reflected "the aroma of Christ" sacrificed on the altar to save the world (2 Cor 2:14-16b). The partitio of the letter in 2:16c-17 declares that Paul's ministry is "sufficient" because it is sincere, non-exploitative, and genuinely authorized by God. This was demonstrated by the success of Paul's ministry to the Corinthians, whose conversion served as "a letter of Christ" (2 Cor 3:3) that, as Paul argues, was superior to any human letter of recommendation. The "new covenant" (2 Cor 3:6) proclaimed in Paul's ministry is not based on human competence but on the Spirit that "gives life." In contrast to the Mosaic ministry such as the super-apostles proclaimed, which placed a veil between God's glory and human sight that only they were allegedly capable of penetrating, Paul and his colleagues minister "with unveiled faces" that enabled access to everyone (3:18). This enables freedom in the Spirit (3:17) as both Paul and his converts gaze upon God's glory reflected in Christ (3:18), rather than claiming to possess such glory in themselves, as the super-apostles did. Since they proclaimed their own glory that gave them the right to lord it over others, Paul declares that "we do not proclaim ourselves; we proclaim Jesus Christ as Lord and ourselves as your slaves for Jesus' sake" (2 Cor 4:5). The genuine gospel is like treasure in earthen vessels (2 Cor 4:7) that remains vulnerable and breakable, as Paul admits to being (2 Cor 4:8-12), but which the super-apostles claim to transcend.

Paul therefore does not lose heart because of his vulnerable ministry (2 Cor 4:16–5:10) in which he is required "to walk by faith and not by sight" (2 Cor 5:7). In contrast to the super-apostles who boasted of their visionary and ecstatic powers, Paul declares that "if we are beside ourselves, it is for God; if we are in our right mind, it is for you" (2 Cor 5:13). In contrast to the super-apostles who touted such experiences as proof of their superiority, Paul had preserved the privacy of his own charismatic experiences in order to serve his congregations in a rational manner, conforming to the self-giving ethos of Christ (2 Cor 5:15). The formal proof ends by rejecting "the human point of view" (2 Cor 5:16) advocated by the super-apostles. The true gospel is presented as a call for reconciliation (2 Cor 5:18-21), which overcomes the war against God as represented by the claims to possess super powers and the resultant right to dominate others.

The peroratio of Letter E in 6:1-13 + 7:2-4 urges the congregation not to reject the grace of God by accepting the propaganda of the super-apostles. The marks of legitimate ministry are reviewed in 2 Cor 6:3-10, in contrast to the superiority claims of the visiting evangelists. The extant portion of the letter ends with an emotional appeal to be reconciled with Paul (2 Cor 6:11-13 + 7:2-4).

THE RHETORICAL SITUATION

When Paul wrote Letter C, the long missive on unity, he had heard the detailed report of "Chloë's people" about the division of the congregation into factions. Whereas he did not seem overly concerned in Letter A with the division of the congregation (1 Cor 11:18), even stating that divisions were necessary in order to be able to identify the genuine people (1 Cor 11:19), by the time Paul wrote

Letter C, he must have been fully aware of how divided the congregation in Corinth was. Thus, he wrote Letter C, still thinking that the main problem was disunity. If Paul could get the congregation to be unified, Paul likely thought, the major problems would be solved. Thus, in Letter C, Paul did not defend himself against charges by Corinthians or anyone else to the effect that he was inferior as an apostle. This rhetorical decision by Paul suggests that Paul did not think he needed to defend himself at that time.

By the time Paul wrote Letter E, his understanding of the situation in the Corinthian congregation had changed. Paul probably believed that Letter C would cause the congregation, which had been deeply divided into factions, to come together into unity. Letter C, like many other letters written by first century Jesus-believers, did not have the desired effect of causing the congregation to become unified.[3] After writing and sending Letter C, Paul hears of invading missionaries (the "super-apostles") who bring letters of recommendation to prove their "sufficiency" in miracle working and spiritual interpretation of scripture. They have won over the congregation and are discrediting Paul's theology and leadership. In response to the criticisms against himself that the congregation has apparently accepted, based on the super-apostles' propaganda, Paul defends the idea of genuine apostolic treasure's being held in earthen vessels and urges reconciliation. He is likely to have thought that Letter C would be effective in unifying the church, so thereafter he asked for the offering for the Jerusalem church to be collected in Letter D. By Letter E, the situation has markedly changed: Paul now knows he must defend himself against the attacks of the people he refers to as the "super-apostles." In Letter E, he compares himself favorably to the super-apostles. We can assume that Paul hoped that Letter E would have the desired effect, which was to get the Corinthian Jesus-believers to reconcile with Paul himself and his ministry. In comparison with Letter C, our Letter E is more serious. Instead of arguing for unity via the standard deliberative appeals to advantage and to honor, as he did in Letters C and D, Letter E shows Paul defending himself, and this strongly suggests that he thought he needed to do so. Letter E reflects a turning point in Paul's relationship with the Corinthians. After Letter E was written and sent, according to our reconstruction, Paul made the painful second visit to Corinth, and that became an even greater turning point in his relationship with the Jesus-believers in Corinth. We will say more about that in chapter 10 of this book.

THE RHETORIC OF LETTER E

The Exordium

In St. Paul's authentic letters, as well as in several other letters attributed to Paul, the *exordium* takes the form of the epistolary prescript, always followed except in Galatians by a thanksgiving prayer, and sometimes a prayer of intercession for the readers. In prayers such as these, the letter writer has (and Paul makes use of) a golden opportunity to gain the goodwill of the audience by honorifically thanking God for the good things that the audience has done in the past and present. The thanksgiving prayers also typically introduce topics that will be dealt with later in the *probatio*.

In the thanksgiving prayer, Paul introduces the themes of sacrifice that will be taken up so prominently in the proofs. One of the activities for which Paul is thankful to God is that God leads "us" in a triumphal procession, in which "we" are offered to God as a burnt sacrifice. This immediately triggers an image of true apostolic activity as sacrificial, rather than triumphant, as presumably the super-apostles allege that it should be. This paradox is further heightened by the fact that the aroma of this sacrifice (2:15) can be smelled by two kinds of people: those who are perishing and those who are being saved. The people who are perishing (the Corinthians, if they follow the super-apostles) are those who interpret this smell as a smell of death; yet at the same time, people who are being saved are those who interpret this smell of burnt sacrifice as a smell of life, a transformed life to be sure (2:16). This issue of whether true ministry involves life or death will be taken up by Paul in his final argument in 5:14-15, as well as in 5:1; and this will be amplified in the list of sufferings in the *peroratio*, 6:3-10. Although prosecution is not directly taken up in this letter (as Paul later will do in Letter F), the fact that Paul teaches that true ministry involves sacrifice, death, and so on, is in itself a condemnation of the ministry of the super-apostles. By the juxtaposition of the two kinds of perceivers of the smell of sacrifice (2:15-16), the audience is invited to be the second kind, the people who perceive that the sacrifice is really "from life to life," that is, to understand the true meaning of sacrifice as opposed to the outward meaning that is obvious to anyone without the inner knowledge of the cultic act. This implies that the super-apostles do not really understand the inner meaning of ministry within the Jesus-believing community; yet again, this condemnation is measured and rather subtle.

A prominent theme in the thanksgiving (2:14f) is that of the procession.[4] Clearly there is the image of a burnt offering, giving off an odor as the sacrificial victim is offered. The incense or perfume that is spread in front of the procession must be used up to be effective. Similarly, Paul's rhetoric is that the apostle's purpose is fulfilled only in his being used up in missionizing. Thus, the very point the super-apostles criticize proves to be the mark of genuine apostolicity. In epiphany processions, there was the figure of the herald, whose "job was to prepare the bystanders for the epiphany of the deity." The herald in such processions called for the bystanders to "make room" in the road for the procession, which followed, which provides an important parallel to the use of the verb χωρέω in Letter E.[5]

THE *PARTITIO*

The abrupt rhetorical question posed at the end of 2:16 initiates a *partitio* that continues through the end of verse 17. This has been difficult for interpreters to understand because it comes too late in the discourse of canonical 2 Corinthians to function as a *partitio*, and because Paul does not provide an immediate answer the question that is posed. This *partitio* in Letter E provides five phrases that relate to the five different parts of the *probatio*. The question, "Who is competent for these things?" relates to the first argument in 3:1-6, which shows Paul is in fact "competent" despite his lack of letters of recommendation that the super-apostles have displayed.[6] The allegation by Paul in 2:17 (which, as one can see, is not even remotely related to the question in 2:16c) states, "We are not, like so many, peddlers of God's word." The phrase "like so many" is not specified, but there can be little doubt that the super-apostles are implied. Yet this is not taken up in prosecution; in the third part of the *probatio*, 4:1-15, we have a defense of Paul, which relates to this allegation. The phrase "as men of sincerity" relates to the second argument in 3:7-18, which shows that Paul is sincere. His ministry has greater glory than that of Moses, so his boldness is appropriate because Paul (as presumably his followers) has an eschatological hope. The next phrase in the *partitio*, "as commissioned by God," has a clear referent in Paul's fourth argument in 5:6-10. Paul's confidence is in God, because (as the first argument also shows) Paul looks to the eternal, invisible things on the basis of his eschatological hope, and because Paul—as a true ambassador of Christ—possesses the virtue of courage, The final phrase in the *partitio*, "in the sight of God, we speak in Christ," relates to the defense of Paul's apostolic office in the fifth argument, 5:11-21, particularly explaining why Paul does the things he does (see especially 5:12c: "what we are is known to God"). The "in Christ" part of the *partitio* phrase relating to this proof is taken up in the final part of the proof, "We beseech you on behalf of Christ." The "in Christ" should, in fact, be taken instrumentally here: "we speak with Christ" or "we speak with the authority given us by Christ." One would not know this from the *partitio* phrase alone; the proof is required to bring out the full implications of "we speak in Christ." But this fifth argument does not follow the pattern suggested by the *partitio* slavishly; in fact, the "message" that "we speak in Christ" is a message of reconciliation. Paul's ministry in general is a ministry of reconciliation (5:19), but the implication at the very end of the proof is that the audience is not just to understand what Paul's ministry is, but actually to be reconciled to God. If the audience has been responding positively to the super-apostles with, presumably, their θεῖος ἀνήρ type of divinizing theology,[7] their understanding of what ministry is would be vastly different from Paul's.[8] Instead of becoming gods, the Corinthian believers are to recognize the significance of the death of Christ, and that they, if they are truly following Christ, come under the category of death to self while becoming a new creation. In Paul's theology, this involves not becoming divine but rather recognizing one's estrangement from God and becoming reconciled to God through Christ.

THE *PROBATIO*

The first argument in the proof, 3:1-6, attempts to show that Paul is "sufficient" or "competent." This argument is introduced by a double *interrogatio* touching the issue of self-recommendation especially through letters. This implies that the issue had been raised by Paul's enemies that Paul did not go around carrying letters of recommendation.[9] Paul then replies that he carries no recommendation letters because he had human letters, the Corinthians themselves. Paul's argumentation here is very sly, because if the Corinthians questioned the quality of Paul's ministry, they then brought into question their own status as Jesus-believers and members of a church that Paul founded. In fact, Paul argues, the letters that Paul has (the Corinthians themselves) are better than the letters of the super-apostles, because Christ is the writer of the letters Paul has (3:3). A second argument for Paul's competence as an apostle is in 3:4-6 that Paul's competence is in God. Paul in fact answers the charge that he is not competent, 3:5, with the allegation that Paul's competence is found in God, "who has made us competent to be ministers of a new covenant" (3:6). Given that Paul has demonstrated his "competence" and has answered in the affirmative the question that he posed in the *partitio* ("Who is competent for these things?"), Paul builds on this conclusion in the second proof.

The second argument, 3:7-18, is subjectively the most difficult part of Letter E, because the reasoning is so convoluted. Perhaps the reasoning is so convoluted because Paul used topics that the super-apostles have already used against him in their own rhetorical efforts to compare Paul negatively to Moses. If Moses was a θεῖος ἀνήρ figure in Hellenistic Judaism, and if the super-apostles were using the topic of "glory" to describe themselves, this would account for Paul's use of the material. In 3:14ff, the exegesis of the Moses / veiling tradition takes a turn toward *refutatio* when Paul states that a veil remains over the Torah when it is read, and on the hearts of the Jews when it is heard, a veil to be removed only by Christ. As Christ removes the veil (for some people and not for others, *cf.* 2:15), the consequence is that for true Pauline Jesus-believers, the veil is removed and they can see the glory of the Lord, 3:18. These arguments in the second proof seem to add up to the conclusion that Paul is sincere because his Gospel is not veiled, but if it is veiled, it is only veiled to those who are unable to see it, again reminding us of the two kinds of people of 2:15. Paul is not only sincere because his Gospel is not veiled; he is also sincere because his boldness (3:12) is appropriate since his ministry has greater glory than that of Moses (3:7-11). Yet, to avoid the charge of ὕβρις, Paul never says that it is his own ministry, which has the glory, but only the ministry of the new covenant (3:7). One should note that the two kinds of recipients in 2:15 are paralleled by the two kinds of recipients in 3:15-18, the "Jews" and people who have the Spirit. This implies that if the super-apostles and their followers alleged that Paul's ministry is not sincere (i.e., that it is "veiled"), Paul's reply is that the super-apostles are either equal to or like the Jews, as the veil lies on their hearts, in Paul's rhetoric. Paul emphasizes that there is no middle ground: their hearts are either unveiled or veiled! Yet Paul is extremely subtle with this rhetorical guilt by association.

The third argument is in 4:1-15. It takes up one of the most important topics in rhetoric: the topic of honor. It corresponds to the allegation in the *partitio* that "we are not, like so many, peddlers of God's word" (2:17). He begins very straightforwardly by saying that he has "renounced disgraceful, underhanded ways" and that he "refuse[s] to practice cunning or to tamper with the word of God" (4:2). This is ostensibly a defense of Paul by Paul himself, but by implication, it is also a prosecution of the super-apostles, since it implies that the super-apostles do these very things. The topic of honor is used reciprocally in 4:2 as Paul commends himself "to every person's conscience in the sight of God." This implies that Paul believes or at least hopes that the audience will be composed of persons of honor, namely the Corinthians. In 4:3-4, there is a small *recapitulatio* of the argument in the previous proof about veiling, to make sure that the Corinthians understood the correct implications of that very complicated argument, that Paul's gospel is "veiled only to those who are perishing" (4:3). Further, Paul argues in 4:5-6 that Paul does not preach himself, but rather Christ. This rhetorically implies that the super-apostles do in fact preach themselves, and probably not as "servants for Jesus' sake" but more like divine representatives of a higher deity. This polemic is further heightened in 4:7-12 as Paul describes his ministry as a treasure in earthen vessels, the earthen vessel symbolizing Paul himself. Paul's life, moreover, is characterized by suffering rather than by a divine aura. But in fact Paul is paradoxically a divine representative of Jesus since he carries the salvific mark of Jesus—the death of Jesus—around in his body, 4:10. By the mere fact that Paul's afflicted human existence symbolizes the death of Jesus, the life of Jesus is also manifested among the signs of death. This strongly suggests a connection with 2:15-16, where both death and life are manifested in the smell of sacrifice, but the people who are ignorant of the cult see and smell only death. Finally in 4:13-15, Paul's honor is defended as

Paul's ministry is argued to be consistent with the Spirit and with Christ and the Father. Note that a doctrine of the Trinity is not being argued here, but the different divine persons are mentioned because the multiplicity of divine witnesses makes for a stronger rhetorical case. Paul is honorable because he, like the Spirit (who inspires sacred scripture) "believed, and so he spoke" (4:13); he is also honorable because he will be raised with Jesus into God's or Jesus' presence (4:14); Paul is finally honorable because his ministry is for the sake of the readers and because their being involved in this ministry increases the thanksgiving to God, as more and more people become a part of it, enlarging the chorus of praise (4:15).

The fourth argument, 4:16–5:10, attempts to show that Paul's confidence is in God and seems to relate to the phrase "as commissioned by God" in the *partitio*, 2:17. The thesis of this proof is that "we do not look to the things that are seen, but to the things that are unseen" since the unseen things are eternal (4:18). In the first argument of this proof (5:1-5), Paul argues that he has an eschatological hope, symbolized by a "house not made with hands, eternal, in the heavens" (5:1). This hope is obviously an *exemplum* of a "thing not seen" as in 4:18. The rest of the first argument is taken up with descriptions of present existence in the light of the eschatological hope, an existence characterized by "groaning" and "anxiety" (5:2-4). The groaning and anxiety symbolize the great difference between the present earthly existence and future heavenly existence, to which Paul looks forward because of the eschatological hope. In 5:5, Paul argues that the basis of the hope is God, "who has prepared us for this very thing," and given the Spirit as a guarantee. The idea of a guarantee is a legal one and would seem to be most consistent with judicial rhetoric since Paul is attempting to prove that his eschatological hope, a "thing not seen," is not in vain.

The second part of this argument, 5:6-10, is extremely interesting. It is based on the previous argument that Paul has an eschatological hope. But in the argument in 5:6-10, Paul argues that he is in possession of the virtue of courage. The possession of this virtue has probative value, not only that Paul has the eschatological hope, but that also that Paul is especially commissioned by God. A reason for this courage is the γνῶσις ("knowledge," though the noun form is not used at 5:6) that Paul and his body are, in their present existence, away from the Lord. This is part of the presupposition of the virtue of courage. Another part is found in 5:8-9, where Paul admits that he would rather be at home with the God; however, since it is not God's will that Paul be in an absolutely fulfilled state of existence, Paul makes it his business to please the Lord (5:9). The gap between Paul's desire to be with the Lord and his present undesirable bodily state is filled by Paul's determination to please the Lord, wherever he finds himself. This very Stoic-sounding determination is a proof of Paul's possession of the virtue of courage. The combination of the eschatological hope and Paul's courage add up to a demonstration of Paul's commission by God. One can speculate here that this is very much in opposition to the theory of ministry of the super-apostles, who would speak of fulfillment in this left, with miracles and ecstatic utterances as proof of already being divine. This would be very much opposite what Paul argues, both in terms of the eschatological hope and in terms of the virtue of courage that Paul needs to keep going during a less-than-perfect present existence. But, if this prosecution of the super-apostles is being done, it is being done rather under the surface and by implication only. This, like many other features of the *probatio* of Letter E, points to a very subtle discourse of judicial rhetoric, and it is probably consistent with Paul's desire for reconciliation with the congregation, a reconciliation, which Paul presumably believes would not be furthered by using invective, as well deserved as it may have been! Paul vilifies here only by implication, by the comparisons, which his argument about his own ministry invites with the ministries of the super-apostles.

The most rhetorically complex argument, the fifth and final one, is found at 5:11-21. We believe that it relates to the phrase from the *partitio*, "in the sight of God we speak in Christ" (2:17). This argument is introduced by a three-part thesis in 5:11: "we persuade human beings," "but what we are is known to God," and "I hope it is also known to your conscience." The three arguments in this section of the proof, 5:12, 5:13-15, and 5:16-21 (note that each one is more complex and longer than the last) seem to relate to each part of the three-part thesis in order. The first argument in 5:12, based on "we persuade human beings" (which is to say, "we practice rhetoric"), is an explanation of Paul's use of rhetoric. Paul wishes to avoid the charge of self-commendation, so he argues that "we are not commending ourselves to you again" (*cf.* 3:1), adding that he is "giving you cause to be proud of us, so that you may be able to answer those who pride themselves on a person's position and not on that person's heart" (*cf.* 5:8-9). Thus, the reason for Paul's use of rhetorical technique in this and other letters, Paul says, is not Paul's ὕβρις but the ὕβρις of others! The old issue of the honor or dishonor of doing rhetoric, which antedates Socrates, remains in the background here. If Paul's rhetoric is thought to be in the least bit dishonorable, the reason for it is the Corinthians' ὕβρις ("but [we are] giving you cause to be *proud* of us") or the ὕβρις of the super-apostles ("so that you may be able to answer those who *pride* themselves on a man's position and not on his heart"), not Paul's, according to this proof. We suspect that this is an answer to a charge of pride on the part of the super-apostles concerning Paul. But we note that the prosecuting side of the rhetoric of this letter is only at the level of implication, since "those who pride themselves" are not positively identified by Paul. In the second argument, 5:13-15, which we believe relates to the portion of the thesis (5:12c), "what we are is known to God," Paul is here answering a charge that he has an unpredictable ministry, and that this reflects a lack of mental stability. This argument is stated by two conditionals, which may be paraphrased, "if we are acting crazy, it is because God has made us act this way; if we are in our right mind, it is for your sake" (5:13). Paul's suspect apostolic behavior is defended here according to traditions in Greek religion refer to divine inspiration as having the result of making the person so inspired, crazy.[10] Paul here explains his questionable behavior on the basis that "the love of Christ controls us" (5:14). This explained in a most interesting way by Paul's eschatological theory in 5:14-15. Paul reasons that since Christ died for all, all have therefore died; and this means that those who are (paradoxically) still alive must live for Christ and not for themselves. Thus, Paul argues, Christ controls his behavior because Paul has died to himself and lives only for Christ (*cf.* Gal 2:20). This therefore implies that to attack Paul's behavior is to attack Christ who controls Paul's behavior; and these would be very dangerous waters for any enemy of Paul to tread, since to attack Christ's control of Paul's behavior allowed the Corinthians to become Jesus-believers. A third argument in 5:16-21 is apparently based on 5:11d: "I hope [what we are] is also known to your conscience." This argument is based on the second argument that Paul has died, and so on. On the basis of Paul's death (to self), Paul now regards "no one from a human point of view" (5:16). Two *exempla* of this statement are given: Paul does not even regard Christ from a human point of view now, and "if anyone is in Christ, that person is a new creation" (5:17). The second *exemplum* has often been taken in an overly spiritualized sense.[11] In the context of this rather too subtle judicial piece, however, the "anyone" has a very subtly defiant tone to it that suggests the dichotomy found in the two kinds of people in 2:15-16, the people who are being saved *versus* the people who are perishing. Paul thus implies that the people who are attacking him and his behavior, which is controlled by Christ, are those who are perishing, since they persist in regarding Paul "from a human point of view." They are people who are not part of the new creation; for them the old has not passed away, nor has the new come. This being the case, their attack on Paul has no basis, since, not being controlled by Christ, they cannot rightly judge Paul who *is* controlled by Christ. But, sad to say, Paul does not state this directly; he only implies it. By the "anyone," Paul's audience is invited to act and to be part of the new creation, the transformed people, for whom indeed "the old has passed away; behold the new has come!" (5:17).

This leads very naturally into the topic of reconciliation, which concludes this proof. Since reconciliation is the overcoming of enmity, Paul's premise is that Christ exposed and overcame the war against God that was expressed in his crucifixion. Calvin Roetzel observes that in 5:21, Paul "recasts and even subverts the legitimacy of the powers that presided over Jesus' condemnation."[12] But rather than condemning these powers and the human race they represent, requiring them to make atonement, Christ died in their behalf to convey the divine reconciliation they could never have earned. As John Fitzgerald shows, "in contrast to the usual view that the offending party must take the first step toward peace, Paul makes 'God, the offended party, the one who takes the initiative in reconciliation.' "[13] The reconciliation that Christ conveys calls for overcoming the conflicts between Paul and his Corinthian adversaries. Not only is Paul's ministerial goal reconciliation; this is also God's task, which he undertook in the Christ-event. Thus, Paul's appeal for reconciliation is not on the basis of his desire alone; it is on the basis of his apostolic office: "So we are ambassadors for Christ, God making his appeal through us" (5:20a).[14] Thus, as a fully commissioned ambassador, for God through Christ controls his behavior, since Paul has died to self, the Apostle is in fact doing his duty when he appeals for reconciliation in 5:20b: "We beseech you on behalf of Christ, be reconciled to God." All this relates to the *partitio* phrase: "in the sight of God, we speak in Christ." Like other statements in the *partitio*, the full implication of this phrase of a few words can only be seen by working through the section of the *probatio* to which it points. Paul's behavior takes place "in the sight of God"; therefore it is blameless. What Paul means when he says "we speak in Christ" is that he speaks with Christ's authority, *cf.* 5.20.

THE *PERORATIO*

This subtly argued *probatio* is amplified further by the *peroratio*, 6:1-13 + 7:2-4. The address, "fellow workers," clearly presupposes the fifth proof and I take it to mean "fellow workers with Christ and/or God." The opening appeal is "not to receive the grace of God in vain," namely, to decide to support Paul's ministry now, rather than waiting to see its result at the Last Judgment. In the context of judicial rhetoric, this is reminiscent of appeals to the judge or jury to make a decision—the right decision—at this time.

The aspect of the *peroratio* that acts as *enumeratio* or *recapitulatio* is found in 6:3-10. The core of the *recapitulatio* is in the long lists of sufferings and antitheses in 6:4-10. These long lists are an exposition of "in every way" (ἐν παντὶ) in 6:4. The lists not only recall the idea of apostolic ministry as sacrifice as in the *exordium* in 2:15-16, but they are in themselves quite dramatic. The antithesis found in the *exordium* of the two kinds of people who perceive the smell of sacrifice differently is renewed and amplified here in the list of antitheses in 6:8-10. Just as the people who do not penetrate to the true meaning of the cult cannot perceive the smell of (presumably) the Apostle's life being offered up as a sacrifice to God, such people also cannot penetrate the mystery of the antitheses, perceiving only the bad things in the last and not the good things; for example, the enemies of Paul perceive only his dishonor and apparent punishment by God, rather than Paul's true honor and the fact that Paul remains alive. Also, the antitheses in 6:8-10 are a beautiful and powerful recapitulation of the topics of the proofs, namely honor (Paul's and the Corinthians'), impostors (i.e., who is a true apostle), ill repute ("what I am is known to God"), death (i.e., death to self and being thus controlled by Christ), and so on. The seventh, eighth, and ninth antitheses in 6:10 do not recapitulate what has gone on in the proof, but serve mainly to round out this impressive list, ending with "possessing everything" (πάντα), which forms a fine *inclusio* with "in every way" (ἐν παντὶ) in 6:4a. The emotional appeal is centered in the final few verses of the extant letter, 6:11-13 + 7:2-4, but it is also contained in the list of sufferings in 6:4b-5. It is reminiscent of the ends of speeches when the defendant is described in terms of how much he or she has suffered; the strong implication is that the people in power should do something to right the situation, namely to acquit the accused.[15] Nevertheless in this letter, Paul is not vindictive. Hence, he does not use *indignatio*, the part of *adfectus* in which the rhetor seeks to excite the emotions of the audience against his accusers.[16] Paul appeals for something much more profound: reconciliation with the Corinthians. This profundity is heightened by the fact that it is consistent with and actually echoes the last part of the fifth proof. The emotional appeal is a strong one in the very last two verses, 7:3-4: "I do not say this to condemn you," and "you are in our hearts, to die together and to live together."

This rhetorical analysis of the letter-fragment 2 Cor. 2:14–6:13 + 7:2-4 as reconstructed by Bornkamm[17] and others shows that this letter-fragment is understandable as a persuasive letter, with the exception of the epistolary prescript which is missing. Its topics, argumentation, and amplification are fully consistent with a situation in which Paul was defending himself from attack. It is also consistent with an historical reconstruction along the lines of Bornkamm, in that other letter fragments found in 2 Corinthians in all likelihood follow later in time than this letter-fragment. In particular, the appearance of Letter F (2 Cor. 10:1-13:13, with 1 Cor 9:1-18 spliced in), a highly sarcastic and bombastic tome, and then the letter of reconciliation (2 Cor. 1:1–2:13 + 7:5-16), is consistent with the historical reconstruction in which the opponents of Paul were quite successful in getting the upper hand in Corinth, until Paul's masterpiece of sarcasm, Letter F, was read. Only after their behavior had been corrected was it possible that a reconciliation might actually take place.[18] If this historical reconstruction is correct, and if our observations about the subtlety of the argumentation Letter E are correct, it appears that Letter E was entirely too subtle to do the job of converting the Corinthians away from their fascination with the super-apostles and to the style of belief and practice taught by their founding apostle, Paul. What was needed, unfortunately, was a sarcastic attack in kind in order to right the situation, which is exactly what we have in Letter F.

THE COHESIVENESS OF LETTER E

Our rhetorical analysis of Letter E confirms the basic rightness of the literary identification of 2 Cor 2:14–6:13 + 7:2-4 as an almost complete letter. Obviously the epistolary prescript is missing; however, from the thanksgiving prayer, which begins in 2:14 to the peroratio in 6:1-13 + 7:2-4, there is a cohesive persuasive discourse, a discourse which is different from 2 Cor 1:1–2:13 and from 7:5-16, and different as well from 2 Cor 10:1–13:13. This confirms the need for partitioning the canonical form of 2 Corinthians, for which we argue in chapter 2 of this book.

Particular points about the rhetoric of Letter E are of interest here. Very notably, there is a coherence between the topics introduced in what we have of the exordium, namely from the thanksgiving prayer onward, and the arguments in the probatio. What is recapitulated in the peroratio points the hearer or reader of this letter back to both the arguments in the probatio as well as their introduction in the exordium. One of the most important ways in which the coherence of the letter, as reconstructed here, is demonstrated is the subject of the irony of true apostleship. Instead of what the super-apostles argued, or would have argued, Paul writes of true apostles' lives being used up in the triumphal procession. Sacrificial ministry means being thought of as worthless by those who do not agree with Paul's kind of apostleship. Yet, as Paul argues, it is precisely the sacrificial nature of his apostleship that is its hallmark. The ministry of those who revel in their glory and demean Paul for his lack of glory is actually the kind of ministry for which neither God nor the community of Jesus-believers have any use. Indeed Letter E argues that there are two kinds of people who see and smell the sacrifice of Paul's life. The two kinds of people see and smell the same thing, yet they perceive it differently. The hearers and readers are offered the chance to decide for Paul's kind of apostolic ministry, or that of his opponents. Paul defends his ministry, not least by comparing his ministry to that of his opponents. Those who heard and/or read this letter in the first century—with the original epistolary prescript and epistolary postscript, which we now do not have—were given the opportunity to decide the case. Yet it was not just about Paul and his ministry as an apostle; it was even more about what it is to be a Jesus-believer and what a congregation of such believers should be like, and what kind of leadership was needed to guide the church in the right direction. The opponents of Paul assuredly had their answer, and Paul had his. So a decision was needed, and Paul was putting the alternatives sharply in the face of the Corinthian church.

As far as we can read the evidence, Letter E as a document of rhetoric was very well crafted, as letters were understood to be, in the middle of the first century. Despite Paul's admired skill in dictating letters, this letter did not have the desired effect. After Paul dictated and sent this letter, he somehow got word that the Corinthians were still divided, for and especially against Paul as their apostle. Hence, the next act in the drama of this congregation's history, it appears, was that Paul made a second visit to the congregation. We will deal with that visit in chapter 11 of this book.

The Rhetorical Arrangement of Letter E

(2 Cor.)	
	I. *Exordium*
(Missing)	(A. Epistolary prescript)
2:14-16b	B. Thanksgiving prayer
2:14	1. Object of thanksgiving: God who acts "in Christ"
	2. Aretology, celebrating the actions of God
	a. Specification of activity: God "leads in triumph"
	b. Means of triumph: spreading the "fragrance" of divine knowledge through the Pauline mission
2:15	3. Explanation of the triumph
	a. The Pauline mission as "the aroma of Christ"
	b. Opposing perceptions of the aroma
	i. Among the "saved"
	ii. Among the "perishing"
2:16a-b	c. The Impact of the aroma
	i. "Death" to those who reject the gospel
	ii. "Life" to those who accept the gospel
2:16c-17	II. *Partitio*
2:16c	A. * Introductory rhetorical question: "who is sufficient" to participate in this mission of life and death?
2:17	B. Paul's propositions concerning himself
	1. *** Stated negatively: "For we are not, like so many, peddlers of God's word"
	2. Stated positively:
	a. ** With reference to integrity: "men of sincerity"
	b. **** With reference to authorization: "commissioned by God"
	c. ***** With reference to accountability: we proclaim Christ "in the sight of God"

3:1–5:21	III. *Probatio*	
3:1-6	A. First proof: that Paul's ministry is "sufficient"*	
3:7-18	B. Second proof: that Paul ministers "with unveiled face"**	
4:1-15	C. Third proof: that Paul is honorable in not preaching "ourselves"***	
4:16–5:10	D. Fourth proof: that Paul "walks by faith and not by sight" in fulfilling his commission****	
5:11-21	E. Fifth proof: that Paul's "ministry of reconciliation" is accountable*****	
6:1-13 + 7:2-4	IV. *Peroratio*	
6:1-2	A. Exhortation: do not receive the grace of God in vain	
6:3-10	B. Recapitulation: the true understanding of apostolic ministry	
6:11-13 + 7:2-4	C. *Adfectus*: an appeal to the emotions to decide in favor of Paul (i.e.. be reconciled to Paul)	
(Missing)	D. (Epistolary postscript)	

(* The asterisks in the five parts of the probatio correspond to the asterisks in the partitio. E.g., the question in 2:16c, "Who is sufficient?" corresponds to 3:1-6.)

THE GENUS OF LETTER E

Letter E is a restrained and elegant example of a persuasive self-defense of Paul. Its arguments are serious, but they are not overdone. Letter E is an example of the *genus* of judicial or forensic rhetoric.

NOTES

1. Paul had referred in 1 Cor 16:7, at the end of Letter C written in the summer of 54, to his plan to depart from Ephesus after Pentecost.
2. Paul B. Duff, *Moses in Corinth: The Apologetic Context of 2 Corinthians 3*, NovTSup 159 (Leiden and Boston: Brill, 2015), argues, especially in pp. 102–17, that the context of Paul's argument about letters of recommendation was that Paul was asked by his Corinthian church members for such letters. Duff argues that Paul's treatment of letters of recommendation in 2 Cor 2:14–6:13 + 7:2-4 does not require that there were invading missionaries or opponents. It is clear that the issue of such

letters was an issue that Paul did not invent. It would not have been to his rhetorical advantage to do so. In the present study, we argue that Letter E is a letter of defense, and the way the rhetoric works is that Paul argues that his ministry was fully valid without such letters—valid enough to convert most if not all of the Corinthian believers. Paul has no such letters because Paul does not need them. It is difficult to see why Corinthian Jesus-believers would ask Paul for recommendation letters if other apostles did not possess such letters. It is interesting to speculate who would have written letters of recommendation that Paul's opponents might carry. Given the interest in Moses's ministry in Letter E, the opponents' letters might well have included a written guarantee of the opponents' fidelity to Torah observance or their consistency with the dominant view in Jewish congregations, or their consistency with what well known apostles like Peter and James taught. Also in Letter E, Paul argues in 5:16 that he does not have and, more importantly, does not need a connection with the human Jesus before his death and resurrection, in order to be considered a genuine apostle, since "we know [Jesus] in this way no longer."

3. Duff, *Moses in Corinth*, argues that the "harsh, admonitory language in 1 Corinthians" (72) was responsible for Paul's need to make a defense in 2 Cor 2:14–6:13 + 7:2-4. Paul thought that 1 Corinthians was Paul's effort to bring about unity, but this effort at unity backfired when Paul later wrote 2 Corinthians 8. "Instead, Paul's aggressive pursuit of the collection for the Jerusalem church caused another flare-up of anger and resentment directed against Paul. . . . By sending the letter now found in 2 Corinthians 8, Paul inadvertently provided just the ammunition that Paul's opponents needed. With the arrival of the letter—an appeal that strongly encouraged the Corinthians complete the collection—it seems that the tide of Corinthian opinion began to turn against Paul. This was primarily because Paul had unilaterally changed the plans for the collection's delivery" (211). Thus Paul's need to defend himself, Duff holds, was primarily due to what Paul had done in his handling of the Corinthian church by long distance, rather than primarily due to the coming of outside opponents into the Corinthian congregation who unilaterally stirred up opposition to Paul.

4. One important interpretive question is whether the procession that Paul writes about is that of a triumphal procession (implying the meaning that Paul and other apostles are being compared with those who were defeated in battle), or whether the kind of procession Paul refers to was a procession that was more generally a religious procession. On the meaning of θριαμβεύειν see the recent monograph by Christoph Heilig, *Reassessing 2 Corinthians 2:14 in its Literary and Historical Context*, BTS 27 (Leuven: Peeters, 2017), especially 32–74. Based on a wide-ranging literary and historical analysis of that verb and its usage, Heilig argues that the primary meaning of the metaphor was military rather than religious. On the relation between the military and religious metaphors, see especially Paul Brooks Duff, "Metaphor, Motif, and Meaning: The Rhetorical Strategy behind the Image 'Led in Triumph' in 2 Corinthians 2:14," *CBQ* 53 (1991): 79–92. Very importantly, Duff shows how the motif, including both the military and the cultic meanings of θριαμβεύειν, become part of Paul's rhetorical strategy in this letter, 2 Cor 2:14–6:14 + 7:2-4. See also Duff's article, "Apostolic Suffering and the Language of Processions in 2 Corinthians

4:7-10," *BTB* 21 (1992): 158–65, in which Duff gives further parallels to epiphany processions in the Greco-Roman world, as well as Duff, *Moses in Corinth*, 93–98.

5. Duff, "Apostolic Suffering," 159–60.

6. If 2 Cor 2:17 were the answer to the question of 2:16c, this would mean that Paul suggested that nobody was "competent" or "sufficient" for ministry to and among Jesus-believers, which is something that Paul was unlikely to argue. More likely is the interpretation that Paul understands himself to be competent and that he understands his opponents to be incompetent. On the question and answer, Rudolf Bultmann in his *The Second Letter to the Corinthians*, edited by Erich Dinkler and translated by Roy A. Harrisville (Minneapolis: Augsburg, 1985), 69, commented: "The question certainly means, 'Who can be such a bearer of the Word, or how can I be such a bearer?' Thus the answer in verse 17 . . . which does not enumerate the qualities required but is rather a confession. But the question is clearly occasioned by the fact that at Corinth Paul's ἱκανότης was contested, as 3:1ff. and particularly 3:5f. indicate, and, of course, as the polemic in verse 17 already shows." Furnish also affirms that the style "abruptly changes" from 2:16a to 2:16b (*II Corinthians*, 190).

7. The understanding of Paul's Corinthian opponents as having a "divine man" type of Christology is well argued by Dieter Georgi in *The Opponents of Paul in Second Corinthians* (Philadelphia: Fortress Press, 1986). On the understanding of the category of "divine man" in general, see Hans Dieter Betz, "Gottmensch II (Griechische-römische Antike und Urchristentum)," in *RAC* 12: 234–312, as well as David L. Tiede, *The Charismatic Figure as Miracle Worker*, SBLDS 1 (Missoula: Scholars Press, 1972), and Carl H. Holladay, *Theios Aner in Hellenistic-Judaism: A Critique of the Use of This Category in New Testament Christology*, SBLDS 40 (Missoula: Scholars Press, 1977).

8. On the self-understanding of Paul's opponents, see especially Georgi, *Opponents*, 229–313.

9. On the issue of the letters of recommendation in 2 Corinthians, see Georgi, *Opponents*, 242–44.

10. See E. R. Dodds, *The Greeks and the Irrational* (Berkeley: University of California Press, 1966).

11. Against an overly spiritualized interpretation of this verse Bultmann comments: "The ἐν Χριστῷ is thus not a formula of mysticism, but rather of eschatology, or it has an eschatological-ecclesiological sense. But along with that the ἐν Χριστῷ marks the believers' new life as an existence which is eschatologically determined. And this eschatological existence is described as a καινὴ κτίσις" (Bultmann, *Second Letter to the Corinthians*, 157).

12. Roetzel, *2 Corinthians*, 83.

13. John T. Fitzgerald, "Paul and Paradigm Shifts: Reconciliation and Its Linkage Group," in *Cracks in an Earthen Vessel*, 253.

14. On Paul's self-understanding as an ambassador, see Robert Jewett, "Romans as an Ambassadorial Letter," *Int* 36 (1982): 5–20. Bultmann, *Second Letter to the Corinthians*, 163–64, comments on 2 Cor. 5:20: "As Christ's messenger and representative, the apostle is also God's messenger and representative, and his labor as διάκονος τῆς καταλλαγῆς belongs to the work of atonement itself. . . . Verse 20 is

thus the most intense expression of Paul's παρρησία, and the οὖν corresponds exactly to the conclusions drawn in 3:12; 4:1, 16; 5:6 and 11."

15. Cicero, *De inventione* 1.106-107.

16. Cicero, *De inventione* 1.100.

17. See Bornkamm, "Vorgeschichte" (reprint in *Geschichte und Glaube II*), 177–78, as well as Bornkamm, *Paul* (New York: Harper & Row, 1971), 244–46.

18. Compare 2 Cor. 13:2 ("if I come again I will not spare them—since you desire proof that Christ is speaking in me!") with the results of the severe letter reported by Paul in the letter of reconciliation in 2 Cor. 7:7f, ("[Titus] telling us of your longing for us, how sorry you are, your zeal for me, so that I was greatly cheered. Because if I caused you pain by letter, I do not regret it.").

Chapter 10

Letter F

Anguish of Heart and Many Tears (2 Cor 10:1–11:9 + 1 Cor 9:1-18 + 2 Cor 11:10-13:13)

AN OVERVIEW OF THE SCHOLARLY DEBATE

The modern scholarly debate[1] on 2 Cor 10-13 began in 1776 with the work of J. S. Semler, who first suggested that chapters 10–13 were in actuality a separate letter from chapters 1–9. This thesis was refined in 1870 in the work of Adolf Hausrath, whose pamphlet *Der Vier-Capitelbrief des Paulus an die Korinther*[2] focused on the profound difference in tone between chapters 1–9 and 10–13. The classic Meyer-Kommentar of Hans Windisch published in 1924 and reprinted in 1970, *Der zweite Korintherbrief*,[3] was based on a partition theory separating 1–9 from 10–13, with chapters 1–7 being separated from chapters 8 and 9 as well. A consensus among Pauline specialists began to grow with the famous article of Günther Bornkamm in 1961, which argued that 2 Cor 1:1–2:13 belonged with 7:2 and what followed it, and that 2:14–6:13 was a separate letter from this.[4] The fragment 6:14–7:1 was argued by Hans Dieter Betz to be an "anti-Pauline fragment,"[5] with its theology generally understood as the polar opposite to the theology of Galatians. Bornkamm's theory enjoys a great deal of acceptance among New Testament scholars, though there is no consensus as to the provenance of 2 Cor 6:14–7:1. The partition theories of Windisch were essentially accepted by Rudolf Bultmann in his incomplete lecture notes on 2 Corinthians, published as a successor to Windisch's Meyer-Kommentar, though made available in English translation in 1985.[6] The partition theory of Bornkamm is likewise accepted in Francis T. Fallon's small commentary of 1980.[7] The detailed Anchor Bible commentary published in 1984 by Victor Paul Furnish clearly accepted 2 Cor 10-13 as a letter separate from 2 Cor 1-9.[8]

The question of who the Corinthian opponents of Paul were has received much attention, largely due to the work of Dieter Georgi and those who have responded to him. Georgi argued in 1964 (English translation 1986[9]) that the opponents of Paul in Corinth understood themselves to be θεῖοι ἄνδρες ("divine men") whose propaganda was that Paul was not a true apostle because of his lack of miracles and other enthusiastic phenomena, along with what was argued to be his poor ability at oral rhetoric.

Although Betz had argued in his 1972 monograph *Der Apostel Paulus und die sokratische Tradition: Eine exegetische Untersuchung zu einer "Apologie" 2 Korinther 10-13*[10] that 2 Cor 10-13 was Paul's ἀπολογία (defense), very much in the tradition of other ἀπολογίαι from the Greek world, and that Paul quite consciously used sarcasm and bombast in this ἀπολογία, Betz did not provide an overall rhetorical analysis as he did for his commentary on Galatians seven years later. This study will provide such an analysis of 2 Cor 10:1–13:13, with the letter fragment 1 Cor 9:1-18 interposed between 2 Cor 11:9 and 11:10. This study, therefore, is the first attempt to explain the rhetoric of Letter F, as reconstructed in the Jewett-Hughes hypothesis.

THE PROVENANCE OF LETTER F

A short time after sending Letter E, Paul visited Corinth in a vain effort to resolve the conflict. This probably occurred in the mid-summer of 55. There is a reference to this "painful visit" (2 Cor 2:1) in Letter G, written a year later in the summer of 56. In Letter G, he declares that he had decided not to make another such visit that might cause further injuries both to Paul and the congregation (2 Cor 7:9). The visiting evangelists had encouraged one of the Corinthian leaders, most likely Gaius,[11] to denounce Paul in an open meeting. When the congregation failed to defend him against these allegations, Paul was bitterly humiliated (2 Cor 12:20-21) and driven into a deep depression (2 Cor 2:13; 7:5-6) that was not relieved until he met Titus in Macedonia a year later with news about reconciliation.[12]

Soon after Paul returned from the painful visit in the late summer or fall of 55, he wrote Letter F, the so-called four-chapter letter, containing 2 Cor 10-13 and some additional material. There are no explicit indications about where this dictation occurred, but in view of the fact that Paul was unable to return to Ephesus,[13] he was probably elsewhere in Asia or in Macedonia. In Calvin Roetzel's summary, Paul sent this "Letter of Tears" (2 Cor 2:4) with Titus "in the hope that he [Titus] could right the floundering mission and restore confidence in his ministry."[14] Since the exordium of this letter was removed by the redactor, the argument starts with an agitated defense of his ministry and a critique of the super-apostles in 10:1-18. While Paul refrains from boasting because it violates the gospel, they boast "beyond limits" (10:14-16) and violate boundaries by invading Paul's missionary sphere.

This is followed by a bitterly sarcastic "fool's speech" in 11:1–12:13 in which Paul foolishly boasts about every detail that the super-apostles have criticized to show that they are the real fools. As L. L. Welborn shows on the basis of classical parallels, the fool's speech enabled Paul "to speak the truth, laughingly."[15] The premise of this brilliant speech is that only fools boast, so that the very act of boasting reveals that the super-apostles are proclaiming "another Jesus" and "another gospel" (11:4). With regard to the criticism that Paul refrained from accepting remuneration from the Corinthians while accepting help from other congregations, he sarcastically apologizes for preaching "free of charge" (11:7), in obvious contrast to the super-apostles. This leads to the extensive discussion of Paul's renunciation of his right to remuneration that is explained by our reconstruction of 1 Cor 9:1-18 as part of the Letter of Tears.

There are significant details in the awkward transition between 2 Cor 11:9 and 10 that reveal the redactor's hand. In verse 10, there is a reference to "this boast" (ἡ καύχησις αὕτη) that Paul will not silence, but the antecedent reference to "this" is missing; the last explicit reference to boasting was back in 10:17 and has nothing to do with remuneration. Commentators make various suggestions about this missing antecedent,[16] attempting to supply what is missing in the Greek text, but the grammatical and literary problem remains. The material that we believe was deleted from 2 Cor 11 contains the missing references: with regard to Paul's renunciation of his apostolic right, "no one is going to take away my boast" (1 Cor 9:15). The term "καύχημα" ("boast") appears in the following verse and the word "reward" appears in 9:17 and 18 to express the properly eschatological alternative to boasting.

There is also a serious discrepancy in tone between 2 Cor 11:9 and 10. The former is a calm report about the Macedonians who supplied Paul's needs in Corinth, ending with the declaration that he would not consent to being a burden to the Corinthians. The style is that of *narratio*, objectively stating the facts of the case. The following verse has a sharply defensive tone, beginning with an oath: "as surely as the truth of Christ is in me,"[17] Paul's boast will not be silenced. In this verse, Paul is defending himself, supported by the most powerful means, namely Christ himself.[18]

When the material from 1 Cor 9:1-18 is restored between 2 Cor 11:9 and 10, the four rhetorical questions requiring the answer "yes" in 1 Cor 9:1 interrogate the Corinthian audience as courtroom witnesses,[19] forcing them to recognize the absurdity of the accusations concerning receiving help from the Macedonians. Paul's aim is to restore his relationship as the apostle to the Corinthians, as 9:2 continues, "If to others I am not an apostle, in fact to you I am. For you are the seal of my apostleship in the Lord." There are smooth transitions on both ends of the material that the redactor deleted from Letter F. In 2 Cor 11:9, Paul was explaining why he would continue to renounce remuneration, and in 1 Cor 9:1, he asks whether he does not have the freedom to make such a decision, while denying that his critics were right in claiming that his behavior demonstrated a lack of apostolic authority. In 2 Cor 11:10, Paul continues the theme of retaining the boast of renouncing remuneration in 1 Cor 9:18. Here are the two transitions that were disturbed by the redactor: from 2 Cor 11:9 to 1 Cor 9:1 and from 1 Cor 9:15 + 18 to 2 Cor 11:10

> in every way I kept myself from being a burden to you, and I will continue to refrain [from being a burden]. Am I not free? Am I not an apostle? Have I not seen Jesus our Lord? Are not you my work in the Lord?
> . . . .
> No one is going to take away my boast. . . . And so what is my reward? That I may present the gospel free of charge so as to make full use of my authority in the gospel. It is the truth of Christ in me that this boast will not be silenced for me in the regions of Achaia.

When the transition to 2 Cor 11:10 is restored, a strengthened case can be made that verse 12 is not the beginning of a new paragraph as some commentators contend.[20] The antecedent to Ὁ δὲ ποιῶ ("but what I am doing") is preaching the gospel free of charge (1 Cor 9:15-18). Paul continues on until 2 Cor 11:15 to accuse those making such perverse allegations as false apostles.

In 2 Cor 11:16–12:13, Paul again plays the fool to show that he can surpass the false claims of the super-apostles. As Calvin Roetzel observes, "Miming the fool, Paul builds a grotesque parody of boasting" as he brags about the tribulations of his ministry.[21] He ironically boasts about his visions and the unresolved thorn in the flesh to remind the Corinthians that in contrast to the super-apostles' triumphalism, "divine grace and the power of Christ manifest themselves in weakness" (2 Cor 12:9).[22] The fool's speech ends with a postscript in 2 Cor 12:11-13 where Paul reiterates that "his weakness in no sense made him inferior to the 'superapostles.' "[23] The letter ends in 12:14–13:10 by admonishing the audience to come to its senses before Paul is forced to come to Corinth as an agent of the "power of God" in punishing evildoers (2 Cor 13:4, 10). He hopes he can come for "building up and not for tearing down" (2 Cor 13:10; cf. 12:19). As Ralph Martin observes, "We will miss the true motivation behind Paul's writing of chaps. 10-13 if we fail to see that he wished to avoid stern action against the Corinthians. Instead, Paul's goal is that chaps. 10-13 will lead the Corinthians to see that they are wrong, and in turn will lead them to repent and accept Paul's ministry and message. If this change would occur, then the apostle would be satisfied."[24]

THE RHETORIC OF LETTER F

Among the standard *genera* of rhetoric (epideictic, deliberative, and judicial), it seems clear that Letter F is an example of judicial rhetoric. In this reconstructed letter, Paul defends himself against his opponents rather less than he prosecutes both his opponents and his Corinthian converts for accepting the arguments of his opponents.

Normally in Pauline letters, the *exordium* includes the epistolary prescript and the thanksgiving prayer, but sadly the *exordium* has been lost in the redactional process that created the canonical 1 and 2 Corinthians. The *probatio* or proofs are extant, and their intent and form are clear: the defense of Paul and the prosecution of Paul's detractors. The *probatio* is in two parts; the first part is 2 Cor 10:1-18, which includes material, which defends the past conduct and the apostolic status of Paul, as well as material, which compares the apostolic ministry of Paul to his opponents. Most interestingly, in 10:10, the slogan what the opponents used to attack Paul's rhetoric has been preserved. Paul quotes it to refute it. Although his letters are quite rightly conceded to be "weighty and strong" (i.e., persuasive), his personal appearance is that of weakness, and his λόγος (oral rhetoric) is "despicable." Paul, like other rhetorical writers, concedes that his public delivery is poor (2 Cor 10:11), though he insists that he is consistent with it "in deed."

The first part of the *probatio* concludes with a comparison of Paul to his opponents. Can we conclude here that Paul has been accused of "overextending" himself through his long-distance missionary work (2 Cor 10:14-17)? If so, Paul protests that his supposed overextension did in fact include the initial conversion of the Corinthians and the founding of their church. Probably against the charge of Paul's opponents that Paul brings no letters of recommendation around to prove his apostolic authenticity (2 Cor 10:10, cf. 2 Cor 3:1-3), Paul replies that self-commendation is of no avail compared with divine commendation.

The second part of the *probatio* is the "foolish discourse" or "fool's speech" in which Paul intentionally plays the role of the fool who is really wise. Betz has pointed out the important parallels between Paul here and the Socratic ἔλεγχος (perhaps best translated as "refutation") in his 1972 monograph. Paul goes to great lengths to justify his speaking as a fool in this proof (2 Cor 11:1-14), even commanding his readers to bear with his foolish talk (2 Cor 11:1b). One reason that his readers should bear with his foolish talk is their past unfaithfulness, culminating in the fact that they have received "another gospel" than the one Paul preached to them; they are compared to the mother of all sin, Eve, whom the serpent beguiled. This implies that the "beguiling" that the Corinthian opponents of Paul have done to the Corinthians is like the "beguiling" that the talking serpent did to Eve in the Garden of Eden (2 Cor 11:3-4), which probably invites the comparison of the Corinthian opponents with Satan (cf. 2 Cor 11:13-15; 12:7).

The first argument proper of the second proof includes a defense by Paul against the charge that he is not an authentic apostle, charges made by the "super-apostles," as Paul quite sarcastically refers to them in 2 Cor 11:5. These charges seem to include the charge that Paul is not a polished preacher (11:6; cf. 10:10), which Paul concedes, although he points out that he is not a "layman" (ἰδιώτης) in γνῶσις. Another charge against Paul is clearly that he is not an authentic apostle because he does not receive financial support from the Corinthians. Paul launches into an extended tirade based on the allegation that he had a perfect right to receive financial support from all his congregations (as he did from his Macedonian congregations, 2 Cor 11:9), but that in Corinth, he intentionally chose not to receive any financial support. According to our partition theory, we read 1 Cor 9:1-18 between 2 Cor 11:9 and 11:10, and when we do so, we have more apologetic material on exactly the same subject from Paul himself in 1 Cor 9.

THE PROBLEM OF 9:1-18

One of the major problems of identifying 9:1-18 as a *digressio* is the fact that its content is clearly judicial: the defense of Paul's right to church support of his lifestyle, and the obvious comparison of his apostolic rights to the rights of other apostles. According to rules of Latin rhetoric, however, the *digressio* was to have the content of "epideiktische Beschreibung" or that of a "Sondernarratio."[25] The apparently related term "transitus" appears to be related to the *narratio*.[26] The material in 1 Cor 9:1-18, because its rhetorical genus is judicial, can be understood in the context of 1 Cor 9:19-24 only with difficulty. "For being free from all myself...." in 1 Cor 9:24 can be seen as either an editorial interpolation by the late first-century editor of the Corinthian correspondence, or as having been in Corinthian Letter C in the first place, so that this was the reason why 1 Cor 9:1-18 was put there in the canonical form of the Corinthian letters. In the context of Letter F, however, 1 Cor 9:1-18 has a clear rhetorical purpose: to justify Paul's practice of not accepting money from the Corinthians because of his voluntarily declining to exercise what was his prerogative, "not making full use of my right in the gospel" (1 Cor 9:18), so that no "obstacle" could be put in the way of the Corinthians' accepting the gospel (1 Cor 9:12b).

1 Cor 9:1-18 fits very well in Letter F for a further rhetorical reason: to insist on one's right to financial support and then to decline to accept this support is quite a foolish thing to do. Therefore, the "foolish discourse" of Paul includes not only his repeated boasting and his later description of a

heavenly journey, most notably without an accompanying transcript of divine revelations (2 Cor 12:2-5), as well as his boast about the fact that his apostolic prayer for a personal healing miracle was intentionally not answered by God (2 Cor 12:7-10), but also includes his insistent demand for a right of which he pointedly does not make use!

After comparing his opponents with Satan in 2 Cor 11:13-15, Paul accuses the Corinthians of already putting up with fools, that is, his opponents (2 Cor 11:19), and we have an interesting list of things Paul says his opponents do to the Corinthians in 11:20. They "consume" the Corinthians (apparently referring to their practice of accepting support), in contrast to Paul's practice), and they "take advantage of" them and "enslave" them as well. Paul goes so far as to say that his Corinthian opponents "hit you in the face," and yet the captive, gullible Corinthians "bear with it gladly" (2 Cor 11:19-20). Apparently the Corinthian opponents had a kind of mesmerizing effect on the Corinthians, in great contrast with Paul's poor oral delivery and his difficult-to-understand letters.

The fourth argument of the second proof shows Paul answering charges against his authenticity as an apostle point by point. Paul claims his Jewish heritage, as well as the fact that he is a διάκονος (apparently an honorable title in Pauline communities from earliest times; cf. 1 Cor 3). This is not particularly foolish. When Paul, however, brings his long list of sufferings as proof of his authenticity, this is both foolish and in accord with traditions of judicial rhetoric attested in Latin rhetoric as far back as Cicero.[27] In judicial rhetoric, it was often the case that the advocate would plead to the judge for mercy based on the sufferings that the accused had received (or that the accused had caused, if the advocate was prosecuting), and here Paul pulls out all the stops in 2 Cor 11:24-29. Significantly, one of the climaxes of this long list of sufferings is his "daily concern for all the churches" (2 Cor 11:29), to which obviously the Corinthians and the opponents of Paul were contributing heavily. In rhetorical perspective, the fact that Paul makes a *tour de force* of his boast of weakness is definitely because of the Corinthian slogan preserved in 2 Cor 10:10 that his "physical presence is weak." In other words, Paul makes the Corinthian accusation into a kind of justification through the prolific use of *exempla* of suffering. This shows a kind of brilliance in rhetorical skill that one does not read every day in either the modern world or the literature of antiquity.

The foolish discourse concludes with an extreme example of the use of sarcasm in 12:1-3. Probably against the Corinthian opponents who claim frequent divine visions and heavenly journeys, Paul boasts about "a man in Christ" (meaning none other than himself) whom, for reasons of modesty, he declines to name in this verse. This heavenly journey, perhaps quite unlike heavenly journeys reported by the Corinthian opponents, included revelations and visions that were so holy that they could not be told, which shows a kind of sarcastic one-upmanship, which Paul is using against his opponents. The final and most devastating example of sarcasm is in 2 Cor 12:7-10, where—apparently as a spoof of the Corinthian opponents who claim dramatic healing miracles—Paul says that he was given a "thorn in the flesh" so that he should not become too elated by heavenly visions (2 Cor 12:7), obviously referring to the heavenly vision of the "man in Christ" of 2 Cor 12:2-5. In order to combat the Corinthian opponents who very likely claim knowledge and mastery of divine things, and who may well pride themselves in the excellence of their physical bodies, Paul tells us that he prayed "three times" to God, asking that the "thorn in the flesh" be taken away. God's answer to this request for the healing miracle was that no such miracle would happen, because God chose to perfect his power in weakness (2 Cor 12:9), and that "my grace is sufficient for you"! Paul sarcastically concluded that his weakness meant real strength in 12:10.

Although the second proof is not completed until 2 Cor 12:13, Paul decisively shifts from foolish talk in 12:11, saying, "I am not in any respect inferior to these super-apostles, even though I am nothing!" which implies that, in Paul's estimation, the super-apostles are actually less than nothing.

In the third and final proof in 2 Cor 12:14–13:10, Paul warns of his impending visit, in which his severity will be unmatched, "since you desire proof that Christ is speaking in me!" Paul will, in his third visit, become severe, rather as he accuses the Corinthian opponents of being at all times (cf. 2 Cor 11:20).

CONCLUSION

Paul's polemical rhetoric in Letter F seems to be unmatched anywhere in the first two centuries of the writings of Jesus-believing communities, except perhaps the biting sarcasm of Tertullian's *Apologeticum*. As far as letters go, it seems that Paul may well have written this most weighty and strong of his letters in order to counter his opponents whose oral rhetoric had already decisively persuaded Paul's most problematic congregation. If the Jewett-Hughes partition theory is correct, Letter G (2 Cor 1:1-2:13 + 7:5-16 + 13:11-13) shows that reconciliation took place after Letter F had been received. In Letter G, Paul refers to an earlier letter, which caused pain to the Corinthians, but of this Paul is not in the least ashamed (2 Cor 7:8). We conclude, as other scholars have, that this painful letter was probably none other than the caustic Letter F, whose rhetoric we have described here.

We conclude here with a few notes on rhetoric and rhetorical criticism of this letter. If rhetoric exaggeration is present in Letter F (as we argue that it is), it would never be to the advantage of a persuasive writer to exaggerate the charges against himself, which means that we should have good confidence in the reconstruction of the charges against Paul in Corinth. A competent rhetor would never seriously defend himself against charges that had not been leveled at himself, and a competent rhetor would never make up the charges preserved in 2 Cor 10:10. Thus, rhetorical criticism represents a real advance over other types of criticism, because it can creatively combine a kind of literary analysis with an analysis of the audience situation or *Sitz im Leben*, which evoked the rhetoric.[28]

A final conclusion of our analysis of Letter F is that it provides an interesting confirmation of the work of the oldest rhetorical critic within Jesus-believing communities, namely St. Augustine of Hippo. In *De doctrina christiana*, book 4, Augustine identified the rhetoric of Paul in 2 Corinthians as being a refutation of "certain persons, pseudo-apostles from among the Jews," who had attacked him.[29] Augustine goes on in the same work to tell his readers that Paul's rhetoric represents a marriage of *sapientia* and *eloquentia*,[30] which we should understand, following Cicero,[31] as Augustine's saying that St. Paul's rhetoric here was both ideal and exemplary. With his Roman rhetorical education and his experience as a teacher of rhetoric, Augustine was fully capable of identifying St. Paul's refutation of opponents when he read it in 2 Corinthians.

The Rhetorical Arrangement of Corinthian Letter F

(Missing)	(I. *Exordium*)
2 Cor 10:1 11:9; 1 Cor 9:1-18; 2 Cor 11:10– 13:10	II. *Probatio*
2 Cor 10:1-18	A. First proof: the defense of Paul

10:1
10:1
	1. Presuppositions
	   a) Address
	      i) Statement of address
	      ii) Basis for address: "courtesy and gentleness of Christ"
	      iii) *Ethos* of sender
	         (A) When present: humble
	         (B) When absent: bold

10:2-6
 	
10:2
 	
10:3-4
	b) Request: not to be forced to be bold "with those who consider that we act according to the flesh"
	      i) Statement of request (based on false understanding of Paul's behavior)
	      ii) Reason for request: Paul's true behavior
	         (A) Behavior in general

10:3		(1) Stated negatively: οὐ κατὰ σάρκα στρατευόμεθα
10:4		(2) Stated negatively: οὐ σαρκικὰ
		(3) Stated positively: ἀλλὰ δυνατὰ τῷ θεῷ
10:4-6		(B) Behavior in particular
10:4		(1) With regard to strongholds: "we tear down"
		(2) With regard to reasonings: "we tear down"
10:5		(3) With regard to "heights raised up against the knowledge of God": "we tear down"
10:6		(4) With regard to thoughts: "we take captive"
		(5) With regard to disobedience: "we are prepared to punish"
10:7		c) Command: "Pay attention to what is in front of your face!"
10:8-21		2. First argument: Paul's defense
10:8		a) Paul's status as a fellow Jesus-believer
		b) Paul's apostolic authority
		i) Statement as conditional boast
		ii) Purpose of authority: "to build up and not to tear down"
		iii) Fulfillment of conditional boast: "I would not be ashamed"
10:9-11		c) Paul's status as a rhetor
10:9		i) Transition from previous section: "Lest I might seem to scare you through letters"
10:10		ii) Rehearsal of the Corinthian slogan concerning Paul
		(A) Quotation formula: "For they say"
		(B) Quotation
		(1) With regard to written rhetoric
		(2) With regard to oral rhetoric
10:11		iii) Paul's response to the slogan
10:12-18		3. Second argument: comparison of Paul to his opponents
10:12a		a) Statement of comparison (stated negatively: "We do not have the audacity to compare ourselves with certain persons who recommend themselves")
10:12b		b) Activities of Paul's opponents
		i) Statement of activities: false comparisons
		ii) Paul's judgment on false comparisons
10:13		c) Activities of Paul
		i) Boasting
		(A) Statement of activity
		(B) Justification of activity
		(1) Negatively: "not beyond the proper limit"
		(2) Positively: "in accord with the measure of the jurisdiction which God has apportioned out"

Letter F

10:14	ii) "Reaching"
	(A) Statement of activity
	(B) Justification of activity: "we reached as far as you with the gospel of Christ"
10:15-17	iii) Further justification of activities
10:15	(A) Of boasting (negatively)
10:16	(B) Of "reaching"(stated as future hope)
10:17	(C) Of boasting(stated with quotation of Jeremiah 9:24)
10:18	d) Summary of argument
	i) Stated negatively: "For the one approved is not the one who recommends himself"
	ii) Stated positively: "but the one whom the Lord recommends"
2 Cor 11:1-9; 1 Cor 9:1-18; 2 Cor 11:10–13:10	B. The foolish discourse
2 Cor 11:1-4	1. Presupposition: justification of speaking as a fool
11:1a	a) Request to bear with Paul
11:1b	b) Command to bear with Paul: "In fact, do put up with me!"
11:2-4	c) Justification of the request to bear with Paul
11:2	i) First justification: Paul's love for the readers
11:3-4	(A) Statement of Paul's love
	(B) Result of love: "I betrothed you to one man"(Christ)
	(C) Purpose of Paul's love: eschatological hope
11:3-4	ii) Second justification: the readers' unfaithfulness
11:3	(A) Statement of Paul's charge: "I fear that . . ."
	(B) Descriptions of unfaithfulness:
	(1) Comparison of Corinthians' unfaithfulness to the biblical exemplum of Eve
	(a) Statement of comparison
	(b) Result of unfaithfulness
11:4	(2) Exempla of Corinthians' unfaithfulness
	(a) Reception of "another Jesus"
	(b) Reception of "another Spirit"
	(c) Reception of "another gospel"(cf. Galatians 1:4-9)
11:5-11	2. First argument: against the inferiority of Paul to the "super-apostles"
11:5	a) Statement of argument: "I consider myself in no way inferior to the 'super-apostles'"
11:6-11	b) Points in defense of Paul, against the charges of his Corinthian opponents
11:6	i) First causa: Paul's oral delivery (cf. 2 Cor 10:10)

	(A) Concession of status of "layman" in oral rhetoric
	(B) Denial of status of "layman" in γνῶσις
11:7-11	ii) Second causa: against the argument that Paul's lack of a church salary means that he is not a true apostle
11:7	(A) Statement of causa as question
11:8-11	(B) Points in defense of Paul
	(1) First point: Paul's practice of not taking a salary from the Corinthians
11:8-9	(a) Statement of point
	(b) Paul's revelation of financial support
	(i) Past
11:9b	(ii) Present
1 Cor 9:1-18	(2) Second point: on Paul's right to financial support from the Corinthian church
9:1-2	(a) By virtue of Paul's status as an apostle
9:3-6	(b) By comparison with prerogatives of other apostles
9:7	(c) By comparison to other occupations
9:8-10	(d) In relation to Scripture (Deuteronomy 25:4)
9:11-12a	(e) Conclusions
9:11	(i) Paul's worth and the Corinthians' advantage
9:12a	(ii) The rights of Paul
9:12b-18	(3) Third point: Paul's non-exercise of his rights as an apostle
9:12b	(a) Statement of non-exercise of rights
	(b) Purpose of non-exercise of rights: "we endure anything rather than put an obstacle in the way of the gospel of Christ"
9:13-14	(c) Reiteration of rights of religious workers to financial support
9:13	(i) In cultic tradition
9:14	(ii) By divine command
9:15-18	(d) Paul's response to his rights
9:15a	(i) Statement of response
	(ii) Purpose of this letter(stated negatively): "nor am I writing to secure any such provision"
9:15b-18	(iii)Reason for response: to retain Paul's "ground for boasting"
9:15b	(1) Statement of reason
9:16-17	(2) identification of ground of boasting
9:18	(3) Paul's reward: "making the gospel free of charge, not making use of my right in the gospel"
2 Cor 11:10-11	(4) divine witness to the truth of Paul's defense

Letter F

11:12-15	3. Second argument: Paul's prosecution of his opponents
11:12	a) Transition from previous section: "What I am doing I will continue to do"
	b) Statement of argument: "in order to deny an opportunity to those who seek an opportunity to be recognized as our equals in what they boast about"
11:13	c) Polemical descriptions of Paul's opponents
	i) "False apostles"
	ii) "Deceitful workmen who disguise themselves as apostles of Christ"
11:14-15	d) Reason for polemical description: *comparatio* to Satan
11:14	i) Statement of reason: "even Satan disguises himself as an angel of light"
11:15	ii) Further implication of *comparatio*: "Their end will correspond to their deeds"
11:16-21a	4. Third argument: Paul's accusation of the Corinthians
11:16-18	a) Reiteration of the setting of the foolish discourse
11:16a	i) Stated negatively: "I say again, let no one think I am a fool"
11:16b	ii) Stated positively: "But should it be otherwise, accept me as a fool, so that I too may boast a little"
11:17-18	iii) Justification of the use of the fool's speech
11:17	(A) Negatively in terms of divine authorship
	(B) Positively because of the boasts of other fools
11:19-21a	b) Charge against the Corinthians
11:19	i) Statement of charge: "You gladly bear with fools"
	ii) Paul's comment on the appropriateness of the charge
11:20	iii) Exempla of Corinthians' errors in accepting false apostles
	(A) The Corinthians' errors: "you bear with it . . ."
	(B) Activities of false apostles in relation to the Corinthians, in Paul's estimation
	(1) Enslavement
	(2) "Consumption"
	(3) Taking advantage
	(4) Presumptuous activity
	(5) "Hitting you in the face"
11:21a	iv) Paul's sarcastic comment on his charges against the false apostles(by way of *comparatio* to himself): "To my shame, I must say, we were too weak for that!
11:21b-33	5. Fourth argument: Paul's authenticity as an apostle
11:21b	a) Statement of argument: "But whatever anyone dares to boast of . . . I dare to boast of that"
	b) Qualification of argument(interposed in above phrase): "I speak as a fool"
11:22-29	c) Points in favor of Paul's authenticity as an apostle

11:22		i) Racial background
		   (A) As "Hebrews"
		   (B) As "Israelites"
		   (C) As "descendants of Abraham"

11:23		ii) Status as διάκονοι Χριστοῦ
		   (A) Statement of status as question
		   (B) Qualification: I am out of my mind to talk like this"

11:23
11:23-29
11:23
		(C) Answer: "I am a better one"
		   (D) Justification of answer: catalog of sufferings
		      (1) "Far greater labors"
		      (2) "Far more imprisonments"
		      (3) "Countless beatings, often nearly fatal"
		         (a) Statement of beatings

11:24-25a 11:24		(b) Description of beatings (i) First description: "Five times I received the 39 lashes from the Jews"
11:25		(ii) Second description: "Three times I was beaten with rods" (iii) Third description: "Once I was stoned"

11:26		(4) "Three times I have been shipwrecked, a day and a night adrift at sea"
		      (5) "Frequent journeys"
		      (6) Dangers
		         (a) "From rivers"
		         (b) "From robbers"
		         (c) "From my own people"(i.e., the Jews)
		         (d) "From Gentiles"
		         (e) "In the city"
		         (f) "In the wilderness"
		         (g) "At sea"
		         (h) "From false brethren"(i.e., false apostles and certain members of the Corinthian church)

11:27		(7) Miscellaneous hardships
		         (a) "Through toil and hardship"
		         (b) "Many sleepless nights"
		         (c) "Often going hungry"
		         (d) "In cold and exposure"

11:29		(8) Ecclesiastical hardships
		         (a) In general: "there is the daily pressure on me of all the churches"
		         (b) In particular
		            (i) Concern for the weak
		            (ii) Concern for the wayward

11:30-33		iii) A sarcastic point

Letter F

11:30	(A) Introduction and qualification of the point: "If I must boast, I will boast of the things that show my weakness"
11:31	(B) Calling on God as witness to truth
11:32-33	(C) A *narratio* of weakness: Paul's escape from King Aretas at Damascus over the wall in a basket
12:1-13	6. Fifth and final argument: a highly foolish and sarcastic boast
12:1	a) Qualification of the boast
	b) Introduction of new argument: "I will go on to visions and revelations of the Lord"
12:2-5	c) A *narratio* of a vision of "a man in Christ" (i.e. Paul)
12:2	i) Introduction of *narratio*: "I know a man in Christ"
	ii) Time of heavenly journey
	iii) Place of heavenly journey: "third heaven"
	iv) Circumstances of heavenly journey: "whether in the body or not, I do not know"
	v) Witness to truth: God
12:3	vi) Place of heavenly journey: "Paradise"
	vii) Reiteration of circumstances of heavenly journey
12:4	viii) Content of what happened on heavenly journey: "he heard things that cannot be told"
12:5	d) Paul's comment on *narration*
	i) Positively: "on behalf of this man I will boast"
	ii) Negatively: "but on my behalf I will not boast, except of my weaknesses"
12:6	e) Paul's comment on the appropriateness of boasting
	i) Positively
	ii) Negatively
12:7-10	f) A boast: a *narratio* of weakness (cf. 10:10!)
12:7	i) Introduction to boast: "to keep me from being too elated by the abundance of revelations (cf. 12:4!)
	ii) Content of weakness: "a thorn in the flesh, a messenger of Satan"
12:8	iii) Paul's initial reaction to it: "Three times I besought the Lord about this, that it should leave me"
12:9	iv) God's response to Paul's prayer for a personal healing miracle: "My grace is sufficient for you, for my power is made perfect in weakness"
12:10	v) Paul's response to divine revelation: boasting in weakness
	(A) First response: "I will all the more gladly boast of my weaknesses"
	(B) Purpose of boasting: "that the power of Christ may rest upon me"
	(C) Second response: contentment with sufferings

	(D) Reason for contentment: "for when I am weak, I am strong"(cf. 10:10!)
12:11-13	g) Conclusions from *narrationes* of "visions and revelations of the Lord (cf. 12:1!)
12:11a	i) Judgment on the Corinthians: "I have been a fool! You forced me to it, for I ought to have been commended by you"
12:11b	ii) Paul's sarcastic evaluation of himself in comparison to other apostles: "For I am not in any respect inferior to these super-apostles, even though I am nothing!"
12:12-13	iii) Paul's decisions about the Corinthians
12:12	(A) On the Corinthians' rejection of Paul as a true apostle (negative)
12:13	(B) On the Corinthians rejection of Paul because of his lack of a church salary: "I myself did not burden you. . . . Forgive me this wrong!"
12:14–13:10	C. Third proof: concerning Paul's impending visit
12:14	1. Introduction to proof
12:14-21	2. Presuppositions
12:14-16	a) The issue of a church salary for Paul
12:14	i) Statement of issue: "I will not be a burden to you"
12:14-16	ii) Paul's purpose in refusing church support
12:14	(A) Paul's desire
	(i) Negative
	(ii) Positive
12:15	(iii) Positive
12:15	(B) Proper response by the Corinthians, stated as a question
12:16	(C) Concession (sarcastic) of Paul's guilt: "I was crafty, as you say, and got the better of you by guile"
12:17-18	b) The issue of Paul's subordinates' taking advantage of the Corinthians(stated as questions)
12:17	i) Paul's indirect advantage
12:18	ii) Advantage of subordinates
12:18	iii) Consistency of Paul and subordinates
12:19	c) The issue of the Corinthians' rejection of Paul and the propriety of his defense
12:20-21	d) Paul's fear of what he may find on his third visit
12:20	i) Statement of fear
12:20-21	ii) Statement of what Paul fears
	(A) The errors of the Corinthians
12:21	(B) The severity of Paul's visit
13:1-4	3. First argument: the necessity of Paul's third visit
13:1	a) Statement of argument
13:1	b) Reason for visit: a principle from the Bible (Deuteronomy 19:15)
13:2-4	c) Paul's projected activity on third visit

13:2	i) As foretold by past warnings: "that if I come again I will not spare them"
13:3	ii) Sarcastic comment on severity of Paul's third visit and Paul's weakness: "—since you desire proof that Christ is speaking in me!"
13:3-4	d) Christ's projected activity on Paul's third visit
13:3-4a	i) By reference to the issue of weakness vs. strength
13:4b	ii) Relationship of Paul to Christ
13:5-10	4. Second argument: necessary preparation for Paul's third visit
13:5	a) Statement of argument as command
13:6-7	b) Result of preparation that Paul hopes for
13:8	c) The necessity of truth
13:9-10	d) The purpose of this letter

NOTES

1. For an excellent history of scholarship on 2 Corinthians, see Victor Paul Furnish, "Corinthians, Second Letter to the," in John H. Hayes, editor, *Dictionary of Biblical Interpretation*, 2 volumes (Nashville: Abingdon Press, 1999), 1.223-7.

2. Heidelberg: Bassermann, 1870.

3. 9th edition (Göttingen: Vandenhoeck & Ruprecht, 1924; reprinted (ed. Georg Strecker) 1970.

4. "Die Vorgeschichte des sogennanten Zweiten Korintherbriefes," reprinted in Bornkamm's *Gesammelte Aufsätze* (Munich: Kaiser, 1971) 4.162-194.

5. Betz, "2 Cor 6:14–7:1," 88–108.

6. Bultmann, *Second Letter to the Corinthians*. For a more recent discussion of the scholarly alternatives as to the literary non-integrity of 2 Corinthians, see the especially clear treatment by Duff, *Moses in Corinth*, 46–51.

7. *2 Corinthians*, NTM (Wilmington: Michael Glazier, 1980).

8. *II Corinthians: Translated with Introduction, Notes, and Commentary*, AB 32A (Garden City, NY: Doubleday, 1984).

9. *The Opponents of Paul in Second Corinthians* (Philadelphia: Fortress, 1986).

10. BHT 45; Tübingen: Mohr Siebeck, 1972.

11. Welborn, *End to Enmity*, 288ff.

12. Welborn, *End to Enmity*, 434–39.

13. See Jewett, *Chronology*, 104; Acts 20:16 makes it likely that Paul was forced to avoid entering Ephesus after the end of his ministry there in the winter of 54–55.

14. Roetzel, *2 Corinthians*, 32.

15. Welborn, *End to Enmity*, 439.

16. See Paul Barnett, *The Second Epistle to the Corinthians*, NICNT (Grand Rapids and Cambridge: Eerdmans, 1997), 519; Murray J. Harris, *The Second Epistle to the Corinthians: A Commentary on the Greek Text*, NIGTC (Grand Rapids: Eerdmans; Bletchley: Paternoster Press, 2005), 764.

17. Bultmann, *zweite Brief*, 208; Collins, *Second Corinthians*, 219; translation by Harris, *Second Epistle*, 763.

18. See Harris, *Second Epistle*, 764; Barnett, *Second Epistle*, 519; Thrall, *2 Corinthians*, 2.687.

19. Collins, *First Corinthians*, 328; Schrage, *erste Brief*, 2.286-88.

20. See Harris, *Second Epistle*, 767.

21. Roetzel, *2 Corinthians*, 108.

22. Roetzel, *2 Corinthians*, 112.

23. Roetzel, *2 Corinthians*, 112.

24. Ralph P. Martin, *2 Corinthians*, 487–88.

25. Lausberg, *Handbuch*, §342.

26. Lausberg, *Handbuch*, §343.

27. Cicero, *De inventione* 1.106-109.

28. See Frank W. Hughes, "The Social Situations Implied by Rhetoric," in Karl P. Donfried and Johannes Beutler, editors, *The Thessalonians Debate: Methodological Discord or Methodological Synthesis?* (Grand Rapids: Eerdmans, 2000), 241–54.

29. Augustine, *De doctrina christiana* 4.7.11; English translation by D. W. Robertson, Jr., Library of Liberal Arts (Indianapolis: Bobbs-Merrill, 1958).

30. *Ibid.*, 4.7.11-12. On Augustine's understanding of Paul's rhetoric, see E. A. Judge, "Paul's Boasting in Relation to Contemporary Professional Practice," *ABR* 16 (1968): 37–50.

31. Cicero, *De oratore* 3.125.

Chapter 11

Letter G

Consolation for the Afflicted (2 Cor 1:1–2:13 + 2 Cor 7:5-16 + 13:11-13)

THE PROVENANCE OF LETTER G

There is a consensus among scholars committed to the partitioning of 2 Corinthians that Paul's hope for a positive response to the severe letter was fulfilled.[1] He meets Titus in Macedonia who brings good news that the Corinthians regret their share in the conflict and wish to be reconciled with Paul. They now have decided to punish the wrongdoer in some way (2 Cor 7:11). But not all of the issues are resolved. Paul once again is forced by circumstances to delay his travel plans to visit Corinth and he needs to explain why he wrote such a fierce letter if he still wanted to be their friend. The biting sarcasm about the Corinthians' willingness to be exploited by the super-apostles caused embarrassment and injured feelings. The congregation was sorely grieved by the conflict and needed to be comforted. Letter G was written in the early summer of 56, probably from Macedonia, to provide consolation and clarification of his own attitude, now that the conflict was over.

Letter G opens with a typical salutation followed by a thanksgiving that starts in 2 Cor 1:3 that states the theme of the letter, that God is "a God of all consolation." Both the Corinthians and Paul have suffered afflictions and share equally in "the comfort of Christ." In verses 8–11, Paul discloses the life-threatening circumstances he had faced in Asia, probably an imprisonment in Ephesus that closed his ministry there in the winter of 54–55, describing the life-threatening experience in Romans 16:3-4.[2] In describing the shared experiences of suffering, Calvin Roetzel explains that "Paul linked arms with his converts in a circle of consolation commissioned to console others in distress."[3]

This thanksgiving section is followed by a formal *partitio* in 1:12-14 that names the three topics of the letter: that Paul's behavior was consistent with the grace of God; that Paul's aim in writing letters, even the letter of tears, was intended to produce understanding of the faith; and that Paul's hope is that both he and the Corinthians will be proud of each other when they face the last judgment. Each of these three arguments is introduced by a short narration of the circumstances that needed to be clarified to achieve the consolation that God intended. In the first argument of 1:15-22, Paul begins the discussion of his travel plans that had to be altered because of circumstances. Neither he nor God were vacillating, saying "Yes!" when they meant "No!," because the gospel Paul and his colleagues brought to Corinth was a reliable expression of God's affirmation. In Christ, "every one of God's promises is a 'Yes'" (2 Cor 1:20). The charismatic endowment of the believers in Corinth confirms this conviction (2 Cor 1:21–22).

The second narration in 1:23–2:4 explains why Paul wrote the letter of tears rather than returning to Corinth after his disastrous visit in which the congregation had repudiated his leadership. The result of Paul's unwillingness "to lord it over your faith" (1 Cor 1:24) was that in the end, the Corinthians stood firm in the faith. Paul goes on to explain the "affliction and anguish of heart, with many tears" that produced this letter (2 Cor 2:4). The need for consolation was clearly on both sides, but Paul is particularly concerned to clarify that his harsh letter was an expression of his love for the congregation. He goes on in 2:5-11 to discuss the congregation's decision to punish the man whose denunciation had marked the low point in Paul's "painful visit." Paul requests that the congregation should "forgive and encourage this person, lest such a person be overcome by excessive grief" (2 Cor 2:7).[4]

In 2 Cor 2:12-13 + 7:5-7, Paul writes a third narration that describes the excruciating anxiety he felt after sending off the harsh "letter of tears." Consolation came with Titus's arrival in Macedonia with good news about the Corinthians' reception of the harsh letter. Although it caused pain in Corinth, Paul will not apologize for writing it because it provoked the congregation "to repentance" (2 Cor 7:9). In 7:10-11, Paul lists the results of the letter, acknowledging that the congregation has shown themselves to be "blameless in the matter" (2 Cor 7:11). This even includes their handling of the matter of the "wrongdoer" in 7:12. This leads to the summary of Paul's argument in 7:13a, which includes both Paul and the Corinthians: "therefore we are consoled."

The formal argument of Letter G ends with a *peroratio* in 7:13b-16, which recapitulates the letter by describing Paul's consolation and the restoration of confidence on all sides. Paul, Titus, and the Corinthians have discovered they can rely on each other. This leads smoothly into the conclusion of Letter G, which in all probability is found in 2 Cor 13:11–13.[5] Consequently, this letter of consolation is the only one of the eight letters that we have in its entirety.[6] Although it posed problems for the later ecclesiastical editors, serving as the frame letter for the redaction of 2 Corinthians, it was apparently successful with its original audience.⁷ Since Paul carried through with his hope to spend the winter of 56-57 in Corinth (2 Cor 1:16; Rom 16:1-23; Acts 20:3), there is good reason to believe that this letter cemented a reliable and productive relationship with the Corinthians. Lawrence Welborn goes even further to conclude that "Paul's reconciliation with the wrongdoer Gaius created the psychological conditions for the last and most productive period in Paul's life as an apostle of Christ,"⁸ when Paul not only wrote the masterful letter to the Romans but also prepared the way for delivering the Jerusalem offering and mounting the Spanish mission.

TRADITIONS OF GRECO-ROMAN RHETORIC

Two handbooks of epideictic rhetoric dating from the late third to early fourth centuries of the Common Era are attributed to Menander Rhetor. One of these interesting works lists a speech of consolation, the λόγος παραμυθητικός, as a kind of speech conventionally composed in the *genus* of epideictic rhetoric.⁹ A more famous epideictic speech is the ἐπιτάφιος (funeral oration),¹⁰ which often included consolation and, as Menander Rhetor tells us, could include various kinds of exhortations and prayers.¹¹ The λόγος παραμυθητικός (consolation speech) itself might include narratives (414.7), and Menander Rhetor gave as an example a narrative of the destruction of cities and nations (414.7-8), in which the orator may speak of "how the change from this life is perhaps to be preferred, since it rids us of troubles, greed, unjust fate" (414.8-10).

In a Hellenistic handbook of letter-writing attributed to Libanius, we learn of the existence of forty-one types of letters, of which the twenty-first is the παραμυθητική, the letter of consolation. In another epistolary handbook attributed to Demetrius, there are twenty-one letter types, of which the fifth is the παραμυθητικός. Both epistolary handbooks gave brief examples of the content of a letter of consolation, and Pseudo-Demetrius's example includes a description of how the writer of the letter shares the grief suffered by the addressee, how sufferings are common to all humanity, and how reason will help the sufferer deal with his or her grief.¹² At about the same time as the development of those two Hellenistic handbooks of letter-writing (heavily influenced by rhetoric as they were), the tradition of Greek rhetoric was being transferred into Latin with some adaptations. An early stage in the transfer of Greek rhetoric into Latin is represented by Cicero's famous handbook *De inventione*. In rhetorical theory (and in most of Cicero's own rhetorical practice), the part of the speech in which one conventionally found appeals to the emotions was the ending of the speech, the *peroratio*. In Cicero's time, there was a conventional understanding that the *peroratio* had two *partes*:

the recapitulation (*recapitulatio*) of the points demonstrated in the speech, and the appeal to the emotions (*adfectus*), which was further subdivided in Latin rhetoric into the arousal of emotions against the opponent (*indignatio*) and the arousal of emotions for the orator and his client's case (*conquestio*). In Cicero's youthful handbook *De inventione* are listed fifteen topics, which could be used in *indignatio*, and sixteen topics, which could be used in *conquestio*. The sixteen commonplaces (*loci communes*) of *conquestio* begin with Cicero's general explanation that such *loci*

> set forth the power of fortune over all men and the weakness of the human race. When such a passage is delivered gravely and sententiously (*graviter et sententiose*), the spirit of man is prepared for pity, for in viewing the misfortune of another he will contemplate his own weakness.[13]

The third such *locus* is that "in which each separate phase of misfortune is deplore"; the example Cicero gives is the example of a father's mourning the death of his son, in which all of the past involvements of the father with the son are rather emotionally recounted.[14] The tenth *locus* of *conquestio* is that in which one's helplessness and weakness and loneliness are revealed."[15] Finally, the sixteenth *locus* is that "in which we show that our soul is full of mercy for others, but still is noble, lofty, and patient of misfortune and will be so whatever may befall."[16] The traditional topics associated with consolation, as mentioned earlier, are used in a part of 2 Corinthians, 1:1–2:13 + 7:5-16, which has been identified by exegetes as a "letter of reconciliation." A more apt description would be "letter of consolation." The situation, which we can reconstruct from the several letters to the Corinthians, shows that Paul's ἦθος was in deep trouble as a result of his absence from the Corinthian church and the presence of the opponents of Paul. From 2 Cor 10:10, we learn that the struggle between Paul and his opponents was to no small degree a rhetorical contest. That Paul could write persuasive letters and finally (i.e., after 2 Cor. 10-13) win over the Corinthians from the clutches of his eloquent opponents is no small tribute to the ancient recognition of the power of his letters, as the earliest known rhetorical critic of Paul, St. Augustine of Hippo, recognized.[17]

THE *EXORDIUM*, 2 COR. 1:1-11

According to rhetorical theory, we expect the *exordium* to introduce the orator and his ἦθος to the audience. The epistolary adaptation of the *exordium* includes what is form-critically identified as the epistolary prescript and the thanksgiving prayer in Pauline and other letters. The prescript in 1:1-2 contains two elements not found in the exordium of 1 Cor 1:1-3, a reference to Timothy and a widened address to the church in Corinth, along "with all the saints in the whole of Achaia." Timothy is not referred to as a coauthor of the letter, but it seems likely in view of the positive references to him in 1 Cor 4:17; 16:10-11 and 2 Cor 1:19 that Paul is trying "to co-opt for himself the goodwill Timothy has garnered with the Corinthians over the years."[18] A similar motive may lie behind the reference to "all of the saints in the whole of Achaia," which would have included Phoebe, the leader of the church in Cenchraea and Paul's patron in the projects of the Jerusalem offering and the Spanish mission.[19] J. Paul Sampley observes that these details "are tilted positively toward enhancing Paul's relations with the Corinthians, a matter of enormous concern throughout 2 Corinthians 1-9."[20]

The form of the thanksgiving prayer allows the letter-writer a golden opportunity to praise the addressees at some length, an opportunity of which Paul usually takes full advantage.[21] This is quite analogous to the traditional function of *captatio benevolentiae* in the *exordium*, as described in several rhetorical handbooks. Exaggeratedly praising language can be used as part of an appeal to acquire the goodwill of the audience. In this case, the audience is indirectly praised for being the beneficiaries of divine blessings imparted in the midst of suffering.

After the epistolary prescript, the thanksgiving prayer (1:3-11) with its lengthy reasons for thanking God unfolds the subjects of the letter: it deals with affliction and comfort. Affliction (θλίψις) comes to "us," from various sources (Paul will identify these sources in great detail in his *narrationes* later); consolation comes from God. The mutuality of Paul's and the Corinthians' suffering of various afflictions is matched by the mutuality of consolation. No matter what the present state of Paul, whether he is "afflicted" or "comforted," he refers the situation to God, Christ, and his ministry to the Corinthians (1:4-6). Afflictions that Jesus-believers suffer can be better borne because of the knowledge that "the sufferings of Christ overflow onto us." Everything works to the ultimate advantage of the Corinthians, their παράκλησις from suffering and their ὑπομονή in the midst of sufferings. Hence, Paul uses the motif of his own and Christ's afflictions as a way of talking about the sufferings experienced by the Corinthians. And he does this for good reason, since in 2 Cor. 2:4, in a *narratio*, he tells us of a letter, which was deeply painful for him to write, written indeed "out of much affliction (ἐκ γὰρ πολλῆς θλίψεως) and anguish of heart, with many tears." There again he talks around the fact that a major reason why he needs to write a letter of reconciliation was his own sarcastic letter (Letter F), which surely must have caused pain, as Paul admits only very late in Letter G (7:8). As a way of dealing with the paradox of writing a letter of reconciliation necessitated in some measure by his own sarcastic letter, it is no accident that Paul introduces the subject of affliction (θλίψις) in the context of shared affliction that "we" experience and, indeed, that Christ experienced.

The *exordium* of this letter in 1:1-11 is an excellent example of *insinuatio*, the introduction of general subjects in the *exordium* in an indirect manner, rather than the direct manner (*principium*)[22] because Paul's strained relationship with the Corinthians would not permit it. The wounded condition of the audience after their reading or hearing the so-called "letter of tears" is graphically described later in this letter by Paul in 7:9-12. So instead of Paul's writing an "I told you so" sort of letter after Letter F had produced its desired effect, Paul's response is similar to that in the sample "letter of consolation" in Pseudo-Libanius' letter-writing handbook: the writer writes that he quite strongly *shares* the sufferings of the reader. Paul perhaps exaggeratedly emphasizes in 1:8-10 how terrible his sufferings were: his missionary journey in Asia resulted in Paul's feeling as if he would not live (1:8) and was under a death sentence (1:9). God's response to Paul's sufferings is found in 1:9-10: God "who raises the dead" delivered Paul "from so deadly a peril" in the past, so that Paul has "hoped (ἐλπίκαμεν) he will deliver us again." The *exordium* concludes with an awkwardly worded request for prayer in 1:11, with the apparent purpose that the thanksgiving to God will be increased because more people will be thanking God.

THE *PARTITIO*, 2 COR. 1:12-14

The *partitio*, 1:12-14, gives an enumeration of the subjects, which are dealt with in the *probatio*. 2 Cor. 1:12 lists the first subject, which concerns his past behavior, that he had acted "with openness" (reading ἁπλότητι with Nestle-Aland, 28th edition) and godly sincerity, not by fleshly wisdom but by the grace of God." The second subject, which concerns the present, is laid out in 1:13-14a, that Paul's teaching by letter is clear and understandable. It is, however, related to Paul's claim to sincerity in 1:12; Paul states in the first case that his personal behavior is consistent with his role as an apostle, and secondly, he states in 1:13a that his teaching by letter is consistent with what the Corinthians can understand. In 1:13b-14a, he gives as an example of his understandable teaching some bit of instruction that they have already understood, possibly the "letter of tears," about which we hear more in this letter. The third subject is listed in 1:14b and concerns the future, that is, the eschatological hope. Like the first subject in 1:12, it is stated in terms of a boast: on the Day of the Lord, the Corinthians and Paul will be able to boast about each other. These three subjects, encompassing the past, the present, and the future, are precisely what are dealt with in the *probatio* of our reconstructed letter.

Letter G

THE *NARRATIO* AND THE *PROBATIO*, 2 COR. 1:15–2:13 + 7:5-13A

Although ancient rhetorical handbooks customarily provided for a separate section of *narratio* between the *exordium* and the *probatio*, rhetorical theory also allowed the more-or-less standard pattern to be altered in favor of omitting the *narratio* or in favor of inserting pieces of *narratio* within other parts of the oration. Particularly in a political debate (in the *genus* of deliberative rhetoric), the "facts" or "events" that could be dealt with in a *narratio* were often well known to the audience, or had been dealt with by other speakers in the debate, so that no repetition would be desirable.[23] On the other hand, a *narratio* broken up into pieces could also be useful in some circumstances.[24] In the *Rhetorica ad Alexandrum*, Pseudo-Aristotle listed two requirements for including a *narratio* within the *exordium*: the oration must be deliberative, and the actions to be narrated must be few in number and well known to the audience.[25] Hence, Pseudo-Aristotle advises that a *narratio* included within other sections of the speech is less an informational "statement of facts" and more a rehearsal of what was already known—a retelling in a way that would help the orator make as persuasive a case as possible in the *probatio*. Quintilian could even say that a *narratio* was a *probatio* "put forward in a continuous form."[26] Hence, Greco-Roman rhetorical theory, as "speaker-oriented" as some modern rhetoricians find it, certainly did make allowances for various situations in which following the elementary rules in a servile way would have resulted in a less persuasive discourse.

When we look for "facts," in 2 Cor. 1:15–2:13 + 7:5-13a, we find little or nothing that the Corinthians did not already know. They already know the fact that Paul has not recently himself been in Corinth (cf. 1:15-16; 1:23–2:4), although they may be unaware of Paul's apostolic travels to Troas and Macedonia (2:12-13 + 7:5-7). They are painfully aware of the fact that Paul sent a "letter of tears" (2:3-5, 9) to the Corinthian church. And they know very well that Titus made a visit after the "letter of tears" had been received (7:7-13) and the Corinthians had been "hurt in God's way" (7:9), meaning that this powerful document of epistolary rhetoric had been effective, changing the Corinthians' policy toward their founding apostle. So this letter concerned itself less with facts or actions and more with attitudes toward and reasons for the things that had already happened and were probably common knowledge in the Corinthian church. Thus, the rhetorical structure of 1:15–2:13 + 7:5-13a, in accordance with Greek rhetorical theory, reveals a section of argumentation containing a three-part *probatio*; preceding each *probatio* is a short section of *narratio*. Each *narratio* serves to give the historical setting of what is to be argued in the *probatio* immediately following.

All three sections of *narratio* contain material, which relates to Paul's travels to Corinth and his relationship with the church there.

The first *narratio*, 1:15-16, tells of Paul's original intention to come to Corinth, within the context of Paul's prospective apostolic mission to Macedonia, and a later return through Corinth in the direction of Judaea. The *probatio* section begins in 1:17a with an *interrogatio*: "Was I vacillating when I wanted to do this?" to which the understood response would be "no." This sentence is a fitting introduction to a proof (1:17-22), which presupposes that Paul's consistency or decisiveness was at issue, exactly what one would expect from the first subject announced in the *partitio* in 1:12, that Paul has behaved "with holiness and godly sincerity." The rest of the proof in 1:17b-22 is a demonstration of Paul's blamelessness and sincerity. Paul continues with another *interrogatio* in 1:17b, asking rhetorically if his behavior is κατὰ σάρκα, like a person who says "Yes, Yes," and also "No, No." Presumably this interesting question means, "Does Paul say 'yes' and 'no' at the same time?" or "Is Paul insincere?" (compare the statement in the *partitio* in 1:12). Paul continues with a defense of his sincerity or consistency, by arguing in a sustained way that his oral rhetoric (λόγος) has not been "yes" and "no," nor has the gospel he preached (1:19) been "yes" and "no," nor has the liturgical "amen," which has been said in the Corinthian church been "yes" and "no." He further grounds his response to the apparent charge of insincerity or inconsistency with a claim to his divine office as apostle: "God establishes us with you in Christ" (1:21). The result of Paul's apostolic office and mission is the Corinthian congregation itself. 2 Cor 1:22 concludes this section of *probatio* with an appeal to the experience of the Corinthian church itself. The logic behind this appeal is that if Paul is not a truly sincere representative of God (as he claims in 1:21), then the baptismal "seal" and the experience of the Holy Spirit in the hearts of the Corinthians at their baptism were not real. All of this section, 1:15-22, argues that Paul had good, honorable intentions to come and make another apostolic visit to the Corinthian church. The sticking point was that he obviously had not done so. This takes us to the next part of the argumentation.

Paul continues with a rather longer *narratio* in 1:23–2:4, where he demonstrates that it was necessary for him, despite his good intentions, to change his travel plans. He calls two witnesses to attest the truth of this statement: first God and second his own soul, 1:23a. Then in 1:23b–2:4, he narrates the specific reasons for the change of plans. Instead of what is argued in 1:17-22 as the reason for his non-visit to Corinth, Paul tells his readers, "it was out of consideration for you that I did not come to Corinth" (1:23b). Then, he explains in 2:1 why such consideration was needed: he "decided not to make another painful visit to you (πάλιν ἐν λύπῃ πρὸς ὑμᾶς ἐλθεῖν)." Although 2:1 does not specify the antecedent of the phrase ἐν λύπῃ (Paul's pain or the

Corinthians' pain), Paul reveals in 2:2-3 that his visit while the Corinthians were in error would have been painful for both Paul and the Corinthians, so that the pain involved would have been mutual. It was, however, to the Corinthians' advantage (a clear deliberative topic) for Paul to have held back from one more painful visit. Then, in 2:3 Paul explains his writing the sharp letter: he presupposed the Corinthians' knowledge that Paul's joy was also their own joy. The mutuality of pain in 2:1-3a together with the mutuality of joy in 2:3b are fitting consequences to the *exordium* of this letter, which states that God comforts "us" so that "we can comfort those who are in every affliction" (1:4). This mutuality is exemplified in 2:4 Paul where concludes this section of *narratio* with his description of the letter, which was so rhetorically effective: it was clearly a sharp letter, but Paul first says he shared the pain, and then later he says his motive in sending the letter was not to cause pain to the Corinthians, but so that they "might know my abundant love" for them. So Paul explains his bitter letter by saying the pain was as much his in writing it as the Corinthians' in reading it. Hence, an important part of what the *exordium* does in this letter is to lead up to a non-apologetic, yet sympathetic, explanation of the "letter of tears" in 2:4.

The *probatio* in 2:5-11 concerns what was to happen in the congregation as they dealt with the offending Jesus-believing brother, by order of Paul in Letter F. Paul's inclusion of this material here gives rise to many kinds of speculation as to what the nature of the offense was, and how Paul dealt with it in the "letter of tears." Some interpreters, including Victor Paul Furnish, argue against identifying the "letter of tears" with 2 Cor 10-13 because 2:3-11 deals predominantly with the Jesus-believing brother who had committed some sort of offense against Paul.[27] However, the original form of Letter F could well have included a condemnation of the man who had wronged Paul (and then later this specific condemnation was edited out when our canonical 2 Corinthians was put together). And, if "it is easier to think of chaps. 10-13 as written in anger rather than sorrow,"[28] one should consider the fact that this letter promoting reconciliation is as persuasive as it is because the use of the conventional topics of consolation, which prominently included the sharing of pain by the friends of those who had been afflicted with some disaster. We conclude that the "letter of tears" was probably the missive lying behind our edited 2 Cor 10-13, because Paul's characterization of that letter in this "letter of reconciliation" is so consistent with this letter's central use of consolation. Precisely as a part of consolation, which was dependent on reconciliation between Paul and the Corinthians, which, in turn, had been dependent on the congregation's fundamentally changing its policy, Paul now orders forgiveness for the offending fellow Jesus-believing. The reason Paul gives is one of the standard topics in funeral speeches: how much grief is really appropriate for those who have suffered. Instead of pointing out the fact that the Corinthian church already has acknowledged the guilt of the offending brother (which they know very well), Paul deals with the offender as someone who has suffered a grievous pain. So, since too much grief is could "overwhelm such a man" (2:7), the order is given for forgiveness. In 2 Cor 2:10, the Corinthian congregation is given authority to forgive sins by Paul, and Paul claims this authority ἐν προσώπῳ Χριστοῦ. Further integration of Paul's rhetoric into the cosmic order is provided by the concluding sentence of this *probatio*, where Paul warns that such a man who remained unforgiven could be an easy target for Satan, on which warning Paul comments, "we are not unaware of his designs."

The third *narratio* includes 2:12-13. We follow Bornkamm and others in believing that 2:12-13 was originally continued in 7:5-7. The first part of the *narratio* includes a description about Paul's perhaps otherwise successful mission work, yet Paul shares more of his sorrow in 2:13: in Troas, there was for Paul "no rest for my spirit, for I did not find Titus." Paul subsequently went to Macedonia. Then, splicing 2:13 to 7:5, we find Paul "having come to Macedonia" and, beautifully parallel to 2:13, we find in 7:5 that Paul had "no rest for my flesh" as a result of "fights without, fears within." This *narratio* thus far has given the setting of Paul's need for consolation by telling the reader of the specifics of Paul's pain. Then, in 7:6-7, we read what happens to pain as the result of divine consolation. God "who consoles the downcast" consoled Paul through the coming of Titus, and in the good news, which Titus brought from Corinth, the fact of the Corinthians' "longing," repentance, and "zeal" for Paul.

The final proof in 7:8-13 is a further explanation of Paul's motives in sending the "letter of tears," in the light of its obvious success in changing the Corinthians' policy toward Paul. Paul has earlier told about his "tears" in writing and sending the letter, yet he can open this proof by saying, "I do not now regret it" (7:8). Paul never positively says he was sorry for sending the letter, although he says that when he "saw that the letter had caused you pain, even if only for a time" he "may have been sorry." Paul, however, argues that the grief, which the Corinthians experienced, was "borne in God's way" (7:10), which caused the Corinthians to demonstrate themselves "blameless in every particular" (7:11). Thus, Paul again restates his goal in sending the "letter of tears" in the light of its rhetorical success, its acceptance by the Corinthians: Paul sent the letter, he says, "so that your eagerness for us might be made clear to you in the sight of God" (7:12), which is among other things a subtle use of the divine passive.

THE *PERORATIO*, 2 COR 7:13B-16

The *peroratio* traditionally combined appeals to the emotions with recapitulation of the arguments of the *probatio*. Paul's appeal to the emotions here is not *indignatio* (stirring the readers against a case made by opponents) but rather *conquestio*, the stirring of emotions in favor of the rhetor and what he has argued. Paul has proceeded so far by sharing with his readers his emotional response to events that have happened in the form of three *narrationes*. Here in 7:13b-16, Paul states his joy in terms of his response to the joy of Titus, and he does so in what seems to be quite exaggerated language: "we rejoiced abundantly at the joy of Titus, because his spirit was refreshed from all of you." This would perhaps have the rhetorical effect of endearing Paul to the readers, as Paul thanked the Corinthian Jesus-believers for refreshing Titus's spirit. Equally important to the function of the *peroratio* is the fact that it carries out the program of the *exordium* by demonstrating that the consolation flowing from "the Father of mercies and the God of all comfort" (1:3) through Paul and to the Corinthians, announced at such great length in the *exordium*, really did occur in this case. By the fact that Paul has been consoled at the reconciliation of the Corinthians to him, and the fact that he says so in this letter, the Corinthians can know that the reconciliation with the founding apostle of their church is real, so that they should have no further worries that Paul is going to make another painful visit. 2 Cor 7:14-16 recapitulates the arguments made by the *narrationes* and *probationes*: the current favorable status of the Corinthians in Paul's eyes, the justification of Paul's boasting to Titus of the Corinthians, the justification of Paul's boasting about Titus to the Corinthians (7.14), the present favorable status of the Corinthians in Titus's eyes (7:15), and a final emotional summary: "I rejoice because I am completely confidant in you" (7:16).

CONCLUSION

Since there is a clear thematic unity, which is matched by a demonstrable unity of rhetorical structure, including an *exordium*, which announces general themes for the letter, worked out in specifics through the *partitio* and later a three-part *probatio*, which is supported by three short *narrationes*, recapitulated by the *peroratio*, and recommendations for specific actions to be taken in the epistolary exhortation, it appears that 1:1–2: 13 + 7:5-16 is an integral letter. Generally speaking, it uses deliberative rhetoric, even though it combines with its standard deliberative appeal to advantage and honor the standard epideictic topic of consolation (which was well known in Greek and Roman rhetoric since the most famous kind of epideictic speech was the funeral oration). The fact that Paul can use topics, which were advised in rhetorical handbooks for two different *genera* of rhetoric attests to (1) the rhetorical creativity of Paul and (2) the fact that deliberative rhetoric (i.e., political speeches) often combined elements of all three *genera* of rhetoric, dealing with actions in the past, the character of various persons, the honor and advantage of cities and groups, as well as a variety of ways to praise and blame, in order to advise groups of people who were empowered to make significant decisions about their own future. Of course, a person who was still learning rhetoric might very well not mix the *genera* of rhetoric. We know, for example, that in the practice of declamation, there was separate terminology for model speeches in two of the three *genera*. A contrived speech in deliberative rhetoric was called a *suasoria*, and a contrived speech in judicial rhetoric was called a *controversia*. The handbooks tell us that declamation was not done in epideictic rhetoric.[29] But if a student of oratory had really mastered the training to which the rhetorical handbooks refer (perhaps through the triad of *imitatio*, theory, and practice)[30] the rules are likely to have been internalized to such an extent that the student of rhetoric knew the rules very well indeed, but was not limited by them. Rhetorical theory tells us primarily what rhetorical teachers were interested in, and it is useful because it indicates the range of possibilities. A well-trained rhetor would know these possibilities and would discover and invent even more through actual practice. To analyze the rhetorical strategies of a discourse, it is necessary to recognize what an author has received through school tradition and what is the author's own composition.[31] Despite the fact that rhetorical critics differ in their most detailed analyses and in their approach to the history of rhetoric, it is clear that a number of scholars have identified "standard" rhetorical structures in Pauline letters, as well as indications that Paul did not limit himself to precepts drawn from textbooks.[32] This dual phenomenon—Paul's agreement with standard features of rhetoric and also Paul's ability to go beyond them, based on the exigence of the situation—suggests that Paul may well have been trained in rhetoric. How else could his letters have been considered by his opponents to be "weighty and strong"?

The Rhetorical Arrangement of Letter G

2 Cor
1:1-11   I. Exordium

1:1-2   A. Epistolary prescript

1:1   1. Superscriptio
               a) Name of sender
               b) Title of sender
               c) Name of co-sender
               d) Title of co-sender
            2. *Adscriptio*
               a) Identification of direct addressees
               b) Identification of indirect addressees: "with all the saints in the whole of Achaia"

1:2		3. *Salutatio*
1:3-11		B. Thanksgiving prayer
1:3-4		1. Object of thanksgiving: God
1:3		a) Identification: "God"
		b) Aretalogy
		(1) With reference to Christ: "father of our Lord Jesus Christ"
1:4		(2) With reference to the topic of consolation
		(a) Statement of aretalogy: "who comforts us in every affliction of ours"
		(b) Purpose of consolation: "so that we can comfort those who are in every affliction"
		(c) Means of consolation: "by means of the consolation with which we have been consoled by God"
1:5-10		2. Reasons for thanksgiving
1:5-6		a) Reasons connected with the present (general)
1:5		(1) Concerning suffering
		(a) Statement of present status of Paul: "the sufferings of Christ overflow onto us abundantly"
		(b) Interpretation of present status of readers: "we share abundantly in comfort also"
1:6a		(2) Concerning affliction
		(a) Statement of present status of Paul: "Whether we are afflicted"
		(b) Interpretation of present status of readers: "it is for your consolation and salvation"
1:6b		(3) Concerning consolation
		(a) Statement of present status of Paul: "whether we are comforted"
		(b) Interpretation of present status of readers: "it is for your comfort, which you experience when you patiently endure the same sufferings that we suffer"
1:7		b) Reason connected with the future: Paul's hope for the future
		(1) Description of hope: "our hope for you is unshaken"
		(2) Presupposition of hope: "as you share in our suffering"
		(3) Content of hope: "you will also share in our consolation"
1:8-10a		c) Reasons connected with the past
1:8		(1) Introduction to the section(disclosure formula and address): "we do not want you to be ignorant, brothers"
		(2) Disclosure: Paul's bad experience in Asia
		(a) Statement of subject of disclosure: "the affliction we experienced in Asia"
		(b) Paul's interpretation of the bad experience
		i) First interpretation (extremely negative)

224   *Chapter 11*

	(a) First statement: "we were so . . . crushed that we despaired of life itself"
1:9	(b) Restatement: "we felt that we had been condemned"
	ii) Second interpretation: bad experience was meant to make Paul trust God
	(a) First statement
	(1) Statement of inter-pretation
	(2) Aretalogy of divinity: "who raises the dead"
1:10a	(b) Restatement: "he delivered us from so deadly a peril"
1:10b	d) Reason connected with the future: Paul's hope for deliverance
	(1) Statement of hope: "and he will deliver us"
	(2) Restatement of hope: "on him we have set our hope that he will deliver us again"

1:11   C. Request for prayer

1:12-14   II. *Partitio* (*enumeratio* of subjects argued in probatio)

1:12   A. First subject (regarding the past): Paul's boast that he has acted blamelessly

   1. Identification of Paul's boast: his conscience
   2. Content of the boast: "that we have behaved in the world and still more toward you, with holiness and godly sincerity, not by fleshly wisdom but by the grace of God"

1:13-14a   B. Second subject: Paul's epistolary teaching is clear and understandable (regarding the present)

1:13a   1. Statement of second subject: "for we do not write to you except what you read and also understand"

1:13b-14a   2. Transition to third subject: "I hope that you will thoroughly understand, just as you have perfectly understood"

1:14b   C. Third subject (regarding the future): the boast of Paul and of the Corinthians should be mutual: "that we will be your boast, just as you will be ours, on the Day of the Lord Jesus"

1:15–2:13
 + 7:5-13a   III. *Probatio*

1:15-16   A. The First *Narratio*: Clarifying Paul's travel plans
1:15   1. Summary of travel plans: "I wanted to come to you first, that you might have a double favor"
1:16   2. First segment of plans: "I wanted to visit you on my way to Macedonia"

Letter G 225

	3. Second segment of plans: "and to come back to you from Macedonia"
	4. Third segment of plans: "and have you send me on my way to Judaea"
1:17-22	B. The first proof: defense of Paul's first formulation of travel plans
1:17a	1. First point (stated as *interrogatio*) about Paul's consistency in his first intention: "Was I vacillating when I wanted to do this?" (understood answer: no)
1:17b	2. Second point: about honor of Paul in changing travel plans
	a) Statement of thesis(as *interrogatio*): "Do I make plans like a worldly man, ready to say Yes, Yes, and also No, No?"
1:18	b) First argument: Paul has not been Yes and No
	(1) Presupposition: "As God is faithful"
	(2) Statement of argument
1:19	c) Second argument: Paul's gospel has not been Yes and No
	(1) Definition of content of gospel: "the Son of God, Jesus Christ, whom we preached among you"
	(2) Specification of preachers of gospel: "Silvanus Timothy and I"
	(3) Statement of argument:
	(a) Negatively: "not Yes and No"
	(b) Positively: "in him it is always Yes"
1:20-22	(4) Further reasons for argument (other parts of the content of Paul's and the Corinthians' faith)
1:20	(a) First reason (Christology): "for all the promises of God find their Yes in him"
	(b) Second reason (liturgical practices of the community in response to Christology): "That is why we say the Amen through him, to the glory of God"
1:21	(c) Third reason (Paul's apostolic office)
	i) Statement of reason: "God establishes us with you in Christ"
	ii) Restatement of reason: "he has commissioned us (=Paul)"
1:22	(d) Fourth reason(baptism and its theological meaning)
	i) First meaning: seal
	ii) Second meaning: Spirit in heart as guarantee
1:23–2:13	C. The second *narratio*: Paul's change of travel plans
1:23	1. Calling of witness to attest to statement of facts
	a) First witness: God
	b) Second witness: "my own soul"

	2. Statement of facts
	a) First statement: "it was out of consideration for you that I did not come to Corinth"
1:24	b) Justification of first statement
	i) Negatively: "not that we lord it over your faith"
	ii) Positively: "we are fellow workers for your joy, for you stand in the faith"
2:1	c) Second statement: "For I made up my mind not to make another visit in pain to you"
2:2	d) Justification of second statement: "If I cause pain to you, who is there to comfort me?"
2:3	e) Third statement: "And I wrote this very thing in order that I might not come and be pained by those who should be cheering me up"
	f) Justification of third statement: "trusting that you were aware that my joy was all of your joy too"
2:4	g) Fourth statement: "For it was out of much tribulation and anxiety of heart, with many tears, that I wrote you"
	h) Justification of faith statement
	i) Negatively: "not to cause you pain"
	ii) Positively: "but that you might know my abundant love for you"
2:5-11	D. The second proof: concerning forgiveness for an offending brother
2:5	1. Introduction to section: "If anyone caused pain, he didn't cause me pain, but in part—not to belabor the point—he caused all of you pain"
2:6	2. Advice concerning the offending brother
	a) With regard to the previous penalty: "The penalty that was agreed on by the general meeting is sufficient"
2:7	b) With regard to present action:
	i) Relationship to previous penalty: "Something very different is needed now"
	ii) Reason for present action (stated negatively): "lest such an overpowering grief overwhelm such a man"
2:8	iii) Statement of present action advised
2:9	c) With regard to Paul's part in the previous penalty: the reason for writing the letter was to test obedience
2:10	d) With regard to present action (forgiveness)
	i) Concerning the forgiveness of the Corinthians and of Paul
	(a) Concerning Paul's concurrence with the Corinthians' forgiveness: "anyone you forgive, I forgive"
	(b) Concerning Paul's authority to forgive: "anyone I forgive, if I should forgive anything, I forgive as a deputy of Christ"
2:11	ii) Concerning the reason for forgiveness: "so that Satan may not defeat us, for we are not unaware of his designs"

2:12-13 + 7:5-7	E. The third *narratio*

2:12	1. Paul's travel to Troas
	   a) Specification of destination: Troas
	   b) Reason for travel
	      i) First reason (mission): "where I was to preach the gospel of Christ"
	      ii) Second reason (mission): "where a door was opened to me in the Lord"

2:13	c) Paul's distress in Troas: "no rest for my spirit, for I did not find Titus" d) Paul's departure from Troas: "but I left them and set out for Macedonia"
7:5-7	2. Paul's travel to Macedonia

7:5	a) Specification of destination: Macedonia
	   b) Paul's distress in Macedonia
	      i) Specification of distress: "our flesh had no rest"
	      ii) Reasons for distress: "we were afflicted in every way—fights without, fears within"

7:6	c) Paul's consolation in Macedonia
	      i) Consoler: God
	         (a) Name of deity: "God"
	         (b) Aretalogy: "who consoles the downcast"
	      ii) Means of consolation: "the arrival of Titus"

7:7	iii) Extent of consolation
	         (a) Concerning Titus: "not only in the coming of Titus"
	         (b) Concerning the Corinthians: "but also in the consolation with which we were consoled about you"
	            (1) Statement of extent
	            (2) Reasons for consolation
	         (a) "Your longing for us"
	         (b) "how sorry you are"
	         (c) "your zeal for me"
	         (c) Summary of extent: "so that this cheered me up"

7:8-13	F. The third proof: an explanation of the "letter of tears"

7:8	1. Paul's attitude in writing the letter
	   a) Present: "I do not now regret it"
	   b) Past: "I may have been sorry when I saw that the letter had caused you pain, even if only for a time"

7:9-11	2. The response to the "letter of tears"
7:9a	a) Paul's reaction to the Corinthians' response: "now I am happy, not because you were hurt, but because you were wounded into repentance"
7:9b	b) The Corinthians' response: "you were hurt in God's way, so that you suffered no damage through us"
7:10	i) Statement of response

	ii) Specification of reason for favorable response: a comparison of:
	(a) Grief borne in God's way
	(b) Grief borne in the world's way
	iii) Specification of the results of the letter
	(a) eagerness
	(b) vindication
	(c) anger
	(d fear
	(E) longing (for Paul)
	(F) zeal
	(G) drive for justice
7:11	iv) Summary of results of the letter: "You demonstrated yourselves blameless in every particular."
7:12-13a	3. Paul's goal in sending the letter
7:12	a) Transition from earlier sections: "Although I wrote you the letter . . ."
	b) Specification of goal
	i) Negatively: "not because of the offender or the offendee"
	ii) Positively: "but so that your eagerness for us might be made clear to you in the sight of God"
7:13a	c) Summary of the goal and its results: "therefore we are consoled"
7:13b-16	IV. *Peroratio* (stated as more narrative, but using both *conquestio* and *recapitulatio*)
7:13b	A. *Conquestio*: Paul's response to the joy of Titus
	1. Statement of Paul's response
	a) Transition from previous section: "Besides being encouraged ourselves"
	b) Specification of Paul's response: "we were delighted beyond everything by seeing how happy Titus is"
	2. Reason for Titus' joy: "that his spirit was refreshed from all of you"
7:14	B. *Recapitulatio*
	1. First point (the favorable present status of the Corinthians in Paul's eyes): "Anything I may have said to him (Titus) to show my pride in you has been justified"
	2. Second point (the honor of Paul): "just as everything we ever said to you was true"
	3. Third point (the honor of Titus): "our boast also in Titus proved true"
7:15	4. Fourth point (the favorable present status of the Corinthians in Titus' eyes)
7:16	5. Summary (the favorable present status of the Corinthians in Paul's eyes, restated): "I rejoice because I am completely confident in you"

13:11-13	V.	Epistolary Conclusion
13:11		A. Summary of letter
13:12		B. Instructions to greet one another, together with greetings from "all the saints"
13:13		C. Final prayer for the readers

NOTES

1. Furnish, *II Corinthians*, 47; Roetzel, *2 Corinthians*, 124.
2. See Jewett, *Romans*, 957–58.
3. Roetzel, *2 Corinthians*, 128.
4. See Welborn, *End to Emnity*, 476–78.
5. Roetzel, *2 Corinthians*, 143–46; see the discussion in notes 110 and following above.
6. See Roetzel, *2 Corinthians*, 125.
7. See Mitchell, "Letters to Corinth," 309.
8. Welborn, *End to Enmity*, 481.
9. Menander Rhetor 413.5–414.30.
10. For a recent general discussion of epideictic rhetoric, see especially the edition and translation of *Menander Rhetor* by D. A. Russell and N. G. Wilson (Oxford: Clarendon Press, 1981), xi–xxxiv. On p. xiii, they list the following as examples of funeral speeches: the speech of Pericles in Thucydides, *History* 2.34ff., the *Menexenus* of Plato, *Oration* 6 of Hyperides, *Oration* 2 of Lysias, and *Oration* 60 of Demosthenes. On the relation of the funeral speech to early rhetoric, see especially Nicole Loraux, *The Invention of Athens: The Funeral Oration in the Classical City*, translated by Alan Sheridan (Cambridge: Harvard University Press, 1986).
11. Menander Rhetor tells us that advice can be a part of a funeral speech (especially advice to children in place of consolation, 421.25-26), as well as exhortation to copy the virtues of the deceased, 421.30-32. The funeral speech may also be "rounded off with a prayer," 422.2-5.
12. English translation of Pseudo-Demetrius's example is found in Stanley K. Stowers, *Letter Writing in Greco-Roman Antiquity*, LEC 4 (Philadelphia: Westminster Press, 1986), 144; Greek original is in *Demetrii et Libanii qui feruntur Τύποι Ἐπιστολικοί et Ἐπιστολιμαίοι Χαρακτῆρης*, edited by Valentinus Weichert (Leipzig: Teubner, 1910), 4–5.
13. Cicero, *De inventione* 1.106 (English translation by H. M. Hubbell, *Cicero. De inventione, De optimo genere oratorum, Topica*, LCL [Cambridge: Harvard University Press, 1949]).
14. Cicero, *De inventione* 1.107.
15. Cicero, *De inventione* 1.109.
16. Cicero, *De inventione* 1.109.
17. St. Augustine, *De doctrina christiana* 4.12.
18. Sampley, "Second Letter," 38.

19. Jewett, "Paul, Phoebe," 144–64.
20. Sampley, "Second Letter," 38.
21. The notable exception is Galatians, where Paul did not include a thanksgiving prayer in the exordium of that letter. The subject and tone of Galatians do not fit the use of a thanksgiving prayer that would be understood to have been expressed with any degree of sincerity.
22. Cicero, *De inventione* 1.20.
23. According to Aristotle, *Ars rhetorica* 3.16.16, in deliberative rhetoric "narrative is very rare, because no one can narrate things to come."
24. Aristotle, *Ars rhetorica* 3.16.1, tells us that in epideictic rhetoric, the narrative "should not be consecutive, but disjointed."
25. *Rhetorica ad Alexandrum* 1438b15-25 and 1436a39-41, respectively.
26. Quintilian, *Institutio oratoria* 4.2.79: "*Aut quid inter probationem et narrationem interest, nisi quod narratio est probationis continua propositio, rursus probatio narrationi congruens confirmatio?*"
27. Furnish, *II Corinthians*, 37.
28. Furnish, *II Corinthians*, 37.
29. On declamation, see especially D. A. Russell, *Greek Declamation* (Cambridge: Cambridge University Press, 1983).
30. *Rhetorica ad Herennium* 1.3: *haec omnia tribus rebus adsequi poterimus: arte, imitatione, exercitatione*; cf. Quintilian, *Institutio oratoria* 3.5.1: *facultas orandi consummatur natura, arte exercitatione, cui partem quartam adiciunt quidem imitationis*.
31. On rhetorical criticism as the identification of an author's rhetorical strategies, see Carl Joachim Classen, *Recht–Rhetorik–Politik: Untersuchungen zur Ciceros rhetorischer Strategie* (Darmstadt: Wissenschaftliche Buchgesellschaft, 1985), especially 11–12.
32. On the other hand, the new book by Michael C. Parsons and Michael Wade Martin, *Ancient Rhetoric and the New Testament: The Influence of Elementary Greek Composition* (Waco: Baylor University Press, 2018), argues in favor of using *progymnasmata* and other elementary rhetorical school exercises as models, rather than models based on the usual arrangement of speeches. Yet the interesting history of declamation, as we have discussed just above, shows that along with the elementary exercises, such as the *progymnasmata*, parts of speeches and whole speeches were part of the instruction in rhetorical schools. We suggest that it is neither necessary nor desirable to set one part of rhetorical instruction over against another, as we compare early Jesus-believing literature in its complexity with Greek and Roman rhetoric in their complexities. See the discussion in Parsons and Martin, especially pp. 1–3 with notes 17 and 18 on p. 11.

Chapter 12

Letter H

An Appeal to the Achaians (2 Cor 9:1-15)

THE PROVENANCE OF 2 COR 9

There are a number of differences between the way the Apostle is using rhetoric for fundraising in 2 Cor 8 and 2 Cor 9.[1] Generally speaking, 2 Cor 8 is mostly concerned with motivating the majority of the Corinthian congregation to be generous, in respect of a collection of money which has substantially not been raised. And generally speaking, a considerably larger portion of 2 Cor 9 is concerned with the rationale for distributing the money and the reliability of those who will carry the money. Given these differences, it is most likely that different historical and even geographical situations are presupposed.[2] In both cases, 2 Cor 8 and 9 utilized the standard topics of deliberative rhetoric: advantage and honor.[3] What was being argued, however, differs substantially in these two letter-fragments.[4] The basic difference between the two parts of the letter-fragments that we have is that 2 Cor 8 is quite clear that the giving by the Corinthian church to Paul's collection for the relief of Jerusalem Christians had stopped, or perhaps that the collection so far had been graced by contributions from only a few church members, meaning that it had not fully taken place by the time Paul wrote 2 Cor 8. Paul did not defend himself in Letters A, B, C, and D, and so we surmise that Paul thought that he did not need to do so, as he wrote those letters. Of course, much had happened after Letter C, his appeal for unity, so that things were different when Paul wrote Letter H. Paul wrote in Letter D: "In this I give my opinion. For this is advantageous to you, whoever not only began to do but also to desire (to do something) since last year. Now, however, complete the task, for just as there was the eagerness that comes from desiring it, let it be fulfilled from what you have" (2 Cor 8:10-11). We translate the correlative pronoun οἵτινες here as "whoever" rather than "you."[5] This seems to relate to the fact that some members of the Corinthian church had already contributed: some members of the congregation "began." Yet probably because of the conflict between most of the Corinthian congregation and Paul, the majority of the Corinthian Christians may well have not yet contributed to this collection. Thus, the Apostle asked the Corinthians to "complete" what "whoever" "began." After the deep conflict between Paul and the Corinthians, which reached its two climaxes in Paul's painful second visit and in Letter F, it would have been difficult for Paul to conclude that the offering for the relief of the Jerusalem Christians was in any condition other than serious doubt. By the time of his dictating and sending his bombastic Letter F, it does not seem likely that Paul thinks the Corinthian Christians have raised a great deal of money at all: he refers to the donors as "whoever began last year," according to 2 Cor 8:10. This is the reason he asked the Corinthian Christians to "complete" the offering, which perhaps had only barely begun before the giving stopped.

The situation in 2 Cor 9 clearly appears to be significantly different from that underlying 2 Cor 8. Betz has identified 2 Cor 9 as an "administrative letter," directed to a different group of Jesus-believers than the church in Corinth. Roetzel in his commentary on 2 Corinthians concurs.[6] In fact, quite unlike Letter D (2 Cor 8), Letter H (2 Cor 9) was written to Christians in Achaia, not those in the city of Corinth per se. Achaia was the Roman province of which Corinth was the capitol, and yet even though Corinth was the capitol, Paul does not mention the city or church of Corinth by name, a church in which he had spent a great deal of time.[7] There is also no mention of any part of the conflict that Paul had suffered with Corinth. Paul chose not to rehearse any of that conflict here as he is writing to a group of churches, perhaps house-churches, in Achaia outside the capitol city. It would not have been to Paul's rhetorical advantage, in the context of this letter to other Achaian Christians, to mention the protracted and bitter struggle between the Corinthian Christians and himself. We do not know whether the Achaians would have known about the Corinthian conflict.[8]

Instead of writing about an offering that has fundamentally not yet been raised, as in 2 Cor 8, Paul writes in Letter H of an offering about which he says, "Achaia has been prepared since last year" (2 Cor 9:2). There is a great administrative difference between an offering, which has substantially not been raised and an offering, which has been raised, but has not been applied to the purpose for which the donors had given money.

Looking at what we have of Letter H, we can see that Paul mentioned that his boasting to the Macedonians about the Achaians' preparedness to give (παρεσκεύασται, "you have been prepared," perfect tense, passive voice) had actually stirred the Macedonians to more giving: "your zeal has stirred the majority of them."

THE RHETORIC OF LETTER H

The situation in which the rhetoric of 2 Cor 9 fits best is that the money has substantially been raised as donations from the group of congregations in Achaia outside Corinth, as 9:1-4 indicates. Paul's rhetorical goal in this letter appears to persuade the Achaians to hand over the money raised to the people who will take it to Jerusalem. Just because the money is raised, or substantially raised, Paul may well be worried that the leaders of the congregations in Achaia will choose not to hand over the offering to Paul and the others who would personally bring the offering to Jerusalem. The Achaian congregations might decide to keep all or part of this offering and apply it to other purposes, perhaps in order to help other congregations other than the Jesus-believers in Jerusalem.

Despite its inclusion in the canonical 2 Corinthians, it is not clear that 2 Cor 9—the remaining fragment of Letter H—has anything directly to do with the congregation in Corinth. Its inclusion in the canonical form of 2 Corinthians appears to us to have come about as a phenomenon of editing. Both Letters D and H, 2 Cor 8 and 2 Cor 9, are about fundraising, so it is not hard to see that in the editing process, these two letter-fragments would have been placed together in the diverse collection known to us as 2 Corinthians.

The way rhetoric is used in 2 Cor 9 is different from its use in 2 Cor 8, even though they are both within the *genus* of deliberative rhetoric. Paul uses the analogy from farming to describe giving and receiving. Notably in 9:6-10, Paul uses analogies that are highly agricultural, which makes sense, given that he is writing to people who are not city people. Those who are stingy in their giving are compared with those who "sow sparingly" (9:6), and they will likewise "reap sparingly." Conversely, those who "sow bountifully" will also "reap bountifully." This is an exhortation not merely to giving, but to generosity. Yet, at the same time as Paul exhorts the Achaians to give generously, he also mentions that they should give "as each person has made up his or mind, not reluctantly or under compulsion, for God loves a cheerful giver" (9:7). Generous giving will bring an advantage to the giver, namely "abundance for every good work" (9:8), so that "you will be enriched in every way for great generosity, which through us will produce thanksgiving to God" (9:11). Indeed, the recipients of the Achaians' generosity "long for you and pray for you, because of the surpassing grace of God in you" (9:14).

So in Corinthian Letter H, 2 Cor 9:1-15, the motivation for giving is not the generosity of the poor Macedonians or of Christ himself, but the mission of the church, namely to help fellow Christians who are in need. Paul uses both standard topics of deliberative rhetoric in 2 Cor 9, just as he did in 2 Cor 8. Paul argues on the basis of honor in 9:2-4. He changes his argumentation to the topic of advantage in vv. 5-14.

So, even though Paul used the same topics of honor and advantage in the two letter-fragments, it is significant that he used them in different ways. This is not surprising in that in both cases, he was exhorting the recipients of his persuasive letters to give for the relief of Jerusalem Christians, which is to say that he was asking them to take a course of action in the present, which would affect the future of the church. In the case of 2 Cor 8, his exhortation to give came, as far as he knew at the time, before the protracted conflict between the Corinthian Christians and himself, perhaps following relatively quickly after Paul responded in Letter C to the detailed reports about disunity from "those of Chloë" (1 Cor 1:11). He probably believed that the disunity in the Corinthian church had probably been resolved, due to his pastoral correction of the Corinthians by means of Letter C. So in Letter D, 2 Cor 8, Paul wrote to ask the Corinthians to collect the money they had promised to collect when Paul made his first visit to Corinth, during which time he founded the church. Paul subsequently made very full use of the topics of consolation in Letter G, which was written to make sure that the Corinthians stayed reconciled to Paul (and to God), and probably also in the hope that they would resume giving to Paul's collection for the relief of fellow Jesus-believers in Jerusalem. In Letter G, Paul seems certain that the reconciliation has really taken place, based on Titus' report, 2 Cor 7:6-16. Paul is quite emphatic in 7:16, the last verse of the fragment of Letter G that we have: "I rejoice that I have confidence in you in every respect."

The letter fragment we identify as Letter H reflects a different situation, and the fact that the same deliberative topics are used as in Letter D is one example that, while Paul does not use any rhetorical handbook slavishly, he seems to know that deliberative argumentation is effective when it uses both standard topics of advantage and honor. Nonetheless, if we were to assume that these two chapters were originally in the same letter of Paul to the Corinthians, it would be rhetorically strange for Paul to have used honor and advantage in chapter 8, and then for him to turn around and use honor and advantage again in chapter 9, yet in different ways. The fact that Paul mentioned the Achaians in 2 Cor 9, instead of the Corinthians,[9] all the while using the two standard topics in quite different ways in the two chapters, confirms that 2 Cor 9 is a fragment from a different letter. It is unfortunate that we do not have certain knowledge of whether the Corinthians ever gave the money to Paul and the other people who were carrying the money to Jerusalem.[10] In Romans 15:26, however, he mentions only the churches in the provinces of Macedonia and Achaia as having given to the offering to help fellow Christians in Jerusalem. No specific mention is made of the Corinthian congregation, which is all the more striking since Paul was spending the winter in Corinth when he wrote Romans. Since the most prominent congregation of Jesus-believers in Greece is not mentioned, when he had spent so much time there, this omission appears to be a good indication that the Corinthians had not completed their share of the offering by the time Paul wrote Romans, in great contrast to the generosity of the Macedonians and the cities in Achaia other than Corinth. Paul, of course, did not miss the irony of the situation that the generous Macedonians were thought to be proverbially poor, in contrast to the apparently stingy Christians living in the major commercial center of Greece. Yet to our best knowledge and belief, Paul's efforts to raise money from the church in the well-to-do city of Corinth probably came to very little, while the relatively poor people of Macedonia and the people of Achaia outside the capitol city of Corinth gave generously. If this conclusion is correct, we may say that, like several other letters of the Corinthian correspondence, which Paul dictated and sent to the Jesus-believers in that city, what we have of Letter D was most likely not persuasive enough, while Letter H, addressed to a different group of Jesus-believers in different locations in Achaia, may have been successful.

By placing the material about the Jerusalem offering in the relative obscurity of 2 Cor 8 and 9, the redaction redirected the thrust of Paul's ministry. Its climax was no longer the long-planned journey to Jerusalem and Rome aimed at reconciliation between Gentile and Jewish believers and the presentation of their message of the gospel to the Roman Empire. It was rather to lead the resistance against the internal enemy, proto-Gnosticism. By ending 1 and 2 Corinthians with climactic affirmations of Pauline leaders and warnings against heresies, the way is prepared for the creation of the Pastoral Epistles. Moreover, as our investigation has demonstrated, every redactional decision involved in the creation of the Corinthian correspondence shows evidence of critical interaction with proto-gnostic ideas.

The Rhetorical Arrangement of Letter H

(Missing)	(I. *Exordium*)
2 Cor 9:1-15	II. *Probatio*
9:1-2	A. Introduction to the proof
9:1	1. First part of introduction: the figure of *praeteritio*: "it is superfluous for me to write anything to you"
9:2	2. Second part of introduction: *captatio benevolentiae*: "I know how eager you are to help; I speak of it proudly to Macedonians: I tell them that Achaia has been ready for a year, and most of them have been fired by your zeal"
9:3-5	B. First argument: the purpose of Paul's sending emissaries to Corinth

236   *Chapter 12*

9:3   1. Statement of argument: "My purpose in sending . . . to ensure that what we have said about you should not prove to be an empty boast"
                             2. Identification of emissaries: "the brothers"
                             3. Further explanation of reasons for sending emissaries
                                a) Paul's desire for the Corinthians: "I want you to be prepared"
                                b) Paul's boast about the Corinthians: ". . . as I told them you were (prepared)"
9:4   c) An *exemplum* of unpreparedness
                                   i) Statement of *exemplum*
                                   ii) Result of *exemplum*: "what a disgrace it will be to us, not to mention you"

9:5   d) Paul's ultimate reason for sending the emissaries: to get the Corinthians prepared for his visit
                                   i) Statement of reason
                                   ii) The *exemplum* of preparedness
                                   iii) The result of the *exemplum*
                                       (A) Stated positively: "it then will be awaiting me as a bounty indeed"
                                       (B) Stated negatively: "and not as an extortion"

9:6-15   C. Second argument: an appeal to give generously

9:6   1. Statement of argument: "This is it: he who sows sparingly will reap sparingly, and he who sows bountifully will reap bountifully"

9:7-15   2. Reasons to support argument
9:7   a) The attitude of giving
                                   i) Stated positively: personal decision about giving
                                   ii) Stated negatively: "there is to be no reluctance, no compulsion, for God loves a cheerful giver"

9:8-15   b) The relationship of God to giving
9:8   i) First part: God's power to give
                                   ii) Second part: the result of God's gift: "thus you will have ample means in yourselves to meet each and every situation, with enough and to spare for every good cause"

9:9   iii) An *exemplum* from Scripture about God's giving
                                       (A) Quotation formula: "thus it is written"
                                       (B) Quotation of Psalm 112:9
9:10   iv) Third part: the gift and its purpose
                                       (A) Identification of giver: "He who provides seed for sowing and bread for eating"
                                       (B) Identification of gift: "will provide seed for you to sow"

9:11-15	(C)	Results of gift
9:11		(1) First result: multiplication of gift
		(2) Second result: bounty for the Corinthians
		(3) Third result: thanksgiving to God
		(a) Statement of result
9:12		(b) Identification of result in terms of the Jerusalem church
		(c) Reiteration of result: thanksgiving to God
		(4) Fourth result: increased honoring of God as a result of the Corinthians' becoming *exempla*
		(a) Statement of result
		(b) Specification of exemplary qualities of Corinthians
		(i) First quality: "how humbly you obey" God
		(ii) Second quality: "how faithfully you confess the gospel of Christ"
9:13		(5) Fifth result (*repetitio*): thanksgiving to God
		(a) Statement of result
		(b) Reason for result: "your liberal contribution to their need and to the general good"
9:14		(6) Sixth result: intercessory prayers for the Corinthians by the Jerusalem church
		(7) Seventh result: the goodwill of the Jerusalem church for the Corinthian church: "their heart will go out to you"
		(a) Statement of result
		(b) Reason for result: "because of the richness of the grace which God has bestowed upon you"
9:15	v)	Conclusion of explanation of relation of God to giving: Paul's own prayer of thanksgiving

NOTES

1. Keith F. Nickle, *The Collection: A Study in Paul's Strategy* (Naperville, IL: Allenson, 1966; reprinted Eugene, OR: Wipf & Stock, 2009), 22, comments: "In the second letter (ch. 9) which followed shortly after, Paul changed the direction of his argument. No longer using the Macedonian response as an example for the Corinthians, he instead somewhat frantically informed them that he had used their earlier enthusiasm and expected (but not yet forthcoming) performance as an example for the Macedonians; an example which was instrumental in the success realized there (vv. 2ff.). This intensification of Paul's anxiety was undoubtedly heightened by the rapid approach of his own trip to Corinth, on which he would be accompanied by the representatives of these same Macedonian churches (v. 4)."

2. See especially Calvin J. Roetzel, *2 Corinthians*, ANTS (Nashville: Abingdon Press, 2007), 147: "Both the timing and the address of 9:1-15 set it apart from the

earlier offering letter in 8:1-24. While the earlier offering letter probably went primarily to Corinth to persuade a distrustful congregation to complete their lagging collection project, this letter is a round robin epistle to the churches of Achaia that, unlike Corinth, have eagerly embraced the offering effort perhaps from the beginning. . . . Whereas chapter 8 signals the beginning of the offering project, chapter 9 declares the offering project is nearing completion. . . . Thus 9:1-15 is no mere doublet of 8:1-24 but is probably an independent and later epistle written for a wider audience."

3. See Frank W. Hughes, "The Rhetoric of Reconciliation: 2 Corinthians 1.1–2.13 and 7.5–8.24," in Duane F. Watson, editor, *Persuasive Artistry: Studies in New Testament Rhetoric in Honor of George A. Kennedy*, JSNTSup 50 (Sheffield: JSOT Press, 1991), 246–61, especially 257–60. At the time of writing that article, we believed that 2 Corinthians 8 was at the end of the "letter of reconciliation." This is a position that we no longer hold.

4. On the historical placement of 2 Corinthians 8 earlier in the sequence of letters, see especially the definitive article by Margaret M. Mitchell, "Letters to Corinth," 307–38, especially 321–33. Concerning 2 Corinthians 9, Mitchell comments, "The storms now passed, Paul leaves debates about epistolary meaning behind, and sets in motion the final stages of the collection for the saints in Jerusalem from all the province of Achaia" (335).

5. *BDAG* gives several meanings of ὅστις, ἥτις, ὅ τι. One of them is "any person, *whoever, every one who*, in a generalizing sense" and another meaning is "undetermined person belonging to a class or having a status, *who, one who*" (729).

6. Roetzel, *2 Corinthians*, 30–33, 147–55.

7. Mitchell, *Paul, the Corinthians and the Birth of Christian Hermeneutics* (Cambridge: Cambridge University Press, 2010), comments: "The very last piece of the correspondence is preserved in what is now 2 Corinthians 9, a final request to the Corinthians and indeed the whole Roman province of Achaia to seal their bond with him and with the Macedonians (whose example Paul had invoked to their anger and regional jealousy back in the early stage [2 Corinthians 8] by joining in the collection effort for the saints in Jerusalem)." Her position presupposes that Paul in mentioning in Achaia in 2 Corinthians 9 is also including the Corinthian congregation.

8. Betz, *2 Corinthians 8 and 9*, comments as follows: "Paul also seems to have had an exceptionally good relationship with the Christians of Achaia. So far as we can tell, the Corinthian crisis was limited to Corinth, while the other Achaian churches maintained an untroubled and loyal relationship to the apostle. For this reason, Paul turned to them when he needed assistance in bringing the collection for Jerusalem to a conclusion" (52).

9. On the many political and social differences between the Corinthians and people from elsewhere in Achaia, see Betz, *2 Corinthians 8 and 9*, 49–53.

10. Nickel comments: "Acts does not inform us whether the collection Paul brought to Jerusalem was well received by the church there or not. It does not even mention if it was delivered. As a matter of fact, the only mention made of the collection at all in Acts is an obscure reference in Paul's speech before Felix (Acts 24.17; cf. 24.26) . . . . Let it suffice to note here that in this one minor allusion the author of Acts either intentionally or ignorantly pictured it as a delivery by Paul of

traditional Jewish contributions from the Diaspora to Jerusalem" (*Collection*, 70). Roetzel, *2 Corinthians*, 156, also comments: "In the end, however, the letters provide no information on how or if the offering was received in Jerusalem. The Acts account suggests that the presentation did not go well (21:17-40). The effort by Paul and his Gentile converts to present the offering in the Temple brought an accusation that he had defiled the holy place (Acts 21:28). He was arrested, charged, and sent to Rome for trial." To these comments, we add our opinion, based on our rhetorical reading of Acts. If the offering from the Gentiles had truly been graciously accepted by Jewish Jesus-believers in Jerusalem, as Paul had surely hoped, it is difficult to think that the writer of Acts would have neglected to point out this joyous event in Jerusalem, which would have foreshadowed the future unity of Gentile and Jewish Jesus-believers. Thus, we fully agree with Dieter Georgi, *Remembering the Poor: The History of Paul's Collection for Jerusalem* (Nashville: Abingdon, 1992), 126: "Had Luke learned of such an announcement, he would certainly have made use of it."

Part Three

REFLECTIONS ON THE REDACTION OF THE ORIGINAL LETTERS

Chapter 13

Redirecting Paul's Ministry

In chapters 2 through 4 of this study, we have examined the evidence in favor of partition theories concerning the composition of both 1 and 2 Corinthians, including our hypothesis of a redaction involving both Corinthian letters. In chapter 5 through 12 of this study, we have looked carefully at the rhetoric of the resultant reconstructed letters and letter-fragments, in the order in which we believe the original letters were dictated and sent by the Apostle Paul. Given our hypothesis of redaction, in this chapter, we wish to state some logical conclusions of the intentional redaction of the original Corinthian letters into the two Corinthian letters we have in the New Testament.

The original Corinthian letters were most likely edited in the late first century or early second century CE. It is reasonable to assume that they were edited, in quite discernible ways, for one or more reasons. The major reason for the redaction which took place was a struggle against what was considered heresy near the time of the end of the first century. Heresies in the second century CE are by no means difficult to imagine since there is so much evidence of them in the extant writings of Jesus-believers in that period. What remains difficult is the identification of one of the several strands of Jesus-believing at any time in the second century as orthodox.[1] It is interesting to note that the most important of the heresiologists, Irenaeus of Lyons, around 180 CE wrote a five-volume work entitled Ἔλεγχος καὶ ἀνατροπὴ τῆς ψευδωνύμου γνώσεως ("On the Detection and Refutation of Knowledge Falsely So-Called"), typically referred to by its Latin title *Adversus haereses* or "Against Heresies" in English. The original Greek title comes from the Pauline corpus, specifically 1 Timothy 6:20: "Timothy, guard what has been entrusted to you. Avoid the profane chatter and contradictions of what is falsely called knowledge." The person to whom the warning against "what is falsely called knowledge" is directed is none other than Timothy, a major hero of the authentic Pauline letters, and in fact one of Paul's closest deputies. The three Pastoral Epistles, 1 and 2 Timothy and Titus, have as their addressees Paul's two closest protégés. Evidently they were considered in Pauline churches to be the ultimate guarantors of Paul's theology and practice, after Paul's martyrdom. They were to Paul what the apostles were to Jesus in the gospels, with the notable difference that Timothy and Titus appear to have been faithful to Paul, quite unlike the original disciples of Jesus, according to the passion narratives in the gospels.

In the late first-century or the early second-century period, a time of multiple and difficult changes in Jesus-believing communities, Timothy and Titus were portrayed in the Pastoral Epistles as well as the Corinthian letters as examples of faithfulness and steadfastness. Examples of steadfastness were particularly important in situations of deep conflicts, which were probably at both the theological and practical levels. At the same time in which Timothy was held up as an example of doctrinal steadfastness, that is, no changes from what Paul himself had taught, people like Demas, Crescens, Alexander the coppersmith, and even Titus (2 Tim 4:9-14) were described as "in love with the present world" (2 Tim 4:9). Since we know that things were unsettled in the Corinthian congregation during Paul's lifetime, the strong likelihood is that life in various Pauline churches was even more unsettled after the Apostle's martyrdom.[2] The Apostle was no longer physically present to correct those who needed correction. His correction of the Corinthian congregation by letter, as we have shown, was difficult and much of the time unsuccessful. It is altogether likely that late first-century Jesus-believers who exercised leadership in Pauline churches would have believed that they needed more help in correcting wayward Jesus-believers now that Paul had been martyred. They required rather more powerful tools to deal effectively with what they understood to be heresy, not just anywhere but specifically within Pauline congregations. This suggests the importance of understanding certain letters of the Pauline corpus not merely as pseudepigrapha but as *Pauline* pseudepigrapha.[3] The fact that they were included within the Pauline corpus indicates their importance to Pauline churches at the times at which they were written and published, the late first century or the early second century, after Paul's martyrdom.

The new letters appearing to be written by Paul should not be considered as afterthoughts in the Pauline corpus. They were part and parcel of what various late first century leaders would have needed to communicate to readers in not just any churches, but *Pauline* churches. It was precisely because Paul was an authority figure in Pauline congregations, and evidently more so after his martyrdom, that the Pastoral Epistles were written and disseminated. The people that would have needed the Pastoral Epistles, of course, were not Timothy and Titus themselves, but the local leadership in Pauline congregations. The new instruction for the new local leadership needed to be in writing. This new instruction could then be circulated along with the older, authentic letters of Paul. They could also be disseminated along with the redacted Corinthian letters, the letters dealing most specifically with congregational problems. Instead of a single letter here or a couple of letters there, a collection of Pauline letters including the redacted 1 and 2 Corinthians and any or all of the Pastoral Epistles could serve as a powerful corrective to both heterodoxy and heteropraxy.

During his lifetime, Paul was hardly an undisputed authority figure in Pauline churches. After his martyrdom, the pseudonymous writings we have in the Pauline collection of letters reflect a different, entirely positive estimation of Paul's authority. Whereas the historical Paul had taught primarily personally and secondarily through his letters, the new *ēthos* of Paul was that he taught through his letters alone. Paul's letters, after his death, were invested with a level of authority that they had never had during the Apostle's lifetime. These letters were not yet part of a closed canon of Holy Scripture, but they were read, discussed, cherished, collected, copied, compared, and recopied, as Colossians 4:16 shows. When there were new problems that had never occurred in Paul's time, pseudonymity was used by writers in Pauline communities, just as pseudonymity was already a typical practice in some of the writings of early Judaism.[4] Part of the phenomenon of pseudonymity is pseudonymity used in letters.[5] The study of the letters of the Pauline corpus since the early nineteenth century has included the discussion and analysis of letters, which are believed to utilize pseudonymity. Excluding Hebrews, the letters in the Pauline corpus, which appear to be the least likely to have been written by Paul, are the Pastoral Epistles.[6]

Among the ecclesiastical concerns of 1 and 2 Timothy and Titus and of Ephesians are two which are of greatest interest to those who examine the Corinthian correspondence. First, there is the interest in portraying Paul as the universal teacher of at least the Gentile church, coupled with the corollary of portraying Paul as a person whose authority and *ēthos* oppose heresy.[7] Second, there is the emphasis in 1 Timothy and Titus on the institution of local congregations, which are headed by ἐπίσκοποι, which we will translate as "bishops." Where Paul had addressed his letter to the Philippians to "those in Philippi, together with bishops and deacons" (τοῖς οὖσιν ἐν Φιλίπποις σὺν ἐπισκόποις καὶ διακόνοις, Philippians 1:1), specifically including a plural number of bishops in the Philippian church, in the Pastoral Epistles, we read "Paul" writing specifically about a single bishop for each congregation. With presumably multiple deacons and perhaps multiple widows per congregation, a team of people doing ministries is implied; yet in the church order written into 1 Timothy and Titus, there is emphatically *one* bishop per church.

In the wider spectrum of Jesus-believing congregations in the late first century was the indisputable fact that the ἀπόστολοι had died. Most of them had died as martyrs. After those who had been with the historical Jesus before his death, as well as those who had experienced the risen Jesus, including Paul and some of the people Paul knows such as the "well known apostles" Andronicus and Junia (Romans 16:7), were no longer around to exercise their authority as apostles in the church, it is clear that the ἐπίσκοποι were placed in the highest positions of authority. Another phenomenon is that the apostles like Paul were traveling evangelists, church-planters, and church-correctors. They successfully spread the Gospel around the Mediterranean Sea and in other places. The authority exercised by traveling church-planters in Paul's time would be exercised after Paul's death by the local head of each congregation, the ἐπίσκοπος, whose title was already in use in the secular world as an "overseer" or "supervisor." Instead of plural ἐπίσκοποι in a local congregation as in Paul's time, there came to be one ἐπίσκοπος in each local congregation. This latter situation is what is clearly reflected in the Pastoral Epistles.[8] This was an extremely significant change in the structure of the congregations from Paul's time to that of the Pastoral Epistles.

Since the ἐπίσκοποι did not originally have the status to exert authority to any extent beyond their local congregation, as the ἀπόστολοι had had, it would have been natural for the local ἐπίσκοπος to fill the vacuum of ecclesial authority that the death of the ἀπόστολοι had created. In the late first-century and early second-century period, when heresies were beginning to flourish, very notably in the permanent absence of the ἀπόστολοι, it is not hard to understand how the increase in the authority of each local ἐπίσκοπος would take place. This shift in the structure of authority involved a change from the charismatic understanding of authority in Paul's time to a structure that can be called hierarchical, with ἐπίσκοποι clearly in charge of local congregations. The written justification and foundation for this shift in authority in Pauline churches is in fact the Pastoral Epistles.

THE LETTER TO TITUS

Several passages in the Pastoral Epistles illustrate the concerns of the late first-century and early second-century Jesus-believing congregations. In the Letter to Titus, there is no thanksgiving prayer, but the letter, after the salutation, opens with a review of Paul's leaving Titus in charge of the church in Crete: that he should "organize what remained to be done, and should appoint πρεσβύτεροι in every town, as I directed you" (1:5). In Titus 1:6-9, there is list of qualifications for πρεσβύτεροι, quite analogous with qualifications for ἐπίσκοποι, διάκονοι, and χῆραι (widows) in 1 Timothy. There is an extended contrast between people who practice good behavior and those who practice bad behavior. Instead of a job description for those in the paid ministry of widows, as in 1 Timothy 5, women are directed to avoid drinking too much alcohol and to teach younger women to love husbands and children (Tit 2:4), indeed being "submissive to their husbands, so that the word of God may not be discredited" (2:5).

THE FIRST AND SECOND LETTERS TO TIMOTHY

Among the Pastoral Epistles, only 2 Timothy is written from incarceration. 2 Timothy is also explicit about Paul having ordained Timothy. With or without ordination, there are various lists of qualifications in 1 Timothy for ἐπίσκοπος (1 Tim 3:1-7), διάκονοι (3:8-13), χῆραι (widows, 5:3-16, and πρεσβύτεροι (presbyters, 5:17-22), yet there is no specification of Timothy in 1 Timothy as having been ordained.

The *ēthos* of Paul is of greatest interest. In 2 Timothy, Paul mentions his trials and troubles, which were numerous. Timothy, however, is to be proud of Paul's troubles, rather than being ashamed of Paul because of his incarceration. 2 Timothy does also mention other coworkers with Paul who have fled, given that Paul was put in jail, apparently awaiting trial. We do not know what crime Paul was charged with, yet several of Paul's traditional coworkers, including Titus, have fled. What exactly does 2 Timothy mean in 4:10-16, especially in 4:10 where "Titus has gone to Dalmatia"? Is the Paul of 2 Timothy accusing Titus of abandonment?

Paul is now not just an apostle: he is now "a herald and apostle and teacher" (2 Tim 1:11). Especially since an ἀπόστολος was understood as primarily a traveling church-planter, on either side of this title are written two other titles not used by Paul before: he is now—especially since he cannot travel outside his incarceration or if indeed he has departed his natural life—primarily a person who both "proclaims" the gospel and also teaches it. His proclamation, in the late first century if not the early second century, after his martyrdom, and even during the last part of his actual incarceration, can only be through his letters, which are apparently in some sort of collection that is available to some Christians. Paul now proclaims and teaches through his letters in what will eventually become the Pauline corpus of letters. If this collection of letters is still in its inception or if it is only a local phenomenon in some Pauline churches, this might very well account for the Acts of the Apostles' silence concerning Paul's letter writing. If Paul has been martyred by the time of 2 Timothy, if not also by the time of 1 Timothy and Titus, he can only speak through his letters and what people in Pauline churches remember of his oral teaching. The physical voice of Paul himself has been stilled, and yet Paul's λόγος, coming in one or more ways (in both letters and oral teaching) from Paul through Pauline churches still speaks.[9] Hence, it continued to be important for the written message of Paul to continue to be read.

Yet in order for that written message of Paul to be received well, Paul's *ēthos* needed modification for the late first century or the early second century of the Common Era. Part of why Paul praises Timothy in 2 Timothy is the fact that Timothy was not ashamed to be associated with Paul, even given his troubles, including his incarceration. Part of Paul's suffering, to be sure, is the fact that he is thought of by some early Christians as one who suffers "as an evildoer" (2 Tim 2:9). Because his reputation has been so besmirched, Paul's *ēthos* needed rehabilitation. What better situation to effect such a rehabilitation Paul's successors (formerly his collaborators) would have thought than appealing to the reality of Paul's martyrdom? The bleakness of Paul's incarceration, despite the efforts of some church people to allow him and his guard to stay in rented accommodations, is countered by the glory of Paul's faithful ministry, in a situation which led to his execution.

The Pastoral Epistles argue for an understanding of Paul as the universal teacher of Jesus-believing communities, and so an important corollary of Paul's role as the universal teacher is the content of what Paul now teaches through his letters, and what Jesus-believing communities are taught by those who minister in them. An important part of what Timothy as well as other ministers of the gospel should be expected to do will be to correct those whose understanding of the faith in Jesus is heretical. Timothy, the ostensible addressee of 2 Timothy, is ordered in writing to correct those who have defective understandings of the faith. There will be theological struggles (2:23) to be sure, and those who have gotten the faith wrong need to be corrected (2:24). Those who disobey are compared with Jannes and Jambres in the Hebrew Bible in the time of Moses (3:8). This comparison of those who are disobedient in Pauline churches with those who disobeyed Moses may perhaps imply a pairing of certain Pauline letters, as far as the writer of 2 Timothy was concerned, with the Hebrew Bible.

THE LETTER TO THE EPHESIANS

Although the Letter to the Ephesians does not share the understanding of church order and offices that one sees in 1 Timothy and Titus, Ephesians does clearly contain the idea of Paul's being the universal teacher of the church. The teaching authority Paul had during his earthly life was now extended and heightened, via one or more collections of Pauline letters. The Paul who could not be present in a particular church because he was at or en route to other churches is now not present anywhere physically because of his martyrdom.

Yet though his body was no longer present, Paul continued to teach through his letters. Ephesians 3:1-13 is the *locus classicus* for a description of Paul's teaching ministry, after his death. Schnelle writes as follows:

> In Ephesians 3:1-13 [Paul] appears as the crucial messenger of revelation for the church (cf. Col. 1:24-29), for he reveals the previously hidden mystery of the granting of salvation to the gentiles (Eph. 3:6, 8), to all humankind, and to the powers (Eph. 3:10). In the memory of his person/his work, the Pauline apostle to the nations appears after his death (Eph. 3:1; 4:1) in a dimension that is significant for salvation history. Paul is the decisive recipient of the revelation of God, which leads to the universal church composed of Jews and people from the nations. . . . The apostleship guaranteed through Paul appears as the norm for the relationship to Christ. . . . Because the apostle is a messenger of the mystery of the gospel (Eph. 6:20), this mystery can be appropriately preached only by him. The recourse to Paul and the associated pseudepigraphic character of Ephesians thus results necessarily from the image of Paul communicated in the letter.[10]

In an article published in 1981, cited by Schnelle, Helmut Merklein examined how the image of Paul was being used in Colossians and Ephesians.[11] Notably, Merklein begins a new section with the statement, "Constitutive for the image of Paul in Colossians and Ephesians is therefore that 'Paul' himself now belongs to the content of proclamation; therefore he belongs within the 'mystery.'"[12] Merklein also points to the relation of what is said about Paul's ministry in 3:1-13 to the image of the church as a building, built upon the foundation of the apostles and prophets, with Christ Jesus as the cornerstone (2:2).[13] Thus in the theology of Ephesians as a whole, Paul in his role as teacher has become part of the mystery, since he interprets and teaches the content of the mystery to those who are privileged to learn from him, no longer in person since his martyrdom, but through the letters by him as they have been handed on to the churches as a central part of the traditions of Jesus-believers. The "foundation of the apostles and prophets" also may imply—by the time Ephesians was written—the heightened status of a collection of Pauline letters, as in Ephesians 2:20 both "the apostles and prophets" make up the foundation of the building, the ἐκκλεσία, which here is not compared to a living, moving body, the body of Christ (as Paul did), but is spoken of as a building, complete with a foundation and a cornerstone.

CONCLUSION

In this chapter, we have shown significant points of contact between two of the manifestations of Pauline theology and practice after the Apostle's martyrdom. Far from there being a major emphasis on Paul's incarceration and death, both the Pastoral Epistles and Ephesians focus their readers' attention on the strongly positive influence Paul had on Gentile Jesus-believing congregations. During his natural lifetime, he founded a number of congregations, and after his martyrdom, the influence of his ministry, especially his theological leadership of churches, continued to grow and develop. The congregations, which, after his death, considered Paul's ministry to be good and fruitful continued to look to Pauline letters for guidance. Leaders in these churches can reasonably be expected to have welcomed written Pauline letters to use to guide and govern congregations when there were questions or conflicts about either old or new practices or teachings. The same forces that caused the Pastoral Epistles and Ephesians to be written were also highly conducive to the profound editing of already existing Pauline letters, such as the several letters to Corinthian believers. In this study, we have shown that it is likely that eight original letters by Paul to Corinthian Jesus-believers were edited in such ways as to display characteristics that addressed concerns that are more likely to have occurred in the second and third generations of Jesus-believers. The editing that took place between the form of the original letters to the congregation in Corinth and the canonical form of the two letters in the New Testament reflects the need for the church to pursue the things that made for stability. This stability, in the opinion of the Pastoral Epistles, needed to include directions both to oppose heresy and to support the theological foundation of right belief and practice.[14] In order to oppose heresy and to create a structure of right belief and practice, there have to be both a foundation and building materials. Paul, as interpreted by certain late first-century or early second-century Jesus-believers, was the foundation, apparently together with his ways of interpreting the scriptures of Judaism. The Deutero-Pauline and Pastoral Epistles, along with the editing of the Corinthian correspondence, as we have shown, were the building materials. Thus, both the Deutero-Pauline letters and the Pastoral letters contributed in their particular ways to the ongoing development of Pauline churches in the late first century and early second century of the Common Era.

NOTES

1. See especially Walter Bauer, *Orthodoxy and Heresy in Earliest Christianity*, translated from the 1964 German reissue and edited by R. A. Kraft and G. Krodel (Philadelphia: Fortress, 1972).

2. Udo Schnelle, *The First One Hundred Years of Christianity: An Introduction to its History, Literature, and Development* (Grand Rapids: Baker Academic, 2020), reminds us of the unsettled nature of several types of Jesus-believing communities: "Between 60 and 70 CE a critical culmination occurred within the history of the

theology of the early church. Problems of both the internal logic of faith and the external influences resulted in the necessity of making a literary and theological new orientation. Three of the most important figures of early Christianity died as martyrs almost contemporaneously shortly before the Jewish War." These three figures were James, the brother of the Lord, Peter, and Paul. "Their deaths constituted a clear turning point for the self-understanding of Christianity, also precipitating a new literature. In place of the eyewitnesses and appearances and the personal activity of the apostles for the expansion of Christianity, the written record now takes the form of the new literary genre of the gospel and of the pseudepigraphic letters (Deutero-Paulines and apostolic letters under the names of Peter, James, and Jude" (299).

3. Raymond F. Collins, *Letters that Paul Did Not Write: The Epistle to the Hebrews and the Pauline Pseudepigrapha*, GNS 28 (Wilmington, DE: Michael Glazier, 1989).

4. John J. Collins, *Apocalypse, Prophecy, and Pseudepigraphy: On Jewish Apocalyptic Literature* (Grand Rapids: Eerdmans, 2015).

5. Jörg Frei, Jens Herzer, Martina Janßen, and Clare K. Rothschild, editors, *Pseudepigraphie und Verfasserfiktion in frühchristlichen Briefen / Pseudepigraphy and Author Fiction in Early Christian Letters*, WUNT 246 (Tübingen: Mohr Siebeck, 2009).

6. On pseudepigraphy in the Pastoral Epistles, see especially Jens Herzer, "Fiktion oder Täuschung? Zur Diskussion über die Pseudepigraphie der Pastoralbriefe," in Frei Herzer et al., *Pseudepigraphie*, 489–536, as well as Frank W. Hughes, "Pseudonymity as Rhetoric." See also Norbert Brox, *Die Pastoralbriefe*, 4th edition, RNT 7/2 (Regensburg: Pustet, 1969). For a positive estimation of Pauline authorship of the Pastorals, see George W. Knight, III, *The Pastoral Epistles*, NIGTC (Grand Rapids: Eerdmans, 1992), as well as Philip H. Towner, *The Letters to Timothy and Titus*, NICNT (Grand Rapids: Eerdmans, 2006).

7. Schnelle, *First One Hundred Years*, comments concerning the Pastoral Epistles as follows: "As the only legitimate proclaimer, Paul himself becomes the content of the preaching so that a soteriological dimension is attributed to his work. . . . As authorized proclaimer and content of the gospel, Paul in the Pastoral Epistles becomes the guarantor of the tradition and the legitimate teacher. He instructs the churches in 'sound teaching': διδασκαλία and παραθήκη designate the totality of what is presented in the Pastorals as preaching and ethical instruction. While the false teachers split the church with their false teaching, Timothy and Titus, along with the churches that are addressed, should hold firmly to the original teaching and to the Scripture . . ." (341). "As a whole, the Pastoral Epistles present an exceedingly vigorous image of Paul who stands up for and battles for his churches as preacher, teacher, pastor, and church organizer. Paul is equally an apostle, church authority, supporter of a collective identity, and the ideal/model of a Christian. His dominant place in the churches does not have to be established by the author of the Pastorals, for he writes in a living Pauline tradition" (342).

8. Hans von Campenhausen, *Ecclesiastical Authority and Spiritual Power in the Church of the First Three Centuries*, translated by J. A. Baker (London: Adam & Charles Black, 1969), 107–8.

9. Hans von Campenhausen, *Ecclesiastical Authority*, 106–23, especially 106–9.
10. Schnelle, *First One Hundred Years*, 339–40.
11. Helmut Merklein, "Paulinische Theologie in der Rezeption des Kolosser- und Epheserbriefes," in Karl Kertelge, editor, *Paulus in den neutestamentlichen Spätschriften*, QD 89 (Freiburg, Basel, Vienna: Herder, 1981), 25–69.
12. Merklein, "Paulinische Theologie," 29.
13. Merklein, "Paulinische Theologie," 33: "Die Kirche ist auferbaut auf dem Fundament der Apostel und Propheten, wobei Christus Jesus der Eckstein ist" (Eph 2,20).
14. Charles H. Talbert, *Ephesians and Colossians*, Paideia Commentaries on the New Testament (Grand Rapids: Baker Academic, 2007), identifies two trajectories of thought in the early church about the role of Paul: "the one that views Paul as an apostle alongside the Twelve, and the one that views Paul as the sole apostle" (104). The Pastoral Epistles, along with Ephesians, Talbert argues, belong to the second trajectory: "As in Ephesians, Paul is *the* apostle and authoritative teacher of the church, 'by the will of God' (2 Tim 1:1; cf. Eph 1:1). . . . The Paul of the Pastorals is an aged spiritual giant. The Paul of Ephesians is the 'father of the Gentile mission.' In these two postapostolic canonical depictions of Paul the emphases are very similar, perhaps because they come from the same Pauline circle." Raymond F. Collins in *Letters That Paul Did Not Write* also comments on Ephesians as follows: "The 'Paul' who is a model is unique nonetheless. The paulinist speaks of the church's apostolic foundation (Eph 2:20; 3:5; 4:11), yet he mentions only one apostle by name. That is Paul 'an apostle of Christ Jesus by the will of God' (Eph 1:1) . . . . An epistle which highlights the apostolic foundation of the church as a key element in the unfolding of the mystery of salvation cites only the apostle Paul by name. . . . Paul's preaching of the gospel has a universal scope" (168–69).

Part Four

HISTORICAL IMPLICATIONS

Chapter 14

The Publication of 1 and 2 Corinthians
From Scroll to Codex

Our thesis about the redaction of 1 and 2 Corinthians throws light on one of the most puzzling features of early Jesus-believing communities. Whereas all of the Jesus-believing writings of the second century, including all of the biblical materials, are in codex form, 98 percent of writings other than those of Jesus-believing communities in that period are in scrolls rather than codices.[1] An even more striking observation is that every Jewish copy of the Hebrew Scriptures was in scroll form, whereas every fragment of the holy books of Jesus believing communities, whether belonging to what was later called the Old or New Testament, was transmitted exclusively in codex form. Since the earliest documents that developed into the New Testament were Pauline letters, undoubtedly written on scrolls, this transition to codex is one of the most remarkable features of the early church. In view of the innate conservatism of religious movements, this transition is particularly puzzling. As is well known, the Jewish tradition never made such a transition, even in the later period when codices became dominant. A distinctive feeling of holiness evoked by the scrolls of Jewish Scriptures continues to the present day. Since the writers involved in the creation of the writings that developed into the New Testament were all profoundly influenced by Judaism, this transition is even more amazing. Harry Y. Gamble writes that "the Christian use of the codex is a genuine anomaly that needs an explanation. Why did the codex come so early to be the favored format for Christian literature but take much longer to gain a similar status among non-Christians?"[2]

Previous efforts to answer this question have been unconvincing. In the discussion thus far, only the positive advantages of codices have been taken into account. Scant attention has been given to the much more serious question as to why the original scroll materials are entirely absent. Among the thousands of examples of New Testament documents, there are only a few fragments in scroll form. David Trobisch lists a few tiny fragments of NT texts on scrolls, none of which appears to be part of an extensive citation.[3] Since the original Pauline letters were in the form of scrolls, which were widely distributed between Pauline congregations, the elimination of these original documents and their replacement by documents on codices cannot have been accidental. A widely supported campaign of suppression was required. This suppression must have occurred at a very early stage in the transmission of Jesus-believing documents and it reflects a conviction that the original form of these documents contained a significant danger for the early church. We return to this issue after evaluating previous suggestions about the alleged practical advantages of codex over scroll.

A seemingly plausible explanation is that since codices were written on both sides of the page, the material cost must have been about half as expensive as documents in scroll format. Several factors render this explanation implausible. In addition to the calculation by T. C. Skeat that reduced this to "a saving of 26% of the cost of the roll format by changing to the codex,"[4] there were increased labor costs in "cutting the sheets from a roll and then stacking and binding them."[5] Moreover, as Roberts and Skeat point out in *The Birth of the Codex*, there are no indications in any New Testament documents of economic concerns expressed by narrow margins or compressed scripts in order to crowd in more letters per page.[6] This alleged economic consideration was thought to be crucial because of the lower-class setting of early congregations, but more recent studies have shown that the leaders of house churches were usually not impoverished.[7] Copies of individual Pauline letters for exchange between churches as reflected in Colossians 4:16 would not have imposed an insuperable burden for patrons of house churches. Economic considerations cannot therefore account for the transition from scroll to codex.

Some scholars have suggested that the codex form was preferred by early Jesus-believers because of its convenience. A codex could be held in one hand and could simply be closed after use rather than being rolled back up to its starting point. As Harry Gamble points out, however, what seems obvious to moderns accustomed to books did not appear to be irksome for persons used to working with scrolls.[8] A related possibility is ease of reference,[9] because a specific text can be more quickly located by opening a codex than by unrolling a scroll. This may seem plausible to modern readers accustomed to working with numbered chapters and verses, but the numbering system developed a millennium later and there is not a single example of references by ancient writers even to page numbers. It appears that the page numbers on some ancient codices were "merely a device for keeping the pages in the right order during the process of binding and—perhaps even more important—to ensure that none were missing."[10] Convenient reference must therefore be discarded as an explanation for the transition from scroll to codex.

A more decisive aspect of convenience may have been ease of carrying. M. McCormick pointed to the superior portability of codices as a factor explaining their preponderance in a movement shaped by itinerant evangelists.[11] For example, the Chester Beatty codex of Numbers and Deuteronomy would have required a scroll 28 meters long, far too large for easy carrying or convenient use.[12] However, as Eric Turner has shown, it was not until the fourth and fifth centuries that Christian codices of this size began to appear.[13] The earliest codices of Jesus-believing literature are so small that their advantage in portability was marginal.[14]

An advantage in comprehensiveness was undoubtedly gained by placing groups of early Jesus-believing writings into codices. To copy all four gospels and Acts in a single volume as in one of the Chester Beatty codices would have been totally impossible on a single scroll. Gregory the Great reported that he was able to place the material from thirty-five rolls onto only six codices.[15] It appears, however, that the concern for comprehensiveness was a relatively late development, because as we noted earlier, all of the early codices are relatively small. These considerations clarify the usefulness of codices in later church history but provide no adequate rationale for the early decision to abandon the scroll form of the earliest writings that came to be viewed as inspired scripture, the Pauline letters. Roberts and Skeat provided an assessment that we believe is appropriate for the entire issue of comprehensiveness:

> As regards the question whether the quality of comprehensiveness may have influenced the early Christians in their choice of codex, the answer must be much the same as in the case of compactness, namely that it is doubtful whether it can have been an important factor as early as A.D. 100.[16]

Since none of these explanations of practical advantages proved convincing, hypothetical links with early Jesus-believing writings have been proposed. This approach was summarized by Harry Gamble, that "some early Christian document of high authority was originally issued in a codex and that the authority of its content carried over to the kind of book in which it was transcribed, and thus the codex was promoted as the standard form of the Christian book."[17] Colin Roberts developed the initial form of such a hypothesis, that Mark's gospel was originally written on the parchment codex in Rome and was later copied into papyrus codices after it arrived in Alexandria.[18] Neither textual critics nor gospel specialists have found this hypothesis plausible,[19] but as Harry Gamble points out, "the basic assumption ... is sound: there must have been a decisive, precedent-setting development in the publication and circulation early Christian literature that rapidly established the codex in Christian use, and it is likely that this development had to do with the religious authority accorded to whatever Christian document(s) first came to be known in codex form."[20] Our hypothesis explains how this came about with the publication of the Corinthian correspondence.

Gamble makes a case that the publication of the Pauline letter corpus was the occasion that first required a codex because its contents would have filled a scroll at least 80 feet long, which was "more than double the maximum length of Greek rolls and roughly three times what may be regarded as a normal length."[21] This calculation rests on the assumption shared by other scholars who coordinate canonical lists with manuscript evidence that there were three forms of this letter corpus: a collection of ten letters arranged according to length; a collection of letters written to seven churches; and Marcion's revised collection that placed Galatians at the beginning.[22] The presence of two other sequences of seven letters in the book of Revelation and the writings of Ignatius make it likely that the original Pauline corpus contained letters to seven churches[23] arranged by length. The two Corinthian letters, understood as a single long document, were probably followed by Romans, Ephesians, Galatians, Philippians, Colossians (with Philemon), and the two Thessalonian letters, making a total of ten.[24] The Chester Beatty papyrus of the early third century contains nine letters in the sequence Romans, Hebrews, 1 and 2 Corinthians, Ephesians, Galatians, Philippians, Colossians, and 1 Thessalonians, with space in the mutilated end to accommodate 2 Thessalonians but not the Pastoral Epistles.[25] When the three Pastoral Epistles were added to the collection, Philemon was moved to the end, thus retaining the structure of ten letters to seven churches, followed by four letters to individual church leaders. Although many of these details are elusive and remain in dispute, Harry Gamble concludes that this publication explains the transition from scroll to codex:

> The coming together of this transcriptional need and religious authority in the Pauline letter collection and nowhere else makes it nearly certain that the codex was introduced into Christian usage as the vehicle of a primitive edition of the *corpus Paulinum*.[26]

This theory by Harry Gamble resolves many of the shortcomings in earlier explanations of the rise of the codex. What it fails to explain is the absence of copies of Paul's letters in their original form. It is clear from Colossians 4:16 that early Pauline congregations were exchanging such letters, in all probability in their original scroll form. There must have been many such documents in circulation within decades of Paul's founding missions. An extremely urgent rationale must have been felt by the second- and third-generation congregations to search out and destroy every copy of Paul's letters in scroll form. This reflects a life and death struggle of sufficient importance to overturn the respect that originally was granted to the Pauline letters, in their original form, as they were circulating among the churches of Greece, Asia Minor, and Rome. None of the previous theories provides a sufficient rationale for this fundamental change from scroll to codex, including its systematic enforcement. The struggle against incipient and early forms of gnosticism provides such a rationale.

The redaction of the letters to Corinth and Rome in the struggle against early heresy among Jesus-believers required a publication in redacted form that would replace the most dangerous Pauline letters that were being employed by teachers perceived to be heretics. The redacted letters needed to be published in a form that would not allow further large-scale editing, which the choice of codex automatically accomplished by being written on both sides of the page. The fact that an early use of codex was in Roman legal collections shows that the advantage of textual reliability was widely recognized. No further alterations of these early codices of the literature of Jesus-believing communities were possible, aside from occasional, brief marginal notes and emendations identified by later textual critics. Once the shift to codex was made, probably in the redacted forms of Paul's letters to Rome and Corinth, it soon came to be recognized in orthodox circles that letters in codex form were authentic while copies in the original scroll form that were still being employed by their opponents were hence heretical. With the later development of various forms of the Pauline letter corpus and gospel collections, this rationale persisted while providing the suitable model for collections of other early Jesus-believing documents. The advantages of portability, price, comprehensiveness, ease of reference, and so forth helped to reinforce the priority of the codex form.[27]

Our study of the redactional process and its relation to competing groups within the Pauline mission field offers some clues to the time and place of the publication of 1 and 2 Corinthians. The likelihood that a portion of Corinthian Letter B left over from the redaction of 1 Corinthians found its way into 2 Corinthians (2 Cor 6:14–7:1) and that a portion from Corinthian Letter F (1 Cor 9:1-18) was excised from material that came to comprise a part of 2 Corinthians makes it quite likely that both letters were edited at approximately the same time. The similarity in redactional method and viewpoint suggests the same person or circle was responsible for both 1 and 2 Corinthians. This conclusion is not contradicted by the fact that 1 Corinthians was much more widely cited in the early part of the second century, as noted by Bornkamm.[28] Mitton had summarized the results of the Oxford Committee's analysis on this point: "It is clear that 1 Corinthians is the letter of Paul which has most clearly impressed itself on the minds of early Christian leaders. This epistle is confidently known early in the second century in the churches of Rome and Asia Minor, and perhaps in Syria."[29] This scholarly consensus correlates exactly with the results of the current study.

The priority of 1 Corinthians is explained by our redactional analysis, namely that the goal of creating the canonical letter was to spike the cannons being fired from Corinthian Letter C, the Pauline letter that served as a manifesto for the opponents of the early catholic movement reflected in the Pastoral Epistles. We have demonstrated that the argumentative situation in the latter decades of the first century accounts for the fact that 1 Corinthians was so energetically copied and distributed. There was less urgency in the distribution of 2 Corinthians, because it dealt with a less crucial issue: countering the anxious depiction of Paul in Letter G. This was achieved by inserting triumphal material from Letter E and adding the authoritative Letter F to the point of emphasis at the end of 2 Corinthians. The resultant image of Paul's apostolic authority was shared by most branches of the Pauline movement, while the burning issues raised by gnostic intellectuals set the agenda and prepared the way for the creation of the Pastoral Epistles.

Our hypothesis about the creation of 1 and 2 Corinthians in codex form also provides the basis for drawing some inferences about the identity of the Pauline school. It must have been a group of disciples who were conversant with the complicated techniques required for the creation and publication of codices. This points to a house church that was engaged in the business of publication. Its leaders must have been involved in extensive debates with proto-gnostics over the proper interpretation of the Pauline letters to the Corinthians. These debates would have revealed not only which Pauline statements were most useful in supporting the proto-gnostic viewpoint but also which passages could be cited in support of the conservative alternative. The agenda for the redaction of the Corinthian correspondence that we have analyzed in this study thus emerged in all probability out of these controversies.

A series of chronological and historical details make it likely that the redaction and publication of the Pauline letters occurred in the decades between 90 and 110 CE and that this process took place somewhere in Rome or Western Asia Minor. The fragment of Titus in Papyus Ryland I 5 provides a *terminus ad quem* in the second century.[30] Michaela Engelmann has made a plausible case that the Pastorals were written in the sequence of 2 Tim, Titus, 1 Tim and that their relationship to each other does not demand a third-generation provenance;[31] a period between the death of Paul in 62 CE and the end of the second generation of believers around 100 thus seems plausible for the writing of the Pastorals. A broad consensus was stated by Günther Zuntz a generation ago and still remains plausible, "that the archetypal *Corpus* was produced about A. D. 100."[32]

In conclusion, it is clear that this observation by Zuntz correlates very well with evidence elsewhere that the basic transition from scroll to codex occurred before or after the end of the first century CE. If Zuntz is correct on this point, the likelihood is that the redaction of the Corinthian correspondence took place in the late first century or the very early second century.

NOTES

1. Colin H. Roberts and T. C. Skeat, *The Birth of the Codex* (Oxford: Oxford University Press, 1983), 73.

2. Harry Y. Gamble, *Books and Readers in the Early Church: A History of Early Christian Texts* (New Haven and London: Yale University Press, 1995), 54; see also William A. Johnson, "The Ancient Book" in Roger S. Bagnall, editor, *The Oxford Handbook of Papyrology* (New York: Oxford University Press, 2009), 256–81, especially 267.

3. See David Trobisch, *Die Endredaktion des Neuen Testaments. Eine Untersuchung zur Entstehung der christlichen Bibel*, NTOA 31 (Göttingen: Vandenhoeck und Ruprecht; Freiburg: Universitätsverlag, 1996), 33.

4. T. C. Skeat, "The Length of the Standard Papyrus Roll and the Cost-advantage of the Codex," *ZPE* 45 (1982): 169–75; 175.

5. Gamble, *Books and Readers*, 54–55.

6. Roberts and Skeat, *Birth*, 46–47.

7. See Meeks, *Urban Christians*, 51 73; Cavan W. Concannon, "The Archaeology of the Pauline Mission," in Mark Harding and Alanna Nobbs, editors, *All Things to All Cultures: Paul Among Jews, Greeks, and Romans* (Grand Rapids: Eerdmans, 2013), 57–83, especially 80.

8. Gamble, *Books and Readers*, 55; Skeat, "Time-Consuming Task," 373–76.

9. Roberts and Skeat, *Birth*, 50–51.

10. Roberts and Skeat, *Birth*, 51.

11. M. McCormick, "The Birth of the Codex and the Apostolic Life-Style," *Scriptorium. Revue internationale des études relatives aux manuscrits* 39 (1985): 150–58.

12. See Roberts and Skeat, *Birth*, 47–48.

13. Eric G. Turner, *The Typology of the Early Codex* (Philadelphia: Fortress, 1977), 82–83.

14. See Gamble, *Books and Readers*, 55.

15. Reported by Roberts and Skeat, *Birth*, 48, from a citation of Gregory, *Epistula*, 5.53a.

16. Roberts and Skeat, *Birth*, 49; see also Gamble, *Books and Readers*, 55.

17. Gamble, *Books and Readers*, 56.

18. Roberts, "Codex," 187–91.

19. See Joseph van Haelst, "Les origines du codex," in Alain Blanchard, editor, *Les débuts du codex. Actes de la journée d'étude organisée à Paris les 3 et 4 juillet 1985 par l'Institut de Papyrologie de la Sorbonne*, Bibliologia: Elementa ad librorum

studia pertinentia, 9 (Brepols: Turnhout, 1989), 13–35, especially 29–31; Gamble, *Books and Readers*, 56–57; as well as commentaries on Mark.

20. Gamble, *Books and Readers*, 58.
21. Gamble, *Books and Readers*, 62–63.
22. Gamble, *Books and Readers*, 59–61; Gamble, *New Testament Canon*, 36–41; Gamble, "The Pauline Corpus and the Early Christian Book," in William S. Babcock, editor, *Paul and the Legacies of Paul* (Dallas: Southern Methodist University Press, 1990), 265–80; Judith M. Lieu, *Marcion and the Making of a Heretic: God and Scripture in the Second Century* (Cambridge: Cambridge University Press, 2015), 234–69, especially 237–42; Frede, "Corpus Paulinum," 292–301; Clabeaux, *A Lost Edition of the Letters of Paul: A Reassessment of the Text of the Pauline Corpus Attested by Marcion*, CBQMS 21 (Washington: Catholic Biblical Association, 1989), 4, 81–87, 103–4, 147–48; Llewelyn and Kearsley, "The Development of the Codex," 249–56; Richards, "The Codex and the Early Collection of Paul's Letters," *Bulletin for Biblical Research* 8 (1998): 151–66; Scherbenske, *Canonizing Paul*, 71–115; for an assessment that takes only the manuscript evidence into account, see Trobisch, *Paul's Letter Collection*, 20–22.
23. See Frede, "Corpus Paulinum," 291.
24. See Gamble, *Books and Readers*, 61.
25. David G. Martinez, "The Papyri and Early Christianity," in Bagnall, editor, *Handbook*, 599–622; 596, citing Eldon Jay Epp, "Issues," 15–37.
26. Gamble, *Books and Readers*, 63.
27. See Johnson, "Ancient Book," 267.
28. Bornkamm, "Vorgeschichte," 33f.
29. Mitton, *Formation*, 22.
30. Martinez, "Papyri," 596, citing Roberts, *Manuscript*, 13; Roberts and Skeat, *Birth of the Codex*, 40–41.
31. Michaela Engelmann, *Unzertrennliche Drillinge? Motivsemantische Untersuchungen zum literarischen Verhältnis der Pastoralbriefe*, BZNW 192 (Berlin & Boston: De Gruyter, 2012), 559–600.
32. Zuntz, *Text*, 279.

Appendices

Appendix I

Summary of the Jewett-Hughes Partition Theory in Relation to the Canonical 1 and 2 Corinthians

JEWETT-HUGHES PARTITION THEORY

Corinthian letters and fragments	Equivalents in the canonical 1 and 2 Corinthians
A	1 Cor 11:2, 17-34a + 1 Cor 11:3-16 + 1 Cor 16:1-4 + 1 Cor 11:34b
B	2 Cor 6:14–7:1 + 1 Cor 6:12–20 + 1 Cor 9:24–10:22 + 1 Cor 15:1–58 + 1 Cor 16:13–24
C	1 Cor 1:1–6:11 + 1 Cor 7:1–8:13 + 1 Cor 9:19–23 + 1 Cor 10:23–11:1 + 1 Cor 12:1–31a + 1 Cor 14:1c–33a + 1 Cor 14:37–40 + 1 Cor 12:31b–13:13 + 1 Cor 16:5–12
D	2 Cor 8:1–24
E	2 Cor 2:14–6:13 + 2 Cor 7:2–4
F	2 Cor 10:1-11:9 + 1 Cor 9:1–18 + 2 Cor 11:10-13:10
G	2 Cor 1:1–2:13 + 7:5–16 + 13:11–13
H	2 Cor 9:1–15

Appendix II
Schematic Representations of the Redactional Process

The Formation of 1 Corinthians

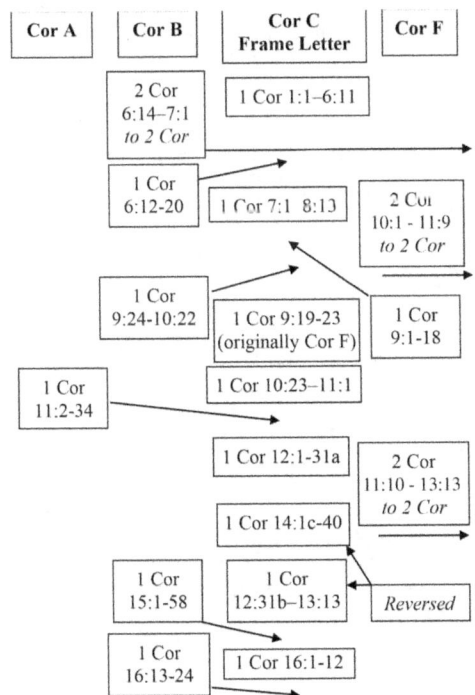

Appendix II

The Formation of 2 Corinthians

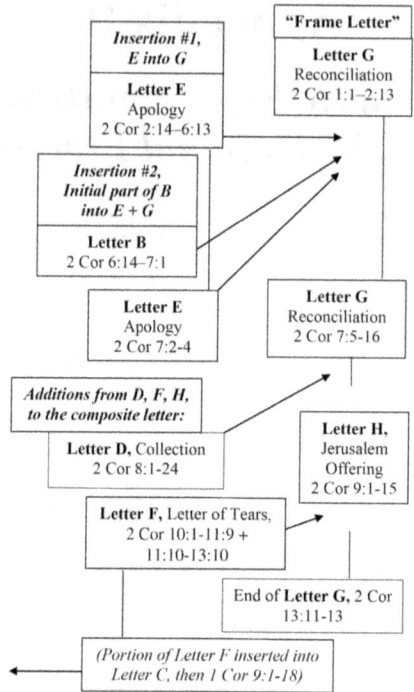

Appendix II

The Result: Canonical 2 Corinthians

1:1–2:13	2:14–6:13	6:14–7:1	7:2-4	7:5-16
From **Letter G**, the Letter of Reconciliation	From **Letter E**, the Letter of Apology	From **Letter B**, the Letter of Bodily Relations	From **Letter E**, the Letter of Apology	From **Letter G**, the Letter of Reconciliation

8:1-24	9:1-15	10:1-11:9 + 11:10-13:10	13:11-13
From **Letter D**, the first Offering Letter	From **Letter H**, the Appeal to the Achaians ("Jerusalem Offering")	From **Letter F**, the Letter of Tears	Conclusion of **Letter G**

Appendix III
Previous Partition and Redaction Theories

Johannes Weiss, *Der erste Korintherbrief* (Kritisch-exegetischer Kommentar zum Neuen Testament; Göttingen: Vandenhoeck & Ruprecht, 1910); *Earliest Christianity: A History of the Period A.D. 30–150* (2 volumes; Harper Torchbooks; New York: Harper, 1959), 356–57:

A:	1 Cor 10:1-23; 6:12-20; 11:2-34; 16:7 (?), 8-9; perhaps 16:20-21; 2 Cor 6:14–2:1
B1:	1 Cor 7:1–8:24; 10:24–11:1, 12:1-31; 13:1-13; 14:1-40; 15:1 58; 16.1-6, perhaps also 16:7 and 16:15-19
B2:	1 Cor 1:1-9; 1:10–6:11; 16:10-14 and perhaps 16:22-24
C:	2 Cor 2:14-6:13; 7:2-4; 10:1-13:13
D:	2 Cor 1:1-2:13; 7:5-16, 9:1-15

Walter Schmithals, *Gnosticism in Corinth: An Investigation of the Letters to the Corinthians* (German original, 1956; Nashville: Abingdon Press, 1971), 100–1, note 30:

A:	2 Cor 6:14–7:1; 1 Cor 6:12-20; 9:24-10:22; 11:2-34; 15:1-58; 16:13-24
B:	1 Cor 1:1-6:11; 7:1–9:23; 10:23–11:1; 12:1–14:40; 16:1-12
C:	2 Cor 2:14–6:13; 7:2-4
D:	2 Cor 10:1–13:13
E:	2 Cor 9:1-15
F:	2 Cor 1:1–2:13; 7:5–8:24

Jean Héring, *The First Epistle of Saint Paul to the Corinthians* (French original, 1948; London: Epworth Press, 1962; *idem, The Second Epistle of Saint Paul to the Corinthians* (French original, 1958; London: Epworth Press, 1967):

A:	1 Cor 1-8; 10:23–11:1; 16:1-4, 10-14
B:	1 Cor 9, 10:1-22; 11-15
C:	2 Cor 10-13
D:	2 Cor 9
E:	2 Cor 1-8

Günther Bornkamm, *Die Vorgeschichte des sogenannten Zweiten Korintherbrief* (Heidelberg: Carl Winter, 1965), as cited by Linda L. Belleville, *Reflections of Glory* (JSNTSup 52; Sheffield: JSOT Press, 1991) 85 note 2:

1:	2 Cor 2:14–6:13; 7:2-4
2:	2 Cor 10:1-13:10
3:	2 Cor 1:1–2:13; 7:5-16; 8:1-24; 13:11-23
4:	2 Cor 9:1-15
5:	2 Cor 6:14-7:1

Wolfgang Schenk, "Der 1. Korintherbrief als Briefsammlung," *Zeitschrift für die neutestamentliche Wissenschaft* 60 (1969): 219–243:

A:	1 Cor 1:1-9; 2 Cor 6:14-7:1; 1 Cor 6:1-11 . . . 11:2-34; 15:1-58; 16:13-24 (Vorbrief = previous letter)
B:	1 Cor 9:1-18, 24-27; 10:1-22; 6:12-20; 5:1-13
C:	1 Cor 7; 8; 9:19-23; 10:23-11:1; 12:1-31a; 14:1c-40; 12:31b-13:13; 16:1-12 (Antwortbrief = answering letter)
D:	1 Cor 1:10-4:21
E:	2 Cor 2:14-6:13; 7:2-4
F:	2 Cor 10:1-13:10 (13?)
G:	2 Cor 1:1-2:13; 7:5-16 (13:11-13?)
H:	2 Cor 8
I:	2 Cor 9

Walter Schmithals, *Die Briefe des Paulus in ihrer ursprünglichen Form* (Zürcher Werkkommentar zur Bibel; Zürich: Theologischer Verlag, 1984):

A:	1 Cor 11:2, 17-34
B:	1 Cor 9:24-10:22; 6:12-20
C:	1 Cor 6:1-11; 2 Cor 6:14-7:1
D:	1 Cor 15:1-58; 16:13-24
E:	1 Cor 11:3-16; 7:1–8:13; 9:12-22; 10:23–11:1; 12:1-31a; 14:1c-40; 12:31b–13:13; 16:1-12 (Antwortbrief = answering letter)
F:	1 Cor 1:1–3:23; 4:14-21
G:	1 Cor 5:1-13

H: 1 Cor 4:1-5; 9:1b-18; 2 Cor 6:3-13; 7:2-4a
J: 2 Cor 4:2-14
K: 1 Cor 4:7-13; 2 Cor 2:14–3:13; 4:16–6:2; Romans 13:12b-14
L: 2 Cor 10:1–13:13 (Tränenbrief = letter of tears)
M: 2 Cor 8:1-24a (Kollektenbrief = fundraising letter)
N: 2 Cor 1:1–2:13 ; 7:5-7, 4b, 8-16; 9:1-15; Romans 5:1b-10 (Freudenbrief = letter of joy)

Philipp Vielhauer, *Geschichte der urchristlichen Literatur: Einleitung in das Neue Testament, die Apokryphen and die Apostolischen Väter* (de Gruyter Lehrbuch; Berlin and New York: Walter de Gruyter, 1975; durchgesehener Nachdruck 1978), 141–53:

A:	1 Cor 11:2-34
B:	the remainder of 1 Cor
C:	2 Cor 2:14–6:13; 7:2-4; 10:1–13:13
D:	2 Cor 1:1-2, 13; 7:5-16; (?) 9:1-15
E:	2 Cor 8:1-24

Dieter Georgi, "Corinthians, Second," in *The Interpreter's Dictionary of the Bible, Supplementary Volume* (Nashville: Abingdon Press, 1976), 183–86:

A:	2 Cor 2:14–6:13 + 7:2-4
B:	2 Cor 10:1–13:13
C:	2 Cor 1:1–2:13 + 7:5-16
D:	2 Cor 8:1-24
E:	2 Cor 9:1-15

Christophe Senft, *La première épître de Saint Paul aux Corinthiens* (Commentaire du Nouveau Testament, deuxième serie, 7; Geneva: Labor et Fides, 1990 [first edition 1979]), 19:

A1:	1 Cor 6:1-11; 15:1-58; 16:13-24
A2:	1 Cor 6:12-20; 11:2-34
B:	1 Cor 5:1-13; 9:24-10:22
C:	1 Cor 7:1-40; 8:1-13; (9:1-18); 9:19-23; 10:23-11:1; 12:1–14:40; 16:1-12
D:	1 Cor 1:1-4:21

Gerhard Sellin, "Hauptprobleme des Ersten Korintherbrief," in *Aufstieg under Niedergang der römischen Welt*, II.25.4 (Berlin and New York: de Gruyter, 1987), 2940–3044 (quotation is from page 2979):

A (Vorbrief):	1 Cor 11:2-34; 5:1-8; 6:12-20; 9:24–10:22; 6:1-11
B (Antwortbrief):	1 Cor 5:9-13; 7:1–9:23; 10:23–11:1; 12:1–14:33a, 37-40; 15; 16
C:	1 Cor 1:1–4:21

Appendix IV

Translations of the Eight Original Letters

CORINTHIAN LETTER A

1 Cor 11:2, 17-34a + 1 Cor 11:3-16 + 1 Cor 16:1-4 + 1 Cor 11:34b

(11:2) Now I praise you because you remember me with respect to everything, just as I handed it on to you, and you are observing these traditions. (11:17) In this, I am telling you, however, I do not praise you: when you come together, it is not for the better but for the worse. (18) First of all, when you are gathered together in the assembly, I am hearing that there are divisions among you, and I believe it in part. (19) For it is necessary that there are differences of opinion among you, in order it may become clear who are genuine among you. (20) Thus, when you gather in the same place, it is not the Lord's supper that you are eating. (21) For each one of you brings along his or her own supper, and one goes hungry and another gets drunk. (22) Do you not have houses of your own to eat and drink in? Or do you despise the church of God so that you look down on those who have nothing? What do I say to you? Am I praising you? For this I do not praise you!

(23) For I received from the Lord what I also passed on to you: the Lord Jesus, on the night he was handed over, took bread, and as he gave thanks, (24) broke the bread and said, "This is my body which is for you: do this in memory of me." (25) In the same manner, he took the cup after supper, saying "This cup is the new covenant in my blood: do this, as often as you drink, in memory of me. (26) For as often as you eat this bread and drink this cup, you proclaim the death of the Lord until he comes."

(27) For this reason, whoever might eat the bread or drink the cup of the Lord in an unworthy manner is guilty of the body and blood of the Lord. (28) Let a person test himself or herself and in this way eat of the bread and drink from the cup. (29) For a person eating and drinking, not discerning the body, eats judgment for himself or herself. (30) This is the reason many of you are weak and sick, and some of you have fallen asleep. (31) If we put ourselves to the test, we will not be judged; (32) being judged by the Lord, let us be instructed, in order that we will not be condemned with the world.

(33) So, my brothers and sisters, when you gather to eat, wait for one another, in order that you do not come under judgment. (34a) If any person is hungry, let that person eat at home, in order that you may not be brought together into judgment.

(11:3) Now I want you to know that the one who is superior to every man is Christ, and the one who is superior to Christ is God. (4) Every man who prays or prophesies while wearing a head covering brings shame on his head. (5) Now every woman praying or prophesying with her head uncovered brings shame on her head. It is one and the same for her to have her head shaved. (6) If a woman will not have her head covered, then let her have her hair cut. So if it is shameful to have her hair cut or to have her head shaved, let her head be covered with hair. (7) For it is not right that a man have his head covered with hair since he is the image and glory of God. A woman, however, is the glory of her husband.

(8) For man did not have his origin from woman, but woman from man. (9) Moreover, man was not created from woman, but woman from man. (10) For this reason, a woman needs to have a symbol of authority on her head, because of the angels. (11) It is clear that there is no place for a woman without a man, just as there is no place for man without a woman in the Lord. (12) For just as woman comes from man, so too man has his origin through a woman. So all things are from God.

(13) Judge for yourselves: Is it proper for a woman to pray to God, uncovered by her hair? (14) Does not nature itself teach you that a man, on the one hand, if he prays with long hair, brings shame upon himself, (15) yet, on the other hand, for a woman it is her glory? Her hair is given [her] for a covering.

(16) If someone wants to be contentious, neither we nor the churches of God have any such custom.

(16:1) Now concerning the collection for the saints, just I directed the churches of Galatia, so you should do as well. (2) On the first day of the week, each one of you should store up something in keeping with what he has gained, in order that when I come, there may have to be collections. (3) When I come around, those whomever you have tested I will send with these letters to take your gift to Jerusalem. (4) If it may be right that I accompany them, they will go with me. (11:34b) The other matters I will sort out when I come.

CORINTHIAN LETTER B

2 Cor 6:14–7:1 + 1 Cor 6:12-20 + 1 Cor 9:24–10:22 +
1 Cor 15:1-58 + 1 Cor 16:13-24

(2 Cor 6:14) Do not be unequally yoked with nonbelievers. For what sharing is there between righteousness and lawlessness, or what fellowship is there between light and darkness? (15) Now what agreement does Christ have with Beliar, or what portion is there for the believer with a nonbeliever? (16) What concord is there for the temple of God with idols? For we are the living temple of God, just as God said:

I will dwell in them and I will walk around with them
    and I will be their God and they will be my people.
(17) Therefore go out from the midst of them
    and separate yourselves, says the Lord,
And touch nothing impure
    and I will receive you
(18) And I will be a father to you and you will be sons and daughters to me, says the Lord almighty."

(7:1) Having thus these promises, beloved ones, let us purify ourselves from every pollution of the flesh and spirit, as we perfect holiness in the fear of God.

(1 Cor 6:12) "All things are allowed me" but not all things are advantageous; "all things are allowed me" but I will not be placed under the authority of anything. (13) "Foods are for the belly, and the belly for food," however, God will indeed destroy them both. The body is not for immorality but for the Lord, and the Lord is for the body. (14) Now God both raised the Lord and will raise us through his power. (15) Do you not know that your bodies are members of Christ? So shall I take the members of Christ and make them members of a prostitute? Not at all! (16) Or do you not know that he who is joined to a prostitute is one body with her? "For the two shall be, he said, one

flesh." (17) He who is joined with the Lord is one spirit (with him). (18) Flee away from sexual immorality! Every sin what a person commits is outside the body. He who commits sexual immorality, however, sins against his own body. (19) Or do you not know that your body is the temple of the Holy Spirit in you, whom you have from God, and you are not your own. (20) You were bought with a price. So glorify God in your body.

(9:24) Do you not know that in a race all the runners run, however one receives the prize? So run that you may receive. (25) Everyone who competes exercises self-control with respect to all things; they, on the one hand, in order to receive a perishable prize while we, on the other hand, receive an immortal one. (26) I therefore do not run aimlessly, as if I were boxing the air; (27) but I train my body hard and enslave it, lest having preached to others I might become worthless.

(10:1) I do not want you to be ignorant, brothers and sisters, that all of our fathers were under the cloud and all of them went through the sea, (2) and all of them were baptized into Moses in the cloud and in the sea, (3) and all of them ate the same spiritual food, (4) and all of them drank the same spiritual drink, for they drank from the same spiritual rock; this rock, however, was Christ. (5) But God was not pleased with the majority of them, for they perished in the desert. (6) Now these things became examples to us, so that we might not be people given over to evil passions, just as those people had passions. (7) Let none become idolators just as some of them were, as it is written, "The people sat down to eat and drink, and they stood up to play." (8) Let us not commit immorality, just as some of them were immoral, and on a single day twenty-three thousand of them fell. (9) Let us not tempt Christ, just as some of them tempted and were killed by snakes. (10) Let us not grumble, just as some of them grumbled and were killed by the Destroyer. (11) These things happened to them by way of example, having been written to advise us, unto whom the end of the ages has come. (12) Therefore, let those who think they stand be careful lest that person fall. (13) You have not suffered a temptation, which is not a common human one. Yet God is faithful, who will not let you be tempted beyond what you can stand, but will provide with the temptation also a way of escape so that you can endure. (14) For this reason, my beloved, flee away from idolatry. (15) I speak as to those who are wise: judge for yourselves what I say. (16) The cup of blessing which we bless, is it not a communion of the blood of Christ? The bread that we break, is it not a communion of the body of Christ? (17) Because there is one bread, we who are many are one body, for all of us share in the one bread. (18) Consider Israel according to the flesh: are not those who eat the sacrifices participants in the altar? (19) So what am I saying? That foods offered to idols are something or that an idol is something? (20) Rather, because of the things they sacrifice, they offer sacrifice to demons and not to God. I do not want you to become partners with demons. (21) It is not possible for you to drink the cup of the Lord and also the cup of demons; it is not possible for you to share in the table of the Lord and the table of demons. (22) Or are we provoking the Lord? We are not stronger than he is.

(1 Cor 15:1) Now I point out to you, brothers and sisters, the gospel which I preached to you, which indeed you received, in which you are standing, (2) through which you are saved, by which word I preached to you—if you are holding it fast; otherwise, if you are not holding it fast, then you believed in vain. (3) For I passed on to you among the things of highest importance, which you also received, that Christ died for our sins according to the Scriptures, (4) and that he was buried and that he was raised on the third day according to the Scriptures, (5) and that he was seen by Cephas along with the twelve. (6) Later he was seen by more than five hundred brothers and sisters at one time, among whom the majority remain alive until now, though some of them fallen asleep. (7) Later he was seen by James, and then by all the apostles. (8) Last of all, as to a baby who was aborted, he appeared also to me. (9) For I am the least of the apostles, indeed unworthy to be called an apostle, because I persecuted the church of God. (10) Yet by the grace of God I am what I am, and the grace of God has not been bestowed on me in vain. Actually I worked harder than all of them—not I but the grace of God, which is with me. (11) So whether it was I or they, so we preached and so you believed.

(12) Now if Christ has been preached as having been raised from the dead, how is it that some of you say that there is no resurrection of the dead? (13) If there is no resurrection of the dead, then Christ was not raised. (14) If Christ was not raised, as a consequence our preaching is in vain, and your faith is in vain. (15) We, however, would be proven to be false witnesses of God, because we testified concerning God that he raised Christ, whom he did not raise if in fact the dead are not raised. (16) For if the dead are not raised, neither was Christ raised. (17) If Christ, however, was not raised, your faith is empty, and you are still in your sins. (18) Consequently those who have fallen asleep in Christ are lost. (19) If it is in this life alone that we have come to hope in Christ, we are of all people most pitiful.

(20) Yet now Christ has been raised from the dead, the firstfruit of those who have fallen asleep. (21) For since death came through a human being, the resurrection of the dead has also come through a human being. (22) For just as all who are in Adam will die, so also all those who are in Christ will

be made alive. (23) Each, however, in its own order: the firstfruit Christ, then those who belong to Christ at his coming. (24) Then will come the end, when the kingdom will be given to God the Father, when every primacy and every authority and every power will be set aside. (25) For it is necessary that he reign until "all his enemies shall be put under his feet." (26) Death is the last enemy to be defeated. (27) For "he will put all things under his feet." Now when it says that all things are subordinated, it is evident that the exception is the one who subordinates all things to himself. (28) When all things are subordinated to him, then the Son himself will be subordinated to the one who subordinates all things to him, in order that God may be all in all.

(29) For otherwise why are people baptized for the dead? If it is really true that the dead are not raised, why indeed be baptized for them? (30) Why, moreover, are we in danger every hour? (31) I suffer death daily, by my boast in you, [brothers and sisters,] which I have in our Christ Jesus our Lord. (32) In human terms, if I have fought wild beasts in Ephesus, what good is that to me? If the dead are not raised, "let us eat and drink, for tomorrow we shall die." (33) Do not be deceived: bad company destroys good habits.

(34) Sober up as you should, and do not sin, for some people possess ignorance of God; I am saying this to your shame. (35) But someone will say: how are the dead raised? With what kind of body do they appear? (36) Fool! What you sow does not come to life unless it dies. (37) And that which you sow is not the body it will become, but a bare grain, perhaps of wheat or some other grain. (38) God, however, gives to each a body just as he willed, and to each of the seeds its own body. (39) All flesh is not the same flesh, but one for people, yet another flesh for a domesticated animal, still another flesh for birds and yet another for fish. (40) There are heavenly bodies, and there are earthly bodies; there is one splendor for heavenly bodies, another splendor for earthly bodies. (41) There is the splendor of the sun, and another splendor of the moon, and still another splendor for stars; star differs from star in splendor. (42) So it is also with the resurrection of the dead. It is sown in corruption, it is raised in immortality. (43) It is sown in dishonor; it is raised in splendor. (44) It is sown a physical body; it is raised a spiritual body. If there is a physical body, there is also a spiritual body. (45) Indeed, just as it is written: "The first man Adam became a living soul"; the last Adam became a living spirit. (46) It is not the spiritual (body), which is first, but the physical one, and then the spiritual. (47) The first man is the man of earth; the second man is from heaven. (48) As the earthly man is, so also are those who are earthly, and as the heavenly man is, so also are those who are heavenly. (49)

And just as we bore the image of the earthly man, so also will we bear the image of the heavenly man.

(50) Now I say this, brothers and sisters: flesh and blood are not able to inherit the kingdom of God; neither does corruption inherit that which is imperishable. (51) Behold, I tell you a mystery: we shall not all sleep, however we shall all be changed, (52) in a moment, in the twinkling of an eye, at the last trumpet. For the trumpet shall sound and the dead shall be raised incorruptible, and we shall be changed. (53) For it is necessary for the corruptible to be clothed with incorruption and the mortal to be clothed with immortality. (54) Now when this corruptible (body) is clothed with incorruption and this mortal (body) is clothed with immortality, the word that is written will come to pass:

Death is swallowed up in victory.
(55) Where, death, is your victory?
Where, death, is your sting?

(56) The sting of death is sin; however, the power of sin is the Law. (57) But thanks be to God who gives us the victory through our Lord Jesus Christ. (58) Therefore, my beloved brothers and sisters, be steadfast, immovable, abounding in the work of the Lord always, knowing that your work is not in vain in the Lord.

(1 Cor 16:13) Be wide awake, stand up in the faith, act like men, be strong. (14) Let everything you do be done in love.

(15) Now I encourage you, brothers and sisters; you are aware of the household of Stephanus that it is the first fruit of Achaia, and it devoted itself for ministry to the saints. (16) Be subject to such people as these and to all who work and labor! (17) I rejoice at the coming of Stephanus and Fortunatus and Achaicus, because they have fulfilled what was lacking in you. (18) They have refreshed my spirit and yours. Therefore read what they bring to you.

(19) The churches of Asia greet you. Aquila and Prisca and the church meeting in their house send you many greetings in the Lord. (20) All the brothers and sisters greet you. Greet one another with a holy kiss.

(21) This greeting is in my, Paul's, hand. (22) If anyone does not love the Lord, let him be cursed. Our Lord, come! (23) The grace of the Lord Jesus be with you. (24) My love be with all of you in Christ Jesus.

CORINTHIAN LETTER C

1 Cor 1:1–6:11 + 1 Cor 7:1–8:13 + 1 Cor 9:19-23 + 1 Cor 10:23–11:1 + 1 Cor 12:1-31a + 1 Cor 14:1c-33a + 1 Cor 14:37-40 + 1 Cor 12:31b–13:13 + 1 Cor 16:5-12

(1 Cor 1:1) Paul, called as an apostle of Christ Jesus through the will of God, together with Sosthenes the brother, (2) to the church of God, which is in Corinth, sanctified in Christ Jesus, called to be saints, with all those who call upon the name of our Lord Jesus Christ in every place, theirs and ours, (3) grace to you and peace from God our Father and our Lord Jesus Christ.

(4) I thank my God always for you because of the grace of God, which has been given you in Christ Jesus, (5) because in every way you have been enriched in him, in every word and all knowledge, (6) just as the witness of Christ has been confirmed in you, (7) so that you are not lacking in any spiritual gift as you wait for the revelation of our Lord Jesus Christ; (8) he will indeed confirm you blameless until the end on the day of our Lord Jesus. (9) God is faithful, through whom you have been called for sharing in his Son Jesus Christ our Lord.

(10) I beseech you, brothers and sisters, through the name of our Lord Jesus Christ, that all of you be in agreement, that there be no divisions among you, that you be built up in the same mind and hold the same opinion. (11) For it has been made clear to me by Chloë's people, my brothers and sisters, that there are quarrels among you. (12) I'm telling you this: that particular ones of you say: "I belong to Paul," or "I belong to Apollos," or "I belong to Cephas," or "I belong to Christ." (13) Is Christ divided? Surely Paul was not crucified for you, nor were you baptized in the name of Paul, were you? (14) I am thankful that I baptized none of you except Crispus and Gaius, (15) so that none of you would say that you were baptized in my name! (16) I did however baptize the household of Stephanus, but beyond that I do not know that I baptized anyone else. (17) For Christ did not send me to baptize but to preach the gospel, not in cleverness of speech, in order that the cross of Christ might not be rendered void.

(18) For the message of the cross is foolishness to those who are perishing, yet to us who are being saved it is the power of God. (19) For it is written:

I will destroy the wisdom of the wise
and the intelligence of the intelligent I will set aside.

(20) Where is the wise person? Where is the scribe? Where is the debater of this era? Has not God made the wisdom of the world foolish? (21) Since in the wisdom of God, the world did not know God by means of wisdom, God was pleased because of the foolishness of the proclamation to save those who believe. (22) Since Jews indeed ask for signs and Greeks seek wisdom, (23) we, however, preach Christ crucified, a stumbling block to Jews, foolishness to Gentiles, (24) yet to those who are called, Jews as well as Greeks, Christ is the power of God and the wisdom of God. (25) For the foolishness of God is wiser than human beings and the weakness of God is stronger than human beings.

(26) For consider your calling, brothers and sisters, that not many of you were wise according to the flesh, not many were powerful, not many nobly born. (27) But God chose the foolish things of the world, in order to shame the wise ones, and God chose the weak things of the world in order to shame the strong, (28) and God chose the lowly and despised things of the world, indeed things that do not exist, in order to nullify things that do exist, (29) so that all flesh is unable to boast before God. (30) Now as a result of this you are in Christ Jesus, who has become our wisdom from God, our righteousness, our holiness, and our redemption, (31) so that just as it is written: "Let the one who boasts, boast in the Lord."

(2:1) When I came to you, brothers and sisters, I came to you not with an abundance of speech or wisdom, as I disclosed to you the mystery of God. (2) For I decided not to know anything among you except Jesus Christ and him crucified. (3) And I was in weakness and with fear and much trembling as I approached you, (4) and my speech and my proclamation were not in persuasive words of wisdom, but in a demonstration of spirit and power, (5) in order that your faith might not be in human wisdom but in the power of God.

(6) Now we do impart wisdom among those who are mature, yet it is a wisdom that neither this age nor the rulers of those age can refute. (7) But we impart the wisdom of God, which has been hidden in mystery, which God decided on before the ages for our glory, (8) a wisdom which none of the rulers of this age knew; for if they had known it, they would not have crucified the Lord of glory. (9) But just as it is written:

The things which neither eye saw nor ear heard,
and never entered into the heart of people,
the things which God prepared for those who love him.

(10) Now God has made a revelation to us through the Spirit. For the Spirit searches all things, even the depths of God. (11) For what human being

knows people or the matters of a person except the Spirit of God? (12) Now we did not receive the spirit of the world but the Spirit which is from God, so that we might know the things which have been given us by God. (13) The things we say are not with the instructed words from human wisdom, but with words taught by the Spirit, interpreting spiritual things to spiritual people. (14) The unspiritual person does not receive the things of the Spirit of God; for they are foolishness to that person, and that person is unable to know them, because these things are judged spiritually. (15) The spiritual person judges all things, yet that person is judged by no one. (16) "For who has known the mind of the Lord; who will advise him?" We, however, have the mind of Christ.

(3:1) Indeed, brothers and sisters, when I came to you, I could not speak to you as spiritual people but as fleshly, as infants in Christ. (2) I fed you milk, not solid food; for you were not ready for it. But you still are not ready, (3) for you are still fleshly. For when there are jealousy and strife among you, are you not fleshly and walking in a human way? (4) For when one of you says, "I belong to Paul," another saying "I belong to Apollos," are you not merely human? (5) What indeed is Apollos? What is Paul? Ministers through whom you came to faith, as the Lord granted to each one. (6) I planted, Apollos watered, but God gave the growth. (7) In this way, neither the planter nor the waterer amount to anything, but it is God who causes growth. (8) The planter and the waterer are one, yet each one will receive his own reward, according to his own labor. (9) For we are God's fellow-workers, God's field; you are God's building. (10) According to the grace of God given me, as a skilled master-builder I laid a foundation, and another person is building on it. Let each person look carefully how he or she builds! (11) For no other foundation can anyone lay other than the foundation, which is Jesus Christ. (12) Now if a certain person builds upon a foundation using gold, silver, precious stones, wood, hay, and stubble, (13) the work of each builder will be identified clearly, for the day will show it, because it will be revealed by fire. And what kind of work each worker did will be tested by fire. (14) If the construction work of a certain person endures, that person will receive a reward. (15) If the work of a particular person burns up, that person will suffer loss, yet he will be saved, however, it will be like going through fire. (16) Do you not know that you are God's temple, and the Spirit of God dwells in you? (17) If a person destroys the temple of God, God will destroy that person. For the temple of God is holy—you are that temple.

(18) Let no person deceive himself or herself. If someone of you thinks that he is wise in this age, let him become a fool, so that he will become wise. (19) For the wisdom of this world is foolishness with God. For it is written:

"He catches the wise in their cunning." (20) And again, "The Lord knows the plans of the wise, that they are empty." (21) Therefore, let no one boast in human beings, for all things are yours, (22) whether Paul or Apollos or Cephas, whether the world or life or death, whether things present or things to come, (23) you are Christ's, and Christ is God's.

(4:1) In this way, let a person consider us as servants of Christ and stewards of the mysteries of God. (2) In this case, moreover it is required of stewards that they be found faithful. (3) This, however, is of the least concern to me, that I should be judged by you on a day appointed by a human court. Actually I do not even judge myself. (4) For there is nothing troubling my conscience; yet I am not justified for this point—the Lord examines me. (5) Therefore, you are not to judge me in anything before the time, until the Lord comes, who will illumine the secrets of darkness and will lay bare the intentions of hearts. And then there will be commendation for each person from God.

(6) I have applied these things, brothers and sisters, to myself and to Apollos because of you, in order that you may learn the saying "nothing beyond what is written," so that no one of you may be puffed up against another person. (7) For who is making a distinction among you? What do you have that you have not received? Now if you did receive it, why do you boast as if you had not received it? (8) Already you are filled; already you have become rich; quite apart from us you have become kings. Indeed, I wish you had become kings, so that we might reign along with you! (9) For it seems to me that God has displayed us apostles in last place, as persons condemned to die: we have become a spectacle in the world, to both angels and human beings. (10) We are fools for Christ; you, however, are wise in Christ! We are weak, yet you are strong. You are honored, but we are dishonored. (11) Until the present moment we are hungry and thirsty, and we go naked and are roughly treated and homeless, (12) and we labor, working with our own hands. When we are reviled, we bless; when we are persecuted, we endure, (13) when we are slandered, we give encouragement. We have become the refuse of the world, the off-scouring of all things, to this very moment.

(14) I am not writing these things to you to make you ashamed, but to counsel my beloved children. (15) For you might have ten thousand instructors in Christ, but not many fathers. For in Christ Jesus I gave birth to you through the gospel. (16) So I urge you, become imitators of me. (17) For this reason, I sent Timothy to you, who is my beloved and faithful child in the Lord, who will remind you of my ways, which are in Christ [Jesus], just as I teach everywhere in every church. (18) There are some who are puffed up, as if I am not coming to you. (19) If the Lord might wish it, I will be coming to you

shortly, and I will find out not the word of those who are puffed up but their power. (20) For the kingdom of God does not consist of talk but of power. (21) What is your wish? For me to come to you with a rod or in love and in a spirit of gentleness?

(5:1) Actually one hears that there is immorality among you, and this immorality is of a sort, which does not happen even among the Gentiles. I speak of the fact that that a certain man is having sex with the wife of his father. (2) And you are puffed up about it, when you ought to be sad, so that he who is doing this would be cast out from the midst of you. (3) For I, though absent in body I am present in spirit, have already come to a decision, as if I were present, about the one who has acted in this way. (4) When you are gathered in the name of [our] Lord Jesus, and my spirit is present with you, with the power of our Lord Jesus, (5) hand over this person to Satan for the destruction of his flesh, so that his spirit may be saved on the day of the Lord. (6) Your boasting is not good! Do you not know that a little yeast leavens the whole loaf? (7) Clean out the old leaven, in order that you may be a new loaf, just as you are now unleavened. For Christ, our Passover has been sacrificed for us. (8) So let us keep the feast, neither with the old leaven nor the leaven of evil and wickedness, but with the unleavened bread of sincerity and truth. (9) I wrote you in my letter not to mingle with immoral people, (10) not meaning the entirety of immoral people in this world, or the covetous, or robbers, or idolaters, for then you would be obliged to leave the world. (11) Now, however, I have written you not to mix with whomever who might be called a brother or sister if this person should be an immoral person or a covetous one, or an idolater, or a verbally abusive person or a drunkard or a robber; with such as these do not share a meal. (12) For it is not my task to judge the outsiders; yet are you not to judge those who are inside? (13) God will judge those outsiders. "Throw the immoral one out from you."

(6:1) Is a certain one of you bold enough to pursue a lawsuit against another, to be judged by the unjust, and not by the saints? (2) Or do you not know that the saints will judge the world? And if the world is to be judged by you, are you unworthy to exercise judgment in these trivial matters? (3) Do you not know that we will judge angels, so why not ordinary matters? (4) If you should have ordinary legal matters, do you appoint as judges those who have no standing in the church? (5) I say this to your shame. Is there really not one wise person among you, who would be able to make a judgment with respect to his brother or sister? (6) But brother or sister files a legal case for judgment against another brother or sister, and this takes place before unbelievers? (7) Are you not already entirely defeated because you have legal cases against each other? Because of this, why not rather be wronged? Why not rather be defrauded? (8) But do you wrong and you defraud, and do you do this to believers? (9) Don't you know that the unrighteous will not inherit the kingdom of God? Don't be deceived! Neither immoral persons nor idolaters, nor adulterers, nor the effeminate, nor sodomites, (10) neither robbers nor the covetous, nor drunkards, nor the verbally abusive, nor swindlers will inherit the kingdom of God. (11) Indeed some of you were one of these. But you were washed, but you were made holy, but you were justified in the name of the Lord Jesus Christ and in the Spirit of our God.

(7:1) Now concerning the matters about which you wrote. It is good for a man not to touch a woman. (2) Yet because of immorality let each man have a wife, and let each woman have her own husband. (3) Let a husband give his wife her due; similarly let a wife give what is due to her husband. (4) A woman does not have authority over her own body, but her husband does; similarly a man does not have authority over his own body, but his wife does. (5) Do not refuse each other, except by mutual agreement for a time, in order that you may dedicate yourselves to prayer, and then come together again, in order that Satan may not tempt you through your lack of self-control. (6) I say this as a concession, not as an order. (7) I would wish all persons to be as I am. But each person has his or her own spiritual gift from God, whatever it truly is.

(8) I say this to the unmarried and widows, it is good for you to remain as I am myself. (9) If, however, they do not have that level of self-control, let them get married for it is better to marry than to burn. (10) To those who are already married, I say—not I but the Lord—a wife should not separate from her husband. (11) If, however, she does separate, let her remain unmarried or let her reconcile with her husband; a husband is not to put away his wife. (12) Now to the rest I say—not I but the Lord—if a brother has an unbelieving wife and she is content to live with him, let him not put her away. (13) And if a woman has an unbelieving husband and he is content to live with her, let her not put him away. (14) For an unbelieving husband is made holy by his wife and an unbelieving wife is made holy by her husband. Otherwise your children would be unclean; now however they are holy. (15) If, however, an unbelieving spouse wishes to separate, let that person separate. The believing husband or wife has not been enslaved to such as these. God has called us to peace. (16) For what do you know, wives: Might you save your husband? Or what do you know, husband: might you save your wife?

(7:17) Let each one of you walk as the Lord has chosen, indeed as the Lord apportioned to each one. And this is how I order matters in all the churches. (18) If a man is circumcised when he is called, let him not hide it. If a man was uncircumcised when he was called, let him not get circumcised. (19) Circumcision means nothing, and uncircumcision means nothing, but what is important is keeping the commandments of God. (20) Each person is to remain in the state in which he was called. (21) If one is a slave when called, never mind. But if you are able to become a free person, it is better to take advantage of it. (22) For he who is called by the Lord as a slave is a freedman of the Lord, and similarly he who is called as a free person is a slave of Christ. (23) You were bought at a price: do not become the slaves of people. (24) Let each person remain as he was when he was called with respect to God.

(25) Concerning virgins, I do not have a command from the Lord, yet I give my opinion as a person who by the mercy of God has been faithful. (26) Thus, I think it is good, because of the disaster that is coming shortly, to be as one is. (27) If a man is married to a woman, let him not seek to end the marriage. If a man is free from a woman, let him not seek a wife. (28) Yet if you get married, you have not sinned, and if a virgin marries a man, she has not sinned. Those who get married will have trouble in the flesh; I, however, would spare you this. (29) Now I say this, brothers and sisters, the time is growing short. So in the meantime, let those who have wives be as if they had no wives, (30) and let those who weep be as those who do not weep; let those who rejoice be as those who do not rejoice; and those who go to the marketplace be as those who have no possessions; (31) and those who make use of the world be as those who do not make use of it. For the form of this world is passing away.

(32) I wish that you would be unencumbered. The unmarried man concerns himself with the Lord's work, how he may be pleasing to the Lord. (33) The married man concerns himself with the affairs of the world, how he may please his wife, (34) and so he is divided. Likewise, the unmarried woman and the virgin concern themselves with the Lord's work, so that they may be holy, both in body and in spirit. The woman who has gotten married is concerned with the affairs of the world, how she may be please her husband. (35) I say this with respect to what is advantageous to you, not in order to put a noose around your neck, but for your good order and your devotion to the Lord, that you may not be distracted. (36) If anyone thinks that they are acting improperly toward a virgin, if the passions are strong, and it ought to be this way, let that person do as he wishes—it is no sin—let them marry. (37) Now the man who has stood firm in his heart, without compulsion, has the power over his own will, and has decided this in his own heart, to take a virgin for himself, will do well, and the one who does not get married will do better. (39) A woman is bound in marriage for such time as her husband is living; when the husband passes away, she is free to marry whom she

wishes, as long as it is in the Lord. (40) Yet whoever remains single will be more blessed, in my opinion. I, however, think that I have the spirit of God.

(8:1) Concerning food sacrificed to idols, we know that all of us possess knowledge. Knowledge puffs up, yet love builds up. (2) If a person supposes himself to have come to know something, that person does not know as it is necessary to know. (3) If a person loves God, that person is known by him. (4) Consequently concerning foods offered in idol worship, we know that there is no true idol in the world and that there is no god other than the one God. (5) For even if there are those that are called gods, whether in heaven or on the earth, thus there are many gods and many lords.

(6) Yet for us there is one God the Father
from whom are all things and for whom we exist,
And one Lord Jesus Christ,
through whom are all things and through whom we exist.

(7) But not all possess knowledge. Some people, however, through being accustomed to idols in former times, eat as if it were meat offered in idol worship, and their weak conscience is defiled. (8) Food, though, will not bring us to God; whoever among us abstains from eating will not fall short, and whoever among us who eats will not have more than enough. (9) Pay attention, however, that this authority of yours does not become a stumbling block to the weak. (10) For if someone should see you, a knowledgeable person, enjoying a meal in the temple of an idol, would not the conscience of the weak brother or sister be encouraged, by seeing you, to eat meat offered in pagan worship? (11) Thus, the weak brother or sister would be destroyed by your knowledge—this brother or sister for whom Christ died. (12) So as you sin against a brother or sister and wound their weak conscience, you are sinning against Christ. (13) For this reason, if food causes my brother or sister to stumble, I would give up meat forever, in order that I might not cause the stumbling of my brother or sister.

(9:19) For though I am free of all things, I have exercised discipline on myself for the sake of all people, in order that I might gain more people. (20) To the Jews I became as a Jew, in order to gain Jews; to those under law I became as one under law, not being myself under law, in order that I might gain those under law. (21) To those outside law, I became as one outside law, though I am not outside God's law but live according to the law of Christ, in order that I might gain those outside the law. (22) To those who were weak, I became weak, in order that I might gain the weak. I have become all things to all people, in order that by all means I might save some. (23) Yet I do all things for the sake of the gospel, in order that I might become a person who shares in it.

(10:23) "All things are permitted," but not all things are advantageous. "All things are permitted" but not all things build up. (24) Let no one seek his own (advantage), but that of the other person. (25) Eat everything that is on sale in the meat market, without asking questions for the sake of conscience. (26) For "the earth is the Lord's, and the fullness of it." (27) If some unbeliever should invite you and you wish to go, eat whatever is placed in front of you without asking questions for the sake of conscience. (28) If, however, someone should say to you, "This was offered to an idol," then don't eat this food, for the sake of the conscience of the person who informed you. (29) I speak not of your own conscience, but of the other person's. For what reason is my freedom to be decided by the conscience of another person? (30) If I give thanks as I eat it, why would I be committing blasphemy because of that for which I have given thanks? (31) In sum, whether you eat or whether you drink, or whatever you do, do all things to God's glory. (32) Do not do anything to offend either Jews or Greeks or the church of God, (33) just as I strive to please all people in all things, not seeking my own advantage but that of many people, in order that they might be saved. (11:1) Imitate me, just as I also imitate Christ.

(12:1) Now concerning spiritual gifts, brothers and sisters, I don't want you to be ignorant. (2) You know that when you were pagans, you were led astray toward idols which do not speak. (3) For this reason, I am making it known to you that nobody by the Spirit of God says, "Jesus be cursed," and nobody is able to say "Jesus is Lord" except by the Holy Spirit.

(4) There are varieties of spiritual gifts, but the same Spirit. (5) And there are varieties of ministries, but the same Lord. (6) And there are varieties of activities, but the same God who causes all activities in all people. (7) To one person is given the manifestation of the Spirit, for that person's advantage. (8) For to one is given the message of wisdom; to another the message of knowledge according to the same Spirit; (9) to another faith by the same Spirit, to another gifts of healings by the one spirit, (10) to another the workings of miracles, to another prophecy, to another the discernments of spirits, to another kinds of languages, to another the interpretation of languages. Now one and the same Spirit works these things, distributing to each person just as he wishes.

(12) For just as the body is one and it has indeed many parts, all of the parts of the body, though many, are one body, and the same is true of Christ. (13) For all of us were in the one Spirit baptized into one body, whether Jews or Greeks, whether enslaved or free people, and we all were given to drink of the one Spirit. (14) For indeed the body is not made up of a single part but of

many. (15) If the foot should say, "Because I am not a hand, I am not part of the body," on this account would it be no part of the body? (16) And if the ear might say, "Because I am not an eye, I am not part of the body," on this account would it be no part of the body? (17) If the entire body were the eye, where would the hearing be? If the entire body were hearing, where would the sense of smell be? (18) Now, however, God has positioned the body parts, each one of them in the body just as he chose. (19) If all things in the body were one part, where would the body be? (20) Now there are many parts, but one body. (21) Thus, the eye cannot say to the hand, "I don't need you," or again the head cannot say this to the feet, "I don't need you." (22) But the parts of the body that seem weaker are necessary parts, (23) and the parts of the body that we suppose to be of lesser honor we invest with surpassing honor, and to our more unpresentable parts we give surpassing honor, (24) which our more presentable parts do not need. But God has composed the body, giving overwhelmingly surpassing honor to it, (25) so that there may be no division in the body, but the parts may have the same concern for each other. (26) If one part suffers, all the parts suffer; if one part is honored, all the parts rejoice together. (27) Now you are the body of Christ, and individually you are parts of it. (28) And so God has put in place in the church first apostles, second prophets, third teachers, then miracle-workers, then gifts of healings, helpful deeds, administrations, and kinds of languages. (29) Are all apostles? Not all are prophets; not all are teachers; not all work miracles. (30) Not all have spiritual gifts of healings. Not all speak in languages; not all interpret. (31) Yet seek the higher spiritual gifts, (14:1c) especially that you may prophesy.

(14:2) The one who speaks in a language does not speak to people but to God; for nobody understands when this person speaks mysteries. (3) The one who prophesies speaks to people to build them up, to encourage, and to console. (4) The one who speaks in a language builds himself up, yet the one who prophesies builds the church up. (5) I wish that all of you would speak in languages, but more especially that you may prophesy; the one who prophesies is greater than the one who speaks in languages, except if there is interpretation, in order that the church may be built up.

(6) Now, brothers and sisters, if I were to come to you speaking in (other) languages, how would I benefit you unless I would speak, whether in a revelation or in knowledge or in prophecy, or in teaching? (7) In the same way, musical instruments give a sound, whether a flute or a lyre; if they make no clear distinction in their tones, how will it be known whether it is flute-playing or lyre-playing? (8) For indeed if a trumpet should play an uncertain sound, who will prepare for battle? (9) In the same way also if you give through a

language a message that is unintelligible, how will what you have spoken be understood? You would be speaking into the air. (10) There are probably ever so many kinds of sounds in the world, and none of them is without meaning. (11) Consequently if I should not know the force of a sound, I would be a barbarian in speaking and the one speaking to me likewise barbarian. (12) In the same way also you, since you are eager to pursue spiritual gifts, that you may excel in the building up of the church.

(13) For this reason, the speaker in a language should pray that they might interpret. (14) If I might pray in a language, my spirit is praying; my mind, however, is unfruitful. (15) So what is this? I will pray in the Spirit, yet I will also pray with the mind. I will sing in the Spirit, yet I will also sing with the mind. (16) So if you bless in the Spirit, as for the one who is in the position of an untrained person, how will he say the "Amen" to your prayer of thanksgiving? In this case, he would not know what you are saying. (17) For though you may give thanks beautifully, in fact the other person would not be edified. (18) I thank God that I speak in languages more than all of you. (19) But in the church I desire to speak five words with my mind, in order that I might make myself understood to others, rather than ten thousand words in a language.

(20) Brothers and sisters, do not be children in understanding but be babies in evil, in order that in understanding you may become perfect. (21) In the Law, it is written:

In other languages and by the lips of other people I shall speak to this people
And in this way they will not listen to me, says the Lord.

(22) Thus, languages exist as a sign not for believers but for unbelievers, while prophecy is not for unbelievers but for believers. (23) If the whole church were gathered at the same place and everybody were speaking in languages, if untrained persons or unbelievers were to enter, wouldn't they say that you are mad? (24) Now if all were prophesying, and some unbeliever or untrained person enters, he would be identified by all, examined by all, (25) the secrets of his heart would become known, and thus falling on his face he would worship God, confessing that "truly God is among you."

(26) Consequently, what is this? When you gather, each person has a psalm, a teaching, a revelation, a language, an interpretation. Let everything be done for upbuilding. (27) When a person speaks in a tongue, there should be two or at most three in turn, and let one interpret. (28) If, however, there should be no one to interpret, let the church be silent, with each person speaking indeed to God. (29) Let two or three prophets speak, and let others discern. (30) If

there is another person sitting there who receives a revelation, let the first person be silent. (31) For you can all prophesy, each one in order, that all may be taught and all may be encouraged. (32) Indeed the spirits of prophets are subject to the prophets, (33a) for God is not a God of disorder but of peace.

(37) If anyone think himself or herself to be a prophet or a spiritual person, let that person understand what I am writing to you, that it is a command of the Lord. (38) If anyone disregards this, let that person be disregarded. (39) Therefore, brothers and sisters, seek to prophesy and do not forbid speaking in languages. (40) Yet let all things be done with decency and in order.

(12:31b) Indeed I am now showing you a way that is better still. (13:1) If I speak with the languages of human beings or of angels, but without love, I have become a noisy gong or a clanging cymbal. (2) Indeed if I might have prophecy and if I might know all mysteries and all knowledge, and if I might possess complete faith so that I might move mountains, if I did not however have love, I would be nothing. (3) If I were to give away all my possessions, and if I should hand over my body so that I could boast about it, if I did not have love, it would be of no advantage to me.

(4) Love is longsuffering; love is kind, love is not filled with jealousy; love is not boastful; love is not puffed up; (5) love is not rude; love does not seek its own way; it is not provoked to wrath; love does not keep a record of evil; (6) it does not rejoice in what is wrong, but it rejoices together with the truth. (7) Love bears all things, love believes all things, love hopes all things, love endures all things.

(8) Love never fails. As for prophecy, it will be set aside. As for languages, they will cease. As for knowledge, it will be set aside. (9) For we know partially, and we prophesy partially; (10) when what is perfect comes, that which is partial will be set aside. (11) When I was a child, I spoke as a child, I thought as a child, I reasoned as a child; when I became a man, I put aside childish things. (12) For now we see in a mirror dimly; then we shall see face to face. Now I know partially; yet then I shall know fully, just as I have been known fully. (13) So now there remain faith, hope, love, these three; yet the greatest of these is love. (14:1) Pursue love.

(16:5) Now I will come to you when I pass through Macedonia. For I am coming through Macedonia; (6) if it turns out so, I may stay with you or I may spend the winter, in order that you may send me off where I may be going. (7) For I don't want to see you just in passing; rather I hope to spend some time with you if the Lord will permit. (8) Yet I will remain in Ephesus until

Pentecost. (9) For a great and effective door has been opened to me, and there are many opponents.

(10) Now if Timothy should come, see to it that he has nothing to fear in you, for he is active in the work of the Lord, as I am. (11) Let no one despise him. Now give him a peaceful sendoff, in order that he may come to me. For I am waiting for him, along with the brothers and sisters. (12) Now concerning the brother Apollos, I have urged him greatly, so that he may come to you along with the brothers and sisters; it was, though, not at all his will to come to you at this time. Yet he will come when he has the opportunity.

CORINTHIAN LETTER D

2 Cor 8:1-24

(8:1) Now I want you to know, brothers, about the grace of God, which has been given to all the churches of Macedonia, (2) because in the midst of a great ordeal of suffering the overabundance of their joy and their deep poverty abounded in an overflow of the riches of their sincerity. (3) They gave according to their means, I am testifying, and indeed beyond their means, (4) of their own accord they earnestly begged us for the privilege of sharing in the ministry to the saints, (5) and beyond what we had hoped they gave themselves first to the Lord and then to us through will of God, (6) so that Titus encouraged us, in order that just as they had begun they also completed this gracious favor for us. (7) But just as you abound in everything, in faith and in speech and knowledge and in all enthusiasm and in the love in you that comes from us, so also may you abound in this gracious gift. (8) I am not giving you an order but am testing the genuineness of your love, because of the enthusiasm of others. (9) For you know of the gift of our Lord Jesus Christ, that though he was rich he became poor, in order that you might be enriched by his poverty. (10) I also give my opinion about this: this is of advantage to you, whoever began a year ago not only to do but to wish to do this. (11) Now, however, complete this work, so that just as you had the willingness of intention, then bring it to completion out of what you have. (12) For if the willingness is present, the gift will be acceptable according to what you have, not according to what you do not have. (13) I do not want there to be relief for others and pain for you, but that there would be equality. (14) At the present moment, your abundance meets the needs of others, in order that their abundance might meet your needs, in which case there would be equality, (15) just as it is written, "The one who had much did not have too much, and the one who had little did not have too little."

(16) Now thanks be to God who has put the enthusiasm for you into the heart of Titus, (17) because he received your encouragement, and he is now more enthusiastic, of his own accord, to come to you. (18) In addition, we sent along with him the brother whose fame in the gospel has spread throughout all the churches. (19) Not only him, but also another man who was handpicked by the churches as our traveling companion to accompany this gracious gift in ministry by us, to the glory of the Lord and thanks to your good will, (20) we are sending this, lest someone will find fault with us in this generous gift which will be ministered by us. (21) For we previously thought that this gift would be good not only in the eyes of the Lord but as far as people are concerned. (22) Now we previously sent to them our brother whom we have tested in many ways and found to be eager many times; yet now he is all the more eager with great confidence in you. (23) As for Titus, he is my partner and fellow worker; as for our brothers, they are the apostles of the churches, the glory of Christ. (24) Therefore, demonstrate your love so that our boasting about you as well will be proved true as you meet these people from the churches.

CORINTHIAN LETTER E

2 Cor 2:14–6:13 + 2 Cor 7:2-4

(2:14) Now thanks be to God who always leads us in triumph in Christ and makes present the fragrance of the knowledge of him through us in every place. (15) This means that we are the aroma of Christ in God among those who are being saved and among those who are perishing: (16) to the latter we are the aroma coming from death and leading toward death, and to the former we are the aroma coming from life and giving life.

Who indeed is competent for these things?
    (17) For we are not, as many are, those who peddle the word of God,
    but as persons of sincerity,
    as those who represent God,
    in the sight of God we speak in Christ.

(3:1) Are we beginning to commend ourselves again? Or we do not need, as certain persons do, letters of recommendation to you or from you, do we? (2) You are our letter written on our hearts, known and read by all persons, (3) it being made manifest that you are a letter of Christ ministered by us, written not in ink but by the Spirit of the living God, not on tablets of stone but on tablets of fleshly hearts.

(4) We have such confidence through Christ in the presence of God. (5) Not because we are competent of ourselves to be reckoned as something that comes from ourselves: but our competence comes from God, (6) who has made us competent to be ministers of a new covenant, a covenant not of the letter but of the Spirit. For the letter kills, while the Spirit gives life. (7) If the ministry of death, carved in letters on stones, was given with glory, so that the children of Israel could not bear to look upon the face of Moses because of the glory of his face, which was fading, (8) how much more will not the ministry of the Spirit be given in glory? (9) For if there was the glory of the ministry of condemnation, how much more glory will there be of the ministry that justifies us with God? (10) For that which had been glorified has not been glorified in this case on account of the surpassing glory. (11) For if it was set aside because of glory, how much greater is that which remains in glory!

(12) And so having this hope we proceed with great boldness, (13) and not like Moses who put a veil over his face so that the children of Israel would not behold the termination of that which was being set aside. (14) But their thoughts were hardened. For until the present day the same veil remains over the reading of the old covenant, a veil which is not removed because in Christ it is set aside. (15) But until the present day, whenever Moses is read, a veil lies over their heart. (16) Now whenever he turned toward the Lord, he set aside the veil. (17) The Lord, however, is the Spirit; where the Spirit of the Lord is, there is freedom. (18) So all of us with unveiled face contemplating the glory of the Lord are being changed into the same likeness from one level of glory to another level of glory, just as it is from the Spirit of the Lord.

(4:1) For this reason, having this ministry, just as mercy has been shown to us, we do not lose heart. (2) But we have renounced the hidden things of which one would be ashamed, neither walking with cunning nor falsifying the word of God, but by the open statement of the truth, we commend ourselves to every person's conscience in the sight of God. (3) Now if our gospel is veiled, it is veiled to those who are perishing; (4) in their case, the god of this age has blinded the minds of the unbelievers so that they might not see the illumination of the knowledge of the glory of Christ, who is the image of God. (5) For it is not ourselves that we preach but Jesus Christ as Lord, and ourselves as your slaves through Jesus. (6) Because it is God who said, "Out of darkness let light shine," who has shone in our hearts for the illumination of the knowledge of the glory of God in the face of [Jesus] Christ.

(7) Now we have this treasure in earthen vessels, in order that the extraordinary quality of the power might be from God and not from us. (8) In

everything we are hard-pressed but not crushed, perplexed but not despairing, (9) pursued but not abandoned, cast down but not destroyed, (10) always bearing the death of Jesus in the body, so that the life of Jesus might be obvious in our body. (11) For we who are alive are always being handed over to death through Jesus, in order that the life of Jesus might also be obvious in our mortal flesh. (12) Thus, death is at work in us; however, life is at work in you. (13) Now having the same spirit of faith according to what is written, "I believed, therefore I spoke," so we are believing and so we are speaking as well, (14) knowing that the one who raised the Lord Jesus will raise us with Jesus and will cause us to stand upright with you. (15) For all things are for your sake, in order that as grace may abound, as it increases because of the multiplication of thanksgiving, to the glory of God.

(16) We therefore do not lose heart. Despite the fact that our outer person is wasting away, our inner nature is being renewed day by day. (17) For at the present, our momentary affliction is bringing about in us in an overwhelming way an extraordinary eternal weight of glory; (18) we do not look to the things that are seen but to those that are unseen; since the things that are seen are temporary, while those that are unseen are eternal.

(5:1) For we know that if the earthly tent in which we live were destroyed, we have a dwelling from God, a house not made with hands, eternal, in the heavens. (2) For in this tent, indeed, we sigh because we desire to be clothed with our dwelling which is from heaven, (3) inasmuch as after having been unclothed we should not be found naked. (4) For we who are in the tent groan, weighed down, because of which we do not wish to be unclothed but to put on more clothes, in order that what is mortal may be swallowed up by life. (5) Now the one who prepares us for this very purpose is God, who gives us of the Spirit as a down payment.

(6) Accordingly, we are always confident and aware that when we are present in the body we are away from the Lord, (7) for we walk by means of faith, not sight. (8) We are confident and we would rather prefer to be away from the body and present with the Lord. (9) Thus, we have as our ambition, whether we are near or far from the body, to be pleasing to him. (10) For all of us must appear before the judgment seat of Christ, in order that each one of us may receive what is coming to us for the things he or she has done by means of the body, whether good or evil. (11) Consequently, knowing the fear of the Lord, we persuade people. Being well known to God, now I hope also to have become well known to your consciences. (12) We are not commending ourselves to you again but, on the contrary, giving you an opportunity to boast about us, in order that you may do this in front of those

who boast face to face but not secretly. (13) For if we are out of our mind, it is because of God; if we are in our right mind, it is for you. (14) For the love of Christ impels us, as we have decided this: that since one died for all, as a result all have died. (15) Indeed he died for all, in order that those who are alive may live no longer for themselves but for the one who died and was raised. (16) Therefore, from now on, we know nobody according to the flesh: if we have known Christ according to the flesh, we know him no longer in that way. (17) Thus, if any person is in Christ, there is a new creation: what is old has passed away; behold what is new has come. (18) Now all these things are from God who has reconciled us to himself through Christ and given us the ministry of reconciliation, (19) since God was in Christ reconciling the world to himself, not keeping a record of their trespasses, and entrusting us with the message of reconciliation. (20) Therefore, we are ambassadors for Christ, since God is making his appeal through us. We beg you for Christ's sake, be reconciled to God! (21) For our sake, he made him to be sin who knew no sin, in order that in him we might become the righteousness of God.

(6:1) So working together, indeed we encourage you not to receive the grace of God in vain. (2) For it says,

At the right time I have heard you
and on the day of salvation I have helped you.

Behold, now is the opportune time: behold, now is the day of salvation! (3) We do not place obstacles in anyone's way, in order that no fault may be found with our ministry. (4) But we do commend ourselves in every way as servants of God: in great endurance, in afflictions, in difficulties, in constraints, (5) in blows, in prisons, in tumults, in labors, in sleepless nights, in fastings, (6) with purity, with knowledge, with forbearance, with kindness, with the Holy Spirit, with sincere love, (7) with the message of truth, with the power of God; holding the weapons of righteousness in the right hand and the left, (8) through honor and dishonor, through a bad reputation and a good reputation, as imposters and as truthful, (9) as ignorant fools and as experts, as dying and, behold, we are alive, as being disciplined and yet not killed, (10) as those in pain and yet always rejoicing, as poor yet making many rich, as having nothing, yet retaining possession of everything.

(11) Our mouth is open to you, Corinthians, our heart is open wide! (12) You have not been restricted by us; however, you have been restricted by your affections. (13) In the same way, in exchange, I speak as to children, open wide your hearts. (7:2) Make room for us. We have wronged no one; we have

corrupted no one; we have cheated no one. (3) I do not speak in condemnation: for I said before that you are in our hearts so that we may die together and live together. (4) Great is my boldness toward you: great is my boasting about you. I am filled with encouragement; I am overwhelmed with joy in all my affliction.

CORINTHIAN LETTER F

2 Cor 10:1-11:9 + 1 Cor 9:1-18 + 2 Cor 11:10-13:10

(10:1) Now I, Paul, ask you, through the humility and gentleness of Christ, I who face-to-face with you am lowly among you, but when far away, I am bold toward you. (2) I ask that when I am present, I may not have to be so bold with the confidence by which I am considered by some who think that we walk according to the flesh. (3) For even when we walk in the flesh, we do not wage war according to the flesh, (4) for the weapons of our warfare are not fleshly, but they have the strength of God to bring down strongholds. We destroy sophistries and we set aside every opposition to the knowledge of God, (5) and we take every thought captive for the obedience of Christ, (6) and are ready to punish every disobedience, when your obedience is complete.

(7) Look at the facts in front of your face. If people have confidence that they are of Christ, let that person consider this again for himself or herself: Just as they say, "I am of Christ," so too are we. (8) For if I were to boast exceedingly more because of our authority, which the Lord gave us for building you up and not for tearing you down, I would not be ashamed. (9) Let me not seem to scare you through letters. (10) "His letters," they say, "are weighty and strong, yet his bodily presence is weak, and his speaking ability is despicable." (11) Let such a person consider this: the kind of person we are through letters when absent is the same kind of person we are when actively present.

(12) For we are not being bold to classify or compare ourselves with some of those who recommend themselves, but they lack understanding in that they measure themselves and compare themselves to themselves. (13) We, however, will not boast beyond limits, but according to the length of the measure, which God portioned out to us, as we reached out as far as you. (14) For as we did not overextend ourselves when we reached out to you, until we arrived where you are with the gospel of Christ, (15) we are not boasting beyond limits in the labors of others, yet having the hope of the growth of your faith, to be magnified according to our assignment in order to bring the gospel (16) to the lands beyond you, not part of the assignment of another in order boast

about what has been accomplished. (17) "Let the one who boasts boast in the Lord." (18) For it is not the one who recommends himself, but the one whom the Lord commends, who is genuine.

(11:1) Would that you bear with me in a bit of foolishness; really, do bear with me! (2) For I am jealous for you with God's jealousy, for I betrothed you as a pure virgin to present you to one husband, to Christ. (3) I fear, however, that perhaps, like the snake deceived Eve in his cunning, your thoughts have been led astray from the simplicity and purity, which lead toward Christ. (4) For if a person comes to you preaching another Jesus than the one whom we preached, or another Spirit than the one whom you received, or another gospel than the one you received, you bear with it well enough.

(5) For I consider myself to be lacking nothing in comparison to the superlative apostles. (6) Now if I am an amateur in speaking, I am not so in knowledge, but in every respect these matters have been made clear in all things to you. (7) Did I commit a sin by becoming lowly in order that you would be exalted, because I preached to you the gospel as a gift from God? (8) I robbed other churches, taking payment so that I could minister to your needs, (9) and when I was present with you and you had nothing I did not burden you at all. For what I needed the brothers and sisters who came from Macedonia supplied, and in every way, I kept myself from being a burden to you, and I will so keep myself.

(1 Cor 9:1) Am I not free? Am I not an apostle? Have I not seen Jesus our Lord? Are not you my work in the Lord? (2) If to others I am not an apostle, certainly to you I am. For you are the seal of my apostleship in the Lord. (3) My defense to those who would interrogate me is this. (4) Do we not have the authority to eat and drink? (5) Do we not have the authority to travel with a Christian woman as other apostles do, such as the brothers of the Lord and Cephas? (6) Or is it only I and Barnabas who have no right to refrain from work? (7) What soldier ever goes to fight at his own expense? Who plants a vineyard and does not eat the fruit of it? Or what shepherd takes care of sheep and does not drink some sheep's milk? (8) Do I not speak these things in a human way, or does not the law also say these things? (9) For it is written in the law of Moses, "You shall not muzzle the ox as it treads the grain." Is it about oxen that God is concerned, (10) or does it really concern us? For it was written for us because "the plowman should plow in hope, and the thresher too, in hope of sharing in the crop." (11) If we sowed spiritual seed with you, will we not reap a great fleshly crop from you? (12) If others enjoy authority among you, should we not do

so even more? But we have not used this authority, yet we endure all things, in order that we may not give any hindrance to the gospel of Christ. (13) Do you not know that they who are of the temple eat the food offered in sacrifice, and that they who concern themselves with the altar share in what is offered there? (14) Thus, also the Lord ordered that those who preach the gospel might make their living from the gospel. (15) I however do not make use of this privilege. I have not written these things so that these things may happen in my case; I would rather die than this. No one is going to take away my boast! (16) For if I should preach the gospel, it is not something I may boast about. For I am under pressure: woe is me if I should not preach the gospel. (17) For if I do this willingly, I have a reward; if I do this unwillingly, I have been entrusted with a commission. (18) And so what is my reward? That I may present the gospel free of charge in order not to make use of my authority in the gospel.

(2 Cor 11:10) It is the truth of Christ in me that this boast will not be silenced for me in the regions of Achaia. (11) Why is this? Because I do not love you? God knows I do!

(12) Now what I am doing, and what I shall continue to do, is that I will cut off a pretext from those who seek a pretext, so that they may be found out in what they boast about, just as we will be found out. (13) For people such as these are false apostles, evil workers, impersonators of apostles of Christ! (14) Indeed it is no wonder: for Satan himself impersonates an angel of light. (15) Thus, it is no great mystery when his ministers masquerade as servants of righteousness; they will come to their end according to what they have done.

(16) I am saying it again: let no one think that I am a fool; yet if I am, it is because you will welcome me, so that I may have a little something to boast about. (17) The things I say, I do not speak according to the Lord but as a person given to foolishness, in this boasting project of mine. (18) While many have boasted according to the flesh, I will also boast. (19) For you, being wise, put up with fools gladly. (20) For you put up with it if someone enslaves you, if someone devours you, if someone takes your goods, if someone puts on airs, if someone strikes you in the face. (21) I say, to my shame, that we were too weak to do that!

Along these lines, however, if anyone is bold—I speak in foolishness—I also am bold. (22) Are they Hebrews? So am I. Are they Israelites? So am I. Are they the seed of Abraham? So am I. (23) Are they ministers of Christ? I am demented to speak this way—I am a better one. I have done far more labors; I have fought far more battles; I have endured far more blows; I have been near death often. (24) From Jews I received the thirty-nine lashes, (25) three times I was beaten with rods, once I was stoned, three times I was shipwrecked; I spent a day and a night adrift at sea. (26) Often on journeys, in dangers from rivers, in dangers from robbers, in dangers from my people, in dangers from Gentiles, in dangers in the city, in dangers in the wilderness, in dangers in the sea, in dangers from false brothers and sisters, (27) in labor and hardship, often through sleepless nights, in hunger and thirst, often going without food, cold and naked. (28) Apart from what I have mentioned, there is the pressure on me every day, the anxiety about all the churches. (29) Who is weak and I am not weak? Who is made to stumble and I am not on fire? (30) If it is necessary to boast, I shall boast about my weakness. (31) The God and Father of the Lord Jesus, he who is blessed to all eternity, knows that I am not lying. (32) In Damascus, the ethnarch King Aretas, ordered a watch on the city of the Damascenes, to take me into custody, (33) and through an window, in a basket, I was let down through the wall, and I escaped his hands.

(12:1) It is necessary to boast, though it will be of no advantage; I will go on to visions and revelations of the Lord. (2) I know a person in Christ who, fourteen years ago, whether in the body or whether not in the body I don't know, God knows, was snatched up to the third heaven. (3) And I know such a person, whether in the body or outside the body I do not know, God knows, (4) that he was snatched up into paradise and he heard inexpressible words, which it is not permitted for a person to speak. (5) Concerning such a man I will boast, yet about myself I will not boast except about weakness. (6) For if I might wish to boast, I will not be a fool, for I will be telling the truth. Now I am restraining myself, so that no one would think me to be anything beyond what one sees in me or hears from me, (7) and because of the surpassing nature of the revelations. For this reason, in order to keep me from being arrogant, a thorn was given me in the flesh, a messenger of Satan, in order to torment me, to keep me from being elated. (8) More than this, three times I pleaded with the Lord that it might go away from me. (9) And he said to me, "My grace is sufficient for you, for power is perfected in weakness. Consequently I will more gladly boast about my weaknesses," in order that the power of Christ may dwell in me. (10) For this reason, I am content in weaknesses, in being insulted, in difficulties, in persecutions, and in constraints, for the sake of Christ; for when I am weak, then I am powerful.

(11) I have been a fool, but you compelled me. For I ought to have been supported by you; for I am not in the least inferior to the superapostles, even though I am nothing. (12) Now the signs of an apostle has been performed among you with all patience—signs and wonders and miracles. (13) For how have you been

treated as inferior to the other churches, except that I was not a burden to you? Forgive me this injustice!

(2 Cor 12:14) Look: I am ready to come to you a third time, and I will not be a burden. For I do not seek what is yours but actually you. For children ought not to save up for their parents, but parents for their children. (15) Now I will gladly spend and be spent for the sake of your souls. If my love for you has been abundant, am I to be loved the less? (16) Now so be it: I did not burden you. But cunning as I am, I took you in. (17) Which one of these I sent to you, through whom I have taken advantage of you? (18) I encouraged Titus and I sent the brother: how did Titus take advantage of you? Have we not walked in the same spirit? Were they not in the footsteps of others?

(19) Formerly you may have thought that we were defending ourselves to you. In God's sight we are speaking in Christ. Now everything, beloved ones, is for building you up. (20) For I am afraid lest when I come I might find you not as I wish, and I might be found by you not as you wish: that perhaps there would be strife, envy, outbursts of anger, disputes, slanders, whispers, self-inflations, and disturbances. (21) When I come to you again, may the Lord not humble me toward you, and may I not have to mourn over many who have sinned previously and have failed to repent of the impurity, immorality, and licentiousness, which they were practicing.

(13:1) I am coming to you a third time: "By the mouth of two or three witnesses every word will be substantiated." (2) As I spoke up and said previously, when I was there a second time and as I am away now, to those who previously sinned and to all the rest: I will not spare you again, (3) since you require proof that I am speaking in Christ, who is not weak toward you but rather is strong in you. (4) For indeed he was crucified in weakness, but he lives in the power of God. Certainly we are weak in him, but we will live with him by the power of God as applied to you.

(5) Examine each other to see if you are in the faith; put each other to the test. Or do you not know that Jesus Christ is in you? Surely you are not unqualified! (6) Now I hope that you know that we are not unqualified. (7) So we pray to God that you do not commit any evil, not so that we might be shown to be unqualified, but that you may do what is good, even though we might remain unqualified. (8) Clearly we can do nothing against the truth but only for the truth. (9) For we rejoice when we are weak, however you may be strong. Indeed we pray for this: your maturation. (10) For this reason, I am writing these things from afar, in order that when I am present I will not have to deal sharply according to the authority, which the Lord gave me for building up and not for tearing down.

CORINTHIAN LETTER G

2 Cor 1:1–2:13 + 7:5-16 + 13:11-13

(1:1) Paul, apostle of Christ Jesus through the will of God, together with our brother Timothy, to the church of God, which is in Corinth, with all the saints in the whole of Achaia, (2) grace to you and peace from God our Father and our Lord Jesus Christ.

(3) Blessed be the God and Father of our Lord Jesus Christ, the father of mercies and the God of all consolation, (4) who consoles us in our every affliction so that we ourselves are able to console those in every affliction through the consolation with which we have been consoled by God. (5) For just as the sufferings of Christ overflow onto us, so too does our consolation overflow through Christ. (6) Now if we are afflicted, it is for the sake of your consolation and salvation; if we are being consoled, it is for the sake of your consolation, which functions in the act of enduring the sufferings, which we suffer. (7) Indeed, our hope for you is firm, knowing that you are sharers of sufferings, so are you also sharers of consolation.

(8) For I do not want you to be ignorant, brothers and sisters, concerning our afflictions, which happened in Asia, because we were crushed by the extraordinary pressure, beyond our power, so that we despaired of living. (9) In fact, in ourselves, we were under a sentence of death, so that we might have trust not in ourselves but in God who raises the dead. (10) But the one who rescued us from so great a peril of death, will indeed save us, the one in whom we have hoped that he will continue to save, (11) while you join in helping us by your prayer, so that from many persons there may be many thanksgivings for us for the spiritual gift to us on your behalf.

(12) For our boast is this: the witness of our conscience, that we behaved in the world, and more assuredly toward you, with the simplicity and sincerity of God, and not in fleshly wisdom, but with the grace of God. (13) For we do not write to you other than what you read or what you understand. Now I hope that you will understand, (14) that just as you have understood us partially, that we will ultimately be your boast just as you will be ours on the day of the Lord Jesus.

(15) In this trust, I wanted to come to you previously, in order that you might receive a second gift, (16) and to come through your city as I traveled to Macedonia, and again to come from Macedonia to you; I wanted to be sent off by you to Judaea. (17) In having this as my purpose, did I therefore

vacillate? Or the things I decided on, according to the flesh, did I do so in order that, for me it might be yes, yes and no, no? (18) Yet God is faithful, because our Lord to you was not yes and no. (19) For God's Son Jesus Christ who was preached by us among you, by myself and Silvanus and Timothy, was not yes and no, but in him it was yes. (20) Such are the promises of God: in him it is yes. For this reason, we say the amen to God for his glory to come through us. (21) Now he who confirmed us with you in Christ and anointed us is God, (22) who sealed us and gave the down payment of the Spirit in our hearts.

(23) Now I call upon God as my witness upon my life, that it was to spare you that I did not come to Corinth. (24) It is not that we lord it over your faith, but that we are fellow workers for your joy. For you have stood in the faith.

(2:1) For I decided on my own part not to make another painful visit to you. (2) For if I cause you pain, who makes me glad except the one who has been caused pain by me? (3) And I wrote the very same thing, in order that by not coming, I would suffer pain from those who should give me joy, trusting in all of you that my joy would the joy of all of you. (4) For out of much affliction and anguish of heart I wrote you, with many tears, not in order that you might suffer pain but that you might know the love which I have, especially for you.

(5) Now if a certain person did cause me pain, it was not I who suffered pain, but at least in part, not to exaggerate, it was all of you. (6) This punishment that has been given by the majority of you is now appropriate for such a person, (7) so that, on the other hand, you should rather forgive and encourage this person, lest such a person be overcome by excessive grief. (8) Therefore, I ask you to confirm your love for him. (9) For it was for this reason that I wrote you, in order that I might know your character, if you are obedient in every way. (10) And so the one you forgive for something, I also forgive. For if I have forgiven something, if there was anything to forgive, it is for your sake, before the face of Christ, (11) in order that we will not be robbed by Satan, for we are not ignorant of his designs.

(12) Now when I came to Troas for the gospel of Christ, when indeed a door was opened for me in the Lord, (13) I had no rest in my spirit since I did not find Titus my brother, but taking leave of them I departed for Macedonia. (7:5) For when we arrived in Macedonia our flesh had no rest, but we were afflicted in every way: quarrels on the outside, fears on the inside. (6) But the God who consoles the downcast consoled us by the arrival of Titus, (7) actually not only by his arrival but also by the consolation with which he was

consoled by you, as he reported to us your longing, your mourning, your zeal for me, so that I rejoiced even more. (8) The fact that I caused you pain in my letter, I do not regret, if I did regret it, for I see that that letter did cause you pain for a while. (9) Now I am glad, not that you suffered pain but that your pain provoked you to repentance. For you were pained in God's way, so that you were in no way damaged by us. (10) For the pain which is in God's way achieves a repentance for salvation, which no one regrets. Now the pain of the world produces death. (11) For behold, the fact of suffering pain in God's way produced in you such eagerness, such defense, such indignation, such fear, such longing, such zeal, and such punishment! In everything you have demonstrated yourselves blameless in the matter. (12) Consequently my writing to you was not because of the one who misbehaved but so that your earnestness, which was for us might be might be made clear to you, before God. (13) For this reason, we have been consoled. Now because of our consolation, more especially because of the joy of Titus, we are joyful that his spirit has been refreshed by all of you. (14) Since I have been boasting somewhat about you, I have not been made ashamed, but as we told you everything truthfully, so too our boast about Titus has been proven to be true. (15) For from the bottom of his heart, he was abundantly reminded by you of the obedience of all of you, how with fear and trembling you received him. (16) I am happy that in every way, I can depend on you.

(2 Cor. 13:11) Finally, brothers and sisters, rejoice, become mature, be encouraged, agree with one another, be at peace, and the God of love and peace will be with you. (12) Greet each other with a holy kiss. All the saints great you.

(13) The grace of the Lord Jesus Christ and the love of God and the communion of the Holy Spirit be with you all.

CORINTHIAN LETTER H

2 Cor 9:1-15

(9:1) Now concerning the ministry to the saints, it is unnecessary for me to write to you. (2) For I know your good will, about which I am boasting to the Macedonians, to the effect that Achaia has been ready since last year, and that your zeal has aroused most of them. (3) Now I have sent the brothers, in order that our boasting about you might not be empty in this matter, so that just as I said, you will be fully prepared. (4) What if I should come along with Macedonians and they should find you unprepared, and we would be ashamed—to say nothing of your shame!—if that should occur? (5) Therefore, I considered it necessary to exhort the brothers, in order to make sure that, when they come ahead to you, they will be fully prepared to bestow the blessing previously promised, so that this will be ready, as a blessing and not as an extortion.

(6) Know this: the person who sows sparingly will reap sparingly and the one who sows bountifully will reap bountifully. (7) Let each person, just as he has made up his mind, do so neither out of pressure nor necessity. "For the Lord loves a cheerful giver." (8) Now may God make every gift overflow onto you, in order that you may have enough of everything, so that you may abound in every good work. (9) Just as it is written, "He distributed; he gave to the poor; his righteousness remains forever." (10) So the one who gives seed to the sower and bread to the eater will supply your need and will cause your seed to abound and to make bountiful the harvest of your righteousness. (11) In everything you have been enriched with all liberality; may this liberality produce our thanksgiving to God. (12) Thus, the ministry of this offering will not only supply the needs of the saints; it will also increase many people's thanksgivings to God. (13) Through the proven character of your ministry, they will glorify God because of the submission of your confession to the gospel of Christ and the sincerity of your partnership with them and with all, (14) and they will pray, yearning for the surpassing grace of God to be bestowed on you. (15) Thanks be to God for his ineffable gift!

Bibliography

Aageson, James W. *Paul, the Pastoral Epistles, and the Early Church*. Library of Pauline Studies. Peabody, MA: Hendrickson, 2008.
Aageson, James W. "The Pastoral Epistles, Apostolic Authority, and the Development of the Pauline Scriptures." Pages 5–26 in Stanley E. Porter, editor, *The Pauline Canon*. Pauline Studies, 1. Leiden: Brill, 2004.
Adams, Edward, and David G. Horrell, eds. *Christianity at Corinth: The Quest for the Pauline Church*. Louisville & London: Westminster John Knox Press, 2004.
Aejmelaeus, Lars. *Streit und Versohnung. Das Problem der Zusammensetzung des 2. Korintherbriefes*. Translated by K.-J. Trabant. Helsinki: Suomen Eksegeettisen Seura, 1987.
Aejmelaeus, Lars. *Schwachheit als Waffe. Die Argumentation des Paulus im "Tränenbrief (2 Kor. 10-13)*. Schriften der finnischen exegetischen Gesellschaft, 78. Helsinki: Finnish Exegetical Society; Göttingen: Vandenhoeck & Ruprecht, 2000.
Aichele, George, et al. *The Postmodern Bible: The Bible and Culture Collective*. New Haven: Yale University Press, 1995.
Aland, Kurt. "The Problem of Anonymity and Pseudonymity in the Christian Literature of the First Two Centuries." *JTS* 12 (1961): 39–49.
Aland, Kurt and Barbara Aland. *The Text of the New Testament: An Introduction to the Critical Editions and to the Theory and Practice of Modern Textual Criticism*. Translated by Erroll F. Rhodes. Grand Rapids: Eerdmans; Leiden: Brill, 1987.
Alexander, Loveday C. A. "Ancient Book Production and the Circulation of the Gospels." Pages 71–111 in Richard Bauckham, editor, *The Gospels for All Christians: Rethinking the Gospel Audiences*. Edinburgh: T & T Clark; Grand Rapids: Eerdmans, 1998.
Allo, E. B. *Saint Paul: Première Épître aux Corinthiens*, 2nd edition. *EBib*. Paris: Gabalda, 1956.
Allo, E. B. *Saint Paul: Seconde Épître aux Corinthiens*, 2nd edition. *EBib*. Paris: Gabalda, 1956.

Amador, J. D. H. "Revisiting 2 Corinthians: Rhetoric and the Case for Unity." *NTS* 46 (2000): 92–111.

Anderson, R. Dean, Jr. *Ancient Rhetorical Theory and Paul: Revised Edition.* CBET 18. Leuven: Peeters, 1998.

Arx, Urs von. "Gibt Paulus in 1 Kor 7 eine Interpretation von Gal 3,28? Zugleich ein Beitrag zur relativen Chronologie der Paulusbriefe." Volume 1, pages 193–221 in Constantine J. Belezus et al., editors, *Saint Paul and Corinth.* Athens: Psichoigos, 2009.

Arzt-Grabner, Peter. "1 Cor. 4:6—A Scribal Gloss?" *Biblische Notizen* 130 (2006): 59–78.

Arzt-Grabner, Peter et al. *1. Korinther.* Papyrologische Kommentare zum Neuen Testament, 2. Göttingen: Vandenhoeck & Ruprecht, 2006.

Aune, David E. *The New Testament in Its Literary Environment.* LEC. Philadelphia: Westminster, 1987.

Bachmann, Philipp. *Der erste Brief des Paulus an die Korinther*, 3rd edition. Kommentar zum Neuen Testament, 7. Leipzig: Deichertsche Verlagsbuchhandlung, 1921.

Bachmann, Philipp. *Der zweite Brief des Paulus an die Korinther*, 4th ed. Kommentar zum Neuen Testament, 8. Leipzig: Deichertsche Verlagsbuchhandlung, 1922.

Bacon, B. W. "The Christ-Party in Corinth." *The Expositor* 47 (1914): 399–415.

Bagnall, Roger S. *Everyday Writing in the Graeco-Roman World.* Sather Classical Lectures, 69. Berkeley: University of California Press, 2011.

Bahr, J. Gordon. "Paul and Letter Writing in the First Century." *CBQ* 28 (1966): 465–77.

Bailey, Kenneth E. *Paul Through Mediterrean Eyes: Cultural Studies in 1 Corinthians.* Downers Grove: InterVarsity, 2011.

Baljon, Johannes Marinus Simon. *De tekst der brieven van Paulus aan de Romeinen, de Corinthiers en de Galatiers als voorwerp van de conjecturaalkritiek beschouwd.* Utrecht: Kemink & Zoon, 1884.

Balz, Horst R. "Anonymität und Pseudepigraphie im Urchristentum. Überlegungen zum literarischen und theologischen Problem der urchristlichen und gemeinantiken Pseudepigraphie." *ZTK* 66 (1969): 403–36.

Barnett, Paul. *The Second Epistle to the Corinthians.* NICNT. Grand Rapids & Cambridge: Eerdmans, 1997.

Barr, David L. *New Testament Story*, 2nd ed. Belmont, CA: Wadsworth, 1995.

Barrett, Charles Kingsley. "Cephas and Corinth." Pages 1–12 in Otto Betz et al., editors, *Abraham unser Vater: Juden und Christen im Gespräch über die Bibel. Festschrift für Otto Michel zum 60. Geburtstag.* AGSU 5. Leiden: Brill, 1963.

Barrett, Charles Kingsley. "Christianity at Corinth." *BJRL* 46 (1964): 269–97.

Barrett, Charles Kingsley. *The First Epistle to the Corinthians*, 2nd ed. HNTC. New York: Harper & Row, 1971.

Barrett, Charles Kingsley. *The Pastoral Epistles in the New English Bible.* Oxford: Clarendon, 1963; reprinted, Grand Rapids: Outreach, 1986.

Barrett, Charles Kingsley. *The Second Epistle to the Corinthians.* HNTC. New York: Harper & Row, 1973.

Barrett, Charles Kingsley. "Pauline Controversies in the Post-Pauline Period." *NTS* 20 (1973–74): 229–45.

Bartchy, S. Scott. *First-Century Slavery and 1 Corinthians 7:21*. SBLDS 11. Missoula: Society of Biblical Literature, 1973.

Barton, Stephen C. "Paul's Sense of Place: An Anthropological Approach to Community Formation in Corinth." *NTS* 32 (1986): 225–46.

Bauer, Walter. *Orthodoxy and Heresy in Earliest Christianity*. Translated from the 1964 German reissue and edited by R. A. Kraft and G. Krodel. Philadelphia: Fortress, 1972.

Baum, Armin Daniel. "Literarische Echtheit als Kanonkriterium in der alten Kirche." *ZNW* 88 (1997): 97–110.

Baum, Armin Daniel. *Pseudepigraphie und literarische Fälschung im frühen Christentum. Mit ausgewählten Quellentexten samt deutscher Übersetzung*. WUNT 2.138. Tübingen: Mohr Siebeck, 1999.

Baumert, Norbert. *Mit dem Rücken zur Wand. Übersetzung und Auslegung des zweiten Korintherbriefes*. Würzburg: Echter, 2008.

Baumert, Norbert. *Sorgen des Seelsorgers. Übersetzung und Auslegung des ersten Korintherbriefes*. Paulus neu gelesen 1. Würzburg: Echter, 2007.

Baumert, Norbert. *Täglich sterben und auferstehen. Der Literalsinn von 2 Kor 4,12—5,10*. SANT 34. Munich: Kösel-Verlag, 1973.

Baumert, Norbert. *Woman and Man in Paul: Overcoming a misunderstanding*. Translated by Patrick Madigan and Linda M. Maloney. Collegeville: Liturgical Press, 1996.

Beardslee, William A. *Literary Criticism of the New Testament*. Philadelphia: Fortress Press, 1970.

Becker, Eve-Marie. *Letter Hermeneutics in 2 Corinthians: Literarkritik and Communication Theory*. JSNTSup 279. London: T & T Clark, 2004.

Becker, Eve-Marie. *Schreiben und Verstehen. Paulinische Briefhermeneutik im Zweiten Korintherbrief*. Neutestamentliche Entwürfe zur Theologie, 4. Tübingen: Francke, 2002.

Becker, Eve-Marie. "Was ist Kohärenz? Ein Beitrag zur Präzisierung eines exegetischen Leitkriteriums." *ZNW* 94 (2003): 97–121.

Beier, Peter. "Geteilte Briefe? Eine kritische Untersuchung der neueren Teilungshypothesen zu den paulinischen Briefen." Dissertation Universität Halle, 1984.

Beker, J. Christiaan. *Heirs of Paul: Paul's Legacy in the New Testament and in the Church Today*. Minneapolis: Fortress, 1991.

Belleville, Linda L. "Continuity or Discontinuity: A Fresh Look at 1 Corinthians in the Light of First-Century Epistolary Forms and Conventions." *EvQ* 59 (1987): 15–37.

Belleville, Linda L. "*Kephale* and the Thorny Issue of Headcovering in 1 Corinthians 11:2-16." Pages 215–32 in Trevor J. Burke and J. Keith Elliott, editors, *Paul and the Corinthians: Studies on a Community in Conflict. Essays in Honour of Margaret Thrall*. NovTSup 109. Leiden & Boston: Brill, 2003.

Belleville, Linda L. "A Letter of Apologetic Self-Recommendation: 2 Cor. 1:8-7:16." *NovT* 31 (1989): 142–63.

Belleville, Linda L. *Reflections of Glory: Paul's Polemical Use of the Moses-Doxa Tradition in 2 Corinthians 3:1-18.* JSNTSup 52. Sheffield: JSOT Press, 1991.
Belleville, Linda L. *2 Corinthians.* IVP New Testament Commentary Series, 8. Downers Grove & Leicester, UK: InterVarsity Press, 1995.
Berger, Klaus. "Almosen für Israel: Zum historischen Kontext der paulinischen Kollekte." *NTS* 23 (1977): 180–204.
Berger, Klaus. *Formgeschichte des Neuen Testaments.* Heidelberg: Quelle & Meyer, 1984.
Bernheim, Pierre-Antoine. "Interpolations in Romans: Loisy, O'Neill and others Revisited." Pages 827–838 in Udo Schnelle, editor, *Letter to the Romans.* BETL 226. Leuven: Peeters, 2009.
Betz, Hans Dieter. *Der Apostel Paulus und die sokratische Tradition. Eine exegetische Untersuchung zu seiner "Apologie" 2 Kor 10–13.* BHT 45. Tübingen: Mohr, 1972.
Betz, Hans Dieter. "Corinthians, Second Epistle to." *ABD* (1992): 1.1148–54.
Betz, Hans Dieter. *Galatians: A Commentary on Paul's Letter to the Churches in Galatia.* Hermeneia. Philadelphia: Fortress, 1979.
Betz, Hans Dieter. *Nachfolge and Nachahmung Jesu Christi im Neuen Testament*, BHT 37. Tübingen: Mohr, 1967.
Betz, Hans Dieter. "2 Cor 6:14-7:1: An Anti-Pauline Fragment?" *JBL* 92 (1973): 88–108.
Betz, Hans Dieter. *2 Corinthians 8 and 9: A Commentary on Two Administrative Letters of the Apostle Paul.* Hermeneia. Philadelphia: Fortress, 1985.
Bieringer, Reimund et al., editors. *2 Corinthians: A Bibliography.* BTS 5. Leuven: Peeters, 2008.
Bieringer, Reimund, editor. *The Corinthian Correspondence.* BETL 125. Leuven: University Press & Peeters, 1996.
Bieringer, Reimund and Jan Lambrecht. *Studies on 2 Corinthians.* BETL 112. Leuven: University Press and Peeters, 1994.
Bieringer, Reimund. "Teilungshypothesen zum 2. Korintherbrief." Pages 67–105 in Reimund Bieringer and Jan Lambrecht, *Studies on 2 Corinthians.* BETL 112. Leuven: University Press and Peeters, 1994.
Bitzer, Lloyd F. "Functional Communication: A Situational Perspective." Pages 21–38 in E. E. White, editor, *Rhetoric in Transition: Studies in the Nature and Uses of Rhetoric.* University Park: Pennsylvania State University Press, 1980.
Bitzer, Lloyd F. "The Rhetorical Situation." *Philosophy and Rhetoric* 1 (1968): 1–14.
Black, C. Clifton. "Keeping up with Recent Studies: Rhetorical Criticism and Biblical Interpretation." *ExpTim* 100 (1989): 252–58.
Black, C. Clifton. "Rhetorical Questions: The New Testament, Classical Rhetoric, and Current Interpretations." *Dialog* 29 (1990): 62–70.
Black, C. Clifton and Duane F. Watson, editors. *Words Well Spoken: George Kennedy's Rhetoric and the New Testament.* Waco: Baylor University Press, 2008.
Blanchard, Alain, editor. *Les débuts du codex. Actes de la journée d'étude organisée à Paris les 3 et 4 juillet 1985 par l'Institut de Papyrologie de la Sorbonne.* Bibliologia: Elementa ad librorum studia pertinentia 9. Brepols: Turnhout, 1989.

Blomberg, Craig L. *1 Corinthians*. NIV Application Commentary. Grand Rapids: Zondervan, 1994.

Blomberg, Craig L. "The Structure of 2 Corinthians 1-7." *CTR* 4 (1989): 3–20.

Bloomquist, L. Gregory. *The Function of Ssuffering in Philippians*. JSNTSup 78. Sheffield: JSOT Press, 1993.

Blumell, Lincoln H. "Travel and Communication in the NT." *NIDB* 5. 652–56.

Boer, Martinus C. de. "The Composition of 1 Corinthians." *NTS* 40 (1994): 229–45.

Boer, Martinus C. de. "Images of Paul in the Post-Apologetic Period." *CBQ* 42 (1980) 359–80.

Boers, Hendrikus. "2 Corinthians 5:14-6:2: A Fragment of Pauline Christology." *CBQ* 64 (2002): 527–47.

Bornkamm, Günther. "The History of the Origin of the So-Called Second Letter to the Corinthians." *NTS* 8 (1962): 258–64.

Bornkamm, Günther. *Paul: Paulus*. Translated by D. M. G. Stalker. New York: Harper & Row, 1971.

Bornkamm, Günther. "Die Vorgeschichte des sogenannten zweiten Korintherbriefes," in *SHAW, Philosophische - historische Klasse*, 2nd Abhandlung. Heidelberg: C. Winter, 1961, pp. 7–36.

Boyarin, Daniel. *A Radical Jew: Paul and the Politics of Identity*. Contraversions: Critical Studies in Jewish Literature, Culture, and Society. Berkeley: University of California Press, 1994.

Brandenburger, Egon. *Adam und Christus: exegetisch-religionsgeschichtliche Untersuchung zu Rom. 5,12-21 (1. Kor. 15)*. WMANT 7. Neukirchen: Neukirchener Verlag, 1962.

Branick, Vincent P. "Source and Redaction Analysis of 1 Corinthians 1-3." *JBL* 101 (1982): 251–69.

Bray, Gerald, editor. *1-2 Corinthians*. Ancient Christian Commentary on Scripture: New Testament, VII. Downers Grove: InterVarsity, 1999.

Brendle, Albert. *Im Prozeß der Konfliktüberwendung: Eine exegetische Studie zur Kommunikationssituation zwischen Paulus und den Korinthern in 2 Kor 1,1-2,13; 7,4-16*. Europäische Hochschulschriften, Series XXIII, Theology, 533. Frankfurt: Peter Lang, 1995.

Breyenbach, Cilliers. "Paul's Proclamation and God's 'Thriambos': Notes on 2 Corinthians 2:14-16b." *Neotestamentica* 24/2 (1990): 257–71.

Brodie, Thomas L. "The Genre of 1 Corinthians: Not a Letter but a Letter Essay." Paper delivered at the Society of Biblical Literature Annual Meeting, 2013.

Brown, Alexandra R. *The Cross and Human Transformation: Paul's Apocalyptic Word in 1 Corinthians*. Minneapolis: Fortress, 1995.

Brown, Raymond E. "Peter." Pages 654–57 in K. Crim, V. P. Furnish, L. R. Bailey and E. S. Bucke, editors, *Interpreter's Dictionary of the Bible, Supplement Volume*. Nashville: Abingdon, 1976.

Brox, Norbert. "Altkirchliche Formen des Anspruchs auf apostolische Kirchenverfassung." *Kairos* 12 (1970): 113–40.

Brox, Norbert. "ΑΝΑΘΗΜΑ ΙΗΣΟΥΣ [1 Kor 12,3]." *BZ* 12 (1968): 103–11.

Brox, Norbert. "Lukas als Verfasser der Pastoralbriefe." *JAC* 13 (1970): 62–77.
Brox, Norbert. *Die Pastoralbriefe*, 4th ed. RNT 7.2. Regensburg: Pustet, 1969.
Brox, Norbert. "Zum Problemstand in der Erforschung der altchristlichen Pseudepigraphie." *Kairos* 15 (1973): 10–23.
Bruce, F. F. *1 and 2 Corinthians*. NCB. Grand Rapids: Eerdmans; London: Marshall, Morgan & Scott, 1971.
Brun, Lyder. "Noch einmal die Schriftnorm I Kor. 4,6." *TSK* 103 (1931): 453–56.
Bünker, Michael. *Briefformular und rhetorische Disposition im 1. Korintherbrief*. GTA 28. Göttingen: Vandenhoeck & Ruprecht, 1984.
Bullmore, Michael A. *St. Paul's Theology of Rhetorical Style: An Examination of 1 Corinthians 2:1-5 in the Light of First Century Graeco-Roman Rhetorical Culture*. San Francisco: International Scholars, 1995.
Bultmann, Rudolf. *Der zweite Brief an die Korinther*. Edited by Erich Dinkler. KEK 6. Göttingen: Vandenhoeck & Ruprecht, 1976.
Bultmann, Rudolf. *The Second Letter to the Corinthians*. Translated by Roy A. Harrisville. Minneapolis: Augsburg, 1985.
Burgess, Theodore C. *Epideictic Literature*. Studies in Classical Philology, 3. Chicago: University of Chicago Press, 1902.
Burgos Núñez, Miguel de. "La Correspondencia de Pablo con las Communidades de Corinto." *Communio* 26 (1993): 33–67.
Burke, Kenneth. *A Grammar of Motives*. Berkeley: University of California Press, 1969.
Cameron, Ron and Merrill P. Miller, editors. *Redescribing Paul and the Corinthians*. Early Christianity and its Literature, 5. Atlanta: Society of Biblical Literature, 2011.
Campbell, Douglas A. "An Anchor for Pauline Chronology: Paul's Flight from 'the Ethnarch of King Aretas' (2 Corinthians 11:32-33)." *JBL* 121 (2002): 279–302.
Carey, Greg and L. Gregory Bloomquist, editors. *Vision and Persuasion: Rhetorical Dimensions of Apocalyptic Discourse*. St. Louis: Chalice Press, 1999.
Carrez, Maurice. *La deuxième Épître de saint Paul aux Corinthiens*. CNT 2.8, Geneva: Labor et Fides, 1987.
Carroll, Kenneth L. "The Expansion of the Pauline Corpus." *JBL* 72 (1953): 230–37.
Castelli, Elizabeth A. *Imitating Paul: A Discourse of Power*. Louisville: Westminster John Knox, 1991.
Castelli, Elizabeth A. *Martyrdom and Memory: Early Christian Culture Making*. New York: Columbia University Press, 2004.
Chiu, José Enrique Aguilar. *1 Cor 12—14. Literary Structure and Theology*. AnBib 166. Rome: Pontificio Istituto Biblico, 2007.
Chow, John K. *Patronage and Power: A Study of Social Networks in Corinth*. JSNTSup 75. Sheffield: JSOT, 1992.
Church, F. Forrester. "Rhetorical Structure and Design in Paul's Letter to Philemon." *HTR* 71 (1978): 17–33.
Ciampa, Roy E. and Brian S. Rosner. *The First Letter to the Corinthians*. Pillar New Testament Commentary. Grand Rapids: Eerdmans, 2010.

Clarke, Andrew D. *Secular and Christian Leadership in Corinth: A Socio-historical and Exegetical Study of 1 Corinthians 1-6.* AGJU 18. Leiden: Brill, 1993.
Clarke, Graham. "'As in all the churches of the saints' (1 Corinthians 14.33).'" *BT* 52 (2001): 144–47.
Cleary, Patrick. "The Epistles to the Corinthians." *CBQ* 12 (1950): 10–33.
Clemen, Carl. *Die Einheitlichkeit der paulinischen Briefe an der Hand der bisher mit Bezug auf sie aufgestellten Interpolations- und Compilationshypothesen.* Göttingen: Vandenhoeck und Ruprecht, 1894.
Clines, David J. A. et al., editors. *Art and Meaning: Rhetoric in Biblical Literature.* JSOTSup 19. Sheffield: JSOT Press, 1982.
Collange, Jean-Francois. *Énigmes de la deuxième épître aux Corinthiens. Étude exégétique de 2 Cor. 2:14-7:4.* SNTSMS 18. Cambridge: University Press, 1972.
Collins, Raymond F. *First Corinthians.* SP 7. Collegeville: Liturgical Press, 1999.
Collins, Raymond F. "The Image of Paul in the Pastorals." *Laval théologique et philosophique* 31 (1975): 147–73.
Collins, Raymond F. *Letters that Paul Did Not Write: The Epistle to the Hebrews and the Pauline Pseudepigrapha.* GNS 28. Wilmington: Glazier, 1989.
Collins, Raymond F. "Pastoralbriefe." 6.988-91 in Hans Dieter Betz et al., editors, *Religion in Geschichte und Gegenwart*, 4th ed. Tübingen: Mohr Siebeck, 2003.
Collins, Raymond F. *The Power of Images in Paul.* Collegeville: Liturgical Press, 2008.
Collins, Raymond F. "Reflections on 1 Corinthians as a Hellenistic Letter." Pages 39–61 in Reimund Bieringer, editor, *The Corinthian Correspondence.* BETL 125. Leuven: University Press & Peeters, 1996.
Collins, Raymond F. *Second Corinthians.* Paideia: Commentaries on the New Testament. Grand Rapids: Baker Academic, 2013.
Collins, Raymond F. *1 and 2 Timothy and Titus: A Commentary.* NTL. Louisville: Westminster John Knox, 2002.
Colwell, Ernest C. *Studies in Methodology in Textual Criticism of the New Testament.* NTTS 9. Leiden: Brill, 1969.
Conzelmann, Hans. *1 Corinthians: A Commentary on the First Epistle to the Corinthians.* Hermeneia. Translated by James W. Leitch. Philadelphia: Fortress, 1975.
Conzelmann, Hans. "Paulus und die Weisheit." *NTS* 12 (1966): 231–44.
Cope, Lamar. "1 Cor. 11:1-16: One Step Further." *JBL* 97 (1978): 435–36.
Costa, C. D. N. *Greek Fictional Letters: A Selection, with Introduction, Translation, and Commentary.* Oxford and New York: Oxford University Press, 2001.
Couchoud, Paul-Louis. "Reconstitution et Classement des Lettres de Saint Paul." *RHR* 87 (1923): 8–31.
Craig, Clarence Tucker. "The First Epistle to the Corinthians: Introduction and Exegesis." Pages 1–262 in Volume 10 of G. A. Buttrick et al., editors, *The Interpreter's Bible.* Nashville: Abingdon Press, 1953.
Crafton, Jeffrey A. *The Agency of the Apostle: A Dramatistic Analysis of Paul's Responses to Conflict in 2 Corinthians.* JSNTSup 51. Sheffield: JSOT, 1991.
Crocker, Cornelia Cyss. *Reading 1 Corinthians in the Twenty-First Century.* London & New York: T & T Clark International, 2004.

Dahl, Nils A. "Der Epheserbrief und der verlorene erste Brief des Paulus an die Korinther." Pages 67–77 in Otto Betz et al., editors, *Abraham unser Vater: Juden und Christen im Gespräch über die Bibel. Festschrift für Otto Michel zum 60. Geburtstag.* AGSU 5. Leiden: Brill, 1963.

Dahl, Nils A. "Paul and the Church at Corinth According to 1 Corinthians 1:10—4:21." Pages 313–35 in W. R. Farmer et al., editors, *Christian History and Interpretation: Studies Presented to John Knox.* Cambridge: Cambridge University Press, 1967.

Danker, Frederick W. *II Corinthians.* Augsburg Commentary on the New Testament. Minneapolis: Augsburg, 1989.

Danker, Frederick W. "Paul's Debt to the 'De Corona' of Demosthenes: A Study of Rhetorical Techniques in Second Corinthians." Pages 262–80 in Duane F. Watson, editor, *Persuasive Artistry: Studies in New Testament Rhetoric in Honor of George A. Kennedy.* JSNTSup 50. Sheffield: Academic Press, 1991.

Dassmann, Ernst. *Der Stachel im Fleisch. Paulus in der früchristlichen Literatur bis Irenäus.* Münster: Aschendorff, 1979.

Dautzenberg, Gerhard. "Der zweite Korintherbrief als Briefsammlung. Zur Frage der literarischen Einheitlichkeit und des theologischen Gefüges 2 Kor 1—8." *Aufstieg und Niedergang der römischen Welt* 25, no. 4 (1987): 3045–66.

Davies, Steven L. *New Testament Fundamentals.* Sonoma, CA: Polebridge, 1994.

Dehandschutter, Boudewijn. "Heresy and the Early Christian Notion of Tradition." *Journal of Eastern Christian Studies* 60 (2008): 7–21.

Deissmann, Adolf. *Paul: A Study in Social and Religious History.* Translated by William E. Wilson. Gloucester: Peter Smith, 1972.

Delling, Gerhard. "*Pleonektes ktl.*" *TDNT* 6 (1968): 266–74.

Delling, Gerhard. *Worship in the New Testament.* Translated by Percy Scott. Philadelphia: Westminster, 1962.

Delobel, Joël. "Coherence and Relevance in 1 Cor 8-10." Pages 177–90 in Raimund Bieringer, editor, *The Corinthian Correspondence.* BETL 125. Leuven: Leuven University Press, 1996.

Delobel, Joël. "1 Cor 11,2-16: Towards a Coherence Interpretation." Pages 369–89 in Albert Vanhoye, editor, *L'Apôtre Paul: Personnalité, style et conception du ministère.* BETL 73. Leuven: Leuven University Presss, 1986.

Deming, Will. "The Unity of 1 Corinthians 5-6." *JBL* 115 (1996): 289–312.

DeSilva, David A. "Measuring Penultimate Against Ultimate Reality: An Investigation of the Integrity and Argumentation of 2 Corinthians." *JSNT* 52 (1993): 41–70.

DeSilva, David A. "Meeting the Exigency of a Complex Rhetorical Situation: Paul's Strategy in 2 Corinthians 1 through 7." *AUSS* 34 (1996): 5–22.

DeSilva, David A. "Recasting the Moment of Decision: 2 Corinthians 6:14-7:1 in Its Literary Context." *AUSS* 31 (1993): 3–16.

Dewey, Arthur J. et al. *The Authentic Letters of Paul: A New Reading of Paul's Rhetoric and Meaning: The Scholars Version.* Salem: Polebridge Press, 2010.

DiCicco, Mario M. *Paul's Use of Ethos, Pathos, and Logos in 2 Corinthians 10-13.* Mellen Biblical Press Series, 31. Lewiston: Mellen Biblical Press, 1995.

Dill, John Allen. "Images of the Apostle Paul in the New Testament Epistles." Unpublished paper, Episcopal Diocese of Pennsylvania School of the Diaconate.
Dinkler, Erich. "Korintherbriefe." *RGG*, 3rd ed., 4.18.
Diringer, David. "Hebrew Writing and the Hebrew Book." Pages 39–50 in Hendrik D. L. Vervliet, editor, *The Book through Five Thousand Years*. New York & London: Phaidon, 1972.
Dodd, Brian J. "Paul's Paradigmatic 'I' and 1 Corinthians 6.12." *JSNT* 59 (1995): 39–58.
Doty, William G. *Letters in Primitive Christianity*. Philadelphia: Fortress, 1973.
Doughty, Darrell J. "The Presence and Future of Salvation in Corinth." *ZNW* 66 (1973): 61–90.
Downs, David J. *The Offering of the Gentiles: Paul's Collection for Jerusalem in its Chronological, Cultural and Cultic Contexts*. WUNT 48. Tübingen: Mohr Siebeck, 2008.
Duff, Jeremy. "A Reconsideration of Pseudepigraphy in Early Christianity." PhD. Dissertation, Oxford University, 1998.
Duff, Jeremy. "P46 and the Pastorals: A Misleading Consensus?" *NTS* 44 (1998): 578–90.
Duff, Paul Brooks. "Apostolic Suffering and the Language of Processions in 2 Corinthians 4:7-10." *BTB* 21 (1992): 158–65.
Duff, Paul Brooks. "2 Corinthians 1-7: Sidestepping the Division Hypothesis." *BTB* 24 (1994): 16–26.
Duff, Paul Brooks. "Metaphor, Motif, and Meaning: The Rhetorical Strategy behind the Image 'Led in Triumph' in 2 Corinthians 2:14." *CBQ* 53 (1991): 79–92.
Duff, Paul Brooks. "The Mind of the Redactor: 2 Cor. 6:14-7:1 in its Secondary Context." *NovT* 35 (1993): 160–80.
Duff, Paul Brooks. *Moses in Corinth: The Apologetic Context of 2 Corinthians 3*, NovTSup 159 Leiden: Brill, 2015.
Duling, Dennis and Norman Perrin. *The New Testament: Proclamation & Paranesis, Myth & History*, 3rd ed. Fort Worth: Harcourt Brace, 1994.
Duling, Dennis. "2 Corinthians 11:22: Historical Context, Rhetoric, and Ethnicity." *HTS* 64 (2008): 819–43.
Dulk, Matthijs den. "I Permit No Woman to Teach Except for Thecla: The Curious Case of the Pastoral Epistles and the *Acts of Paul* Reconsidered." *NovT* 54 (2012): 176–203.
Dunderberg, Ismo. "Body Metaphors in 1 Corinthians and in the Interpretation of Knowledge (NHC XI,1)." *Actes du huitieme Congres international d'etudes coptes* 2 (2007): 833–47.
Dungan, David L. "The New Testament Canon in Recent Study." *Int* 29 (1975): 339–51.
Du Toit, Andrie B. "Vilification as a Pragmatic Device in Early Christian Epistolography." *Bib* 75 (1994): 402–14.
Eastman, David L. *Paul the Martyr: The Cult of the Apostle in the Latin West*. Writings from the Greco-Roman World Supplement Series, 4. Atlanta: Society of Biblical Literature, 2011.

Ehrman, Bart. *The New Testament: A Historical Introduction to the Early Christian Writings*. Oxford: Oxford University Press, 1997.

Elliott, Mark W. "The Triumph of Paulinism by the Mid-Third Century." Pages 244–56 in Michael F. Bird and J. R. Dodson, editors, *Paul and the Second Century*. LNTS 212. London & New York: T. & T. Clark, 2011.

Emmerling, Christian August Gottfried. *Epistula Pauli ad Corinthios posterior graece perpetuo commentario illustrata*. Leipzig: J. A. Barth, 1823.

Engberg-Pedersen, Troels, editor. *Paul Beyond the Judaism / Hellenism Divide*. Louisville: Westminster John Knox Press, 2003.

Engberg-Pedersen, Troels, editor. *Paul in His Hellenistic Context*. Minneapolis: Fortress, 1995.

Engelmann, Michaela. *Unzertrennliche Drillinge? Motivsemantische Untersuchungen zum literarischen Verhältnis der Pastoralbriefe*. BZNW 192. Berlin & Boston: De Gruyter, 2012.

Epp, Eldon Jay. "The Codex and Literacy in Early Christianity and at Oxyrhynchus: Issues Raised by Harry Y. Gamble's *Books and Readers in the Early Church*." *CRBR* 10 (1997): 15–37.

Eriksson, Anders. "Elaboration of Argument in 1 Cor 15:20-34." *SEÅ* 64 (1999): 101–14.

Eriksson, Anders. "Special Topics in 1 Corinthians 8—10." Pages 272–301 in Stanley E. Porter and Dennis L. Stamps, editors, *The Rhetorical Interpretation of Scripture: Essays from the 1996 Malibu Conference*. JSNTSup 180. Sheffield: Sheffield Academic Press, 1999.

Eriksson, Anders. *Traditions as Rhetorical Proof. Pauline Argumentation in 1 Corinthians*. ConBNT 29. Stockholm: Almqvist & Wiksell International, 1998.

Esch-Wermeling, Elisabeth. *Thekla—Paulusschulerin wider Willen? Strategien der Leserlenkung in den Theklaakten*. NTAbh 53. Münster: Aschendorff, 2008.

Esler, Philip F. *Conflict and Identity in Romans*. Minneapolis: Fortress Press, 2003.

Esler, Philip F. *The First Christians in Their Social Worlds: Social-Scientific Approaches to New Testament Interpretation*. London & New York: Routledge, 1994.

Ewald, Heinrich. *Die Sendschreiben des Apostels Paulus übersetzt und erklärt*. Göttingen: Dieterischen Buchhndlung, 1857.

Farla, Piet. "The Rhetorical Composition of 1 Cor 8,1—11:1." *ETL* 80 (2004): 144–66.

Fascher, Erich. *Der erste Brief des Paulus an die Korinther*, 3rd ed. THKNT 7. Berlin: Evangelische Verlagsanstalt, 1990.

Fee, Gordon D. *The First Epistle to the Corinthians*. NICNT. Grand Rapids: Eerdmans, 1987.

Filson, Floyd V. "The Second Epistle to the Corinthians: Introduction and Exegesis." Pages 263–425 in volume 10 of G. A. Buttrick, editor, *The Interpreter's Bible*. New York and Nashville: Abingdon Press, 1953.

Fiorenza, Elisabeth Schüssler. "Rhetorical Situation and Historical Reconstruction in 1 Corinthians." *NTS* 33 (1987): 386–403.

Fisher, Fred. *Commentary on 1 and 2 Corinthians*. Waco: Word, 1975.

Fitzgerald, John T. *Cracks in an Earthen Vessel: An Examination of the Catalogues of Hardships in the Corinthian Correspondence.* SBLDS 99. Atlanta: Scholars Press, 1988.

Fitzgerald, John T. "Paul, the Ancient Epistolary Theorists, and 2 Corinthians 10—13. The Purpose and Literary Genre of a Pauline Letter." Pages 190–200 in David L. Balch, et al., editors, *Greeks, Romans, and Christians: Essays in Honor of Abraham J. Malherbe.* Minneapolis: Fortress, 1990.

Fitzgerald, John T. "Paul and Paradigm Shifts: Reconciliation and Its Linkage Group." Pages 241–62, 316–25 in Troels Engberg-Pedersen, editor, *Paul Beyond the Judaism / Hellenism Divide.* Louisville: Westminster John Knox Press, 2003.

Fitzmyer, Joseph A. "A Feature of Qumran Angelology and the Angels of I Cor. XI.10." *NTS* 4 (1957–58): 48–58.

Fitzmyer, Joseph A. *First Corinthians: A New Translation with Introduction and Commentary.* Anchor Yale Bible 32. New Haven & London: Yale University Press, 2008.

Fitzmyer, Joseph A. "Qumran and the Interpolated Paragraph in 2 Cor 6,14-7,1." *CBQ* 23 (1961): 271–80.

Foster, Paul. "Justin and Paul." Pages 108–25 in Michael F. Bird and J. R. Dodson, editors, *Paul and the Second Century.* LNTS 212. London & New York: T & T Clark, 2011.

Foster, Paul. "The Oldest Surviving Manuscript of the Bible." *ExpTim* 122 (2011): 543–45.

Franklin, Eric. *Luke: Interpreter of Paul, Critic of Matthew.* JSNTSup 92. Sheffield: JSOT Press, 1994.

Frede, H. J. "Die Ordnung der Paulusbriefe." *SE* 6 (1973): 122–27 (= TU 112).

Frend, W. H. C. *Martyrdom and Persecution in the Early Church: A Study of a Conflict from the Maccabees to Donatus.* New York: New York University Press, 1967.

Frenschkowski, Marco. "Der Text der Apostelgeschichte und die Realien antiker Buchproduktion." Pages 87–107 in Tobias Nicklas et al., editors, *The Book of Acts as Church History: Text, textual traditions and ancient interpretations.* BZNW 120. Berlin: de Gruyter, 2003.

Friedrich, Gerhard. "Christus, Einheit und Norm der Christen. Das Grundmotiv des 1. Korintherbriefs." *KD* 9 (1963): 235–58.

Friedrich, Gerhard. "Die Gegner des Paulus im 2. Korintherbrief." Pages 181–215 in in Otto Betz et al., editors, *Abraham unser Vater: Juden und Christen im Gespräch über die Bibel. Festschrift für Otto Michel zum 60. Geburtstag.* AGSU 5. Leiden: Brill, 1963.

Frisius, Mark A. "Interpretive Method and Theological Controversy: Tertullian's Use of the Pastoral Epistles, Hebrews, James, 1 and 2 Peter, and Jude," Ph.D. dissertation, The Catholic University of America, 2009.

Flatt, Johann Friedrich von. *Vorlesungen über die beyden Briefe Pauli an die Korinther.* Tübingen, 1827.

Freed, Edwin. *The New Testament: A Critical Introduction.* Belmont, CA: Wadsworth, 1991.

Funk, Robert W. "The New Testament as Tradition and Canon." Pages 151–86 in Robert W. Funk, *Parables and Presence: Forms of the New Testament Tradition*. Philadelphia: Fortress Press, 1982.

Furnish, Victor Paul. *II Corinthians: Translated with Introduction, Notes, and Commentary*, AB 32A. Garden City, New York: Doubleday, 1984.

Furnish, Victor Paul. *The Theology of the First Letter to the Corinthians*. New Testament Theology. Cambridge: Cambridge University Press, 1999.

Gamble, Harry Y. *Books and Readers in the Early Church. A History of Early Christian Texts*. New Haven and London: Yale University Press, 1995.

Gamble, Harry Y. "The Pauline Corpus and the Early Christian Book." Pages 265–80 in William S. Babcock, editor, *Paul and the Legacies of Paul*. Dallas: Southern Methodist University Press, 1990.

Gamble, Harry Y. "The Redaction of the Pauline Letters and the Formation of the Pauline Corpus." *JBL* 94 (1975): 403–18.

Gamble, Harry Y. *The Textual History of the Letter to the Romans*. SD 42. Grand Rapids: Eerdmans, 1977.

Garland, David E. *1 Corinthians*. BECNT. Grand Rapids: Baker Academic, 2003.

Garland, David E. *2 Corinthians*. NAC 29. Nashville: Broadman and Holman, 1999.

Gavigan, James et al., editors. *St. Paul's Epistles to the Corinthians*. The Navarre Bible. Dublin: Four Courts Press, 1991.

Georgi, Dieter. *Die Geschichte der Kollekte des Paulus für Jerusalem*. Hamburg-Bergstedt: Herbert Reich Evangelischer Verlag, 1965.

Georgi, Dieter. *The Opponents of Paul in Second Corinthians*. Philadelphia: Fortress, 1986.

Georgi, Dieter. *Remembering the Poor: The History of Paul's Collection for Jerusalem*. Translated by Ingrid Racz. Nashville: Abingdon Press, 1992.

Georgi, Dieter. "First Letter to the Corinthians." Pages 180–83 in K. Crim, V. P. Furnish, L. R. Bailey and E. S. Bucke, editors, *Interpreter's Dictionary of the Bible, Supplement Volume*. Nashville: Abingdon, 1976.

Georgi, Dieter. "Second Letter to the Corinthians." Pages 183–86 in K. Crim, V. P. Furnish, L. R. Bailey and E. S. Bucke, editors, *Interpreter's Dictionary of the Bible, Supplement Volume*. Nashville: Abingdon, 1976.

Gese, Michael. *Das Vermächtnis des Apostels. Die Rezeption der paulinischen Theologie im Epheserbrief*. WUNT 2.99. Tübingen: Mohr Siebeck, 1997.

Getty, Mary Ann. *First Corinthians, Second Corinthians*. Collegeville Bible Commentary 7. Collegeville: Liturgical Press, 1983.

Gilchrist, J. M. "Paul and the Corinthians—The Sequence of Letters and Visits." *JSNT* 34 (1988): 47–69.

Given, Mark D. *Paul's True Rhetoric: Ambiguity, Cunning, and Deception in Greece and Rome*. Emory Studies in Early Christianity 7. Harrisburg: Trinity Press International, 2001.

Gnilka, Joachim. "2 Cor 6:14–7:1 in the Light of the Qumran Texts and the Testaments of the Twelve Patriarchs." Pages 48–68 in Jerome Murphy-O'Connor, editor, *Paul and Qumran: Studies in New Testament Exegesis*. Chicago: Priory, 1968.

Gnilka, Joachim. "Paränetische Traditionen im Epheserbrief." Pages 397–410 in Albert Descamps et al., editors, *Mélange bibliques en homage au R. P. Béda Rigaux*. Gembloux: Duculot, 1970.

Goguel, Maurice. *Introduction au Nouveau Testament. Les épitres pauliniennes.* Volume IV. Paris: Editions Ernest Leroux, 1926.

Gooch, Peter David. *Dangerous Food: 1 Corinthians 8-10 in Its Context.* Waterloo: Wilfrid Laurier University, 1993.

Goodspeed, Edgar J. "The Editio Princeps of Paul." *JBL* 64 (1945): 193–204.

Goodspeed, Edgar J. *A History of Early Christian Literature.* Revised and enlarged by Robert M. Grant. Chicago: University of Chicago Press, 1966.

Goulder, Michael. "2 Cor 6:14-7:1 as an Integral Part of 2 Corinthians." *NovT* 36 (1994): 47–57.

Gräbe, Petrus J. *The Power of God in Paul's Letters.* WUNT 2.123. Tübingen: Mohr Siebeck, 2000.

Grässer, Erich. "Paulus, der Apostel des Neuen Bundes (2 Kor. 2,14-4,6. Der Anlass der Apologie und ihre Beziehung zum Briefganzen." Pages 7–77 in L. De Lorenzi, editor, *Paolo. Ministro dell Nuovo Testamento (2 Cor 2,14-4,6).* Serie Monografica di Benedictina, 9. Rome: Benedictina Editrice, 1987.

Gräßer, Erich. *Der zweite Brief an die Korinther. Kap 1,1-7,16."* ÖTK 8.1. Gütersloh: Gütersloher Verlagshaus, 2002.

Grässer, Erich. *Der zweite Brief an die Korinther. Kap 8,1-13,13.* ÖTK 8.2. Gütersloh: Gütersloher Verlagshaus, 2005.

Grafton, Anthony. *Forgers and Critics: Creativity and Duplicity in Western Scholarlship.* Princeton: Princeton University Press, 1990.

Grant, Robert M. *Heresy and Criticism: The Search for Authenticity in Early Christian Literature.* Louisville: Westminster John Knox, 1993.

Grant, Robert M. *Paul in the Roman World: The Conflict at Corinth.* Louisville: Westminster John Knox Press, 2001.

Gray, Patrick and Gail R. O'Day, editors. *Scripture and Traditions: Essays on Early Judaism and Christianity in Honor of Carl R. Holladay.* NovTSup 129. Leiden & Boston: Brill, 2008.

Grosheide, F. W. *The First Epistle to the Corinthians.* NICNT. Grand Rapids: Eerdmans, 1983.

Gruber, Maria Margareta. *Herrlichkeit in Schwachheit. Eine Auslegung der Apologie des Zweiten Korintherbriefes 2 Kor 2,14—6,13.* FB 89. Würzburg: Echter Verlag, 1998.

Haelst, Joseph van. *Catalogue des papyrus litteraires Juifs et Chretiens.* Paris: Publications de la Sorbonne, 1976.

Haelst, Joseph van. "Les origines du codex." Pages 13–35 in Alain Blanchard, editor, *Les débuts du codex. Actes de la journée d'étude organisée à Paris les 3 et 4 juillet 1985 par l'Institut de Papyrologie de la Sorbonne.* Bibliologia. Elementa ad librorum studia pertinentia 9. Brepols: Turnhout, 1989.

Hafemann, Scott J. *2 Corinthians.* NIV Application Commentary. Grand Rapids: Zondervan, 2000.

Hafemann, Scott J. *Suffering and Ministry in the Spirit: Paul's Defense of His Ministry in II Corinthians 2:14-3:3.* Grand Rapids: Eerdmans, 1990.
Hagge, H. "Die beiden Überlieferten Sendschreiben des Apostels Paulus an die Gemeinde zu Korinth." *Jahrbücher für protestantische Theologie* 2 (1876): 481–531.
Hall, David R. *The Unity of the Corinthian Correspondence.* JSNTSup 251. London & New York: Clark, 2003.
Halmel, Anton. *Der Vierkapitelbrief im zweiten Korintherbrief des Apostels Paulus.* Essen: Baedeker, 1894.
Halmel, Anton. *Der zweite Korintherbrief des Apostels Paulus.* Halle: Niemeyer, 1904.
Hanges, James Constantine, *Paul, Founder of Churches: A Study in Light of the Evidence for the Role of "Founder-Figures" in the Hellenistic-Roman Period.* WUNT 292. Tübingen: Mohr Siebeck, 2012.
Harrill, J. Albert. *Paul the Apostle: His Life and Legacy in Their Roman Context.* Cambridge: Cambridge University Press, 2012.
Harrington, Daniel J. *Light of All Nations: Essays on the Church in New Testament Research.* GNS 3. Wilmington: Glazier, 1982.
Harris, Murray J. *The Second Epistle to the Corinthians: A Commentary on the Greek Text.* NIGTC. Grand Rapids: Eerdmans; Bletchley: Paternoster Press, 2005.
Harris, Stephen. *The New Testament: A Student's Introduction*, 2nd ed. Mountain View: Mayfield, 1995.
Harrison, James R. *Paul and the Imperial Authorities at Thessalonica and Rome: A Study in the Conflict of Ideology.* WUNT 2.273. Tübingen: Mohr Siebeck, 2011.
Hartin, Patrick J. *Apollos: Paul's Partner or Rival? Paul's Social Network: Brothers and Sisters in Faith.* Collegeville: Liturgical Press, 2009.
Hartke, Wilhelm. *Die Sammlung und die älteste Ausgaben der Paulusbriefe.* Bonn: Georgi, 1917.
Hasler, Victor. *Die Briefe an Timotheus und Titus (Pastoralbriefe).* Zürcher Bibelkommentare. Zurich: Theologischer Verlag, 1978.
Hausrath, Adolf. *Der Apostle Paulus*, 2nd ed. Heidelberg: Bassermann, 1872.
Hausrath, Adolf. *Der Vier-Kapital-Brief des Paulus an die Korinther.* Heidelberg: Bassermann, 1870.
Hay, David M., editor. *Pauline Theology*, Volume II: *1 & 2 Corinthians*. Minneapolis: Fortress Press, 1993.
Hays, Richard B. *The Conversion of the Imagination: Paul as Interpreter of Israel's Scripture.* Grand Rapids: Eerdmans, 2005.
Hays, Richard B. *First Corinthians.* IBC. Louisville: Westminster John Knox, 1997.
Hays, Richard B. *Echoes of Scripture in the Letters of Paul.* New Haven & London: Yale University Press, 1989.
Heckel, Ulrich. *Kraft in Schwachheit. Untersuchung zu 2. Kor 10-13.* WUNT 2/56. Tübingen: Mohr Siebeck, 1993.
Hegermann, Harald. "Der geschichtliche Ort der Pastoralbriefe." *Theologische Versuche* 2 (1970): 47–64.

Heil, John Paul. *The Rhetorical Role of Scripture in 1 Corinthians.* SBLMS 15. Atlanta: Society of Biblical Literature, 2005.

Heine, Susanne. *Frauen der frühen Christenheit. Zur historischen Kritik einer feministischen Theologie.* Göttingen: Vandenhoeck und Ruprecht, 1986.

Heinrici, C. F. G. *Der erste Brief an die Korinther*, 8th ed. Göttingen: Vandenhoeck & Ruprecht, 1896.

Héring, Jean. *The First Epistle of Saint Paul to the Corinthians.* Translated by A. W. Heathcote and P. J. Allcock. London: Epworth, 1962.

Héring, Jean. *The Second Epistle of Saint Paul to the Corinthians.* London: Epworth, 1967.

Hester, James D. and J. David Hester, editors. *Rhetorics in the New Millennium: Promise and Fulfillment.* SAC. New York and London: T & T Clark International, 2010.

Hilgenfeld, Adolf. "Die korinthische Zwischenreise und der Viercapitelbrief des Paulus an die Korinthier." *ZWT* 42 (1899): 1–19.

Hilgenfeld, Adolf. *Historisch-kritische Einleitung in das Neue Testament.* Leipzig: Fues's Verlag (R. Reisland), 1875.

Hoegen-Rohls, Christina. "Wie klingt es, wenn Paulus von Neuer Schöpfung spricht? Stilanallytische Beobachtungen zu 2 Kor 5,17 und Gal 6,15." Pages 143–53 in Peter Müller et al., editors, *". . . was ihr auf dem Weg verhandelt habt." Beiträge zur Exegese und Theologie des Neuen Testaments. Festschrift für Ferdinand Hahn zum 75. Geburtstag.* Neukirchen-Vluyn: Neukirchener Verlag, 2001.

Holland, Glenn. "Paul's Use of Irony as a Rhetorical Technique." Pages 234–48 in Stanley E. Porter and Thomas H. Olbricht, editors, *The Rhetorical Analysis of Scripture: Essays from the 1995 London Conference.* JSNTSup 146. Sheffield: Sheffield Academic Press, 1997.

Holland, Glenn. "Speaking Like a Fool: Irony in 2 Corinthians 10—13." Pages 250–64 in Stanley E. Porter and Thomas H. Olbricht, editors, *Rhetoric and the New Testament: Essays from the 1992 Heidelberg Conference.* JSNTSup 90. Sheffield: JSOT, 1993.

Holmes, Michael W. "Paul and Polycarp." Pages 57–69 in Michael F. Bird and J. R. Dodson, editors, *Paul and the Second Century.* LNTS 212. London & New York: T & T Clark, 2011.

Holsten, Carl. *Das Evangelium des Paulus. I. 1. Die Briefe an die Gemeinden Galatiens und der ersten Brief an die Gemeinde in Korinth.* Berlin: Reimer, 1880.

Holtzmann, Heinrich Julius. "Das gegenseitige Verhältniss der beiden Korintherbriefe." *ZWT* 22 (1879): 455–92.

Holtzmann, Heinrich Julius. *Die Pastoralbriefe, kritisch und exegetisch behandelt.* Leipzig: Wilhelm Engelmann, 1880.

Hooker, Morna D. "'Beyond the Things Which Are Written': An Examination of I Cor IV.6." *NTS* 10 (1963–64): 127–32.

Horn, Curtis Kent. "Pseudonymity in Early Christianity: An Inquiry into the Theory of Innocent Deutero-Pauline Pseudonymity." Ph.D. dissertation, Southwestern Baptist Theological Seminary, 1996.

Horn, Friedrich Wilhelm. "Zur Literarkritik der Paulusbriefe." Pages 745–63 in C. Breytenbach, editor, *Paulus, die Evangelien und das Urchristentum. Beiträge von und zu Walter Schmithals zu seinem 80. Geburtstag.* AGJU 54. Leiden & New York: Brill, 2004.

Horsley, Richard A. *1 Corinthians.* ANTC. Nashville: Abingdon Press, 1998.

Horsley, Richard A. "'How Can Some of You Say That There Is No Resurrection of the Dead?' Spiritual Elitism in Corinth." *NovT* 20 (1978): 203–31.

Horsley, Richard A. "Paul's Assembly in Corinth: An Alternative Society." Pages 371–95 in Daniel N. Schowalter and Steven J. Friesen, editors, *Urban Religion in Roman Corinth: Interdisciplinary Approaches.* HTS 53. Harvard University Press, 2005.

Horsley, Richard A. *Wisdom and Spiritual Transcendence at Corinth: Studies in First Corinthians.* Eugene, OR: Cascade, 2008.

Houlden, J. L. *The Pastoral Epistles: I and II Timothy, Titus.* TPI New Testament Commentary. London: SCM; Philadelphia: Trinity Press International, 1989 reprint of the 1976 edition.

Howard, W. F. "I Cor 4.6." *ExpTim* 33 (1922): 479–80.

Hughes, Frank W. *Early Christian Rhetoric and 2 Thessalonians.* JSNTSup 30. Sheffield: JSOT Press, 1989.

Hughes, Frank W. "The Rhetoric of Reconciliation: 2 Corinthians 1.1-2:13 and 7.5-8.24." Pages 246–61 in Duane F. Watson, editor, *Persuasive Artistry: Studies in New Testament Rhetoric in Honor of George A. Kennedy.* JSNTSup 50. Sheffield: Academic Press, 1991.

Hughes, Frank W. "Corinthian Letter C as a Document of Rhetoric." Presented at the Pauline Epistles Section, Society of Biblical Literature Annual Meeting at Anaheim, 1989.

Hughes, Frank W. "Rhetorical Criticism and the Corinthian Correspondence." Pages 336–50 in Thomas H. Olbricht and Stanley E. Porter, editors, *The Rhetorical Analysis of Scripture: Essays from the 1995 London Conference.* JSNTSup 146. Sheffield: Sheffield Academic Press, 1997.

Hughes, Philip E. *The Second Epistle to the Corinthians.* NICNT. Grand Rapids: Eerdmans, 1962.

Hultgren, Arland J. *I-II Timothy, Titus.* With *II Thessalonians* by Roger Aus. Augsburg Commentary on the New Testament. Minneapolis: Augsburg, 1984.

Hultgren, Stephen H. "2 Cor 6.14-7.1 and Rev 21.3-8: Evidence for the Ephesian Redaction of 2 Corinthians." *NTS* 49 (2003): 39–56.

Hunt, Allen Rhea. *The Inspired Body: Paul, the Corinthians, and Divine Inspiration.* Macon: Mercer University Press, 1996.

Hurd, John Coolidge. "Good News and the Integrity of 1 Corinthians." Pages 38–62 in L. Ann Jervis and Peter Richardson, editors, *Gospel in Paul: Studies on Corinthians, Galatians and Romans for Richard N. Longenecker.* JSNTSup 108. Sheffield: Sheffield Academic Press, 1994.

Hurd, John Coolidge. *The Origin of 1 Corinthians.* New edition. Macon: Mercer University Press, 1983.

Hurtado, Larry W. *The Earliest Christian Artifacts: Manuscripts and Christian Origins.* Grand Rapids: Eerdmans, 2006.

Hussein, Mohamed A. *Vom Papyrus zum Codex. Der Beitrag Ägyptens zur Buchkultur.* Munich: Süddeutscher Verlag, 1972.
Hyldahl, Niels. "Die Frage nach der literarischen Einheit des Zweiten Korintherbriefes." *ZNW* 64 (1973): 289–306.
Hyldahl, Niels. Letter of 1979 replying to Robert Jewett's article on the redaction of 1 Corinthians.
Inkelaar, Harm–Jan. *Conflict over Wisdom: The Theme of I Corinthians 1 - 4 Rooted in Scripture.* CBET 63. Leuven & Walpole: Peeters, 2011.
Isaak, Jonathan M. "Situating the 'Letter to the Hebrews' in early Christian History." PhD. Dissertation, McGill University, 1999.
Jacobs, Lambert D. "Establishing a New Value System in Corinth: 1 Corinthians 5—6 as Persuasive Argument." Pages 374–87 in Stanley E. Porter and Thomas H. Olbricht, editors, *The Rhetorical Analysis of Scripture: Essays from the 1995 London Conference.* JSNTSup 146. Sheffield: Sheffield Academic Press, 1997.
Jegher-Bucher, Verena. "'The Thorn in the Flesh' / 'Der Pfahl im Fleisch': Considerations about 2 Corinthians 12.7-10 iin Connection with 12.1-13." Pages 388–97 in Stanley E. Porter and Thomas H. Olbricht, editors, *The Rhetorical Analysis of Scripture: Essays from the 1995 London Conference.* JSNTSup 146. Sheffield: Sheffield Academic Press, 1997.
Jeremias, Joachim. *Die Briefe an Timotheus and Titus*, NTD 9, Göttingen: Vandenhoeck & Ruprecht, 1975.
Jervis, L. Ann. "'But I Want You to Know. . . .' Paul's Midrashic Intertextual Response to the Corinthian Worshippers (1 Cor xi.2-16)." *JBL* 112 (1993): 231–46.
Jervis, L. Ann and Peter Richardson, editors. *Gospel in Paul: Studies on Corinthians, Galatians and Romans for Richard N. Longenecker.* JSNTSup 108. Sheffield: Sheffield Academic Press, 1994.
Jewett, Robert. *A Chronology of Paul's Life.* Philadelphia: Fortress, 1979.
Jewett, Robert. "Chronology, New Testament." Pages 165–66 in Paul J. Achtemeier, editor, *Harper's Bible Dictionary.* San Francisco: Harper & Row, 1985.
Jewett, Robert. "Chronology, New Testament." Pages 193–98 in John H. Hayes, editor, *Dictionary of Biblical Interpretation.* Nashville: Abingdon Press, 1999.
Jewett, Robert. "Corinth, Corinthian Correspondence." Pages 290–94 in Volume 1 of Everett Ferguson et al., editors, *Encyclopedia of Early Christianity*, revised edition. New York: Garland, 1997.
Jewett, Robert. *Paul's Anthropological Terms: A Study of Their Use in Conflict Settings.* AGJU 10. Leiden: Brill, 1971.
Jewett, Robert. "Paul." Volume2, pages 881–85 in Everett Ferguson et al., editors, *Encyclopedia of Early Christianity*, revised edition. New York: Garland, 1990. New York: Garland, 1997.
Jewett, Robert. "Paul's Dialogue with the Corinthians . . . and Us." *QR* 13 (1993): 89–112.
Jewett, Robert. "Paul, Phoebe, and the Spanish Mission." Pages 144–64 in P. Borgen et al., editors, *The Social World of Formative Christianity and Judaism: Essays in Tribute to Howard Clark Kee.* Philadelphia: Fortress Press, 1988.

Jewett, Robert. "The Redaction of I Corinthians and the Trajectory of the Pauline School." *Journal of the American Academy of Religion,* Supplement 46 (1978): 389–444.
Jewett, Robert. Review of W. Schmithals, *Paul and the Gnostics* and *Gnosticism in Corinth* in *JBL* 93 (1974): 630–32.
Jewett, Robert. *Romans: A Commentary.* Hermeneia. Minneapolis: Fortress, 2007.
Jewett, Robert. *Romans: A Short Commentary.* Minneapolis: Fortress, 2013.
Jewett, Robert. *The Thessalonian Correspondence: Pauline Rhetoric and Millenarian Piety.* FF. Minneapolis: Fortress Press, 1986.
Johnson, Luke Timothy. *The First and Second Letters to Timothy: A New Translation with Introduction and Commentary.* AB 35A. New York: Doubleday, 2001.
Johnson, Luke Timothy. *Letters to Paul's Delegates: 1 Timothy, 2 Timothy, Titus.* The New Testament in Context. Valley Forge: Trinity Press International, 1996.
Johnson, William A. "The Ancient Book." Pages 256–81 in Roger S. Bagnall, editor, *The Oxford Handbook of Papyrology.* New York: Oxford University Press, 2009.
Jonas, Hans. *The Gnostic Religion: The Message of the Alien God and the Beginnings of Christianity*, 2nd rev. ed. Boston: Beacon, 1963.
Jones, F. Stanley. *"Freiheit" in den Briefen des Apostels Paulus. Eine historische, exegetische und religionsgeschichtliche Studie.* GTA 34. Göttingen: Vandenhoeck und Ruprecht, 1987.
Jones, Ivor H. "Rhetorical Criticism and the Unity of 2 Corinthians: One 'Epilogue', or More?" *NTS* 54 (2008): 496–524.
Joubert, Stephan. "Behind the Mask of Rhetoric: 2 Corinthians 8 and the Intra-Textual Relation between Paul and the Corinthians." *Neotestamentica* 26 (1992): 101–12.
Joubert, Stephan. "Managing the Household: Paul as *Paterfamilias* of the Christian Household Groups in Corinth." Pages 213–23 in Philip F. Esler, editor, *Modelling Early Christianity.* London: Routledge, 1995.
Joubert, Stephan. *Paul as Benefactor: Reciprocity, Strategy and Theological Reflection in Paul's Collection.* WUNT 2.124; Tübingen: Mohr Siebeck, 2000.
Jülicher, Adolf. *An Introduction to the New Testament.* Translated by Janet Penrose Ward. London: Smith, Elder, & Co., 1904.
Käsemann, Ernst. *Commentary on Romans.* Translated by G. W. Bromiley. Grand Rapids: Eerdmans, 1980.
Käsemann, Ernst. *Die Legitimität des Apostels. Eine Untersuchung zu II Korinther 10—13.* Libelli, 33. Darmstadt: Wissenschaftliche Buchgesellschaft, 1956.
Käsemann, Ernst. *Das Neue Testament als Kanon: Dokumentation und kritische Analyse zur gegenwärtigen Diskussion.* Göttingen: Vandenhoeck & Ruprecht, 1970.
Käsemann, Ernst. "Paul and Nascent Catholicism: Distinctive Protestant and Catholic Themes Reconsidered." *JTC* 3 (1967): 14–27.
Kammler, Hans-Christian. *Kreuz und Weisheit. Eine exegetische Untersuchung zu 1 Kor 1,10-3,4.* WUNT 159. Tübingen: Mohr Siebeck, 2003.
Karris, Robert J. "The Background and Significance of the Polemic of the Pastoral Epistles." *JBL* 92 (1973): 549–64.

Karris, Robert J. *The Pastoral Epistles.* NTM 17. Wilmington: Glazier, 1984. Second printing of the 1979 edition.

Keck, Leander E., and Victor Paul Furnish. *The Pauline Letters.* Interpreting Biblical Texts. Nashville: Abingdon, 1984.

Keener, Craig S. *1-2 Corinthians.* New Cambridge Bible Commentary. Cambridge and New York: Cambridge University Press, 2005.

Kennedy, George A. *The Art of Persuasion in Greece.* Princeton: Princeton University Press, 1963.

Kennedy, George A. *The Art of Rhetoric in the Roman World 300 B. C.—A. D. 300.* Princeton: Princeton University Press, 1972.

Kennedy, George A. *Classical Rhetoric and Its Christian and Secular Tradition from Ancient to Modern Times.* Chapel Hill: University of North Carolina Press, 1980.

Kennedy, George A. *Greek Rhetoric under Christian Emperors.* Princeton: Princeton University Press, 1983.

Kennedy, George A. *New Testament Interpretation Through Rhetorical Criticism.* Chapel Hill: University of North Carolina Press, 1984.

Kenyon, F. G. *The Text of the Greek Bible*, 3rd edition revised and augmented by A. W. Adams. Studies in Theology. London: Duckworth, 1975.

Kertelge, Karl, editor. *Das kirchliche Amt im Neuen Testament.* Wege der Forschung, 189. Darmstadt: Wissenschaftliche Buchgesellschaft, 1977.

Kertelge, Karl. *"Rechtfertigung" bei Paulus. Studien zur Struktur und zum Bedeutungsgestalt des Paulinischen Rechtfertigungsbegriff.* NTAbh, 3. Münster: Aschendorff, 1967.

Kertelge, Karl, editor. *Paulus in den neutestamentlichen Spätschriften.* QD 89. Freiburg et al.: Herder, 1981.

Kilpatrick, George D. "Conjectural Emendations in the New Testament." Pages 349–60 in Eldon Jay Epp and Gordon J. Fee, editors, *New Testament Textual Criticism: Its Significance for Exegesis: Essays in Honour of Bruce M. Metzger.* Oxford: Clarendon Press; New York: Oxford University Press, 1981.

Kidd, Reggie M. *Wealth and Beneficence in the Pastoral Epistles.* SBLDS 122. Atlanta: Scholars Press, 1990.

Kim, Byung–mo. *Die paulinische Kollekte.* Texte und Arbeiten zum neutestamentlichen Zeitalter 38. Tübingen and Basel: Franke, 2002.

Kistemaker, Simon J. *Exposition of the First Epistle to the Corinthians.* New Testament Commentary. Grand Rapids: Baker, 1993.

Kistemaker, Simon J. *Exposition of the Second Epistle to the Corinthians.* New Testament Commentary. Grand Rapids: Baker, 1997.

Klaiber, Walter. *Der erste Korintherbrief.* Die Botschaft des Neuen Testaments. Neukirchen-Vluyn: Neukirchener Theologie, 2011.

Klaiber, Walter. *Der zweite Korintherbrief.* Die Botschaft des Neuen Testaments. Neukirchen-Vluyn: Neukirchener Theologie, 2012.

Klauck, Hans-Josef. *Die antike Briefliteratur und das Neue Testament. Ein Lehr- und Arbeitsbuch.* Uni-Taschenbücher, 2022. Paderborn: Ferdinand Schöningh, 1998.

Klauck, Hans–Josef. *Hausgemeinde und Hauskirche im frühen Christentum.* SBS 103. Stuttgart: Katholisches Bibelwerk, 1981.

Klauck, Hans–Josef. *Herrenmahl und hellenistischer Kult. Eine religionsgeschichtliche Untersuchung zum ersten Korintherbrief.* NTAbh 15. Münster: Aschendorff, 1982.

Klauck, Hans–Josef. *1. Korintherbrief*, 4th ed. Kommentar zum Neuen Testament mit der Einheitsübersetzung. NEchtB 7. Würzburg: Echter Verlag, 2000.

Klauck, Hans–Josef. *2. Korintherbrief*, 3rd ed. Kommentar zum Neuen Testament mit der Einheitsübersetzung. NEchtB 8. Third edition. Wurzburg: Echter-Verlag, 1994.

Klein, Hans. "Die Begründung für den Spendenaufruf für die Heiligen Jerusalems in 2Kor 8 und 9." Pages 104–30 in Dieter Sänger, editor, *Der zweite Korintherbrief. Literarische Gestalt - historische Situation - theologische Argumentation. Festschrift zum 70. Geburtstag von Dietrich-Alex Koch.* FRLANT 250. Göttingen: Vandenhoeck & Ruprecht, 2012.

Kleine, Werner. *Zwischen Furcht und Hoffnung. Eine textlinguistische Untersuchung des Briefes 2 Kor 1-9 zur wechselseitigen Bedeutsamkeit der Beziehung von Apostel und Gemeinde.* BBB 141. Berlin & Wien: Philo, 2002.

Kloha, Jeffrey John. "A Textual Commentary on Paul's First Epistle to the Corinthians." Volumes 1–4. Dissertation, The University of Leeds, 2006.

Knox, John. *Philemon among the Letters of Paul. A New View of Its Place and Importance.* New York: Abingdon, 1935.

Koch, Dietrich-Alex. "'. . . bezeugt durch das Gesetz und die Propheten.' Zur Funktion des Schrift bei Paulus." Pages 13–24 in Friedrich Wilhelm Horn, editor, *Hellenistisches Christentum. Schriftverständnis—Ekklesiologie--Geschichte* . NTOA / SUNT 65. Göttingen: Vandenhook und Ruprecht, 2008.

Koch, Dietrich-Alex. "Kollektenbericht,'Wir' Bericht und Itinerar. Neue (?) Überlegungen zu einem alten Problem." Pages 318–39 in Friedrich Wilhelm Horn, editor, *Hellenistisches Christentum . Schriftverständnis—Ekklesiologie—Geschichte* . NTOA / SUNT 65. Göttingen: Vandenhook und Ruprecht, 2008.

Koch, Dietrich-Alex. *Die Schrift als Zeuge des Evangeliums: Untersuchungen zur Verwendung und zum Verständnis der Schrift bei Paulus,* BHT 69. Tübingen: Mohr, 1986.

Koester, Helmut. *Introduction to the New Testament*, two volumes. Berlin: Walter de Gruyter, 1987.

Koester, Helmut. *Paul and His World: Interpreting the New Testament.* Minneapolis: Fortress, 2007.

Kooten, Geurt Hendrik van. *Cosmic Christology in Paul and the Pauline School: Colossians and Ephesians in the Context of Graeco-Roman Cosmology, with a New Synopsis of the Greek Texts.* WUNT 2.171. Tübingen: Mohr Siebeck, 2003.

Kremer, Jacob. *Der Erste Brief an die Korinther.* RNT. Regensburg: Friedrich Pustet, 1997.

Krentz, Edgar. "Logos or Sophia. The Pauline Use of the Ancient Dispute between Rhetoric and Philosophy." Pages 277–90 in John T. Fitzgerald et al., editors, *Early Christianity and Classical Culture.* NTTS 110. Leiden: Brill, 2003.

Kruse, Colin G. *2 Corinthians: An Introduction and Commentary.* TNTC. Downers Grove: IVP Academic; Nottingham: Inter-Varsity, 1987.

Kugel, James L. and Rowan A. Greer. *Early Biblical Interpretation.* LEC. Philadelphia: Westminster, 1986.
Kuhn, Heinz Wolfgang. "The Wisdom Passage in 1 Corinthians 2:6-16 between Qumran and Proto-Gnosticism." Pages 240–53 in Daniel K. Falk et al., editors, *Sapiential, Liturgical and Poetical Texts from Qumran: Published in Memory of Maurice Baillet.* Leiden & Boston: Brill, 2000.
Lambrecht, Jan. "Rhetorical Criticism and the New Testament." *Bijdragen. Tijdschrift voor philosophie en theologie* 50 (1989): 239–53.
Lambrecht, Jan. *Second Corinthians*, SP 8. Collegeville: Liturgical Press, 1998.
Lampe, Peter. "Can Words Be Violent or Do They Only Sound That Way? Second Corinthians: Verbal Warfare from Afar as a Complement to a Placid Personal Presence." Pages 223–39 in J. Paul Sampley and Peter Lampe, editors, *Paul and Rhetoric.* T & T Clark Biblical Studies. New York & London: T & T Clark, 2010.
Lampe, Peter. "The Corinthian Eucharistic Dinner Party: Exegesis of a Cultural Context (I Cor. 11:17-34)." *Affirmation* 4/2 (1991): 1–15.
Lampe, Peter. "The Parties in Corinth (1 Corinthians 1-4)." Pages 85–86 in Lukas Vischer, Ulrich Luz, and Christian Link, editors, *Unity of the Church in the New Testament and Today.* Grand Rapids & Cambridge: Eerdmans 2010.
Lang, Friedrich. *Die Briefe an die Korinther.* NTD 7. Göttingen: Vandenhoeck & Ruprecht, 1986.
Lang, Friedrich Gustav. *2 Korinther 5,1-10 in der neueren Forschung.* BGBE 16. Tübingen: Mohr, 1973.
Lausberg, Heinrich. *Handbuch der literarischen Rhetorik*, 4th ed. Stuttgart: Steiner, 2008.
Legault, André. "Beyond the Things which are Written (I Cor IV: 6)." *NTS* 18 (1971–72): 227-31.
Leipoldt, Johannes. *Die Frauen in den antiken Welt and in Urchristentum.* 2nd ed. Leipzig: Kohler & Ameland, 1955.
Lewis, Jack P., editor. *Interpreting 2 Corinthians 5:14-21: An Exercise in Hermeneutics.* Lewiston: Mellen, 1989.
Lewis, Naphtali. *Papyrus in Classical Antiquity.* Oxford: Clarendon, 1974.
Lewis, Scott M., S. J. *"So that God May Be All in All." The Apocalyptic Message of 1 Corinthians 15,12-34.* TGST 42. Rome: Editrice Pontificia Universita Gregoriana, 1998.
Liddell, H. G. and R. Scott. *A Greek-English Lexicon.* Revised by H. S. Jones and R. McKenzie. Oxford: Clarendon, 1968.
Lietzmann, Hans. *An die Korinther I/II*, 5th ed., edited and expanded by Werner Georg Kümmel. HNT 9. Tübingen: Mohr, 1949.
Lightfoot, J. B. *Biblical Essays.* London & New York: Macmillan, 1893.
Lightfoot, J. B. "The Mission of Titus to the Corinthians." *Journal of Classical and Sacred Philology* 2 (1955): 194–205. Reprinted as pages 271–84 in J. B. Lightfoot, *Biblical Essays.* London & New York: Macmillan, 1893.
Lightfoot, J. B. *Notes on Epistles of St. Paul: I-II Thessalonians, I Corinthians 1-7, Romans 1-7, Ephesians 1:1-14.* Edited by J. R. Harmer. Grand Rapids: Baker, 1980; reprint of the 1895 edition.

Lim, T. H. "Not in Persuasive Words of Wisdom, but in the Demonstration of the Spirit and Power." *NovT* 29 (1987): 137–49.

Lindemann, Andreas. *Der erste Korintherbrief.* HNT 9.1. Tübingen: Mohr Siebeck, 2000.

Lindemann, Andreas. ". . . an die Kirche in Korinth samt allen Heiligen in ganz Achaia" Zu Enstehung und Redaktion des "2. Korintherbriefs." Pages 131–59 in Dieter Sänger, editor, *Der zweite Korintherbrief. Literarische Gestalt - historische Situation - theologische Argumentation. Festschrift zum 70. Geburtstag von Dietrich-Alex Koch.* FRLANT 250. Göttingen: Vandenhoeck & Ruprecht, 2012.

Lindemann, Andreas. *Der Kolosserbrief.* Zürcher Werkkommentar. Zürich: Theologischer Verlag, 1983.

Lindemann, Andreas. *Paulus im ältesten Christentum. Das Bild des Apostels und die Rezeption der paulinischen Theologie in der frühchristlichen Literatur bis Marcion.* BHT 58. Tübingen: Mohr Siebeck, 1979.

Lindemann, Andreas. "Die Sammlung der Paulusbriefe im 1. und 2. Jahrhundert." Pages 321–51 in Jean-Marie Auwers et al., editors, *The Biblical Canons. Fiftieth Colloquium Biblicum Lovaniense ... July 25 to 27 2001.* BETL 163. Leuven: Leuven University Press, 2003.

Lindgård, Fredrik. *Paul's Line of Thought in 2 Corinthians 4:16-5:10.* WUNT 2.189. Tübingen: Mohr Siebeck, 2005.

Linton, Olof. "'Nicht über das hinaus, was geschrieben ist (1 Kor. 4,6)." *Theologische Studien und Kritiken* 102 (1930): 425–37.

Lisco, Heinrich. *Die Entstehung des zweiten Korintherbriefs.* Berlin: Schneider, 1896.

Lisco, Heinrich. *Vincula Sanctorum. Ein Beitrag zur Erklärung der Geffangenschaftsbriefe des Apostels Paulus.* Berlin: Schneider, 1900.

Litfin, Duane. *St. Paul's Theology of Proclamation: 1 Corinthians 1-4 and Greco-Roman Rhetoric.* Cambridge and New York: Cambridge University, 1994.

Llewelyn, S. R., with R. A. Kearsley. "The Development of the Codex." *New Documents Illustrating Early Christianity* 7 (1994): 249–56.

Llewelyn, S. R., with R. A. Kearsley. "Letters in the Early Church." *New Documents Illustrating Early Christianity* 7 (1994): 48–55.

Löning, Karl. "Paulinismus in der Apostelgeschichte." Pages 202–32 in Karl Kertelge, editor, *Paulus in den neutestamentlichen Spätschriften.* QD 89. Freiburg et al.: Herder, 1981.

Logan, Alastair H. B. *Gnostic Truth and Christian Heresy: A Study in the History of Gnosticism.* Edinburgh: T & T Clark, 1996.

Lohse, Eduard. "Christusherrschaft und Kirche im Kolosserbrief." *NTS* 11 (1964–65): 203–16.

Lohse, Eduard. *Colossians and Philemon: A Commentary on the Epistles to the Colossians and to Philemon.* Translated by William R. Poehlmann and Robert J. Karris. Hermeneia. Philadelphia: Fortress, 1971.

Loisy, Alfred. "Les épîtres de S. Paul." *Revue d'histoire et de literature religieuses* 7 (1921): 213–50.

Loisy, Alfred. *Les Livres du Nouveau Testament.* Paris: Émile Nourry, 1923.

Long, Fredrick J. *Ancient Rhetoric and Paul's Apology: The Compositional Unity of 2 Corinthians*. SNTSMS 131. Cambridge: Cambridge University Press, 2004.
Long, Fredrick J. "Handout of Major Forensic Oratorical Featurres of 2 Corinthians." Seminar Paper, Society of Biblical Literature, 2000.
Lüdemann, Gerd. *Opposition to Paul in Jewish Christianity*. Translated by M. Eugene Boring. Minneapolis: Fortress, 1989.
Lührmann, Dieter. "Erwägungen zur Geschichte des Urchristentums." *EvT* 32 (1972): 452–67.
Lull, David J. *1 Corinthians*. Chalice Commentaries for Today. St. Louis: Chalice Press, 2007.
Lyons, George. *Pauline Autobiography: Toward a New Understanding*. SBLDS 73. Atlanta: Scholars Press, 1985.
MacDonald, Dennis Ronald. "A Conjectural Emendation of 1 Cor 15:31-32: or the Case of the Misplaced Lion Fight." *HTR* 93 (1980): 265–76.
MacDonald, Dennis Ronald. *There Is No Male and Female: The Fate of a Dominical Saying in Paul and Gnosticism*. HDR 20. Philadelphia: Fortress, 1987.
MacDonald, Dennis Ronald. *The Legend and the Apostle: The Battle for Paul in Story and Canon*. Phildelphia: Westminster, 1983.
MacDonald, Margaret Y. *The Pauline Churches: A Socio-Historical Study of Institutionalization in the Pauline and Deutero-Pauline Writings*. SNTSMS 60. Cambridge: University Press, 1988.
MacRae, George W. *Studies in the New Testament and Gnosticism*. GNS 26. Wilmington: Glazier, 1987.
Machalet, Christian. "Paulus und seine Gegner. Eine Untersuchung zu den Korintherbriefen." *Theokratia* 2 (1973): 183–202.
Mack, Burton L. *Rhetoric and the New Testament*. GBS. Minneapolis: Fortress Press, 1990.
Mack, Burton L. *Who Wrote the New Testament? The Making of the Christian Myth*. San Francisco: Harper, 1995.
Malherbe, Abraham J. "Determinism and Free Will in Paul: The Argument of 1 Corinthians 8 and 9." Pages 231–55 in Troels Engberg-Pedersen, editor, *Paul in His Hellenistic Context*. Minneapolis: Fortress, 1995.
Malherbe, Abraham J. *Paul and the Popular Philosophers*. Minneapolis: Fortress, 1989.
Malherbe, Abraham J. *Social Aspects of Early Christianity*, 2nd edition enlarged. Philadelphia: Fortress, 1983.
Malina, Bruce J. and John J. Pilch. *Social-Science Commentary on the Letters of Paul*. Minneapolis: Fortress, 2006.
Maly, Karl. *Mündige Gemeinde: Untersuchungen zur Pastoralen Führung des Apostels Paulus im 1. Korintherbrief*. SBM 2. Stuttgart: Katholisches Bibelwerk, 1967.
Marshall, Peter. *Enmity in Corinth: Social Conventions in Paul's Relations with the Corinthians*. WUNT 2.23. Tübingen: Mohr Siebeck, 1987.
Martin, Dale B. *The Corinthian Body*. New Haven: Yale University Press, 1995.
Martin, Ralph P. *2 Corinthians*. WBC 40. Waco: Word Books, 1986.

Martin, Troy W. "Invention and Arrangement in Recent Pauline Rhetorical Studies: A Survey of the Practices and the Problems." Pages 48–118 in J. Paul Sampley and Peter Lampe, editors, *Paul and Rhetoric*. T. & T. Clark Biblical Studies. New York and London: T. & T. Clark, 2010.

Marxsen, Willi. *Introduction to the New Testament: An Approach to its Problems*. Translated by G. Buswell; Oxford: Basil Blackwell, 1968; reprinted Philadelphia: Fortress, 1980.

Matera, Frank J. *II Corinthians. A Commentary*. NTL. Louisville and London: Westminster John Knox, 2003.

Mayerhoff, Ernst Theodor. *Der Brief an die Colosser, mit vornehmlicher Berücksichtigung der drei Pastoralbriefe, kritisch geprüft*. Edited by J. L. Mayerhoff. Berlin: Schultze, 1836.

Mazal, Otto. *Geschichte der Buchkultur*. Graz: Akademische Druck- und Verlagsanstalt, 1999.

McCant, Jerry W. *2 Corinthians*. Readings: A New Biblical Commentary. Sheffield: Sheffield Academic Press, 1999.

McCormick, M. "The Birth of the Codex and the Apostolic Life-Style." *Scriptorium. Revue internationale des études relatives aux manuscrits* 39 (1985): 150–58.

McGinn, Sheila E. "*Exousian echein epi tēs kephalēs*: 1 Cor 11:10 and the Ecclesial Authority of Women." *Listening* 31 (1996): 91–104.

McDonnell, M. "Writing, Copying, and Autograph Manuscripts in Ancient Rome." *ClQ* 46 (1996): 469–91.

Meade, David G. *Pseudonymity and Canon. An Investigation into the Relationship of Authorship and Authority in Jewish and Earliest Christian Tradition*. WUNT 39. Tübingen: Mohr Siebeck, 1986.

Mearns, Christopher L. "Early Eschatological Development in Paul: The Evidence of 1 Corinthians." *JSNT* 22 (1984): 19–35.

Meeks, Wayne A. *The First Urban Christians: The Social World of the Apostle Paul*. New Haven and London: Yale University Press, 1983.

Meeks, Wayne A. "The Image of the Androgyne: Some Uses of a Symbol in Earliest Christianity." *HR* 13 (1974): 165–208. Reprinted as pages 3–54 in Allen R. Hilton and H. Gregory Snyder, editors, *In Search of the Early Christians: Selected Essays*. New Haven and London: Yale University Press, 2002.

Meiser, Martin, and Uwe Kühneweg, et al. *Proseminar II. Neues Testament— Kirchengeschichte, Ein Arbeitsbuch*. Stuttgart: Kohlhammer, 1999.

Merk, Otto. "Literarkritik II." *Theologische Realenzyklopädie* 21 (1991): 222–33.

Merk, Otto. "Redaktionsgeschichte / Redaktionskritik II. Neues Testament." *TRE* 28 (1997): 378–84.

Merklein, Helmut. "Die Einheitlichkeit des ersten Korintherbriefes." Pages 345–75 in Helmut Merklein. *Studien zu Jesus und Paulus*. WUNT 43. Tübingen: Mohr Siebeck, 1987.

Merklein, Helmut. "Die Einheitlichkeit des ersten Korintherbriefes." *ZNW* 75 (1984): 153–83.

Merklein, Helmut. *Der erste Brief an die Korinther: Kapitel 1—4.* ÖTK 7.1. Gütersloh: Gütersloher Verlagshaus Gerd Mohn; Würzburg: Echter Verlag, 1992.

Merklein, Helmut. *Der erste Brief an die Korinther: Kapitel 5,1—11,1.* ÖTK 7.2. Gütersloh: Gütersloher Verlagshaus Gerd Mohn; Würzburg: Echter Verlag, 2000.

Merklein, Helmut, edited by Marlis Gielen. *Der erste Brief an die Korinther: Kapitel 11,2—16,24.* ÖTK 7.3. Gütersloh: Gütersloher Verlagshaus Gerd Mohn; Würzburg: Echter Verlag, 2005.

Merz, Annette. *Die fiktive Selbstauslegung des Paulus. Intertextuelle Studien zur Intention und Rezeption der Pastoralbriefe.* NTOA 52. Göttingen: Vandenhoeck & Ruprecht; Fribourg: Academic Press, 2004.

Metzger, Bruce M. *The Canon of the New Testament: Its Origin, Development, and Significance.* Oxford: Clarendon, 1987.

Metzger, Bruce M. *A Textual Commentary on the Greek New Testament.* New York: United Bible Societies, 1971.

Meyer, Heinrich August Wilhelm. *Critical and Exegetical Hand-Book to the Epistles to the Corinthians.* Translated by Douglas Bannerman and William P. Dickson. Preface and explanatory notes by Talbot W. Chambers. New York: Funk & Wagnalls, 1884.

Michaelis, Wilhelm. "Teilungshypothesen bei Paulusbriefen—Briefkompositionen and ihr Sitz im Leben." *TZ* 14 (1958): 321–26.

Mihaila, Corin. *The Paul—Apollos Relationship and Paul's Stance toward Greco-Roman Rhetoric: An Exegetical and Socio-historical Study of 1 Corinthians 1 – 4.* Library of Christian Studies, 402. London & New York: Clark, 2009.

Millard, Alan R. *Reading and Writing in the Time of Jesus.* Sheffield: Sheffield Academic Press, 2000.

Mitchell, Margaret M. *Paul, the Corinthians, and the Birth of Christian Hermeneutics.* Cambridge and New York: Cambridge University Press, 2010.

Mitchell, Margaret M. "The Corinthian Correspondence and the Birth of Pauline Hermeneutics." Pages 17–53 in Trevor J. Burke and J. K. Elliott, editors, *Paul and the Corinthians: Studies on a Community in Conflict: Essays in Honour of Margaret Thrall.* NovTSup 109. Leiden: Brill, 2003.

Mitchell, Margaret M. *Paul and the Rhetoric of Reconciliation: An Exegetical Investigation of the Language and Composition of 1 Corinthians.* Louisville: Westminster/Knox, 1991.

Mitchell, Margaret M. "Paul's Letters to Corinth: The Interpretive Intertwining of Literary and Historical Reconstruction." Pages 307–38 in Daniel N. Schowalter and Steven J. Friesen, editors, *Urban Religion in Roman Corinth: Interdisciplinary Approaches.* HTS 53. Harvard University Press, 2005.

Mitchell, Margaret M. "Re-examining the 'Aborted Apostle': An Exploration of Paul's Self-Description in First Corinthians 15.8." *JSNT* 25 (2002–03): 469–85.

Mitton, Charles Leslie. *The Formation of the Pauline Corpus of Letters.* London: Epworth Press, 1955.

Moessner, David P. et al., editors. *Paul and the Heritage of Israel: Paul's Claim upon Israel's Legacy in Luke and Acts in the Light of the Pauline Letters.* LNTS 452. New York: T & T Clark International, 2012.

Moffatt, James. *The First Epistle of Paul to the Corinthians*. New York and London: Harper & Brothers, 1959.
Morris, Leon. *1 Corinthians: An Introduction and Commentary*. TNTC. Downers Grove: IVP Academic; Nottingham: Inter-Varsity, 2007. Reprint of the 1958 edition.
Moss, Candida R. "Current Trends in the Study of Early Christian Martyrdom." *BSR* 41 (2012): 22–29.
Moulton, James Hope, and George Milligan. *The Vocabulary of the Greek Testament, Illustrated from the Papyri and other Non-literary Sources*. London: Hodder & Stoughton, 1914–1929; reprinted, Grand Rapids: Eerdmans, 1985.
Mounce, William D. *Pastoral Epistles*. WBC 46. Nashville: Thomas Nelson, 2000.
Mount, Christopher. "1 Corinthians 11:3-16: Spirit Possession and Authority in a Non-Pauline Interpolation." *JBL* 124 (2005): 313–40.
Mowry, Lucetta. "The Early Circulation of Paul's Letters." *JBL* 63 (1944): 73–86.
Müller, Paul-Gerhard. "Der Paulinismus in der Apostelgeschichte. Ein forschungsgeschichtliche Überblick." Pages 157–201 in Karl Kertelge, editor, *Paulus in den neutestamentlichen Spätschriften*. QD 89. Freiburg et al.: Herder, 1981.
Müller-Bardorff, Johannes. *Paulus—Wege zu didaktischer Erschließung der paulinischen Briefe*. Gütersloh: Gütersloher Verlags-Haus Mohn, 1970.
Münch, Stephan. *Das Geschenk der Einfachheit. 2 Korinther 8,1-15 und 9,6-15 als Hinführung zu dieser Gabe*. FB 126. Würzburg: Echter Verlag, 2012.
Munck, Johannes. *Paul and the Salvation of Mankind*. Translated by Frank Clarke. Richmond: John Knox, 1959.
Munro, Winsome. *Authority in Paul and Peter: The Identification of a Pastoral Stratum in the Pauline Corpus and 1 Peter*. SNTSMS 45. Cambridge: Cambridge University Press, 1983.
Munro, Winsome. "Interpolation in the Epistles: Weighing Probability." *NTS* 36 (1990): 431–43.
Murphy, James J. "Early Christianity as a 'Persuasive Campaign': Evidence from the Acts of the Apostels and the Letters of Paul." Pages 90–99 in Stanley E. Porter and Thomas H. Olbricht, editors, *Rhetoric and the New Testament: Essays from the 1992 Heidelberg Conference*. JSNTSup, 90. Sheffield: Sheffield: JSOT Press, 1993.
Murphy-O'Connor, Jerome. "Corinthian Slogans in 1 Cor 6:12-20." *CBQ* 40 (1978): 391–96.
Murphy-O'Connor, Jerome. *Keys to First Corinthians: Revisiting the Major Issues*. Oxford /New York: Oxford University Press, 2009.
Murphy-O'Connor, Jerome. *1 Corinthians*. Wilmington: Michael Glazier, 1980.
Murphy-O'Connor, Jerome. "Interpolations in 1 Corinthians." *CBQ* 48 (1986): 81–94.
Murphy-O'Connor, Jerome. *Keys to Second Corinthians: Revisiting the Major Issues*. Oxford: Oxford University Press, 2010.
Murphy-O'Connor, Jerome. "The Non-Pauline Character of 1 Corinthians 11:2-16?" *JBL* 95 (1976): 615–21.
Murphy-O'Connor, Jerome. *Paul: A Critical Life*. Oxford: Clarendon, 1996.

Murphy-O'Connor, Jerome. "Paul and Macedonia: The Connection between 2 Corinthians 2.13 and 2.14." *JSNT* 25 (1985): 99–103.
Murphy-O'Connor, Jerome, editor. *Paul and Qumran: Studies in New Testament Exegesis.* Chicago: Priory, 1968.
Murphy-O'Connor, Jerome. "Sex and Logic in 1 Cor 11:2-16." *CBQ* 42 (1980): 482–500.
Murphy-O'Connor, Jerome. *St. Paul's Corinth: Texts and Archeology.* Wilmington: Michael Glazier, 1983.
Murphy-O'Connor, Jerome. *The Theology of the Second Letter to the Corinthians.* New Testament Theology. Cambridge: Cambridge University Press, 1991.
Nickle, Keith F. *The Collection: A Study in Paul's Strategy.* SBT 48. London: SCM; Naperville: Allenson, 1966.
Nielsen, Charles M. "The Status of Paul and His Letters in Colossians." *PRSt* 12 (1985): 103–22.
O'Brien, Peter Thomas. *Introductory Thanksgivings in the Letters of Paul.* NovTSup 49. Leiden: Brill, 1977.
Oeming, Manfred and A. – R. Pregla. "New Literary Criticism." *TRu* 66 (2001): 1–23.
Oliveira, Anacleto de. *Die Diakonie der Gerechtigkeit und der Versöhnung in der Apologie des 2. Korintherbriefes: Analyse und Auslegung von 2 Kor 2,14– 4,6; 5,11–6,10.* NTAbh 21. Münster: Aschendorff, 1990.
O'Mahony, Kieran. *Pauline Persuasion: A Sounding in 2 Corinthians 8-9.* JSNTSup 199. Sheffield: Sheffield Academic Press, 2000.
O'Neill, John C. "Glosses and Interpolations in the Letters of St Paul." Pages 379–86 in Elizabeth A. Livingstone, editor, *Studia Evangelica VII.* TU 126. Berlin: Akademie-Verlag, 1982.
Orr, William F. and James Arthur Walther. *1 Corinthians: A New Translation: Introduction with a Study of the Life of Paul, Notes, and Commentary.* AB 32. Garden City: Doubleday, 1976.
Osten-Sacken, Peter von der. "Die Apologie des paulinischen Apostolats in 1 Kor 15:1-11." *ZNW* 64 (1973): 245–62.
Pagels, Elaine H. "Exegesis of Genesis 1 in the Gospels of Thomas and John." *JBL* 118 (1999): 477–96.
Pagels, Elaine H. *The Gnostic Paul: Gnostic Exegesis of the Pauline Letters.* Philadelphia: Fortress, 1975; reprinted, Philadelphia: Trinity Press International, 1992.
Parsons, Michael C., and Michael Wade Martin, *Ancient Rhetoric and the New Testament: The Influence of Elementary Greek Composition.* Waco: Baylor University Press, 2018.
Pascuzzi, Maria. *Ethics, Ecclesiology and Church Discipline: A Rhetorical Analysis of 1 Corinthians 5.* TGST 32. Rome: Editrice Pontificia Universita Gregoriana, 1997.
Pascuzzi, Maria A. *First and Second Corinthians.* New Collegeville Bible Commentary: New Testament 7. Collegeville: Liturgical Press, 2005.
Pearson, Birger A. *Ancient Gnosticism: Traditions and Literature.* Minneapolis: Fortress Press, 2007.

Pearson, Brook W. R. "New Testament Literary Criticism." Pages 241–66 in Stanley E. Porter, editor, *Handbook to Exegesis of the New Testament.* NTTS 25. Leiden: Brill, 1997.

Penny, Donald N. "The Pseudo-Pauline Letters of the First Two Centuries." PhD dissertation, Emory University, 1979.

Perkins, Pheme. *First Corinthians.* Paideia: Commentaries on the New Testament. Grand Rapids: Baker Academic, 2012.

Perry, Peter S. *The Rhetoric of Digressions: Revelation 7:1-17 and 10:1—11:13 and Ancient Communication.* WUNT 2.268. Tübingen: Mohr Siebeck, 2009.

Pervo, Richard I. *The Making of Paul: Constructions of the Apostle in Early Christianity.* Minneapolis: Fortress, 2010.

Pesch, Rudolf. *Paulus ringt um die Lebensform der Kirche. Vier Briefe an die Gemeinde Gottes in Korinth. Paulus neu gesehen.* Herderbücherei, 1291. Freiburg: Herder, 1986.

Pesch, Rudolf. *Paulus kämpft um sein Apostolat. Drei weitere Briefe an die Gemeinde Gottes in Korinth.* Freiburg: Herder, 1987.

Peterson, Brian K. *Eloquence and the Proclamation of the Gospel in Corinth.* SBLDS 163. Atlanta: Scholars Press, 1998.

Pétrement, Simone. *A Separate God: The Christian Origins of Gnosticism.* Translated by Carol Harrison. San Francisco: Harper, 1990.

Pfitzner, V. C. *Paul and the Agon Motif: Traditional Athletic Imagery in the Pauline Literature.* NovTSup 16. Leiden: Brill, 1967.

Pierson, Allard and S. A. Naber. *Verisimilia: laceram conditionem Novi Testamenti exemplis illustrarunt et ab origine repetierunt.* Amsterdam: Van Kampen, 1886.

Pietersen, Lloyd K. *The Polemic of the Pastorals: A Sociological Examination of the Development of Pauline Christianity.* JSNTSup 264. London and New York: T & T Clark International, 2004.

Pitta, Antonio. "Il 'discorso del pazzo' o periautologia immoderate? Analisi retorico-letteraria di 2 Cor 11,1-12—12,18." *Bib* 87 (2006): 493–510.

Plank, Karl A. *Paul and the Irony of Affliction.* SemeiaSt. Atlanta: Scholars Press, 1987.

Plummer, Alfred. *The Second Epistle of Paul the Apostle to the Corinthians.* Cambridge: University Press, 1912.

Pogoloff, Stephen M. *Logos and Sophia: The Rhetorical Situation of 1 Corinthians.* SBLDS 134. Atlanta: Scholars Press, 1992.

Pokorný, Petr. *Colossians: A Commentary.* Translated by Siegfried S. Schatzmann. Peabody: Hendrickson, 1991.

Popkes, Wiard. "Leadership: James, Paul, and their Contemporary Background." Pages 323–54 in Bruce Chilton and Craig Evans, editors, *The Missions of James, Peter, and Paul: Tensions in Early Christianity.* NovTSup 115. Leiden & Boston: Brill, 2005.

Popkes, Wiard. "Traditionen und Traditionsbrüche im Jakobusbrief." Pages 143–70 in J. Schlosser, editor, *The Catholic Epistles and Tradition.* Leuven: University Press, 2004.

Porter, Stanley E., editor. *Paul and His Opponents.* Pauline Studies, 2. Leiden: Brill; Atlanta: Society of Biblical Literature, 2005.

Porter, Stanley E. "Paul and the Pauline Letter Collection." Pages 19–36 in Michael F. Bird and J. R. Dodson, editors, *Paul and the Second Century*. LNTS 212. London and New York: T & T Clark, 2011.

Porter, Stanley E., editor. *The Pauline Canon*. Pauline Studies, 1. Atlanta: Society of Biblical Literature, 2004.

Porter, Stanley E. "Paul of Tarsus and his Letters." Pages 533–85 in Stanley E. Porter, editor, *Handbook of Classical Rhetoric in the Hellenistic Period 330 B.C. -- A.D. 400*. Leiden: Brill, 1997.

Porter, Stanley E. and Thomas H. Olbricht, editors. *The Rhetorical Analysis of Scripture: Essays from the 1995 London Conference*. JSNTSup 146. Sheffield: Sheffield Academic Press, 1997.

Porter, Stanley E. and Thomas H. Olbricht, editors. *Rhetoric and the New Testament: Essays from the 1992 Heidelberg Conference*. JSNTSup 90. Sheffield: JSOT Press, 1993.

Porter, Stanley E. and Thomas H. Olbricht, editors. *Rhetoric, Scripture and Theology: Essays from the 1994 Pretoria Conference*. JSNTSup 131. Sheffield: Sheffield Academic Press, 1996.

Porter, Stanley E. "When and How Was the Pauline Canon Compiled? An Assessment of Theories." Pages 95–127 in Stanley E. Porter, editor, *The Pauline Canon*. Pauline Studies, 1. Leiden: Brill, 2004.

Preisker, Herbert. "Zur Komposition des zweiten Korintherbriefes." *TBl* 5 (1926): 154–57.

Price, Robert M. "Apocryphal Apparitions: 1 Corinthians 15:3-11 as a Post-Pauline Interpolation." Pages 69–104 in Robert M. Price et al., editors, *The Empty Tomb: Jesus beyond the Grave*. Amherst: Prometheus Books, 2005.

Price, Robert M. "The Evolution of the Pauline Canon." *HvTSt* 53 (1997): 36–67.

Prior, Michael. *Paul the Letter-Writer and the Second Letter to Timothy*. JSNTSup 23. Sheffield: JSOT Press, 1989.

Probst, Hermann. *Paulus und der Brief. Die Rhetorik des antiken Briefes als Form der paulinischen Korintherkorrespondenz (1 Kor 8 - 10)*. WUNT 2.45. Tübingen: Mohr Siebeck, 1991.

Prümm, Karl. *Diakonia Pneumatos. Theologische Auslegung des zweiten Korintherbriefes*. Rome et al.: Herder, 1962–67.

Quast, Kevin. *Reading the Corinthian Correspondence: An Introduction*. New York: Paulist, 1954.

Quinn, Jerome D. "P[46] –The Pauline Canon?" *CBQ* 36 (1974): 379–85.

Radermacher, Ludwig, editor. *Artium scriptores (Reste der voraristotelischen Rhetorik)*. Österreichische Akademie der Wissenschaften, Philosophisch-historische Klasse, Sitzungsberichte 227.3. Vienna: Rohrer, 1951.

Rakogy, Waldemar. "Was Paul Indeed to Meet Titus in Troas? In Connection with 2 Cor 2,12-13 and 7,5-6." Pages 307–12 in José Enrique Aguilar Chiu et al., editors, *Bible et Terre Saincte. Mélanges Marcel Beaudry*. Bern et al.: Peter Lang, 2008.

Rasimus, Tuomas. "Anathema Iesous (1 Cor 12:3)? Origen of Alexandra on the Ophite Gnostics." Pages 797–821 in Louis Painchaud and Paul-Hubert Poirier, editors, *Coptica — gnostica — manichaica: Mélanges offerts à Wolf-Peter Funk*.

Quebec: Les Presses de l'Universite Laval; Louvain and Paris: Éditions Peeters, 2006.

Reed, Jeffrey T. *A Discourse Analysis of Philippians: Method and Rhetoric in the Debate over Literary Integrity*. JSNTSup 136. Sheffield: Sheffield Academic Press, 1997.

Reicke, Bo. *Re-examining Paul's Letters: The History of the Pauline Correspondence*. Edited by David P. Moessner and Ingalisa Reicke. Harrisburg: Trinity Press International, 2001.

Rensberger. David. K. "As the Apostle Teaches: The Development of the Use of Paul's Letters in Second-Century Christianity." Ph.D. dissertation, Yale University, 1981.

Reynolds, L. D. and N. G. Wilson. *Scribes and Scholars: A Guide to the Transmission of Greek and Latin Literature*. Oxford: Clarendon, 1974.

Richards, E. Randolph. *Paul and First-Century Letter Writing: Secretaries, Composition and Collection*. Downers Grove: InterVarsity Press, 2004.

Richards, E. Randolph. *The Secretary in the Letters of Paul*. WUNT 42. Tübingen: Mohr Siebeck, 1991.

Richardson, Peter. "On the Absence of 'Anti-Judaism' in 1 Corinthians." Volume 1, pages 59–74 in Peter Richardson with David Granskou, editors, *Anti-Judaism in Early Christianity. I. Paul and the Gospels*. Studies in Christianity and Judaism, 2. Waterloo: WLU Press, 1986.

Reid, Robert Stephen. "*Ad Herennium* Argument Strategies in 1 Corinthians." *JGRChJ* 3 (2006): 192–222.

Rengstorf, Karl Heinrich, with Ulrich Luck. *Das Paulusbild in der neueren deutschen Forschung*. Wege der Forschung, 24. Darmstadt: Wissenschaftliche Buchgesellschaft, 1982.

Richards, E. Randolph. "The Codex and the Early Collection of Paul's Letters." *BBR* 8 (1998): 151–66.

Richards, E. Randolph. *Paul and First-Century Letter Writing: Secretaries, Composition and Collection*. Downers Grove: InterVarsity, 2004.

Roberts, Colin Henderson. "The Ancient Book and the Ending of St Mark." *JTS* 40 (1939): 253–57.

Roberts, Colin Henderson. "The Christian Book and the Greek Papyri." *JTS* 50 (1949): 155–68.

Roberts, Colin Henderson and T. C. Skeat. *The Birth of the Codex*. Oxford: Oxford University Press, 1983.

Robertson, Archibald and Plummer, Alfred. *A Critical and Exegetical Commentary on the First Epistle of St. Paul to the Corinthians*. ICC. New York: Scribners, 1911.

Robertson, C. K. *Conflict in Corinth: Redefining the System*. StBibLit 42. New York: Lang, 2001.

Robinson, James M., and Helmut Koester. *Trajectories through Early Christianity*. Philadelphia: Fortress, 1971.

Roetzel, Calvin J. *2 Corinthians*. ANTC. Nashville: Abingdon Press, 2007.

Rolland, Philippe. "La structure littéraire de la deuxième epître aux Corinthiens." *Bib* 71 (1990): 73–84.

Ross, J. M. "Not Above What is Written: A Note on 1 Cor. 4:6." *ExpTim* 82 (1970–71): 215–17.
Rowston, Douglas J. "The Most Neglected Book in the New Testament." *NTS* 21 (1975): 554–63.
Rudolf, Kurt. *Gnosis: The Nature and History of Gnosticism*. Translated by Robert McLachlan Wilson et al. San Francisco: Harper & Row, 1983.
Ruef, John. *Paul's First Letter to Corinth*. Westminster Pelican Commentaries. Philadelphia: Westminster, 1977.
Sabatier, A. *The Apostle Paul: A Sketch of the Development of His Doctrine*. Translated by A. M. Hellier, edited with an essay on the Pastoral Epistles by George G. Findlay, 3rd ed. London: Hodder and Stoughton, 1896.
Sänger, Dieter. "'Jetzt aber führt auch das Tun zu Ende' (2Kor 8,11). Die korinthische Gemeinde und die Kollekte für Jerusalem." Pages 257–82 in Dieter Sänger, editor, *Der zweite Korintherbrief. Literarische Gestalt - historische Situation - theologische Argumentation. Festschrift zum 70. Geburtstag von Dietrich-Alex Koch.* FRLANT 250. Göttingen: Vandenhoeck & Ruprecht, 2012.
Sänger, Dieter, editor. *Der zweite Korintherbrief. Literarische Gestalt - historische Situation - theologische Argumentation. Festschrift zum 70. Geburtstag von Dietrich-Alex Koch.* FRLANT 250. Göttingen: Vandenhoeck & Ruprecht, 2012.
Sahlin, Harald. "Emendationsvorschläge zum griechischen Text des Neuen Testamemts III." *NovT* 25 (1983): 73–88.
Sampley, J. Paul. "The First Letter to the Corinthians." *The New Interpreter's Bible*, ed. Leander E. Keck (Nashville: Abingdon, 2002): 10.771–1003.
Sampley, J. Paul. "The Second Letter to the Corinthians." Volume 11, pages 1–180 in L. E. Keck, editor, *The New Interpreter's Bible*. Nashville: Abingdon, 2000.
Sampley, J. Paul and Peter Lampe, editors. *Paul and Rhetoric*. T & T Clark Biblical Studies. New York; London: T & T Clark, 2010.
Sand, Alexander. "Überlieferung und Sammlung der Paulusbriefe." Pages 11–24 in Karl Kertelge, editor, *Paulus in den neutestamentlichen Spätschriften. Zur Paulusrezeption im Neuen Testament*. QD 89. Freiburg et al.: Herder, 1981.
Sanders, E. P. *Paul: The Apostle's Life, Letters, and Thought*. Minneapolis: Fortress, 2015.
Sandt, H. van de. "1. Kor. 11,2-16 als een retorische eenheid." *Bijdragen. Tijdschrift voor philosophie en theologie* 49 (1988): 410–25.
Sass, Gerhard. "Noch einmal: 2 Kor 6,14–7,1. Literarkritische Waffen gegen einen 'unpaulinischen' Paulus?" *ZNW* 84 (1993): 36–64.
Savage, Timothy B. *Power through Weakness: Paul's Understanding of the Christian Ministry in 2 Corinthians*. SNTSMS 86. Cambridge: Cambridge University Press, 1996.
Saw, Insawn. *Paul's Rhetoric in First Corinthians 15: An Analysis Utilizing the Theories of Classical Rhetoric*. Lewiston: Mellen Biblical Press, 1995.
Scarborough, Jason M. "The Making of an Apostle: Second and Third Century Interpretations of the Writings of Paul." Ph.D. dissertation, Union Theological Seminary, New York, 2007.

Schadewaldt, Wolfgang. "Der Brief bei den Griechen. Ein Instrument des Humanen." Pages 31–42 in E. Hora and E. Kessler, editors, *Studia Humanitatis. Ernesto Grassi zum 70. Geburtstag*. Munich: Fink, 1973.

Schäfer, K. Th. "Marcion und die ältesten Prologe zu den Paulusbriefen." Volume 1, pages 135–50 in Patrick Granfield and Josef A. Jungmann, editors, *Kyriakon. Festschrift Johannes Quasten*. Münster: Aschendorff, 1973.

Schenk, Wolfgang. "Der 1. Korintherbrief als Briefsammlung." *ZNW* 60 (1969): 219–43.

Schenk, Wolfgang. "Korintherbriefe." *TRE* 19 (1990): 620–40.

Schenke, Hans-Martin. "Das Weiterwirken des Paulus and die Pflege seines Erbes durch die Paulus-Schule." *NTS* 21 (1974–75): 505–18.

Schenke, Hans-Martin and Karl Martin Fischer. *Einleitung in die Schriften des Neuen Testaments. I. Die Briefe des Paulus und Schriften des Paulinismus*. Gütersloh: Gütersloher Velagshaus, 1978.

Scherbenske, Eric W. *Canonizing Paul: Ancient Editorial Practice and the Corpus Paulinum*. Oxford: Oxford University Press, 2013.

Schlarb, Egbert. *Die gesunde Lehre: Häresie und Wahrheit im Spiegel der Pastoralbriefe*. Marburger theologische Studien, 28. Marburg: Elwert, 1990.

Schmeller, Thomas. "Der ursprüngliche Kontext von 2 Kor 6.14-7.1. Zur Frage der Einheitlichkeit des 2. Korintherbriefs." *NTS* 52 (2006): 219–38.

Schmeller, Thomas. "Die Cicerobriefe und die Frage nach der Einheitlichkeit des 2. Korintherbriefes." *ZNW* 95 (2004): 181–208.

Schmeller, Thomas. *Der zweite Brief an die Korinther*. EKKNT 8.1. Neukirchen-Vluyn: Neukirchener Theologie; Ostfildern: Patmos-Verlag, 2010.

Schmid, Ulrich. "Die Buchwerdung des Neuen Testaments. Über den Zusammenhang von Textgeschichte und Kanongeschichte." *Wort und Dienst* 27 (2003): 217–32.

Schmiedel, Paul Wilhelm. *Die Briefe an die Thessalonicher und an die Korinther*. Hand-Commentar zum Neuen Testament, 2. Freiburg & Leipzig: Mohr (Siebeck), 1891.

Schmithals, Walter. "Die Abfassung und ältesten Sammlung der paulinischen Hauptbriefe." Pages 175–200 in Schmithals, *Paulus und die Gnostiker. Untersuchungen zu den kleinen Paulusbriefen*. TF 35. Hamburg-Bergstedt: Herbert Reich Evangelischer Verlag, 1965.

Schmithals, Walter. *Die Briefe des Paulus in ihrer ursprünglichen Form*. Zürich: Werkkommentare zur Bibel, 1984.

Schmithals, Walter. *Die Gnosis in Korinth: Eine Untersuchung zu den Korintherbriefen*, 3rd edition. FRLANT 66. Göttingen: Vandenhoeck & Ruprecht, 1979.

Schmithals, Walter. *Gnosticism in Corinth: An Investigation of the Letters to the Corinthians*. Translated by John E. Steely. Nashville: Abingdon, 1971.

Schmithals, Walter. "Die Korintherbriefe als Briefsammlung." *ZNW* 64 (1973): 263–88.

Schmithals, Walter. "Methodische Erwägungen zur Literarkritik der Paulusbriefe." *ZNW* 87 (1996): 51–82.

Schmithals, Walter. *Paul and the Gnostics*. Nashville: Abingdon Press, 1972.

Schmithals, Walter. "Die Sammlung der Paulusbriefe." *ThViat* 15 (1982): 11–22.

Schmidt, Ulrich. *"Nicht vergeblich empfangen"! Eine Untersuchung zum 2. Korintherbrief als Beitrag zur Frage nach der paulinischen Einschätzung des Handelns*. BWANT 162. Stuttgart: Kohlhammer, 2004.
Schmitz, Wolfgang. "Buch/Buchwesen." *RGG*, 4th ed., 1 (1998): 1813–16.
Schneider, Sabastien. *Vollendung des Auferstehens. Eine exegetische Untersuchung von 1 Kor 15,51-52 und 1 Thess 4,13-18*. FB 97. Würzburg: Echter Verlag, 2000.
Schnelle, Udo. *Einführung in die neutestamentliche Exegese*, 5th ed. Göttingen: Vandenhoeck & Ruprecht, 2000.
Schnelle, Udo. *Apostle Paul: His Life and Theology*. Translated by M. Eugene Boring. Grand Rapids: Baker Academic, 2005.
Schowalter, Daniel N., and Steven J. Friesen. *Urban Religion in Roman Corinth: Interdisciplinary Approaches*. HTS 53. Cambridge: Harvard University Press, 2005.
Schrage, Wolfgang. *Der erste Brief an die Korinther*, 4 volumes. EKKNT 7.1-4. Zürich & Düsseldorf: Benziger Verlag; Neukirchen-Vluyn: Neukirchener Verlag, 1991–2001.
Schreiber, Alfred. *Die Gemeinde in Korinth. Versuch einer gruppendynamischen Betrachtung der Entwicklung der Gemeinde von Korinth auf der Basis des ersten Korintherbriefes*. NTAbh 12. Münster: Aschendorff, 1977.
Schröter, Jens. "Die Apostelgeschichte und die Entstehung des neutestamentlichen Kanons. Beobachtungen zur Kanonizierung der Apostelgeschichte und ihrer Bedeutung als kanonischer Schrift." Pages 395–427 in Jean-Marie Auwers et al., editors, *The Biblical Canons. Fiftieth Colloquium Biblicum Lovaniense ... July 25 to 27 2001*. BETL 163. Leuven: Leuven University Press, 2003.
Schütz, John Howard. "Apostolic Authority and the Control of Tradition: I Cor. xv." *NTS* 15 (1969): 439–57.
Schütz, John Howard. *Paul and the Anatomy of Apostolic Authority*. Cambridge: University Press, 1975.
Schulz, Siegfried. "Maranatha und Kurios Jesus." *ZNW* 53 (1962): 125–44.
Schweitzer, Albert. *The Mysticism of Paul the Apostle*. Translated by William Montgomery, foreword by Jaroslav Pelikan. Baltimore and London: Johns Hopkins University Press, 1998.
Schweizer, Eduard. *The Letter to the Colossians: A Commentary*. Minneapolis: Augsburg, 1982.
Scott, Ernest Findlay. *The Pastoral Epistles*. New York: Harper and Brothers, 1936.
Scott, James M. *2 Corinthians*. NIBCNT. Peabody: Hendrickson; Carlisle: Paternoster, 2003.
Segal, Alan F. *Paul the Convert: The Apostolate and Apostasy of Saul the Pharisee*. New Haven and London: Yale University Press, 1990.
Sellin, Gerhard. "Hauptprobleme des ersten Korintherbriefes." *Aufstieg und Niedergang der römischen Welt* II, 25/4 (1987): 2940–3044.
Sellin, Gerhard. *Der Streit um die Auferstehung der Toten: Eine religionsgeschichtliche und exegetische Untersuchung von 1. Korinther 15*. FRLANT 138. Göttingen: Vandenhoeck & Ruprecht, 1986.

Sellin, Gerhard. "1 Korinther 5-6 und der 'Vorbrief' nach Korinth." *NTS* 37 (1991): 535–58.
Semler, Johann Salomo. *Paraphrasis II. Epistolae ad Corinthios*. Halae Magdeburgicae: Hemmerde, 1776.
Senft, Christophe. *La première Épître de Saint-Paul aux Corinthiens*, 2nd ed. CNT 7. Geneva: Labor et Fides, 1990.
Serna, Eduardo de la. "Los orígenes de 1 Corintos." *Bib* 72 (1991): 192–216.
Shanks, Monte Allen. "Papias and His Witness to the Development of the New Testament." Ph.D. dissertation, Southern Baptist Theological Seminary, 2008.
Sibinga, Joost Smit. "The Composition of 1 Cor 9 and Its Context." *NovT* 40 (1998): 136–63.
Sint, Josef A. *Pseudonymität im Altertum. Ihre Formen und ihre Gründe*. Innsbruck: Wagner, 1960.
Skeat, T. C. "The Length of the standard papyrus roll and the cost-advantage of the codex." *ZPE* 45 (1982): 169–75.
Skeat, T. C. "The Origin of the Christian Codex." *ZPE* 102 (1994): 263–68.
Skeat, T. C. "Roll *versus* Codex: A New Approach." *ZPE* 84 (1990): 297–98.
Smit, Joop F. M. *"About the Idol Offerings": Rhetoric, Social Context and Theology of Paul's Discourse in First Corinthians 8:1—11:1*. CBET 27. Leuven: Peeters, 2000.
Smit, Joop F. M. "Argument and Genre of 1 Cor 12—14." Pages 211–30 in Stanley E. Porter and Thomas H. Olbricht, editors, *Rhetoric and the New Testament: Essays from the 1992 Heidelberg Conference*. JSNTSup 90. Sheffield: JSOT, 1993.
Smit, Joop F. M. "'Do Not Be Idolaters': Paul's Rhetoric in First Corinthians 10:1-22." *NovT* 39 (1997): 40–53.
Smit, Joop F. M. "Epideictic Rhetoric in Paul's First Letter to the Corinthians 1-4." *Bib* 84 (2003): 184–201.
Smit, Joop F. M. "1 Cor 8,1-8: A Rhetorical Partitio: A Contribution to the Coherence of 1 Cor 8,1-11,1." Pages 577-91 in Raimund Bieringer, editor, *The Corinthian Correspondence*. BETL 125. Leuven: Leuven University Press, 1996.
Smit, Joop F. M. "'What is Apollos? What is Paul?' In Search for the Coherence of First Corinthians 1:10-4:21." *NovT* 44 (2002): 231–51.
Snyder, Glenn E. *Acts of Paul: The Formation of a Pauline Corpus*. WUNT 352. Tübingen: Mohn Siebeck, 2013.
Snyder, Graydon F. *First Corinthians*, Faith Community Commentary. Macon: Mercer University Press, 1993.
Snyder, Graydon F. "The *Tobspruch* in the New Testament." *NTS* 23 (1976-77): 117–20.
Snyman, Andries H. "1 Corinthians 1:18-31 from a Rhetorical Perspective." *AcT* 29 (2009): 130–44.
Snyman, Andries H. "Persuasion in 1 Corinthians 1:1-9." *Verbum et Ekklesia* 30 (2009): 1–6.
Soards, Marion L. *1 Corinthians*. NIBCNT 7. Peabody: Hendrickson, 1999.
Söding, Thomas. *Das Liebesgebot bei Paulus. Die Mahnung zur Agape im Rahmen der paulinischen Ethik*. NTAbh 26. Münster: Aschendorff, 1995.

Söding, Thomas, with Christian Münch. *Wege der Schriftauslegung: Methodenbuch zum Neuen Testament.* Freiburg: Herder, 1998.

Spencer, Aïda Besançon. *Paul's Literary Style: A Stylistic and Historical Comparison of II Corinthians 11:16-12:13, Romans 8:9-39, and Philippians 3:2-4:13.* Lanham: University Press of America, 1998.

Speyer, Wolfgang. "Fälschung, literarische." *RAC* 7 (1969): 236–77.

Speyer, Wolfgang. *Die literarische Fälschung im heidnischen und christlichen Altertum. Ein Versuch ihrer Deutung.* Handbuch der Altertumswissenschaft, 1.2. Munich: C. H. Beck, 1971.

Speyer, Wolfgang. "Religiöse Pseudepigraphie und literarische Fälschung im Altertum." *JAC* 8–9 (1965–66): 88–125.

Spicq, Ceslaus. *Agape in the New Testament*, 3 volumes. New York: Herder, 1965–6; reprinted, Eugene, OR: Wipf & Stock, 2006.

Spicq, Ceslas. "Comment Comprehendre ΦΙΛΕΙΝ dans 1 Cor. xvi, 22?" *NovT* 1 (1957): 200–04.

Stamps, Dennis L. "Rhetorical Criticism and the Rhetoric of the New Testament Criticism." *Journal of Literature and Theology* 6 (1992): 268–79.

Stamps, Dennis L. "Rethinking the Rhetorical Situation: The Entextualization of the Situation in New Testament Epistles." Pages 193–210 in Stanley E. Porter and Thomas H. Olbricht, editors, *Rhetoric and the New Testament: Essays from the 1992 Heidelberg Conference.* JSNTSup 90. Sheffield: JSOT, 1993.

Stamps, Dennis L. "Rhetorical Criticism of the New Testament." Pages 129–69 in Stanley E. Porter and D. Toombs, editors, *Approaches to New Testament Study.* JSNTSup 120. Sheffield: JSOT, 1995.

Stamps, Dennis L. "The Theological Rhetoric of the Pauline Epistles: Prolegomenon." Pages 249–59 in Stanley E. Porter and Dennis L. Stamps, editors, *The Rhetorical Interpretation of Scripture: Essays from the 1996 Malibu Conference.* JSNTSup 180. Sheffield: Sheffield Academic Press, 1999.

Standaert, B. "La rhétoric ancienne dans Saint Paul." Pages 78–92 in Albert Vanhoye, editor, *L'Apôtre Paul: Personnalité, style et conception du ministère.* BETL 73. Leuven: Leuven University Presss, 1986.

Standhartinger, Angela. "Colossians and the Pauline School." *NTS* 50 (2004): 572–93.

Stanley, Christopher D., *Arguing With Scripture: The Rhetoric of Quotations in the Letters of Paul.* New York: T & T Clark International, 2004.

Stanley, Christopher D., editor. *Paul and Scripture: Extending the Conversation.* ECL 9. Atlanta: Society of Biblical Literature, 2012.

Ste. Croix, G. E. M. de. *Christian Persecution, Martyrdom, and Orthodoxy.* Edited by Michael Whitby and Joseph Streeter. Oxford and New York: Oxford University Press, 2006.

Stegman, Thomas D., S.J. *Second Corinthians.* Catholic Commentary on Sacred Scripture. Grand Rapids: Baker Academic, 2009.

Steinmann, M. "Römisches Schriftwesen. Einleitung in die lateinische Philologie." Pages 74–91 in F. Graf, editor, *Einleitung in die Altertumswissenschaft.* Stuttgart: Teubner, 1997.

Stephens, Susan A. "Book Production." Volume 1, pages 421–36 in Michael Grant and Rachel Kitzinger, editors, *Civilization of the Ancient Mediterranean: Greece and Rome*. New York: Scribners, 1988.

Stephenson, Alan M. G. "A Defence of the Integrity of II Corinthians." Pages 82–97 in Kurt Aland, editor, *The Authorship and Integrity of the New Testament*. Theological Collections, 4. London: SPCK, 1965.

Stephenson, Alan M. G. "Partition Theories on II Corinthians." Pages 639–46 in F. L. Cross, editor, *Studia Evangelica II*. TU 87. Berlin: Akademie Verlag, 1964.

Stewart-Sykes, Alistair. "Ancient Editors and Copyists and Modern Partition Theories: The Case of the Corinthian Correspondence." *JSNT* 61 (1996): 53–64.

Still, Todd D. "Shadow and Light: Marcion's (Mis)construal of the Apostle Paul." Pages 91–107 in Michael F. Bird and J. R. Dodson, editors, *Paul and the Second Century*. LNTS 212. London and New York: T & T Clark, 2011.

Stockhausen, Carol. *Letters in the Pauline Tradition*. MBS 13. Wilmington, DE: Michael Glazier, 1989.

Stockhausen, Carol Kern. *Moses' Veil and the Glory of the New Covenant: The Exegetical Substructure of II Cor. 3,1-4,6*. AnBib 116. Rome: Pontificio Instituto Biblico, 1989.

Stowers, Stanley K. *Letter Writing in Greco-Roman Antiquity*. LEC. Philadelphia: Westminster, 1986.

Stowers, Stanley K. "Peri men gar and the Integrity of 2 Cor. 8 and 9." *NovT* 32 (1990): 340–48.

Straatman, Jan Willem. *Kritische studien over den 1en Brief van Paulus aan de Korinthiers: met een naschrift over de verklaring van I Kor. 9, vs. 1-3 door den Hoogl. J. J. Prins verdedigd in zijn geschrift: "De getuigenis van den apostel Paulus aangaande's Heeren opstanding uit de dooden nader overwogen*, 2 volumes. Groningen: Van Griffen, 1863–1865.

Strecker, Georg. *History of New Testament Literature*, translated by Calvin Kaatter and Hans-Joachim Mollenhauer. Harrisburg: Trinity Press International, 1997.

Strecker, Georg. "Paulus in nachpaulinischer Zeit." *Kairos* 12 (1970): 208–16. Reprinted Pages 311–19 in Georg Strecker, *Eschaton und Historie: Aufsätze*. Göttingen: Vandenhoeck & Ruprecht, 1979.

Streete, Gail Corrington. "Discipline and Disclosure: Paul's Apocalyptic Asceticism in 1 Corinthians." Pages 81–94 in Greg Carey and L. Gregory Bloomquist, editors, *Vision and Persuasion: Rhetorical Dimensions of Apocalyptic Discourse*. St. Louis: Chalice, 1999.

Strugnell, John. "A Plea for Conjectural Emendation in the New Testament, with a Coda on 1 Cor 4:6." *CBQ* 36 (1974): 543–58.

Suhl, Alfred. *Paulus und seine Briefe. Ein Beitrag zur paulinische Chronologie*. Studien zum Neuen Testament 11. Gütersloh: Gütersloher Verlagshaus, 1975.

Sumney, Jerry L. *Identifying Paul's Opponents: The Question of Method in 2 Corinthians*. JSNTSup 40. Sheffield: JSOT Press, 1990.

Sumney, Jerry L. "Studying Paul's Opponents: Advances and Challenges." Pages 7–58 in Stanley E. Porter, editor, *Paul and His Opponents*. Atlanta: Society of Biblical Literature, 2005.

Sundberg, Albert C., Jr. "Canon Muratori: A Fourth-Century List." *HTR* 66 (1973): 1–41.
Sundberg, Albert C., Jr. "Canon of the NT." Pages 136–40 in K. Crim, V. P. Furnish, L. R. Bailey and E. S. Bucke, editors, *Interpreter's Dictionary of the Bible, Supplement Volume*. Nashville: Abingdon, 1976.
Sundberg, Albert C., Jr. "Muratorian Fragment." Pages 609–10 in K. Crim, V. P. Furnish, L. R. Bailey and E. S. Bucke, editors, *Interpreter's Dictionary of the Bible, Supplement Volume*. Nashville: Abingdon, 1976.
Sundermann, Hans-Georg. *Der schwache Apostel und die Kraft der Rede. Eine rhetorische Analyse von 2 Kor 10 – 13*. Europäische Hochschulschriften Reihe, 23, Theologie 575. Frankfurt et al.: Lang, 1996.
Talbert, Charles H. *Luke and the Gnostics: An Examination of the Lucan Purpose*. Nashville: Abingdon, 1966.
Talbert, Charles H. *Reading Corinthians: A Literary and Theological Commentary*. Revised edition. Macon: Smyth & Hewys, 2002.
Taylor, N. H. "The Composition and Chronology of Second Corinthians." *JSNT* 44 (1991): 67–87.
Taylor, Nicholas. *Paul, Antioch and Jerusalem: A Study in Relationships and Authority in Earliest Christianity*. JSNTSup 66. Sheffield: JSOT Press, 1992.
Theissen, Gerd. *The Social Setting of Pauline Christianity: Essays on Corinth*. Edited and translated and with an introduction by John H. Schütz. Philadelphia: Fortress Press, 1982.
Thiselton, Anthony C. *The First Epistle to the Corinthians: A Commentary on the Greek Text*. NIGTC. Grand Rapids: Eerdmans, 2000.
Thompson, Michael B. *Transforming Grace; A Study of 2 Corinthhians*. Oxford: The Bible Reading Fellowship, 1998.
Thraede, Klaus. *Einheit, Gegenwart, Gespräch. Zur Christianisierung antiker Brieftopoi*. Dissertation, Bonn, 1967.
Thraede, Klaus. *Grundzüge griechisch-römische Brieftopik*. Zetemata, 48. Munich: Beck, 1970.
Thrall, Margaret E. *A Critical and Exegetical Commentary on the Second Epistle to the Corinthians*, 2 volumes. ICC. Edinburgh: T. & T. Clark, 1994, 2000.
Thrall, Margaret E. "The Problem of II Cor. vi. 14 - vii. 1 in Some Recent Discussion." *NTS* 24 (1977–78): 132–48.
Thurén, Lauri. *Derhetorizing Paul: A Dynamic Perspective on Pauline Theology and the Law*. Harrisburg: Trinity Press International, 2002.
Towner, P. H. "Gnosis and Realized Eschatology in Ephesus (of the Pastoral Epistles): and the Corinthian Enthusiasm." *JSNT* 31 (1987): 95–124.
Trible, Phyllis. *Rhetorical Criticism: Context, Method, and the Book of Jonah*. Minneapolis: Fortress, 1994.
Trobisch, David. *Die Endredaktion des Neuen Testaments. Eine Untersuchung zur Entstehung der christlichen Bibel*. NTOA 31. Göttingen Vandenhoeck und Ruprecht; Freiburg: Universitätsverlag, 1996.
Trobisch, David. *Die Entstehung der Paulusbriefsammlung. Studien zu den Anfängen christlicher Publizistik*. NTOA 10. Göttingen Vandenhoeck und Ruprecht; Freiburg: Universitätsverlag, 1989.

Trobisch, David. *Paul's Letter Collection: Tracing the Origins.* Minneapolis: Fortress, 1994.

Trompf, G. W. "On Attitudes toward Women in Paul and Paulinist Literature: 1 Cor 11:3 – 16 and Its Context." *CBQ* 42 (1980): 196 – 215.

Trummer, Peter. "Corpus Paulinum—Corpus Pastorale. Zur Ortung der Paulustradition in den Pastoralbriefen." Pages 122–45 in Karl Kertelge, editor, *Paulus in den neutestamentlichen Spätschriften.* QD 89. Freiburg et al.: Herder, 1981.

Trummer, Peter. *Die Paulustradition der Pastoralbriefe.* BBET 8. Frankfurt et al.: Peter Lang, 1978.

Tuckett, Christopher. *Reading the New Testament: Methods of Interpretation*, 4th ed. London: SPCK, 1994.

Turner, Eric G. *Greek Papyri: An Introduction.* Oxford: Clarendon, 1968.

Turner, Eric G. *The Typology of the Early Codex.* Philadelphia: Fortress, 1977.

Twomey, Jay. *2 Corinthians: Crisis and Conflict.* Phoenix Guides to the New Testament, 8. Sheffield: Sheffield Phoenix Press, 2013.

Unnik, Willem C. Van. "De la règle Μήτε προσθεῖναι μήτε ἀφελεῖν dans l'histoire du canon." *VC* 3 (1949): 1–36.

Vegge, Ivar. *2 Corinthians—A Letter about Reconciliation: A Psychagogical, Epistolographical and Rhetorical Analysis.* WUNT 2. 239. Tübingen: Mohr Siebeck, 2008.

Verbrugge, Verlyn D. *Paul's Style of Church Leadership Illustrated by his Instructions to the Corinthians on the Collection: To Command or not to Command.* San Francisco: Mellen Research University Press, 1992.

Verhoef, Eduard. "Pseudepigraphic Paulines in the New Testament." *HvTSt* 59 (2003): 991–1005.

Verhoef, Eduard. "The Senders of the Letters to the Corinthians and the Use of 'I' and 'We.'" Pages 417–25 in Raimund Bieringer, editor, *The Corinthian Correspondence.* BETL 125. Leuven: Leuven University Press, 1996.

Verner, David C. *The Household of God: The Social World of the Pastoral Epistles.* SBLDS 71. Chico: Scholars Press, 1983.

Vielhauer, Philipp. *Geschichte der urchristlichen Literatur. Einleitung in das Neue Testament, die Apokryphen und die Apostolischen Väter.* De Gruyter Lehrbuch. Berlin & New York: de Gruyter, 1975, reprinted 1978.

Vischer, Lukas. *Die Auslegungsgeschichte von 1. Kor. 6,1-11.Rechtsverzicht und Schlichtung.* BGBE 1. Tübingen: Mohr Siebeck, 1955.

Völter, Daniel. *Paulus und seine Briefe. Kritische Untersuchungen zu einer neuen Grundlegung der paulinischen Briefliteratur und ihrer Theologie.* Strasbourg: Heitz, 1905.

Vos, Johan S. "Die Argumentation des Paulus in 1 Kor. 1.10-3.4." Pages 87–119 in Bieringer, Reimund, editor, *The Corinthian Correspondence.* BETL 125. Leuven: University Press & Peeters, 1996.

Walker, Donald Dale. *Paul's Offer of Leniency (2 Cor 10:1): Populist Ideology and Rhetoric in a Pauline Letter Fragment.* WUNT 2.152. Tübingen: Mohr Siebeck, 2002.

Walker, William O., Jr. "1 Corinthians 11:2-16 and Paul's Views Regarding Women." *JBL* 94 (1975): 94–110.
Walker, William O., Jr. "1 Corinthians 15:29-34 as a Non-Pauline Interpolation." *CBQ* 69 (2007): 84–103.
Walker, William O., Jr. *Interpolations in the Pauline Letters*. JSNTSup 213. Sheffield: Sheffield Academic Press, 2001.
Walker, William O., Jr. "The Vocabulary of 1 Corinthians 11:3-16: Pauline or Non-Pauline?" *JSNT* 35 (1989): 75–88.
Wall, Robert W. "The Function of the Pastoral Letters within the Pauline Canon of the New Testament: A Canonical Approach." Pages 27–44 in Stanley E. Porter, editor, *The Pauline Canon*. Pauline Studies, 1. Leiden: Brill, 2004.
Wallis, P. "Ein neuer Auslegungsversuch der Stelle I. Kor. 4,6." *TLZ* 75 (1950): 506–08.
Wanamaker, Charles A. "A Rhetoric of Power: Ideology and 1 Corinthians 1-4." Pages 115–37 in Trevor J. Burke and J. Keith Elliott, editor, *Paul and the Corinthians: Studies on a Community in Conflict. Essays in Honour of Margaret Thrall*. NovTSup 109. Leiden: Brill, 2003.
Wanamaker, Charles A. "'By the Power of God.' Rhetoric and Ideology in 2 Corinthians 10-13." Pages 194–221 in David B. Cowler et al., editors, *Fabrics of Discourse: Essays in Honor of Vernon K. Robbins*. Harrisburg et al.: Trinity Press International, 2003.
Warren, David Harold. "The Text of the Apostle in the Second Century: A Contribution to the History of Its Reception." Th.D. dissertation, Harvard University, 2001.@ #15
Watson, Duane F. "The Contributions and Limitations of Greco-Roman Rhetorical Theory for Constructing the Rhetorical and Historical Situations of a Pauline Epistle." Pages 125–51 in Stanley E. Porter and Dennis L. Stamps, editors, *The Rhetorical Interpretation of Scripture: Essays from the 1996 Malibu Conference*. JSNTSup 180. Sheffield: Sheffield Academic Press, 1999.
Watson, Duane F. "1 Corinthians 10:23-11:1 in the Light of Greco-Roman Rhetoric: The Role of Rhetorical Questions." *JBL* 108 (1989): 301–18. #10
Watson, Duane F., editor. *Persuasive Artistry: Studies in New Testament Rhetoric in Honor of George A. Kennedy*. JSNTSup 50. Sheffield: Academic Press, 1991.
Watson, Duane F. "Paul's Rhetorical Strategy in I Corinthians 15." Pages 231–49 in Stanley E. Porter and Thomas H. Olbricht, editors, *Rhetoric and the New Testament: Essays from the 1992 Heidelberg Conference*. JSNTSup 90. Sheffield: JSOT, 1993.
Watson, Duane F. "Paul's Boasting in 2 Corinthians 10-13 as Defense of his Honor: A Socio-Rhetorical Analysis." Pages 260–75 in Anders Eriksson, Thomas H. Olbricht, and Walter Übelacker, editors, *Rhetorical Argumentation in Biblical Texts: Essays from the Lund 2000 Conference*. ESEC. Harrisburg: Trinity International, 2002.
Watson, Duane F. "The Three Species of Rhetoric and the Study of the Pauline Epistles." Pages 25–47 in J. Paul Sampley and Peter Lampe, editors, *Paul and Rhetoric*. T & T Clark Biblical Studies. New York and London: T & T Clark, 2010.

Watson, Duane F. and Alan J. Hauser, editors. *Rhetorical Criticism of the Bible: A Comprehensive Bibliography with Notes on History and Method.* BibInt 4. Leiden: Brill, 1994.

Watson, Francis. "2 Cor. x.-xiii and Paul's Painful Letter to the Corinthians." *JTS* 35 (1984): 324–46.

Webb, William J. *Returning Home: New Covenant and Second Exodus as the Context for Second Corinthians 6.14-7.1.* JSNTSup 85. Sheffield: JSOT, 1993.

Wedderburn, A. J. M. "The Problem of the Denial of the Resurrection in I Corinthians xv." *NovT* 23 (1981): 229–41.

Wegner, Mark I. "The Rhetorical Strategy of 1 Corinthians 15." *CurTM* 31 (2004): 438–55.

Weiss, Johannes. "Beiträge zur Paulinischen Rhetorik." Pages 165–248 in *Theologische Studien: Herrn Wirk. Oberkonsistorialrath Professor D. Bernard Weiss zu seinem 70. Geburtstage dargebracht.* Göttingen: Vandenhoeck & Ruprecht, 1897.

Weiss, Johannes. *Earliest Christianity: A History of the Period A. D. 30-150.* Books I-II. Edited by F. C. Grant. New York: Harper and Row, 1959. Reprint of the 1937 edition.

Weiss, Johannes. *Earliest Christianity: A History of the Period A. D. 30-150.* Books III-V. Completed after the author's death by Rudolf Knopf. Edited by F. C. Grant. New York: Harper and Row, 1959. Reprint of the 1937 edition.

Weiss, Johannes. *Der erste Korintherbrief*, 9th ed. KEK 5. Göttingen: Vandenhoeck & Ruprecht, 1910.

Weiss, Johannes. Review of Anton Halmel, *Der Vierkapitelbrief im zweiten Korintherbrief des Apostels Paulus* (Essen: Baedeker, 1894), in the *TLZ* 17 (1894): 512–14.

Weiße, Christian Hermann. *Philosophischer Dogmatik oder Philosophie des Christentums.* Leipzig: Hirzel, 1855.

Weitzman, Kurt. "Illustrated Rolls and Codices in Greco-Roman Antiquity." Pages 165–76 in Handrik D. L. Vervliet, editor, *The Book through Five Thousand Years.* New York & London: Phaidon, 1972.

Welborn, L. L. *An End to Enmity: Paul and the "Wrongdoer" of Second Corinthians.* BZNW 185. Berlin and New York: De Gruyter, 2011.

Welborn, L. L. "On the Discord in Corinth: 1 Corinthians 1-4 and Ancient Politics." *JBL* 106 (1987): 85–111.

Welborn, L. L. "The First Letter of Paul to the Corinthians." Pages 1999–2000 in Michael D. Coogan, editor, *The New Oxford Annotated Bible, fully revised fourth edition. New Revised Standard Verion.* New York: Oxford University Press, 2010.

Welborn, L. L. "The Identification of 2 Corinthians 10-13 with the 'Letter of Tears.'" *NovT* 37 (1995): 138–53.

Welborn, L. L. "Like Broken Pieces of a Ring: 2 Cor 1,1-2,13; 7,5-16 and Ancient Theories of Literary Unity." *NTS* 42 (1996): 559–83. Reprinted, pages 95–131 in L. L. Welborn, *Politics and Rhetoric in the Corinthian Epistles.* Macon: Mercer University Press, 1997.

Welborn, L. L. *Paul, the Fool of Christ: A Study of 1 Corinthians 1-4 in the Comic-philosophic Tradition.* JSNTSup 293. London: T & T Clark International, 2005.

Welborn, L. L. *Politics and Rhetoric in the Corinthian Epistles.* Macon: Mercer University Press, 1997.
Wendland, Heinz-Dietrich. *Die Briefe an die Korinther.* NTD 7. Göttingen: Vandenhoeck & Ruprecht, 1968.
Wenschkewitz, Hans. *Die Spiritualisierung der Kultusgriffe. Tempel, Priester und Opfer im Neuen Testament.* Angelos-Beiheft 4. Leipzig: Pfeiffer, 1932.
White John L. *The Apostle of God: Paul and the Promise of Abraham.* Peabody: Hendrickson, 1999.
White John L. *The Form and Function of the Body of the Greek Letter: A Study of the Letter-Body in the Non-Literary Papryi and in Paul the Apostle.* Missoula: Scholars Press, 1972.
White John L. *Light from Ancient Letters.* Philadelphia: Fortress, 1986.
White John L. "A Note on Zenon's Letter Filing." *BASP* 13 (1976): 129–31.
Wickert, Ulrich. "Einheit und Eintract der Kirche im Präskript des ersten Korintherbriefes." *ZNW* 50 (1959): 73–82.
Widmann, Hans. "Herstellung und Vertrieb des Buches in der griechisch-römischen Welt." Pages 546–640 in Volume 8.3–4 of Bertold Hack and Bernhard Wendt, editors, *Archiv für Geschichte des Buchwesens.* Frankfurt: Buchhändler-Vereinigung GmbH, 1967.
Widmann, Martin. "Die vier Phasen des Konflikts zwischen Paulus und den Korinthern: Eine Rekonstruktion der Korrespondenz insbesondere des Thesenbriefs der Korinther und des Antwortbriefs des Paulus." Pages 799–833 in Oswald Bayer and G. U. Wanzeck, editors, *Festgabe für Friedrich Lang zum 65. Geburtstag am 6. September 1978.* Tübingen: Evangelisch-Theologisches Seminar der Universität, Typescript, 1978.
Widmann, Martin. "1 Kor 2 $^{6-16}$: Ein Einspruch gegen Paulus." *ZNW* 70 (1979): 44–53.
Wilckens, Ulrich. *Weisheit und Torheit. Eine exegetisch-religionsgeschichtliche Untersuchung zu 1. Kor. 1 und 2.* Beiträge zur historischen Theologie 26. Tübingen: Mohr, 1959.
Wilder, Amos N. *Early Christian Rhetoric: The Language of the Gospel.* Cambridge: Harvard University Press, 1971. Reprint of the 1964 edition.
Willis, Wendell L. "An Apostolic Apologia? The Form and Function of 1 Corinthians 9." *Journal for the Study of the New Testament* 24 (1985): 33–48.
Wilson, Robert McLachlan. "Gnosticism." Pages 164–81 in Dan Cohn-Sherbok and John M. Court, editors, *Religious Diversity in the Graeco-Roman World.* The Biblical Seminar 79. Sheffield: Sheffield Academic Press, 2001.
Wilson, Robert McLachlan. "Gnosis at Corinth." Pages 102–14 in M. D. Hooker and S. G. Wilson, editors. *Paul and Paulinism: Essays in Honour of C. K. Barrett.* London: SPCK, 1982.
Windisch, Hans. *Der zweite Korintherbrief.* Kritisch-exegetischer Kommentar über das Neue Testament 6. Edited by Georg Strecker. Göttingen: Vandenhoeck & Ruprecht, 1970.

Winter, Bruce W. *After Paul Left Corinth: The Influence of Secular Ethics and Social Change.* Grand Rapids: Eerdmans, 2001.

Winter, Bruce W. *Philo and Paul Among the Sophists: Alexandrian and Corinthian Responses to a Julio-Claudian Movement,* 2nd ed. Grand Rapids: Eerdmans, 2002.

Winter, Bruce W. *Roman Wives, Roman Widows: The Appearance of New Women and the Pauline Communities.* Grand Rapids: Eerdmans, 2003. #5 #7 #8

Winter, Bruce W. "The 'Underlays' of Conflict and Compromise in 1 Corinthians." Pages 139–55 in Trevor J. Burke and J. Keith Elliott, editor, *Paul and the Corinthians: Studies on a Community in Conflict. Essays in Honour of Margaret Thrall.* Novum Testamentum Supplement 109. Leiden: Brill, 2003.

Wire, Antoinentte C. *The Corinthian Women Prophets: A Reconstruction through Paul's Rhetoric.* Minneapolis: Fortress, 1990.

Wischmeyer, Oda. *Der höchste Weg: Das 13. Kapitel des 1. Korintherbriefes.* SNT 13. Gütersloh: Mohn, 1981.

Witherington, Ben III. *Conflict and Community in Corinth: A Socio-Rhetorical Commentary on 1 and 2 Corinthians.* Grand Rapids: Eerdmans, 1995.

Witherington, Ben III. *New Testament Rhetoric: An Introductory Guide to the Art of Persuasion iin and of the New Testament.* Eugene: Cascade, 2009.

Wolff, Christian. *Der erste Brief des Paulus an die Korinther,* 2nd ed. Theologischer Handkommentar zum Neuen Testament 7. Leipzig: Evangelische Verlagsanstalt, 2011. Two volumes.

Wolff, Christian. *Der zweite Brief des Paulus an die Korinther,* 2nd ed. Theologischer Handkommentar zum Neuen Testament 8. Leipzig: Evangelische Verlagsanstalt, 2011.

Wolter, Michael. *Die Pastoralbriefe als Paulustradition.* Forschungen zur Religion und Literatur des Alten und Neuen Testaments 146. Göttingen: Vandenhoeck & Ruprecht, 1988.

Wouters, A. "From Papyrus Roll to Papyrus Codex: Some Technical Aspects of the Ancient Book Fabrication." *Manuscripts of the Middle East* 5 (1990–91 [1993]): 9–19.

Werde, Wilhelm. *Die Echtheit des zweiten Thessalonicherbriefes.* Texte und Untersuchungen 9.2. Leipzig: Hinrichs, 1903.

Wright, N. T. *Colossians and Philemon.* Tyndale New Testament Commentaries. Leicester: Inter-Varsity; Grand Rapids: Eerdmans,

Wright, N. T. *Paul in Fresh Perspective.* Minneapolis: Fortress, 2005.

Wuellner, Wilhelm. "Epistolography and Rhetoric in 1 Corinthians." SNTS paper 1988.

Wuellner, Wilhelm. "Greek Rhetoric and Pauline Argumentation." Pages 177–88 in William R. Schoedel and Robert L. Wilken, editors, *Early Christian Literature and the Classical Intellectual Tradition: In honorem Robert M. Grant.* Théologie Historique 54. Paris: Etudes Beauchesne, 1979.

Wünsch, Hans-Michael. *Der paulinische Brief 2 Kor 1 - 9 als kommunikative Handlung. Eine rhetorisch-literaturwissenschaftliche Untersuchung*. Theologie 4. Münster: Lit-Verlag, 1996.

Yeo, Khiok-Khng. *Rhetorical Interaction in 1 Corinthians 8 and 10: A Formal Analysis with Preliminary Suggestions for a Chinese, Cross-Cultural Hermeneutic*. Leiden: Brill, 1995.

Young, Frances, and Ford, David F. *Meaning and Truth in 2 Corinthians*. London, 1987.

Zeilinger, Franz. *Krieg und Friede in Korinth: Kommentar zum 2. Korintherbrief des Apostels Paulus*, 2 volumes. Vienna et al.: Böhlau, 1992–97.

Zeller, Dieter. *Der erste Brief an die Korinther*. Kritisch-exegetischer Kommentar über das Neue Testament 5. Göttingen: Vandenhoeck & Ruprecht, 2010.

Zmijewski, Josef. *Paulus, Knecht und Apostel Christi. Amt und Amtsträger in paulinischer Sicht*. Stuttgart: Katholisches Bibelwerk, 1986.

Zmijewski, Josef. *Der Stil der paulinischen "Narrenrede". Analyse der Sprachgestaltung in 2 Kor 11,1—12,10 als Beitrag zur Methodik von Stiluntersuchungen neutestamentlicher Texte*. Bonner biblische Beiträge 52. Cologne and Bonn: Hanstein, 1978.

Zuntz, Günther. *The Text of the Epistles: A Disquisition upon the Corpus Paulinum*. British Academy Schweich Lectures, 1946. London: British Academy/Oxford University Press, 1953.

Subject Index

2 Corinthians, disunity, 11–23

Apostolic Conference (Jerusalem), 114

Cicero, 6
codex, 255–61
collections of money, 114

Demosthenes, 6

editing of Corinthian correspondence, 243, 250
Ephesians, Letter to the, 248–49

factionalism in the Corinthian church, 160–61
frame letter, 3

generosity, 30
genus/genera of rhetoric, 15, 17–18
Gnosticism/proto-Gnosticism, 86–91

hairstyles, 112–13, 115

Jerusalem offering, 11

libertinism, sexual, 122, 125–28, 156

literary criticism, 43–57
Lord's Supper, 87, 109, 111, 115–16

Macedonians, 169

partition theories, 58–72
Pastoral Epistles, 26–32, 34, 88, 90–91, 100–101, 243–48, 260
Pauline corpus, 8
pseudonymity, 8

Qumran community, 20

redaction criticism, 7, 21, 24, 85–86, 91–101
resurrection of the dead, rejection of, 123, 128–34, 136, 151–54, 157–59
rhetoric, 4, 134, 154–55, 161, 169–70, 177–88, 197–201, 211–22, 233–35
rhetoric of letters, 5–7

scroll, 255–59
silencing of women, 51–52

tolerance, 30
travel plans, Paul's, 14, 54, 56, 62, 64, 67, 69, 75

Author Index

Allo, E. B., 77n2, 119n11, 146n21, 146n36, 148n96
Amador, J. D. H., 17–18, 38nn32–33, 38n34, 38nn36–38

Bachmann, Philipp, 80n91, 146n19
Barnett, Paul, 19, 39n58, 42n146, 209n16
Barr, David L., 22, 40n100
Barrett, C. K., 36n8, 40n106, 41n125, 42n143, 80n92, 80n94, 95, 102n2, 103n19, 103n28, 103n32, 114, 119n1, 120n38, 131, 145n12, 146n36, 146n38, 147n51, 147n57, 147n61, 148n66, 148n72, 165n6
Bauer, Walter, 41n131, 250n1
Baumert, Norbert, 21
Becker, Eve-Marie, 21, 82
Belleville, Linda L., 38n40, 82n137, 120n44
Berger, Klaus, 173n11, 173n12
Betz, Hans Dieter, 9n1, 11, 21–23, 31, 35n2, 36nn3–4, 37n14, 38n35, 40n97, 40n116, 41n124, 41n136, 83n142, 103n28, 145n7, 146n18, 167, 173n8, 173n15, 173nn17–18, 173n20, 191n7, 193–94, 232, 238nn8–9
Bieringer, Reimund, 19, 36n5, 39n57, 145n7
Bitzer, Lloyd F., 15, 36n9, 37nn10–11

Bloomquist, L. Gregory, 37n16
Bornkamm, Günther, 16, 20–26, 28, 30, 39n77, 40n115, 40n118, 40nn120–22, 41nn126–27, 80n89, 81n112, 192n17, 193, 209n4, 259
Brandenburger, Egon, 145n12, 148n92
Brendle, Albert, 36n9
Brown, Raymond E., 102n11
Brox, Norbert, 41n130, 102n4, 102n8
Bruce, F. F., 77n11
Bultmann, Rudolf, 23, 36n7, 40n115, 191n6, 191n11, 191n14, 193, 209n6, 210n17
Bünker, Michael, 149n99
Burgos Núñez, Miguel de, 63, 81n115

Campenhausen, Hans von, 251n8, 252n9
Carey, Greg and L. Gregory Bloomquist, editors. *Vision and Persuasion: Rhetorical Dimensions of Apocalyptic Discourse*. St. Louis: Chalice Press, 1999
Castelli, Elizabeth A., 41n128
Church, F. Forrester, 37n15
Ciampa, Roy E., 132, 148n76, 148n82, 148n87, 149n105, 149n109, 149n119
Clabeaux, John J., 262n22
Classen, Carl Joachim, 230n31
Collange, Jean-Francois, 21
Collins, John J., 251n4

Collins, Raymond F., 9n3, 41n130, 79n62, 81n112, 82nn136–37, 82nn139–40, 83n143, 83n157, 102n10, 110, 119n13, 119n20, 119n23, 119n30, 119nn34–35, 120nn43–44, 120nn46–47, 120n50, 145n1, 146n20, 146n23, 146n29, 146n39, 147n41, 149nn96–97, 149n101, 149n102, 149n111, 173n9, 173n16, 210n17, 210n19, 251n3, 252n14
Concannon, Cavan W., 261n7
Conzelmann, Hans, 78n15, 78n33, 78n37, 79n46, 79n57, 79n60, 79n62, 79n69, 80n90, 103n21, 103n30, 119n1
Couchoud, Paul-Louis, 36n6, 58, 63, 81n117
Craig, Clarence Tucker, 79n63, 79n67, 79n71, 82n130

Danker, Frederick W., 38n40, 173n15
Dautzenberg, Gerhard, 21, 39n80
Davies, Steven L., 22, 40n99
Delobel, Joël, 111
DeSilva, David A., 16–17, 37n9, 38n28, 38nn30–31
Dinkler, Erich, 58, 81n112
Dodd, Brian J., 83n144, 145n2
Dodds, E. R., 191n10
Donahue, John R., 10n6
Duff, Paul B., 189n2, 190nn3–4, 191n5, 209n6
Duling, Dennis, 22, 40n98

Ehrman, Bart, 10n8, 22, 40n91
Emmerling, Christian August Gottfried, 36n6
Engelmann, Michaela, 260, 262n31
Eriksson, Anders, 146n40, 147n48, 148n65, 148nn74–75, 149n98, 149n100, 149nn115–16, 150nn122–23
Esler, Philip F., 20, 39n71

Fee, Gordon D., 78n38, 103n27, 111, 119nn3–4, 119n14, 119n16, 119n35, 149n96

Filson, Floyd V., 41n142
Fiorenza, Elisabeth Schüssler, 37n9, 113, 119n24, 119n29
Fischer, Karl Martin, 22, 40n93, 81n112
Fitzgerald, John T., 38n40, 191n13
Fitzmyer, Joseph A., 20, 41n135, 54, 78n15, 78n31, 79n71, 83nn146–48, 119n17, 119n28, 119n32, 126, 129, 132, 145nn5–6, 146n20, 146nn23–24, 146n28, 146n33, 147nn49–50, 147n55, 148n65, 148n71, 148n77, 148n79, 148n81, 148nn83–84, 148n88, 149n95, 149n101, 149n104, 149nn108–9, 149n112, 149n115
Frede, H. J., 262nn22–23
Freed, Edwin, 22, 40n88
Frei, Jörg, 251n5
Frend, W. H. C., 41n128
Furnish, Victor Paul, 22, 40n87, 41n141, 42n145, 42nn150–51, 173n7, 193, 209n1, 229n1, 230nn27–28

Gamble, Harry Y., 255–58, 261n2, 261n5, 261n8, 261n14, 261n17, 262nn20–22, 262n24, 262n26
Garland, David E., 19, 39n59, 77n10, 79n60, 165n5, 168, 173n10, 173n14
Georgi, Dieter, 39n78, 41n123, 79n66, 82nn126–27, 82n130, 191nn7–9, 194
Gnilka, Joachim, 20
Goguel, Maurice, 11, 35n2, 58, 63, 81n118
Goulder, Michael, 16, 38n26
Gräßer, Erich, 22, 40n101
Gruber, Maria Margareta, 21, 38n40, 39n81, 41n128

Haelst, Joseph van, 261n19
Hafemann, Scott J., 19, 38n40, 39n63
Hagge, H., 63, 81n109
Hall, David R., 18–19, 39n50
Halmel, Anton, 36n6
Hanson, A. T., 41n130
Harris, Murray J., 19, 39n64, 40n90, 42n149, 209n16, 210nn17–18, 210n20
Harris, Stephen, 22

Hays, Richard B., 119n6, 126, 129, 146n27, 147n41, 147nn52–53, 147n60, 148n68, 149n96
Heckel, Ulrich, 38n40
Heilig, Christoph, 40n122, 190n4
Heinrici, C. F. G., 149n96
Héring, Jean, 81n112, 102n15, 149n96
Herzer, Jens, 251n5, 251n6
Holland, Glenn, 38n40
Hooker, Morna D., 119n24
Horn, Friedrich Wilhelm, 19, 39n56
Horsley, Richard A., 39n70, 45, 49, 77n7, 78n16, 78n41, 78n43, 79n44, 102n7, 110, 113, 118, 119n15, 119n31, 120n49, 147n59, 148n69
Hughes, Frank W., ix–xi, 9, 9n5, 37n17, 102n9, 164n2, 210n28, 238n3, 251n6
Hughes, Philip E., 42n486
Hultgren, Stephen, 20, 22, 39nn68–69, 40n102
Hurd, John C., Jr., 58, 80nn85–86, 81n112, 119n2, 146n20
Hyldahl, Niels, 16, 38n25

Janßen, Martina, 251n5
Jeremias, Joachim, 103n33
Jewett, Robert, ix–xi, 36n9, 37n13, 37n17, 39n72, 40n119, 41nn133–34, 42n153, 80nn78–79, 80n95, 80n97, 82n129, 82n132, 82n134, 102n6, 103n24, 120nn40–41, 145n12, 148nn85–86, 148nn90–91, 149n113, 165n8, 173n19, 191n14, 209n13, 229n2, 231n19
Johnson, William A., 261n2
Jones, Ivor H., 19, 38nn44–48, 39n49
Joubert, Stephan, 173n14
Judge, E. A., 210n30

Kearsley, R. A., 262n22
Kistemaker, Simon J., 19, 39n62, 120n37
Klauck, Hans-Josef, 82n139, 120n46
Klein, Hans, 40n115
Knight, George W., III, 251n6

Koester, Helmut, 22, 40n95, 41n129, 87, 102nn4–5, 103n16

Lambrecht, Jan, 19, 39n57, 39n61
Lampe, Peter, 82nn138–39, 120nn45–46
Lang, Friedrich, 80n77, 80nn81–82
Lausberg, Heinrich, 164n1, 165n7, 210nn25–26
Liddell, H. G., 41n132
Lietzmann, Hans, 78n23, 79n60, 83n144, 103n22, 119n6, 119n11, 145n2, 146n21
Lieu, Judith M., 262n22
Lincoln, Andrew T., 10n7
Lindemann, Andreas, 19, 39n52, 119n35
Llewelyn, S. R., 262n22
Loisy, Alfred, 36n7, 58, 63, 81n110
Long, Fredrick J., 18–19, 38n39, 38nn41–43
Loraux, Nicole, 229n10
Lull, David J., 77n10

MacDonald, Dennis Ronald, 82n137, 120n44
Mack, Burton L., 147n43
Martin, Dale B., 145n8, 148n68, 148n75
Martin, Michael Wade, 230n32
Martin, Ralph P., 210n24
Martin, Troy W., 9
Martinez, David G., 262n30
Marxsen, Willi, 22, 40n94, 81n112
McCormick, M., 257, 261n11
McGinn, Sheila E., 119n24
Meeks, Wayne A., 20, 39n70m, 82n137, 120n44, 261n7
Meiser, Martin, 19, 39n54
Merklein, Helmut, 19, 39n55, 249, 252nn12–13
Merz, Annette, 102n13, 103n29
Meyer, Heinrich August Wilhelm, 77n11, 79n70
Milligan, George, 132n41
Mitchell, Margaret M., 22, 36n8, 40nn105–9, 40n113, 44–54, 57,

77n5, 77nn8–9, 78nn17–19, 78n25, 78nn28–29, 78nn34–35, 78n40, 79n49, 79n54, 79n58, 79n61, 79n68, 79n74, 80n84, 83n151, 83nn153–54, 114, 120n39, 146n22, 146n40, 147n45, 149n115, 165n5, 167–68, 173n1, 173nn5–6, 238n4, 238n7
Mitton, Charles Leslie, 10n7
Moffatt, James, 119n28
Morris, Leon, 120n37
Moss, Candida R., 41n128
Moulton, James Hope, 41n132
Mount, Christopher, 80n75
Müller-Bardorff, Johannes, 81n112
Murphy-O'Connor, Jerome, 81n120

Nickle, Keith F., 237n1, 238n10

Oliveira, Anacleto de, 38n40, 146n19

Pagels, Elaine H., 91, 102n12, 148n94
Parsons, Mikeal C., 230n32
Perkins, Pheme, 79n60, 79n71
Perrin, Norman, 22, 40n98
Pervo, Richard I., 22, 40n103
Pesch, Rudolf, 21, 63, 81n114
Pfitzner, V. C., 146n31, 146n34
Pietersen, Lloyd K., 102n10
Plummer, Alfred, 41n142, 42n146, 83n144, 120n36, 146n21
Pokorný, Petr, 10n7
Preisker, Herbert, 36n7
Probst, Hermann, 78n21

Reumann, John, 37n16
Richards, E. Randolph, 262n22
Roberts, Colin Henderson., 256–57, 261n1, 261n6, 261n9, 261n10, 261n12, 261nn15–16, 261n18, 262n30
Robertson, Archibald, 42n146, 83n144, 120n36, 145n2, 146n21
Robinson, James M., 41n129, 87, 102n5, 103n16
Roetzel, Calvin J., 22, 40n105, 40nn110–13, 42n154, 173nn13–14, 191n12, 196, 209n14, 210nn21–23, 229n3, 229nn5–6, 232, 237n2, 238n6
Rosner, Brian S., 132, 148n76, 148n82, 148n87, 149n105, 149n107, 149n119
Rothschild, Clare K., 251n5
Rudolf, Kurt, 83n156, 145n12, 148n93
Russell, D. A., 229n10, 230n29

Sampley, J. Paul, 9n2, 78n15, 132, 145n15, 145n17, 146n25, 146n31, 146n40, 148nn72–73, 229n18, 230n20
Sandt, H. van de, 119n1, 120n50
Saw, Insawn, 149n115
Schenk, Wolfgang, 21, 36n3, 39n79, 58–61, 80nn87–88, 80n96, 80n98, 92, 93, 102n14, 103n18
Schenke, Hans-Martin, 22, 40n93, 81n112
Scherbenske, Eric W., 262n22
Schlarb, Egbert, 91, 102n9
Schmeller, Thomas, 19, 39n66, 39n73, 39nn74–76
Schmiedel, Paul Wilhelm, 78n22
Schmithals, Walter, 21–22, 36n6, 58, 61–62, 66, 80n99, 80n101, 81nn103–4, 83n148, 83n156, 92, 102n6, 103n17, 145n6
Schnelle, Udo, 19, 39n53, 249, 250n2, 251n7, 252n10
Schrage, Wolfgang, 45, 77n14, 79nn64–65, 82n131, 82n135, 83nn147–48, 83n150, 83n155, 102n7, 118, 119n7, 119n12, 119n18, 119n20, 119n22, 119n33, 120n42, 120n50, 145nn5–6, 145n10, 146n20, 146nn23–24, 146nn30–33, 146n36, 146n38, 147nn42–43, 147n46, 147n58, 147n60, 147n63, 147n65, 147n70, 147n78, 147nn88–90, 149n103, 149n106, 149n110, 149n118, 150n120, 164n3, 165n4
Schulz, Siegfried, 150n123
Schweitzer, Albert, 126, 146n26
Schweizer, Eduard, 86, 102n1
Scott, Ernest Findlay, 97, 103n25

Author Index

Scott, James M., 19, 39n60
Scott, Robert, 132n41
Sellin, Gerhard, 63–66, 81n112, 82nn122–24, 145n8
Semler, Johann Salomo, 11–12, 35n1, 193
Senft, Christophe, 63, 78n30, 81n113, 119n1
Skeat, T. C., 256, 261n6, 261nn8–10, 261n12, 261nn15–16, 262n30
Smit, Joop F. M., 146n40
Snyder, Graydon F., 75, 83n152, 103n26
Söding, Thomas, 19, 39n51
Spicq, C., 95, 103nn19–20
Stamps, Dennis L., 37n9
Stegman, Thomas D., 19, 39n65
Stephenson, Alan M. G., 16, 37n24
Stirewalt, M. Luther, 82n132
Stockhausen, Carol, 38n40
Stowers, Stanley K., 229n12
Strecker, Georg, 86, 102n3
Suhl, Alfred, 53, 62, 79n65, 80n94, 81nn105–6
Sundermann, Hans-Georg, 38n40

Talbert, Charles H., 120n37, 252n14
Taylor, N. H., 22, 40n96
Theissen, Gerd, 83n141, 120n48
Thiselton, Anthony C., 80n97, 81n108, 102n7, 127, 129, 135, 145n9, 146n20, 146n23, 146nn34–35, 147n42, 147n54, 148n67, 148n80, 148n84, 149nn114–15
Thrall, Margaret E., 16, 22, 32, 38n27, 40n89, 41n138, 42n144, 42n147, 42n152
Towner, Philip H., 251n6
Trobisch, David, 256, 261n3, 262n22
Trompf, G. W., 78n42
Turner, Eric G., 257, 261n13
Twomey, Jay, 39n67

Verbrugge, Verlyn D., 167, 173nn3–4
Vielhauer, Philipp, 22, 39n85, 40n117, 80n75, 81n112

Walker, Donald Dale, 21, 39n83
Walker, William O., Jr., 78n42, 82n128
Wanamaker, Charles A., 22, 40n92
Watson, Duane F., xi, 9n4, 15, 37n9, 37n12, 37n18, 147nn43–44, 147n56, 149n115, 149n117
Watson, Francis, 22, 40n86
Weiss, Johannes, 15, 36n6, 37n19, 37n21, 44–51, 54–55, 58, 62–63, 77n1, 77nn3–4, 77nn12–13, 78n20, 78nn26–27, 78n30, 78n32, 78n36, 78n39, 79n45, 79n48, 79n50, 79nn52–53, 79n56, 79n59, 79nn72–73, 80n76, 80n83, 80n93, 81n102, 81nn107–8, 82n133, 83n145, 92, 93, 103n23, 103nn30–31, 119n11, 131, 145n3, 146n21, 147n46, 147n64, 147n75, 148n75, 157
Welborn, L. L., 15, 21–22, 37n20, 37nn22–23, 38n29, 40n104, 63, 81n111, 83n149, 195, 209nn11–12, 209n15, 229n4, 229n8
Wendland, Heinz-Dietrich, 21, 39n84, 77n2
Widmann, Martin, 63, 81n119
Wilckens, Ulrich, 83n156
Wilson, N. G., 229n10
Windisch, Hans, 36n7, 41n137, 41n142, 193
Winter, Bruce W., 108, 119nn8–9, 110n10
Wire, Antoinentte C., 82n137, 120n44
Wischmeyer, Oda, 165n5
Witherington, Ben, III, 173n16
Wolff, Christian, 149n96, 149n114
Wolter, Michael, 102n10

Yeo, Khiok-Khng, 63, 81n116

Zeilinger, Franz, 145nn13–16, 145nn18–19
Zuntz, Günther, 260–61, 262n32
Zwaan, Johannes de, 58, 81n112

Index of Biblical Citations

HEBREW BIBLE

Genesis
1:26-27, 123
2:7, 133
2:17, 135
2:24, 126
3:14, 135
3:19, 135

Leviticus
26:12, 124

Numbers
14, 127

Deuteronomy
25:4, 101
32:21, 48

Isaiah
25:8, 135
27:13, 149n105
43:6, 124
52:11, 124

Jeremiah
31:9, 124
32:38, 124

Ezekiel
20:34, 124
20:41, 12
37:27, 124

Joel
2:1, 149n105

Zephaniah
1:14-16, 149n105

Ecclesiastes
7:5, 83n152

NEW TESTAMENT

Matthew, 7
18:35, 148n89
23:28, 148n89
24:33, 148n89

Mark, 7
9:45, 76

Acts
13:1-3, 72
18:1-3, 115
18:12-17, 72, 115
20:3, 71, 213

20:16, 209
21:17-40, 239n10
24:17, 238n10
24:26, 238n10

Romans, 6, 15
6, 124
12:4-5, 111
15:26, 234
16:1-23, 213
16:3, 175
16:3-4, 211
16:7, 246
16:17-20, 24, 31, 43
16:25-27, 43

1 Corinthians, 3, 5, 9, 11
1–3, 109
1:1, 88
1:1-9, 81n118, 151–52
1:1-10, 56
1:5, 158–59, 170
1:5-6, 88
1:7, 88
1:1–4:21, 3, 10n8, 48, 55, 58, 65, 69, 71, 108–9, 111–12
1:10, 76, 152
1:10ff., 108
1:10-12, 67
1:10-14, 75
1:10-17, 108
1:10–4:21, 60, 67, 75, 108
1:11, 60, 69, 234
1:11-12, 160
1:11ff., 60
1:11–4:21, 153, 158
1:1–6:11 + 7:1–8:3 + 9:19-23 + 10:23–11:1 + 12:1-31a + 14:1c-40 + 12:31b–13:13 + 16:5-12, 69
1:11-17, 154
1:11-31, 153
1:12, 75, 77, 136, 154
1:13, 108
1:14-17, 88
1:18-31, 70, 109, 154

1:26, 75
1:26-31, 158
1:30, 88
2–3, 161
2:1-5, 70, 154
2:1-9, 109
2:2-5, 75
2:5, 158
2:6-15, 154
2:6-16, 70, 158
2:7, 88
2:10–3:4, 109
2:15, 88
2:16, 88
3, 160–62, 199
3:1-3a, 70, 155
3:1-4, 162
3:2, 161–62
3:3b-17, 70
3:4, 154
3:5, 77, 161
3:5-7, 88
3:6, 77
3:6-7, 162
3:6-15, 155
3:16, 89
3:18–4:5, 70, 155
3:22, 77
4:1-21, 59
4:5, 155
4:6, 77
4:6-10, 158
4:6-13, 70, 155
4:8, 130
4:8-13, 89
4:14-16, 75
4:14-21, 70, 155
4:17, 215
4:17-21, 59
4:18, 59, 65
4:18-19, 65
4:19, 56
4:19-21, 65–66
4:20, 65
4:21, 65, 75

Index of Biblical Citations

5, 65, 83n149
5:1, 64, 66
5:1-2, 158–59
5:1-5, 66
5:1-8, 62, 64, 70, 89, 159
5:1-13, 59, 64, 75, 161
5:1–6:11, 153, 155
5:1–14:39, 153
5:1-2, 161
5:2, 65
5:8, 64
5:9, 23, 68, 74, 121
5:9-10, 75
5:9-13, 59, 64, 70
5:13, 62
5:17-21, 59
6, 59
6:1, 59–60, 64
6:1-11, 60–62, 64, 70, 75
6:1-20, 47
6:2, 59
6:2-3, 156
6:8, 156
6:9-10, 59, 156
6:9-11, 89, 156
6:11, 62, 89, 94, 97–98
6:11-12, 44, 69, 71
6:12, 57, 64, 74, 98, 121, 125
6:12-20, 44–45, 55, 57, 59–62, 64, 68, 75, 85, 87, 97–98, 115, 122, 126–27, 160
6:13, 74, 122, 125
6:13-20, 135
6:14, 125
6:15, 126
6:15-16, 126
6:15-17, 121
6:15-18, 75, 98, 122
6:15-20, 126
6:16, 126
6:16-17, 74
6:17-20, 126
6:18, 135
6:19, 59, 122, 126
6:20, 126
6:21, 61

6:20–7:1, 44–45, 71
7, 113
7:1, 53, 62, 69, 75–76, 89, 97–98, 156
7:1-7, 45, 64
7:1-24, 57, 70, 156, 157
7:1-40, 62, 98
7:1–9:23, 64
7:3-4, 76
7:6, 98
7:7, 76, 89, 98
7:9, 76
7:12, 157
7:16, 98
7:17, 98
7:20, 76
7:21, 76
7:24, 98
7:25-40, 57, 70
7:38, 89
8, 46, 60, 65, 89, 93
8:1, 53, 109, 132
8:1-13, 57, 60, 64, 69–70, 72, 76, 157–58
8:1-13 ǀ 9:12-23 + 10:23–11:1, 152, 157
8:1-18, 157
8:1–11:2, 49
8:4-6, 157
8:7, 89, 132
8:7-13, 46
8:13, 47
8:13–9:1, 45, 71–72, 103n30
8:18, 100
9, 59, 101
9:1, 77n10
9:1-2, 66, 195
9:1-18, 195, 259
9:3, 71
9:3ff., 66
9:4, 100
9:7, 101
9:9, 101, 195
9:10, 101, 195
9:1-18, 23, 45–47, 55, 60, 62, 65–66, 72, 94, 100, 194–96, 198–99
9:11, 66

9:12, 66, 198
9:15, 195
9:15-18, 196
9:16, 66
9:17-18, 66, 195
9:18-19, 46–47, 71–72, 100
9:18-24, 60, 198
9:19, 47, 65, 100
9:19-22, 46–47
9:19-23, 48, 60, 70, 76, 100, 157
9:19-24, 198
9:19–10:22, 64
9:21, 96
9:23, 47, 62, 65, 97
9:23-24, 69, 71
9:24, 126
9:24-27, 47, 57, 60, 68, 97, 101, 126
9:24–10:22, 55, 61, 64, 75, 85, 87, 96, 100, 115, 122
9:25, 126, 135
9:26-27, 127
10, 59–60, 89
10:1, 127
10:1-8, 128
10:1-13, 57, 68, 127
10:1-22, 56–57, 59, 65, 69, 72
10:22, 61, 64
10:1-23, 47
10:6, 74, 127
10:6-13, 135
10:7, 97
10:7-13, 127
10:8, 97
10:10, 127
10:11, 127
10:12, 97, 128
10:12-13, 127
10:13, 136
10:14, 97, 122
10:14-22, 68–69, 128
10:14–11:1, 57
10:16, 121, 128
10:20-21, 74, 121
10:21, 122, 128
10:21-29, 94

10:22, 128
10:22-23, 47–48, 69, 71
10:23, 57, 65, 69, 72, 76
10:23ff., 157
10:23-29, 96
10:23–11:1, 48, 57, 65, 69–70, 72, 76, 78n31
10:24, 65
10:29b-30, 90
10:33, 48, 76
11, 55, 68, 71, 109, 111, 120n50
11:1, 65, 98–99
11:1-2, 48–49, 67, 71
11:2, 48, 55, 68, 108, 116, 118
11:2-3, 49
11:2ff., 66
11:2, 23, 87, 99, 107, 110
11:2, 17-34a + 11:3-16 + 16:1-4 + 11:34b, 67, 73, 115
11:2-34, 58–62, 64, 66, 86, 98–99
11:3, 110, 115
11:3-15, 110
11:3-16, 49, 57, 80n75, 99, 111, 113, 116
11:3, 73, 107, 111
11:4-6, 110, 118
11:6, 111, 118
11:7, 111, 118
11:8, 73, 110, 111, 115
11:9, 111
11:10, 111, 118
11:11, 110, 112, 115
11:12, 110, 112, 115
11:13, 118
11:13-15, 112
11:14-15, 112
11:16, 113, 118
11:17, 107–9, 110, 114, 116, 118
11:17-34, 49, 57, 69, 108, 111, 116
11:18, 61, 67, 73, 107–8, 115, 118, 176
11:18-19, 3, 7, 10n8, 67, 73, 108, 115, 153, 160
11:18-22, 108–9
11:18-34, 48, 98, 109
11:19, 67, 108–9

Index of Biblical Citations

11:20, 110
11:21, 110, 118
11:22, 73, 109–10, 116, 118
11:23ff., 109
11:23-25, 49, 87, 109
11:23-26, 99
11:23-33, 109
11:24–12:2, 67
11:25, 110
11:26, 109
11:27-31, 118
11:29, 87, 109, 118
11:33, 74, 116
11:33-34, 79n46, 109, 118
11:34, 50, 55, 61, 64, 68, 110, 114, 118
11:34–12:1, 49–50, 67, 71
12, 76
12–14, 53, 57, 65, 90, 98–99, 112
12:1, 49, 53
12:1-30, 98, 99
12:1-31a, 70
12:3, 76
12:4-30, 50
12:7, 90, 99
12:8, 158
12:9, 158
12:12, 111
12:14, 90
12:14ff., 66
12:15, 66
12:27-30, 157
12:28, 90
12:29-30, 72
12:31, 51
12:31–13:1, 50, 71, 157–59
12:31a, 72
12:31b–13:13, 71, 76, 161
13, 7, 50, 51, 85, 92, 93, 161, 165n5
13:1, 90
13:2, 51
13:3, 162
13:4, 159, 161
13:4-5, 161
13:4-7, 77, 162
13:5-6, 158

13:6, 161
13:7, 90, 93
13:8-10, 159
13:11, 90, 155, 161–62
13:11-12, 77
13:12, 71
13:13–14:1, 51, 71
14, 76, 85, 92–93
14:1, 51, 72
14:1-5, 158
14:1-25, 76
14:1c-33a, 70
14:2-19, 158
14:5, 99
14:18, 99
14:21-23, 158
14:22-25, 158
14:24, 72
14:26-33a, 90
14:29, 90
14:31, 90
14:32-37, 52
14:33a-34, 51–52, 71, 79n55
14:34-35, 51–52
14:33b-36, 51, 99, 100
14:36-37, 52, 71, 79n66
14:37-40, 52, 70, 158
14:39, 94, 95
14:40, 53, 65, 94
14:40–15:1, 69
14:40–15:2, 52–53
15, 65, 92, 148n94, 160
15:1, 65, 128
15:1-2, 135
15:1-8, 87
15:1-11, 53
15:1-57, 68
15:1-58, 53, 55, 57, 59, 75, 96, 122, 124
15:2, 128–29, 135
15:3, 96
15:3-7, 96
15:3-11, 128
15:3-57, 128
15:10-11, 129
15:11, 128

15:12, 123
15:12-19, 129
15:14, 128, 135
15:15, 96
15:17, 68, 135
15:17-19, 128
15:19, 96, 135
15:20-28, 129–30
15:22, 135
15:22-28, 136
15:29-34, 130–31
15:30-32, 136
15:32, 53
15:32-34, 136
15:33, 135
15:34, 149n97
15:35, 122, 132
15:37-41, 132–33
15:42, 134
15:42-44, 133
15:44, 148n90
15:45-46, 74, 122
15:45-49, 130
15:46, 76, 123
15:46-47, 73, 87, 115
15:48-49, 134
15:49, 149n97
15:50-57, 68, 134–35
15:58, 54, 68, 88, 96, 128, 136, 149n97, 149n115
15:58–16:1, 53, 69, 71
16:1, 73, 85, 114–15
16:1-2, 167
16:1-4, 53–54, 56–57, 68, 95, 113–14, 168
16:1-12, 65
16:1-24, 54
16:2, 54, 114
16:2-3, 56, 118
16:2-4, 113
16:3-4, 67
16:3-11, 59
16:4, 79n67
16:4-5, 53–54, 69, 71
16:5-8, 54, 56

16:5-11, 57
16:5-12, 77, 94
16:5-12, 54, 56, 71
16:7, 189n1
16:7-8, 75
16:8, 56
16:10-11, 59, 215
16:12, 57, 94
16:12-13, 54–55, 69, 71
16:13, 65
16:13-14, 81n118, 136
16:13-18, 54
16:13-23, 69
16:13-24, 85, 88, 95, 123
16:15, 95, 136
16:15-18, 57, 68, 74, 121
16:15-24, 68
16:16, 75, 88, 95
16:17-18, 136
16:18, 88, 95, 122
16:19-24, 81n118, 137
16:20, 33
16:22, 95
16:22, 24, 68, 88

2 Corinthians, 3, 5, 9, 13, 15–16, 18, 25
1-7, 17
1–9, 12, 17, 19–20, 22, 193, 215
1:1-11, 214
1:1–2:13, 18, 193
1:1–2:13 + 7:5-16, 186, 214
1:1–2:13 + 7:5-16 + 13:11-13, 4, 5, 12, 15, 22–23, 200, 211–13, 221
1:1–2:13 + 7:5–8:24, 14, 20, 24, 167
1:1-3, 214
1:1-11, 216
1:3, 211, 221
1:3-11, 215
1:4, 219
1:4-6, 215
1:8, 175
1:8-10, 216
1:8-11, 211
1:11, 216
1:12, 218

Index of Biblical Citations

1:12-14, 18, 211, 216
1:15-16, 154, 216, 218
1:15-22, 212, 218
1:15–2:13 +7:5-13a, 217
1:16, 14, 213
1:17, 14, 218
1:17-22, 218
1:19, 215, 218
1:20, 212
1:21-22, 212, 218
1:23, 18, 218
1:23–2:4, 154, 212, 217–18
1:24, 212
1:24–2:2, 14
2:1, 194, 218
2:1-3, 219
2:2-3, 219
2:3, 219
2:3-5, 217
2:3-11, 219
2:4, 11, 14, 167, 212, 215
2:5-11, 212, 219
2:7, 212, 220
2:9, 217
2:10, 220
2:12-13, 18
2:12-13 + 7:5-7, 212, 220
2:13, 16, 18, 25, 194, 220
2:13-14, 29
2:14, 18
2:14-15, 178
2:14-16, 175
2:14–7:3, 17
2:14–6:13, 193
2:14–7:4, 16, 20, 36n6
2:14–6:13 + 7:2-4, 4, 21–24, 28, 175–77, 186–87, 189n2, 190nn3–4
2:15, 178, 180–81
2:15-16, 178, 181, 184–85
2:16, 178, 191n6
2:16-17, 175, 179
2:17, 181, 182–83, 191n6
3:1, 175, 183
3:1-3, 197
3:1-6, 179–80, 191n6

3:3, 176, 180
3:4-6, 180
3:5, 180
3:6, 176, 180
3:7, 180
3:7-11, 180
3:7-18, 179–80
3:12, 181, 192n14
3:14ff., 180
3:15-18, 180
3:17, 176
3:18, 176, 180
4:1, 192n14
4:1-15, 181
4:2, 181
4:3-4, 181
4:5, 176
4:5-6, 181
4:7, 176
4:7-12, 181
4:8-12, 176
4:10, 181
4:13-15, 181
4:14, 182
4:15, 182
4:16, 192n14
4:16–5:10, 176, 182
4:18, 182
5:1, 178, 182
5:1-5, 182
5:2-4, 182
5:5, 182
5:6-10, 179, 182
5:7, 176
5:8-9, 182–83
5:9, 182
5:11, 184, 192n14
5:11-21, 179, 182
5:11–7:1, 18
5:12, 179, 183
5:13, 176, 184
5:13-15, 183
5:14, 184
5:14-15, 178, 184
5:15, 176

5:16, 176, 184
5:16-21, 183–84
5:17, 184
5:18-21, 176
5:19, 179
5:20, 185, 191n14
5:21, 184
6:1-13 + 7:2-4, 176, 185, 187
6:3-10, 176, 178, 185
6:3-13, 62
6:4, 185–86
6:4-5, 186
6:4-10, 185
6:5, 128
6:8-10, 185–86
6:11–7:2, 13
6:11-13 + 7:2-4, 176, 186
6:13, 30
6:13-14, 18–19, 29, 69
6:13–7:2, 16
6:14, 121, 124, 127
6:14, 16, 41n124, 74
6:14-15, 62
6:14-16, 124
6:14–7:1, 4, 16–18, 20–21, 23, 25–26, 30, 36n6, 59–62, 66, 68, 85, 87, 122, 128, 146n18, 193
6:14–7:1 + 1 Cor 6:12-20 + 1 Cor 9:24–10:22, 123–24
6:14–7:1 + 1 Cor 6:12-20 + 1 Cor 9:24–10:22 + 1 Cor 15:1-58 + 1 Cor 16:13-24, 68, 75, 121, 259
6:15, 122
6:15-16, 74, 121
6:16, 59, 124
6:16-18, 124
7, 167
7:1, 60, 124–25, 135
7:1-2, 18–19, 29, 69
7:2-4, 62
7:2-16, 18
7:3-4, 186
7:4, 17
7:4-5, 29
7:4-16, 17

7:5, 16–17, 220
7:5-6, 194
7:5-7, 220
7:5-16, 187
7:6-7, 220
7:6-15, 32
7:6-15, 234
7:7-8, 192n18
7:8, 200, 215
7:8-13, 220
7:9, 194, 212, 217
7:9-12, 216
7:10-13, 212, 220
7:11, 211
7:12-16, 31
7:13-15, 14
7:13-16, 212, 220–21
7:14-16, 221
7:15, 32
7:16, 31
7:16–8:1, 16
8, 81n109, 167, 173n14, 231–35, 238n7
8–9, 18, 22
8:1, 170
8:1-3, 32
8:1-5, 32, 168
8:2, 170
8:3, 170
8:4, 169
8:1-15, 169–70
8:1-24, 23, 25, 30–31, 167–68, 238n2
8:6, 22, 32, 74, 114, 168
8:7, 170
8:7-8, 168
8:8, 168, 170
8:9, 170
8:10, 170, 232
8:10-11, 231
8:11, 168
8:13, 170
8:13-14, 168
8:16-23, 13, 32, 168–70
8:20, 167
8:24, 168
8:24–9:1, 11

9, 11, 17, 20, 231–25, 237n1, 238n4, 238n9
9:1-4, 233
9:1-15, 23–25, 30, 32, 231–35
9:2, 232
9:2-4, 233
9:5-14, 233
9:6, 233
9:6-10, 233
9:6-15, 30
9:7-8, 233
9:9, 30
9:11, 233
9:13, 30
9:14, 233
9:14-15, 17
9:15, 196
9:15–10:1, 16
9:18, 196
10, 17
10:1, 11
10:1ff., 17
10–13, 12, 17, 19–22, 66, 186–87, 193–94, 196, 214, 210, 219
10:1-18, 194, 197
10:1–12:13 + 1 Cor 9:1-18 + 2 Cor 12:14–13:13, 5, 23, 72, 186, 193–201
10:4-6, 27
10:5, 27
10:10, 197–99, 201, 214
10:14-17, 197
10:17, 197
10:14, 122
10:14-16, 194
10:17, 195
10:21, 122
11, 195
11:1, 197
11:1-14, 197
11:1–12:13, 195
11:3, 27
11:3-4, 197
11:4, 27, 195
11:5, 198
11:6, 198
11:7, 195
11:9, 198
11:9-10, 195–96
11:10-12, 196
11:13-15, 24, 198–99
11:19-20, 199
11:20, 199–200
11:24-29, 199
12:1-3, 199
12:2-5, 199–200
12:7, 198, 200
12:7-10, 199–200
12:9, 196, 200
12:10, 200
12:11, 200
12:11-13, 196
12:11–13:10, 19
12:13, 200
12:13-14, 23, 66, 198
12:14, 14
12:14ff., 66
12:14–13:10, 196, 200
12:18, 22
12:19, 19, 196
12:20, 33
12:20-21, 194
12:21, 28
12:21–13:1, 14
12:25, 33
13:2, 192n18
13:2-4, 32
13:4, 196
13:5, 28
13:9, 32
13:10, 33, 196
13:11, 22, 32, 34
13:11-13, 22, 32, 81n118, 212
13:13, 34
13:14, 23

Galatians, 6, 9n1, 15
2:3, 114
2:20, 184
3:28, 52, 115
6:11-17, 24

Ephesians, 7
1:1, 252n14
2:2, 249
2:20, 249, 252nn13–14
3:5, 252n14
3:1-13, 249
4:1, 249
4:11, 252n14
5, 20
6:20, 249

Philippians, 15
1:1, 245
1:12-14, 175
2:19ff., 59

Colossians, 7
1:24-29, 249
4:16, 86, 245

1 Thessalonians, 6
3:1-10, 59
5:6, 149n118

2 Thessalonians, 6, 15
2:2, 8

1 Timothy
1:6ff., 96
1:8-10, 27
1:9, 41n140
1:10, 29
1:12, 29
2:13-14, 27
2:19, 28
3:1-7, 247
3:8-13, 247
3:15, 88
4:2, 89
5:3-16, 247
5:17-18, 30
5:17-22, 247
5:18, 95, 101
6:3-5, 27
6:11-20, 88

6:12, 29
6:20, 243
6:20-21, 34

2 Timothy
1:1, 252n14
1:4, 29
1:7, 29
1:11, 247
1:12, 29
1:13-14, 34
2:1, 29
2:1-2, 28
2:3, 29
2:6, 95
2:8, 28
2:9, 248
2:16-17, 27
2:23-4, 248
2:25-26, 27
3:2, 41n140
3:6, 92
3:8, 248
3:10, 88
3:11, 29
4:1-5, 88
4:3-4, 28
4:5, 29
4:6-8, 29
4:9, 244
4:9-14, 244
4:10-16, 247
4:14, 26
4:15-17, 26
4:17-18, 29

Titus
1:1, 26
1:5, 246
1:6, 41n140
1:6-9, 246
1:8, 97
1:10-11, 26
1:13-14, 26
2:1, 35

2:2, 88
2:4, 247
2:5, 95, 247
2:9, 95
2:14, 96
2:15, 35
2:15–3:1, 27
2:18, 87
3:1, 41n140, 95
3:3, 41n140
3:10-11, 27
3:13-14, 30, 32, 95

Philemon, 15
22, 175

Hebrews
13:9ff., 25

James

1 Peter, 91

2 Peter, 91
1:6, 97
3:2ff., 25
3:15f., 91

1 John

2 John

3 John

Jude
12, 92
17ff., 25

Revelation
21:3-8, 20
22:11, 15, 18f., 25

About the Authors

Frank W. Hughes is an Episcopal priest and has served churches in central Pennsylvania and western Louisiana. He was a senior lecturer in New Testament studies at Codrington College in Barbados, in affiliation with the University of the West Indies. He is the author of *Early Christian Rhetoric and 2 Thessalonians* (1989), which was his dissertation supervised by Robert Jewett, along with many other studies of the use of rhetoric in the Pauline corpus of the New Testament. He is a member of the Society of Biblical Literature, Studiorum Novi Testamenti Societas, and the Anglican Association of Biblical Scholars.

Robert Jewett was theologian-in-residence at St. Mark's United Methodist Church in Lincoln, Nebraska, formerly guest professor of New Testament at the University of Heidelberg, and Harry R. Kendall professor of New Testament interpretation emeritus at Garrett-Evangelical Theological Seminary. He was well known as a scholar of the Pauline letters. He was the author of numerous books, both scholarly and popular, in New Testament studies and American religious and cultural history, including *Romans: A Short Commentary* (2013), *Romans* (2008), *Mission and Menace: Four Centuries of American Religious Zeal* (2008), *The Thessalonian Correspondence* (1986), and *A Chronology of Paul's Life* (1979).

www.ingramcontent.com/pod-product-compliance
Lightning Source LLC
Chambersburg PA
CBHW071358300426
44114CB00016B/2102